Compositional Evolution

The Vienna Series in Theoretical Biology
Gerd B. Müller, Günter P. Wagner, and Werner Callebaut, editors

The Evolution of Cognition, edited by Cecilia Heyes and Ludwig Huber, 2000

Origination of Organismal Form: Beyond the Gene in Developmental and Evolutionary Biology, edited by Gerd B. Müller and Stuart A. Newman, 2003

Environment, Development, and Evolution: Toward a Synthesis, edited by Brian K. Hall, Roy D. Pearson and Gerd B. Müller, 2004

Evolution of Communication Systems: A Comparative Approach, edited by D. Kimbrough Oller and Ulrike Griebel, 2004

Modularity: Understanding the Development and Evolution of Natural Complex Systems, edited by Werner Callebaut and Diego Rasskin-Gutman, 2004

Compositional Evolution: The Impact of Sex, Symbiosis, and Modularity on the Gradualist Framework of Evolution, Richard A. Watson, 2005

Compositional Evolution

The Impact of Sex, Symbiosis, and Modularity on the Gradualist Framework of Evolution

Richard A. Watson

A Bradford Book
The MIT Press
Cambridge, Massachusetts
London, England

This book was set in Times New Roman on 3B2 by Asco Typesetters, Hong Kong.

Library of Congress Cataloging-in-Publication Data

Watson, Richard A., 1968– .
Compositional evolution : the impact of sex, symbiosis, and modularity on the gradualist framework of evolution / Richard A. Watson.
p. cm.—(Vienna series in theoretical biology. A Bradford Book.)
Includes bibliographical references.
ISBN 978-0-262-23243-2 (hc : alk. paper), 978-0-262-53809-1 (pb)
1. Evolution (Biology)—Mathematical models. 2. Computational biology. 3. Evolutionary Computation.
I. Title. II. Series.
QH371.3.M37W38 2006
576.8—dc22

2005043852

To Laura Dominguez Poveda

Contents

Preface

Computer science and biology have a lot to offer each other. My background is in computer science, and like a growing number of researchers I work at the interface of computer science and biology. There is considerable interest at this interface both in using biological systems as inspiration to develop new computational methods (*bio-inspired computation*) and in using computational modeling techniques to assist in the understanding of biological systems (*computational biology*). Although bio-inspired computation does not always assist in the understanding of the biology that inspired it, and computational biology models do not always require new insights on the part of the computer scientist, in some fortuitous cases, work in these fields helps progress both disciplines together. This kind of synergistic result occurs when the biological system or principle being studied is fundamentally an algorithmic or computational process. Some biological processes stand out as obvious candidates for such research. For example, in the science of cognition, the development of artificial neural networks has provided new approaches to solving computational problems and also changed our view of the kind of processes that might go on in the cortex. Another candidate is the science of evolution; but despite notable successes in the use of evolutionary computation techniques for problem solving and design, the underlying principles of evolution by natural selection as most of us understand them today are not significantly different in an *algorithmic* sense, that is, in the sense of a formal step-by-step procedure, from those that Darwin laid out nearly a century and a half ago.

Evolution by natural selection occurs whenever individuals show variation in reproductive success that can be inherited (heritable variation). Variants that reproduce more effectively increase in number, and those that do not, don't. Accordingly, variations of the existing individuals that are *fitter*, in this sense, come to replace those that are less fit. In this manner, although the variations are random, selection acting on them will produce directed change. The underlying algorithmic principle here is *random mutation hill climbing*, the linear, or sequential, accumulation of random changes, each one a fitness improvement over the last.

Darwin believed that each random change must be small and that a progression of "successive slight variations" was required for any adaptation (1859). After both the "Modern Synthesis" of the 1930s (Fisher 1930), when Mendelian genetics (Mendel 1866) was integrated with Darwinian natural selection (Darwin 1859), and the discovery of the molecular structure of DNA in the 1950s (Watson and Crick 1953), it was clear that natural selection could act on whatever heritable variation occurred and that this may come about by spontaneous point mutation introduced by DNA replication errors, or sexual recombination, or any mechanism of genetic variation. These genetic changes may be any size in principle but the process is still fundamentally the linear accumulation of random genetic changes. This is what I shall refer to as the *gradualist framework of evolution*. It includes, in principle, random genetic changes of any size, but given that large random genetic changes seem much more likely than small changes to destroy the proper functioning of a well-adapted organism, it is generally assumed that most adaptive changes will be small ones. Nonetheless, fitness improvements from large genetic changes are not categorically excluded in this framework. It is the linear successive improvement by random variation that defines the framework, not the size of the genetic variations involved. It might be useful to mention straight away that *saltationism* (Goldschmidt 1940), *punctuated equilibria* (Gould and Eldredge 1977), and *neutral theory* (Kimura 1983) are, as I will discuss, all included in this definition of the gradualist framework because they are not different algorithmically—although they differ in opinion about the expected size, rate, and fitness effect of random variations respectively, they all agree that evolution by natural selection is based on the sequential accumulation of random variations. Indeed, the rejection of saltationism results from the implausibility of large random beneficial changes under such an algorithmic process.

Some mechanisms of genetic variation do produce large genetic changes and sometimes these do produce something adaptive. Sexual hybridization of different species sometimes creates successful new species (Rieseberg et al. 2003); lateral or horizontal gene transfer (Mazodier and Davies 1991), widespread in single-celled organisms (Doolittle 2000), has resulted in the rapid adaptation of antibiotic resistance, for example (Ochman, Lawrence and Groisman 2000); and one of the most extraordinary events in evolutionary history was the origin of the intracellular organelles, such as mitochondria and chloroplasts, through the union of genetic material from symbiotic bacteria (Margulis 1970). Are these mechanisms accommodated by the gradualist framework of evolution? Is linear sequential improvement sufficient to describe these processes properly? I argue that they are not.

Notably, mechanisms like sex, lateral gene transfer, and symbiogenesis (the genesis of new species through symbiosis) are not merely a different source of random genetic changes that happen to be large and occasionally adaptive (increasing fitness). These mechanisms involve not the *linear* accumulation of random genetic changes but rather the coming together of genetic material that has been preadapted in different lineages—different individuals, subpopulations, or species. Accordingly, the genetic variations that they produce are not "undirected" random genetic changes—but rather "directed" by prior selection. The more important question is: does it matter whether adaptive genetic variations were selected for in parallel lineages and subsequently brought together, rather than selected serially in a single lineage? The finding of this book is that yes, it does matter. These mechanisms do not introduce anything magical or teleological to the process of evolution by natural selection, but they change the underlying algorithmic principles of evolution, and they cannot be accommodated by the gradualist framework.

In this book I will show that these mechanisms enable *compositional evolution* and that this is algorithmically distinct from the gradualist framework of evolution. One particularly important consequence of this distinction can be seen in how it impacts our understanding of which types of systems are evolvable and which are not. This is illustrated by examining the class of complex systems that compositional evolution can produce but gradual evolution cannot. I show that, in principle, certain kinds of complex adaptations that are pathologically difficult for gradual evolution can be produced easily by compositional evolution. I define an example complex system that has difficult dependencies between different parts of the system that prevent linear incremental improvements in fitness. This system is not only *unevolvable* (not evolvable) under the strict gradualist assumption of small genetic changes, but also unevolvable through the linear accumulation of random genetic changes *of any size*. Nonetheless, a compositional process can exploit the underlying modular structure and evolve systems of this type easily.

The differences between compositional evolution and gradual evolution derive from the fact that they have different underlying algorithmic principles. The algorithmic principle of gradual evolution is simply *hill climbing*, whereas the algorithmic principle underlying compositional evolution is *divide-and-conquer problem decomposition*. The method of solving a problem by decomposing it into more manageable subproblems is a familiar and intuitive concept in design and engineering. But whereas this is usually assumed to require top-down knowledge of how to decompose a problem, in this book I show that it can be applied "bottom up" in an evolutionary process. When this algorithmic distinction is understood, we see that it is no longer appropriate to try to force mechanisms like sex, lateral gene transfer, and symbiogenesis into the linear paradigm of the gradualist framework. Instead we must expand the framework of evolution by natural selection to include a greater range of algorithmic possibilities.

Because evolution by natural selection is fundamentally an algorithmic concept, work in extracting inspiration from biology for computational methods has the potential to feed back into the biology that inspired it. The goals of this book are therefore explicitly interdisciplinary: to elucidate the algorithmic principles underlying evolutionary mechanisms to answer existing questions in computer science, and to provide food for thought about our understanding of the biological processes of evolution.

It turns out that arguments about whether events such as symbiogenesis require us to modify our conception of how evolution works have been going on for nearly a century (Famintsyn 1907; Merezhkovsky 1909; Wallin 1927; Margulis 1970, 1993b). More recently, symbiogenesis is included as one of several fundamental transitions in evolution where entities that were formerly reproductively independent became reproductively dependent (Maynard Smith and Szathmary 1995), forming a new entity at a higher level of organization. But thus far the fact of such events in nature has not been permitted to significantly influence the fundamental ideas about how evolution works. In this book I use the tools of complexity theory and algorithmics to support the claim that these mechanisms should expand our ideas about how evolution works in a fundamental sense.

In evolutionary computation there has been a similarly heated debate about whether the *genetic algorithm*, a computational problem-solving technique based loosely on evolution by natural selection, offers any fundamentally interesting problem-solving capability or whether it is just an unnecessarily complicated form of mutation hill climbing. In particular, the potential role of sexual recombination, or crossover, has been central in this debate. The claims within computer science about the ability of crossover to put together well-adapted subsets of genetic material to form well-adapted individuals not only provide a question worth answering in its own right, but moreover, this issue is algorithmically analogous to the potential of symbiogenesis to put together well-adapted simple entities to form well-adapted entities at a new level of organization. Some of the results I develop in this work build on ideas that were familiar in evolutionary computation but previously not well supported formally; in providing clear resolutions to these questions I also provide a computational framework for understanding sex and symbiogenesis as part of a spectrum of compositional mechanisms.

Following these motives, this book offers: (1) a model of sexual recombination using a genetic algorithm that shows that it is algorithmically distinct from mutation hill-climbing methods; (2) a model of symbiogenesis and the major evolutionary transitions that shows that such processes are also a fundamentally different class of adaptive process from the gradualist evolutionary framework of linear incremental improvement; and (3) a framework for understanding both symbiogenesis and sexual recombination as instances of a general class of mechanisms that I have termed compositional evolution: evolutionary processes involving the combination of systems or subsystems of semi-independently preadapted genetic material. This is contrasted with the gradualist framework of evolution that depends on the linear or sequential accumulation of random modifications.

Readers in several related fields may therefore find this book useful. For researchers in evolutionary computation there are results addressing the benefit of sexual recombination or crossover, the "building-block hypothesis" and which problems are difficult or easy for the genetic algorithm, "cooperative coevolution," the maintenance of diversity in evolving populations, and "linkage learning." For researchers in evolutionary biology the models presented provide tools to think about gradualism in evolution, the benefit of recombination, the evolution of cooperation, serial endosymbiosis theory, and the major evolutionary transitions. For readers interested in combinatorial optimization and machine learning in general, the algorithms developed here provide a heuristic bottom-up divide-and-conquer method that enables automatic problem decomposition and automatic module acquisition in an appropriate problem domain. And researchers in complex systems are provided with models addressing modularity and decomposability in dynamical systems, especially hierarchically modular systems.

The book has three parts. The first part (chapters 1 through 3) provides an overview of the arguments set forth in this book, reviews the gradualist framework of evolution and its impact on our understanding of evolvability, and reviews the compositional mechanisms exhibited in evolutionary biology and the analogous principles used in evolutionary computation. This part of the book provides the background in evolutionary biology and evolutionary computation necessary to see how the research questions in both fields are similar and how they complement one another.

The second part (chapters 4 through 8) provides the computational models that illustrate my argument. Chapter 4 provides a definition of a modular complex system designed to exemplify the different adaptive capabilities of gradual and compositional mechanisms. The following three chapters then examine the evolution of this system under different evolutionary scenarios. Those scenarios use three different variation mechanisms. Chapter 5 discusses spontaneous point mutation—which provides only gradual evolution. Chapter 6 discusses sexual recombination—which can sometimes provide compositional evolution depending on properties of population diversity and genetic architecture. Chapter 7 presents a mechanism of symbiotic encapsulation—which allows less restricted compositional evolution. The last chapter of this part, chapter 8, provides a formal analysis that shows how these compositional mechanisms scale with the size of the system being evolved.

In the third part of the book, chapter 9 discusses how compositional evolution enables the scaling up of evolutionary processes, and the conceptual components behind the compositional models. And chapter 10 discusses the impact it has on our understanding of natural evolution and, similarly, the utility of evolutionary computation methods for problem solving and design.

Throughout the book I have attempted to draw the ideas in evolutionary computation and evolutionary biology closer together to help foster continued exchange between the disciplines. I find it hard to imagine working in one field without being excited by the other, and I hope that some of my enthusiasm for the two rubs off. There is much exciting work to be done to bring evolutionary computation and evolutionary biology closer together so that the full benefits of insights and results in each can inform and stimulate the other. A meeting of evolutionary computation and evolutionary biology, like compositional events in evolutionary history, has the potential to produce many synergistic effects.

Acknowledgments

The development of the research in this book has benefited from the invaluable input of many people. A lot of the ideas took shape while I was at Brandeis University in Jordan Pollack's group known as DEMO—the Dynamical and Evolutionary Machine Organization. My thanks to Jordan and the many members of that group past and present including Alan Blair, Paul Darwen, Hugues Juillé, Pablo Funes, Ofer Melnik, Elizabeth Sklar, Gregory Hornby, Sevan Ficici, Simon Levy, Anthony Bucci, Hod Lipson, Edwin de Jong, and Shivakumar Viswanathan—most notably, Sevan; several of the most critical insights in the work would not have become clear without his input and relentless and rigorous encouragement to get to the heart of the matter.

Many members of the evolutionary computation community have taken the trouble to share insights and provide perspective: Inman Harvey, Dave Cliff, Jason Noble, Peter Todd, Una-May O'Reilly, Alden Wright, Martin Oates, Torsten Reil, Josh Knowles, Rob Shipman, Mark Ebner, and Hugo Touchette. Particular thanks to my thesis committee who provided the guidance that can only be provided by those with experience and expertise in their fields: Gunter Wagner, Dave Waltz, and Ken De Jong.

My research at the Organismic and Evolutionary Biology department at Harvard provided some background in evolutionary biology necessary to complement that which I had learned in computer science. My thanks to John Wakeley for taking in a cross-disciplinary migrant, making me welcome, and providing a tremendously challenging and rewarding environment. Thanks to Alex Platt, Christina Muirhead, Guillaume Achaz, Josh Cherry, and in particular Daniel Weinreich, who caused me to get to the bottom of things I thought I already understood, but didn't really.

Finally, I would like to thank Judy Feldmann and Todd Nudelman, for their fantastic attention to detail in preparation of the final manuscript, together with Bob Prior and the other staff at MIT Press that have made this book possible.

Some number of these people have been fruitful colleagues and collaborators, and many of them have become my friends. But the love that supports me in these endeavors, and in all things, comes from a particular fellow academic, my wife, Laura Dominguez. My love and thanks to her for her endless support. My indebted thanks to all.

Series Foreword

Biology is becoming the leading science in this century. As in all other sciences, progress in biology depends on interactions between empirical research, theory building, and modeling. But whereas the techniques and methods of descriptive and experimental biology have dramatically evolved in recent years, generating a flood of highly detailed empirical data, the integration of these results into useful theoretical frameworks has lagged behind. Driven largely by pragmatic and technical considerations, research in biology continues to be less guided by theory than seems indicated. By promoting the formulation and discussion of new theoretical concepts in the biosciences, this series intends to help fill the gaps in our understanding of some of the major open questions of biology, such as the origin and organization of organismal form, the relationship between development and evolution, and the biological bases of cognition and mind.

Theoretical biology has important roots in the experimental biology movement of early twentieth-century Vienna. Paul Weiss and Ludwig von Bertalanffy were among the first to use the term *theoretical biology* in a modern scientific context. In their understanding the subject was not limited to mathematical formalization, as is often the case today, but extended to the conceptual problems and foundations of biology. It is this commitment to a comprehensive, cross-disciplinary integration of theoretical concepts that the present series intends to emphasize. Today theoretical biology has genetic, developmental, and evolutionary components, the central connective themes in modern biology, but also includes relevant aspects of computational biology, semiotics, and cognition research, and extends to the naturalistic philosophy of sciences.

The Vienna Series grew out of theory-oriented workshops organized by the Konrad Lorenz Institute for Evolution and Cognition Research (KLI), an international center for advanced study closely associated with the University of Vienna (http://kli.ac.at). The KLI fosters research projects, workshops, archives, book projects, and the journal *Biological Theory*, all devoted to aspects of theoretical biology, with an emphasis on integrating the developmental, evolutionary, and cognitive sciences. The series editors welcome suggestions for book projects in these fields.

Gerd B. Müller, University of Vienna, KLI
Günter P. Wagner, Yale University, KLI
Werner Callebaut, Hasselt University, KLI

1 Introduction

If it could be demonstrated that any complex organ existed which could not possibly have been formed by numerous, successive, slight modifications, my theory would absolutely break down.
—Charles Darwin, 1859

Conventionally, evolution by natural selection is almost inseparable from the notion of accumulating successive slight variations. Notions of *gradualism* are deeply ingrained in evolutionary thought and strongly influence our ideas about what kinds of systems are evolvable and which are not. The very idea of large adaptive genetic changes is considered *unevolutionary*. Indeed, attacking the plausibility of a linear succession of incrementally improving protosystems is a common form of criticism of evolutionary theory from Paley (1802) to Behe (1996), while asserting the plausibility of such a succession is a common form of defense (Dawkins 1996).

In natural evolution there are a number of mechanisms that provide exceptional forms of genetic change. For example, the eukaryotic cell (from which all plants and animals are descended) has organelles (such as mitochondria and chloroplasts) that were formed from the genetic integration of previously separate species of bacteria. In these events, groups of organisms, formerly living in close symbiotic relationship, were thus transformed into a new individual at a new level of organization (Margulis 1970). It was suggested as early as 1909 (by Merezhkovsky) that such symbiotic mechanisms, by bringing together the genetic material of two genetically distinct organisms, provide an alternative to gradual evolutionary change. Similarly, on a less dramatic but more frequent scale, sexual recombination has the potential to bring together sets of coadapted genes from genetically distinct parents providing a large genetic change that would be extremely unlikely from spontaneous point mutations applied to either parent alone.

There has been disagreement about what impact such mechanisms should have on our understanding of evolutionary processes. Some suggest that the genetic integration of symbionts cannot be very important in understanding evolutionary processes in general simply because such events are rare. Also, sex is usually restricted to populations that are genetically similar so the opportunity for radical genetic change seems low. Moreover, for both sexual and symbiotic integration, it still seems likely that any large genetic change would more likely be disastrous than beneficial. And finally, even if it were the case that a particular adaptation resulted from genetic integration of different individuals, this might not be a substantive challenge to gradualism since the genetic material provided by each of the component individuals was (presumably) evolved gradually.

The biological fact of the genetic mechanisms is not disputed, and neither is their role in enabling significant innovation such as the eukaryote cell. It is also clear that large genetic changes could be selected for by natural selection if they were beneficial, and mechanisms such as these provide large genetic changes that have evidently, at least sometimes, been beneficial. Accordingly, it might seem that these mechanisms do not require any fundamental change to the gradualist framework of evolution by natural selection. However, a change is required.

In these mechanisms, genetic material is adapted in parallel in different individuals, subpopulations, or species, and subsequently brought together. Thus the genetic changes produced by such events are quite unlike the random genetic changes of, for example, those produced by spontaneous genetic mutations. This parallel adaptation enables these mechanisms to evolve systems that cannot be evolved through the linear accumulation of random genetic changes. Such a process does not introduce anything teleological into evolution, and it still sits squarely within the framework of evolution by natural selection. But it causes us to separate evolution by natural selection from the assumption of gradual change—not merely from the assumption of strict gradualism, involving only "successive slight variations," but from the linear accumulation of random changes *of any size*.

This book uses *evolutionary computation* models to aid in the understanding of these processes. Since the 1970s, considerable interest has developed within computer science in computational optimization methods based loosely on Darwinian natural selection. Work in *evolutionary algorithms*, EAs, is a highly active and rapidly growing field—the most well-known variety being *genetic algorithms*, GAs. Within this field there is considerable interest in the possibility of methods that encapsulate primitive functional units into higher-order components that can be reused in subsequent evolution, which has obvious parallels with these biological mechanisms. There is also significant controversy over the supposed utility of sexual recombination, or *crossover*, in such algorithms; whether it affords any special problem-solving utility or whether spontaneous point mutation alone is just as good. In this book, by providing an answer to these computational questions we also gain an increased understanding of the adaptive capacity of sex and other compositional mechanisms in nature. A computer science approach is useful, not just for providing a modeling tool, but moreover in providing theoretical tools. Algorithmics and complexity theory provide the means to properly formalize our questions and identify differences in adaptive processes in a fundamental sense. In particular, this enables us to pose and answer a formal version of the following question: What kind of complex systems (if any) can be evolved with compositional mechanisms that cannot be evolved through gradual evolution?

The answer to this question depends on *modularity*.[1] I identify a particular form of modular complexity, where subsystems can be evolved semi-independently despite important intermodule dependencies. Systems with this kind of modularity cannot be evolved by gradual evolution because resolving the interdependencies between modules may require making specific large genetic changes. In fact, this class of system typifies characteristics that are pathological for gradual evolution: the corresponding fitness landscape is highly rugged, has many local optima creating broad fitness saddles, and includes "irreducibly complex" adaptations that cannot be reached by a linear succession of randomly modified protosystems. However, an evolving process with compositional mechanisms does not necessarily have the same restrictions. With compositional mechanisms that enable preadapted genetic material from different individuals to be combined, genetic material from another individual can provide specific large genetic changes, enabling continued adaptation. I provide results of simulations to show that this class of modular system is easily evolvable under compositional evolution and not evolvable under gradual evolution. Thus, certain kinds of complex systems, considered unevolvable under the gradualist framework of evolution, are easily evolvable under compositional evolution.

The fact that compositional evolution can provide evolutionary adaptation that is not possible in the gradualist framework causes us to rethink our notions of evolvability (how easy or difficult it is for systems to evolve) and reassess the potential of sex and symbiosis in evolutionary innovation. The simulations and analytic results show us that there are fundamental differences in the adaptive capacities of these mechanisms, and help us to understand the conditions under which compositional mechanisms provide an adaptive advantage.

This book has two main objectives: first, to present and develop the above argument that sex, symbiosis, and other compositional mechanisms move beyond the normal "linear accumulation of random changes" dogma in evolutionary theory, giving new results and theoretical work to support this view; and second and more generally, to foster interdisciplinary exchange between evolutionary biology and evolutionary computation, showing how some of the deepest questions in each of these disciplines can be approached with the tools and insights of the other.

1.1 Gradual and Compositional Evolution

I propose the term *compositional evolution* to refer to evolutionary processes involving the combination of systems or subsystems of semi-independently preadapted genetic material. A family of such mechanisms exists including sex, hybridization, lateral gene transfer, allopolyploidy, and mechanisms of "symbiotic encapsulation" such as endosymbiosis, the genetic integration of symbionts (symbiogenesis), or other mechanisms that encapsulate a group of simple entities into a complex entity at

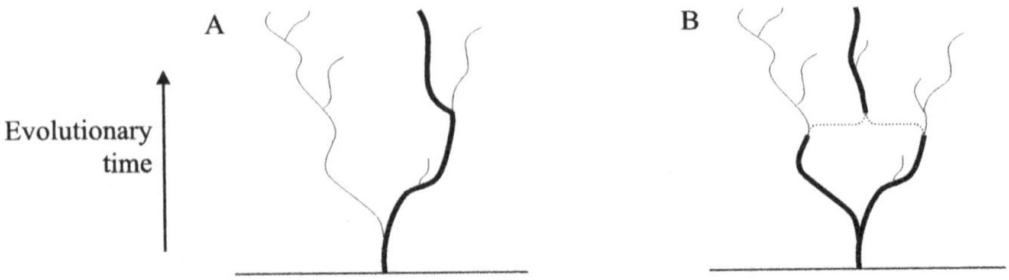

Figure 1.1
Gradual and compositional evolutionary processes. (a) The linear accumulation of random changes under the normal framework of gradual evolutionary adaptation produces the familiar branching ancestral tree. (b) In compositional evolution, in addition to the normal branching process of gradual evolution, there is also the occasional creation of a new entity from the combination of preadapted genetic material from different individuals. This creates a new entity that may be genetically distant from both donor individuals.

a higher level of organization, as exhibited in several of the major transitions in evolution.

In contrast, the familiar gradualist framework of evolution refers to mechanisms that sequentially accumulate random variations in genetic material, that is, the new genetic material introduced by such changes has not been preadapted elsewhere as a set. Thus gradual evolution is driven predominantly by small modifications, that is, "successive slight modifications" (Darwin 1859), though not exclusively so, in principle. This forms the basis of the normal understanding of evolutionary change. Chapter 2 details the background of the gradualist framework of evolution and the established notions of evolutionary difficulty that, in fact, depend on this framework.

Figure 1.1 shows a schematic comparison of ancestral relationships in gradual evolution and compositional evolution. Gradual evolution produces the familiar ancestral "tree" phylogeny (Haeckel 1876). Note that for any extant entity produced by gradual evolution there is a single linear path (shown in bold) linking it to the root of the tree via a succession of (small) random changes. In contrast, individuals descended from a compositional event cannot be traced to the root of the tree via a single linear path of gradual changes. Instead it is correct to respect the true multiple-inheritance origin of this new lineage producing a disconnected ancestral graph where the links to the root of new subtrees (shown by dashed lines) are of a different kind to the rest of the graph. Specifically, not only are they two-to-one edges (connecting two nodes to a new third) but more significantly they do not indicate a succession of gradually changing intermediates.

It is useful to compare this depiction with other nontree diagrams of ancestral relationships that have been offered previously for various events at different scales from horizontal gene transfer to symbiogenesis (e.g., Doolittle 2000; Rivera and

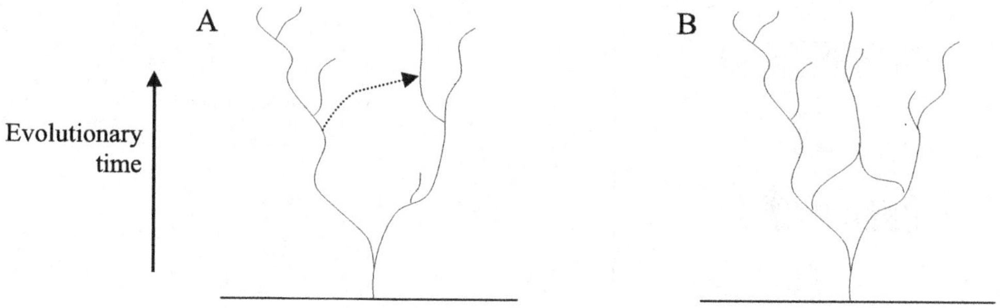

Figure 1.2
Other depictions of compositional events. (a) An ancestral tree with "exceptions." (b) A nontree graph.

Lake 2004; Margulis 1970). Some of these diagrams depict all entities as fitting within a tree and then add "exceptional" cross-links that indicate the exchange of genetic material from one branch across to another (e.g., Doolittle 2000; Kim and Salisbury 2001)—see figure 1.2a. This depiction obscures the fact that the entities thus created are not a small modification of either ancestral donor even though they may be (very much) more similar to one than the other. Others depict the connections that bring lineages together as smooth transitions (of the same type that draw branches apart in differentiation) (e.g., Margulis 1970; Rivera and Lake 2004)—see figure 1.2b. However, if the horizontal dimension of this diagram is supposed to represent genetic (or phenotypic) diversity then this depiction is misleading since it is not the case that the donors of genetic material in a compositional event evolve toward one another gradually becoming genetically or phenotypically similar until they become indistinct and form a single lineage. Even Doolittle, who proposes "uprooting the tree of life" in light of evidence for horizontal gene transfer, uses a depiction of ancestral relationships near the base of the graph using a uniform style of link in the form of figure 1.2b (despite challenging the adherence to a single common ancestor at the root of the tree). Even though the unusual mechanisms of genetic variation are included in these figures, these seemingly subtle issues in fact reveal a strong adherence to trees with linear branching (Kim and Salisbury 2001) and thus gradualist assumptions. Of course, a "median tree" is a useful construct for many purposes, especially when the fraction of genetic material laterally transferred or composed is small, but a strict tree discards information relevant to compositional mechanisms, and a tree with added cross-links is somewhat inconsistent in what the edges of such a graph represent.

The genetic variation mechanisms underlying gradual and compositional evolution are shown in figure 1.3 and figure 1.4, respectively. Note that the genetic changes

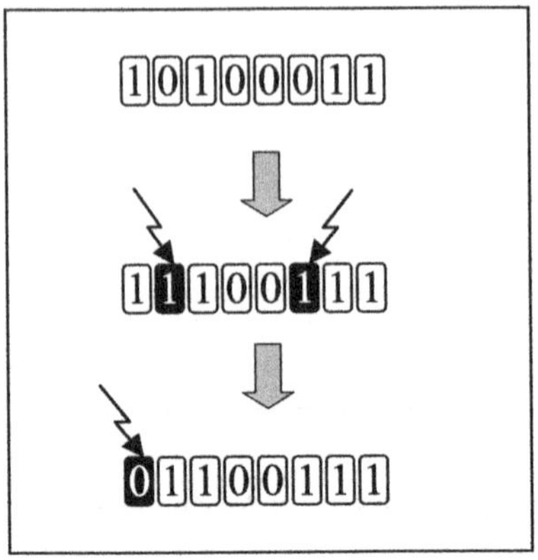

Figure 1.3
Gradual evolution via spontaneous point mutation. Each row represents an individual; each box represents a gene; the value (0 or 1) in each box represents the different forms, or *alleles*, each gene may have. The position of each gene is referred to as a *locus*, and the combination of alleles at all loci defines an organism's *genotype*. When the genetic material is copied during reproduction, errors may be spontaneously introduced—these are genetic *mutations*. Thus the descendents (shown in successive rows) have genotypes that differ in one or more alleles. Under mutational variation, newly introduced genetic material (shown in black) is random.

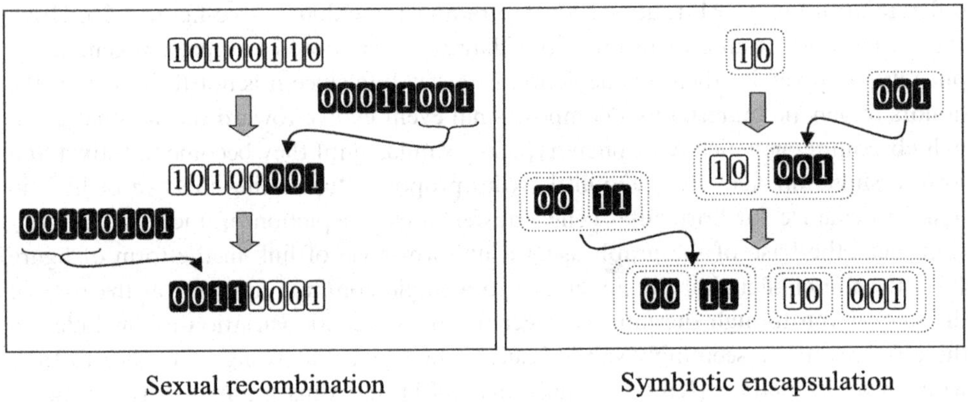

Figure 1.4
Mechanisms of compositional evolution. Left: sexual recombination: sections of genetic material may be transferred as a set from one individual to another. Right: hierarchical encapsulation of symbiotic groups: preadapted sets of genetic material may be assembled by endosymbiosis. In both mechanisms, newly introduced genetic material has already been subject to selection. An interesting difference between these mechanisms that is expanded in the models that follow is that whereas the size of individuals remains constant under sexual recombination, the size of individuals grows under symbiotic encapsulation.

produced by spontaneous point mutation may be large, affecting numerous loci simultaneously, if mutation rates are high. And presumably, there is some nonzero chance that such large changes may be beneficial. But since the genetic changes from mutation are random, beneficial large genetic changes are likely to be rare and evolution is driven predominantly by the accumulation of small modifications. The primary form of gradual variation mechanism in nature is spontaneous genetic mutation, but other forms of genetic variation acting on one individual (or involving genetically similar individuals) may also produce genetic changes that can be accommodated in the gradualist framework.

Of course, spontaneous point mutation as depicted in figure 1.3 is also involved, if not required, for creating the diverse individuals undergoing the compositional change shown in figure 1.4. But the fact remains that compositional mechanisms enable large genetic changes that (unlike changes from spontaneous point mutation, whether they be large or small) are not arbitrary changes in the genetic material of the recipient—rather, the changes that are thus enabled are informed by prior adaptation of the donor individual. The results of such processes are not formed by the gradual accumulation of small changes, or random changes of any size, to either of the ancestral types.

Compositional mechanisms, such as those depicted in the previous figure, form part of a general evolutionary process of subdivision and integration. Abstractly, a process of subdivision and integration exhibits the following components. Evolving entities of different types are evolved in parallel lineages—that is, the population of evolving entities is *subdivided.* Subsequently, some mechanism of *integration* composes genetic material from different lineages together into a new entity. After integration, integrated genetic material reproduces together. Figure 1.5 shows a schematic of this process.

Mechanisms of subdivision and integration are seen at different scales in natural systems. Specifically, at the single-species scale, the separate lineages involved may be subpopulations of a given species, semi-isolated perhaps by virtue of spatial location, and the mechanism of integration may be provided by migration and sexual recombination. At the multispecies scale, the separate lineages may be reproductively isolated species, and integration may occur through horizontal gene transfer or endosymbiosis. Several of the major transitions in evolution share the characteristic that "entities that were capable of independent replication before the transition can replicate only as part of a larger whole after it" (Maynard Smith and Szathmary 1995); and this notion is important in providing the idea that processes of composition may occur through several increases in scale.

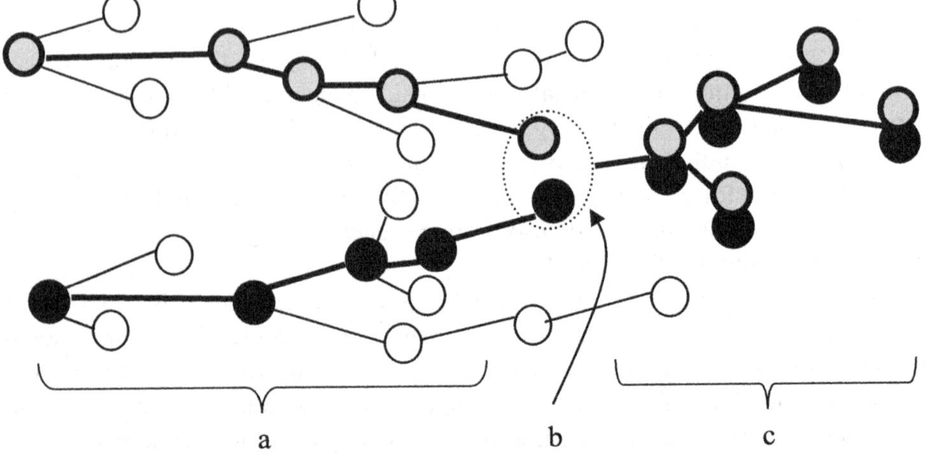

Figure 1.5
Subdivision and integration in compositional evolution. A number of reproductive entities, shown by nodes, in different lineages. Lines in the graph represent ancestral relationships with evolutionary time progressing from left to right: (a) two particular lineages (light shading and dark shading) progress independently in a subdivided population; (b) some mechanism of integration, such as sexual recombination or symbiotic encapsulation, composes together preadapted subsets of genetic material from the previously separate lineages; (c) the integrated genetic material is now replicated together. The integration of genetic material from subdivided populations will occur repeatedly in compositional evolution.

In evolutionary biology, the single-species scale is relevant to models such as shifting balance theory (Wright 1977), and the multispecies scale is relevant to models such as serial endosymbiosis theory (Margulis 1993a). In evolutionary computation, the single-species scale is relevant to issues such as diversity maintenance methods, the utility of crossover, and the building-block hypothesis (Holland 1975, 2000; Goldberg 1989)—and the multispecies scale is relevant to models such as cooperative coevolution (Potter 1997) and the explicit encapsulation of primitive components into reusable composites in models such as automatic module acquisition (Angeline and Pollack 1993).

1.2 The Algorithmic Paradigms of Evolution

I claim a fundamental distinction between gradual and compositional evolution based on the likelihood of evolving certain kinds of complex systems. The basic intuitions here are provided by analogy with well-known classes of optimization algorithms in computer science. In optimization, different kinds of optimization algo-

Table 1.1
Algorithmic classes and their evolutionary analogues.

Dependency of variables	Arbitrary interdependencies	Modular interdependencies	Few/weak interdependencies
Landscape	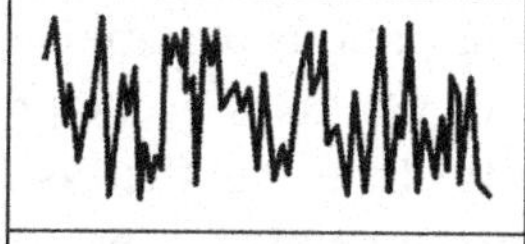	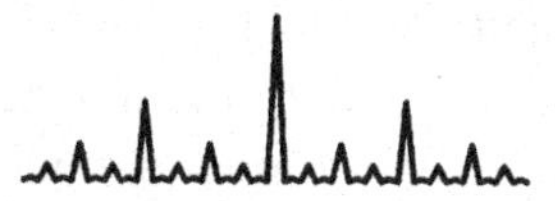	
Algorithmic paradigm	exhaustive search, random search	divide-and-conquer problem decomposition	hill-climbing—accumulation of small variations
Complexity	K^N	N^K	KN
Evolutionary analogue	"impossible"/ "intelligent design"	compositional evolution	gradual evolution

rithms are suitable for different kinds of problems according to the assumptions we have about the dependencies between the problem variables being optimized. A dependency between variables occurs when the optimal setting for one variable is dependent on the setting of other variables. Table 1.1 outlines three main classes of assumptions and the algorithm types that are appropriate for each of them. Starting with the leftmost column, when we have no knowledge of the nature or structure of interdependencies between the problem variables we might assume that the dependencies are arbitrarily difficult. Such dependencies create a random, highly rugged fitness surface, and the appropriate algorithmic paradigms for this class of problem are exhaustive search or random search. Neither of these methods uses any assumptions about the problem domain to guide or reduce the search necessary and therefore the expected time to find high-fitness configurations of variables with these methods is proportionate to the size of the entire search space. The total number of possible configurations for a problem that has N variables, each being able to take one of k values, is k^N. This is an exponential function of N. It means that the size of the search space grows very rapidly with the number of problem variables and a search method that has an operating time proportional to this is feasible only when the number of problem variables is small. In computer science, we say that the computational complexity of a method like this is exponential. This is a very important categorization because it means that the method is infeasible for large problems.

At the other extreme, addressing the rightmost column, we may in other cases hold different assumptions about the interdependencies of variables—in this case, that interdependencies between variables are weak or few. This creates a relatively smooth and generally monomodal fitness landscape, where the appropriate algorithmic paradigms are "greedy" algorithms making incremental improvements, and the simple class of "hill-climbing" algorithms which climb the local gradient in the fitness landscape. When the assumption of weak interdependencies between variables is correct, the expected time to find high-fitness configurations of variables is at worst linear, that is, simply proportionate to the number of variables in the problem. This is a very different class of computational complexity. It means that as N increases, the difficulty of solving the problem increases proportionately—a problem with $2N$ variables is only twice as difficult as problem with N variables. Unlike exponential complexity, this kind of increase is quite manageable and is feasible even for large N.

These two cases—on the one hand, arbitrary interdependencies and exponential time complexity, and on the other hand, weak interdependencies and linear time complexity—represent the naive extremes of the possibilities that might occur in a problem domain. These extremes correspond closely to extreme positions prevalent in evolutionary thought: specifically, if one assumes that the interdependencies between components of a natural system are arbitrarily difficult and complex then it is inconceivable that that system evolved (or at least, the size of such systems that can be achieved with "uninformed" processes is limited); in contrast, if one assumes that the interdependencies between the components of a natural system are weak or few then such systems are easily explained by the normal gradualist model of evolutionary change. Note, however, that if a search method is applied to an inappropriate problem type it will not succeed. For example, when a hill-climber is applied to a problem with arbitrarily difficult interdependencies it will not find high-fitness solutions in less than exponential time (and will generally perform worse than random search because it will follow local gradients that, in this case, will be uninformative). This is why large complex problems with arbitrary interdependencies are unevolvable under the gradualist framework of evolution.

In between these two extremes there are many other possibilities for the number, structure, and nature of variable interdependencies, and in optimization there are important algorithmic paradigms that address this range. One possibility for the interdependencies of variables is that there may be strong and numerous interdependencies but that these dependencies may have a particular structure—for example, a modular structure. It is not so obvious how to represent the high-dimensional landscape of a modular problem domain in the simple one-dimensional caricatures used here, but as we will see later, although they may appear to be as rugged and unforgiving as landscapes with arbitrarily complex interdependencies, the properties of semi-independence among problem variables create significant structure that can be exploited. The algorithmic paradigm that is appropriate for problems of this class broadly includes those known as "divide-and-conquer" techniques. Divide-and-conquer optimization is a form of problem decomposition that utilizes the modular structure of a problem by breaking it into smaller subproblems that are easier to solve, and using solutions to these subproblems to compose a solution to the problem as a whole. For example, if a problem can be divided into two equal halves then each requires time exponential in $N/2$ (i.e., half the number of problem variables), at worst. If each subproblem can be further decomposed, and so on, the time complexity of the whole process can be reduced to polynomial time—that is, the time to optimize the entire problem is some polynomial function of the number of variables in the problem. This means that although large problems are not as easy to solve as when the complexity is linear, they are still a lot easier than when the complexity is exponential, and they remain feasible for large N. Consider how the values $2N$ (linear), N^2 (polynomial), and 2^N (exponential) grow with increasing N. In computational complexity theory, the most important distinction is whether the complexity of a method is exponential or less than exponential—if a method takes exponential time it is simply infeasible for large problems, but if it is polynomial (or less) it is feasible for large problems. So, when applied to problems of a suitable type, hill-climbing and divide-and-conquer methods are feasible for large N.

Following these broad algorithmic classes, the basis of the central claim in this book is that compositional evolutionary mechanisms can provide adaptation akin to divide-and-conquer problem decomposition under certain circumstances. This means that some kinds of large complex systems that could not feasibly be evolved under the gradualist framework are nonetheless evolvable. As is the case for divide-and-conquer methods in general, the adaptive advantage of compositional mechanisms will depend on the structure of interdependencies in the problem domain—in particular, the presence of a modular interdependency structure. If such a structure is present, then compositional mechanisms may provide a form of adaptation that lies in between, yet is fundamentally distinct from, either of the extreme scenarios mentioned above.

The possibility of compositional evolution, and the fundamental distinction from gradual evolution, shares underlying intuitions with some previous work (e.g., Bermudes and Margulis 1985; Margulis 1993a). But the association of these intuitive ideas with this algorithmic class has not been previously developed, nor have formal analyses of the relevant combinatorics been developed in evolutionary theory. In computer science, the underling intuition here is basically that which underlies the building-block hypothesis, which has been present in evolutionary computation, more or less explicitly, since its inception (Holland 1975, 2000). But despite several attempts to demonstrate the validity of the hypothesis (e.g., Mitchell, Holland, and Forrest 1995; Forrest and Mitchell 1993b), this has proved difficult. Chapter 3 details the relevant background on concepts relevant to compositional evolution that appear under various guises through both the evolutionary biology and evolutionary computation literature.

In large part, the difficulty in formalizing the possible impact of compositional evolution in natural evolution, and the difficulty of demonstrating optimization of a compositional style in artificial evolution, stems from an inadequate understanding of modularity. In the next subsection, I introduce a class of complex systems that is sufficient to properly exemplify the difference in the adaptive capacities of gradual and compositional mechanisms.

1.3 Complex Systems with Modular Interdependency and Their (Un)evolvability

A system can be understood as *modular* if it can be described in terms of subsets of variables that are semi-independent (Callebaut 2005, p. 6). Here we are interested in whether modular subsystems have a semi-independent effect on fitness. If this is the case then it will be possible for them to evolve semi-independently. But usually the utility of a module is not independent of context; it may depend strongly on the state of the rest of the system. Accordingly, a module that is fit in one context may be very different from a variant of that module that is fit in another context, and getting the right modules together may be critically important for fitness. We understand a system to be modular not because it has weak dependencies between subsystems, but because the modules encapsulate the internal complexity of subsystems and thereby reduce the dimensionality of the system. I call the property of having modules with significant intermodule dependencies *modular interdependency*.

In this kind of system, changing a module to resolve intermodule dependencies may require changing many genes simultaneously. Accordingly, gradual evolution is unable to resolve the interdependencies between modules and is thus unable to find high-fitness configurations of the system. In contrast, compositional mechanisms can in principle "swap in" a module that has been preadapted in another individual. Compositional mechanisms that are able to discover and manipulate modules effectively are thereby able to search combinations of modules and satisfy intermodule dependencies more effectively.

Chapter 4 details a particular class of system exhibiting modular interdependency and builds on this to illustrate the distinction between gradual and compositional evolution. I start with a basic pairwise relationship between variables: specifically, I

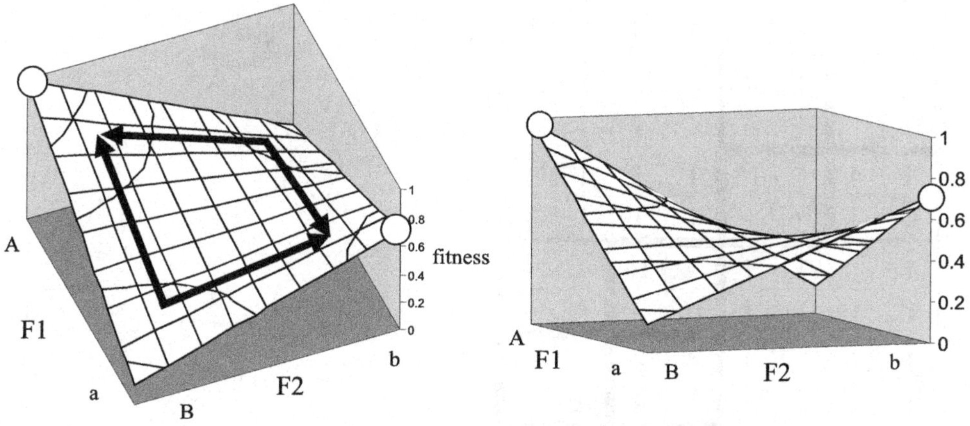

Figure 1.6
A fitness saddle created by interdependency between two variables. A system of two variables, or features, F1 and F2, showing nonadditive fitness interaction or epistasis. Left: The surface shows a fitness landscape and the overlaid arrows show the paths of increasing fitness that can be followed by changing one feature at a time. Right: This particular kind of interaction creates a fitness saddle that is shown more clearly on the rotated view of the same surface. This fitness saddle creates two optima indicated by the large dots located at AB and ab. An algorithm that arrives at ab cannot cross the fitness saddle to AB without changing both features at once.

define the fitness interactions between two variables such that a "fitness saddle" is created. This is illustrated in figure 1.6.

I then use this pairwise interdependency over a larger system of variables to define a system with modular interdependency. Figure 1.7 illustrates an example system exhibiting modular interdependency. The highly regular and symmetric construction used in this particular example enables us to see clearly the underlying structure that is important (though the regularities of this example are not, in fact, required). The dependency matrix on the left of the figure shows the strength of pairwise dependencies between eight problem variables, and the graph on the right depicts the same relationships. Sets of dependencies with equal strengths are indicated by appropriate borders in the table, and by the number of edges and (approximately) by the spatial proximity of nodes in the graph. The fitness of a given configuration for the system of eight variables can be calculated from the sum of pairwise interactions (as per figure 1.6) weighted by the corresponding entry in the dependency matrix.

The salient feature of this structure is that there are subsets of variables in which the variables are more strongly dependent on other variables within their own subset than on variables in other subsets. This creates a dependency matrix where the large

	1	2	3	4	5	6	7	8
1	-	16	4	4	1	1	1	1
2	16	-	4	4	1	1	1	1
3	4	4	-	16	1	1	1	1
4	4	4	16	-	1	1	1	1
5	1	1	1	1	-	16	4	4
6	1	1	1	1	16	-	4	4
7	1	1	1	1	4	4	-	16
8	1	1	1	1	4	4	16	-

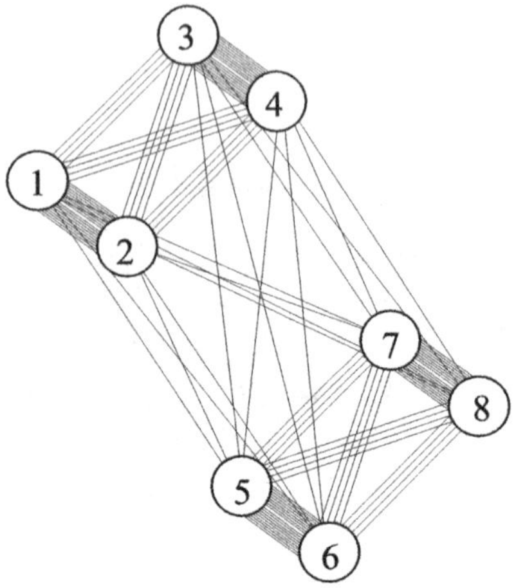

Figure 1.7
A system of variables exhibiting modular interdependency.

values are diagonalizable. But significantly, the values of the matrix that are off the diagonal, representing the strength of dependencies of variables across modules, are nonzero. Clearly, the structure of dependencies in this example system are not just modular but also hierarchically modular—that is, there are clusters and subclusters of more strongly interdependent variables. This potentially allows an adaptive mechanism that is capable of exploiting modularity to decompose the system recursively, or equivalently, to compose together subsolutions repeatedly. This kind of hierarchical decomposability is closely related to the notion of nearly decomposable systems discussed by Simon (1969).

This kind of system may be interpreted in different ways as appropriate for different domains. For example, we may interpret the graph on the right of figure 1.7 as the network structure of a dynamical system where the future state of each variable is dependent both on itself and the state of connected nodes (in the style of "random Boolean networks," Kauffman 1993). A biological example using a dynamical interpretation equates each variable with a gene, and interdependencies between variables may represent transcription factor interactions that "upregulate" or "downregulate" one another. In this interpretation, the fitness of different configurations corresponds to the stability of attractors in the gene expression dynamics. An alternate interpretation is that subsets of genes interact during development to control the attributes of higher-level features, and sets of these interact to create still higher-level features, and so on. If the interaction between genes in one subset and genes in another subset can

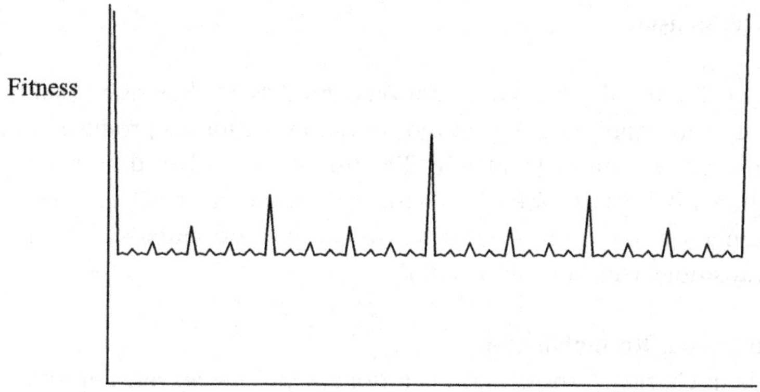

Figure 1.8
A particular cross section through the fitness landscape of a system with modular interdependency. See section 5.1 for details.

be understood through the interaction of their respective higher-level features, then the system will exhibit modular interdependency.

This system of modular interdependency is particularly suited to supporting the general point—that certain kinds of complex systems that are considered unevolvable under the gradualist framework of evolution are easily evolvable under compositional evolution. Its clear modular structure makes it very easy for a compositional mechanism to adapt; however, it also exhibits all the properties usually associated with evolutionary difficulty. Specifically, it creates a highly rugged fitness landscape with an exponential number of local fitness peaks; the peaks are separated by broad fitness saddles (in fact the higher the fitness of a peak the further it is to the next peak of higher fitness); high-fitness configurations of the system are irreducibly complex (in the sense that any small change to the configuration causes a catastrophic decrease in fitness); and finally, there is no guaranteed path of monotonically increasing fitness leading to high-fitness configurations in this system. Figure 1.8 shows a cross section through the fitness landscape created by a complex system with modular interdependency that illustrates most of these features. However, all of these concepts of evolutionary difficulty are dependent on the assumption of gradual evolution. Chapter 5 shows that this kind of system cannot be evolved by a gradual evolutionary process, regardless of the mutation rate that is used. In contrast, when such a system is evolved under compositional evolution these properties of the system do not create evolutionary difficulty. This result depends on the presence of appropriate modularity, a property that gradual evolution cannot exploit but compositional evolution can.

1.4 Compositional Mechanisms

This book provides two highly abstract computational models to illustrate a sufficient set of mechanisms and conditions for compositional evolution to produce systems with hierarchical modular interdependency. The first model is based on sexual recombination (see figure 1.4, left); the second is based on symbiotic encapsulation—the hierarchical encapsulation of symbiotic groups inspired by endosymbiosis and the major evolutionary transitions (see figure 1.4, right).

Composition Based on Sexual Recombination

The simulation models in chapter 6 show that evolutionary processes with appropriate population diversity and variation provided by sexual recombination are able to provide compositional evolution. Specifically, a form of genetic algorithm using sexual recombination, is able to quickly and reliably find the global optima in this problem class. Different individuals in the population discover different modules, and sexual recombination is able to "swap in" modules from one individual to another to discover better combinations of modules that resolve the dependencies between these modules. This provides our first successful example of compositional evolution.

However, the ability of sexual recombination to search combinations of modules is strongly dependent on assumptions about the "genetic map," the placement or ordering of genes on the chromosome (see figure 1.9). In linear chromosomes, a system of genes must be mapped to positions on the chromosome, and the distance between genes in this ordering affects the likelihood that they will co-occur in offspring produced by recombining with other chromosomes. Ideally, features (nodes in the graph of figure 1.7) which are functionally interdependent (shown by numerous interaction lines) will be next to each other on the chromosome (figure 1.9, left). In this case, sexual recombination (in some circumstances) will be able to recombine subsystems effectively. However, without such a favorable situation, functionally interdependent subsets of genes may be arbitrarily positioned on the chromosome (figure 1.9, right). I'll call this a "random genetic map." In this case, sexual recombination is unable to recombine subsystems effectively—even though different well-adapted modules may have been discovered in different members of the population, they cannot be extracted as a unit and recombined effectively. In biological systems, the position of genes might be adaptively reordered, but in engineering domains where the interdependencies of variables are not known *a priori*, we cannot assume a favorable ordering of genes on the chromosome.

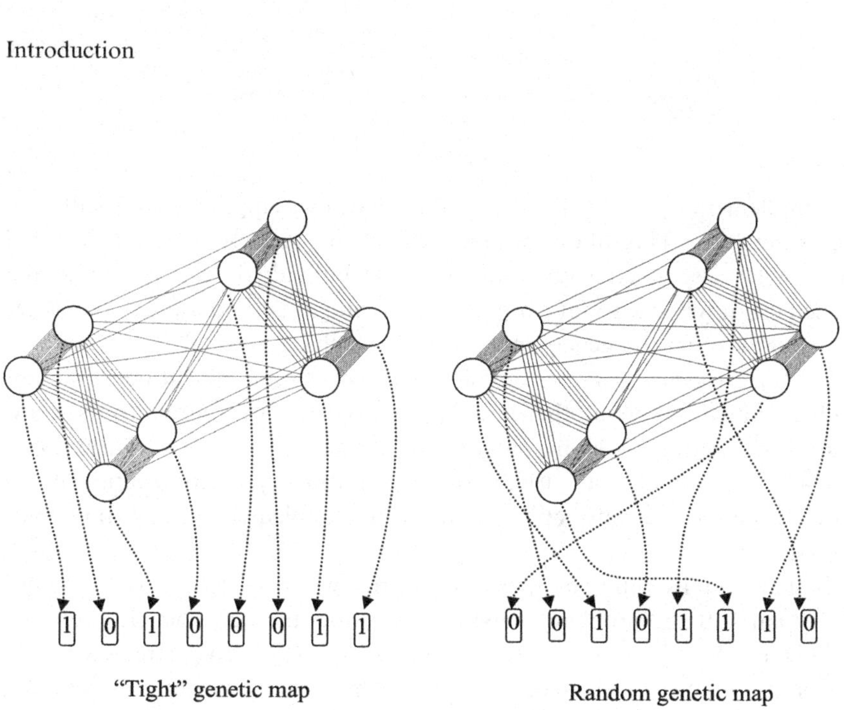

Figure 1.9
The correspondence (or not) of the genetic map with epistatic dependencies. The graph of nodes represents the strength of fitness dependencies of genes (subsets of genetic material) in the evolving system—this is modular in both cases. In a "tight" genetic map the modularity of fitness dependencies corresponds well with the strength of physical linkage between genes. However, if the position of genes in the genetic map is arbitrary (random genetic map) the physical linkage of genetic material does not correspond well with the fitness modularity of genetic material.

Composition Based on Symbiotic Encapsulation

Despite the limitations of composition based on sex, the ability of compositional mechanisms to exploit the structure of problems with modular interdependency is not necessarily dependent on assumptions about the favorable positioning of genes on the chromosome. In chapter 7, I provide a novel model of evolutionary adaptation based on the encapsulation of coadapted simple entities into a new whole. This symbiotic encapsulation model is derived from a mechanism of symbiogenesis or endosymbiosis rather than sexual recombination, and enables compositional evolution in more general circumstances than that provided by sexual recombination.

The salient distinction between sexual recombination and symbiotic encapsulation for our purposes is that whereas sexual recombination produces an offspring by taking, on average, half the genetic material from one parent and half the genetic material from a second parent, symbiotic encapsulation may simply take the union of genetic material from both donor individuals. Naturally, this is most productive when the expression of genetic material from the two parents is not mutually exclusive. Accordingly, the model of this mechanism allows for the possibility of entities that specify complementary characteristics rather than overlapping or mutually exclusive genetic material. This allows whole individuals to represent a functional module that can be assembled with another whole individual, and precludes the need for a mechanism like sex to take a part of one individual and a part of another where it is necessary to use the genetic map to bias which parts to take.

The model is also *coevolutionary*—involving the evolution of entities that are evaluated in the context of one another and thereby coadapt. In contrast to the common adversarial relationships seen in many coevolutionary models (e.g., Hillis 1992; Reynolds 1994; Pollack and Blair 1998), the coevolutionary relationships we are most interested in here occur between entities having complementary adaptive abilities (see Sigmund 1998).

The idea is that initially different specialist entities will evolve to cover different complementary parts of the problem domain. Over time, the dependencies between specialists will be resolved by forming unions between specialists to create new reproductive entities at a higher level of organization. This process repeats, discovering larger alliances until a complete solution is found—a generalist that solves all modules and resolves all intermodule dependencies in the hierarchical problem structure.

This model must accommodate entities of increasing size, as entities of many levels of organization are modeled together, and thus requires a means to prevent large suboptimal generalists from competitively excluding optimal specialists. This proved to be a critical aspect of the model and required methods that step outside frameworks previously familiar in evolutionary computation. The model developed, the "symbiogenic evolutionary adaptation model," or SEAM (to invoke the notion of joins), uses a selection scheme that explicitly respects the *context sensitivity* of an entity's fitness. That is, a proposed solution to a module may be good in one context and not in another, in the same way that the fitness of an organism is strongly dependent on environment. Selection in a varied environment may prevent competitive exclusion of one type of entity by another if the niches they inhabit are distinct, but in the case where one entity is fitter than another in all environments we may assume that the former will competitively exclude the latter. This is modeled explicitly in SEAM by retaining multidimensional measures of fitness coming from the performance of a specialist in different contexts, and applying selection conservatively using the "Pareto dominance" criterion. This provides an abstract form of automatic niching in an ecosystem of different species and replaces the normal single-dimensional fitness selection familiar in single-species models.

SEAM is able to properly identify and optimize the modules in this class of problem automatically and assemble them together to find larger modules repeatedly. It is thus able to quickly and reliably find globally optimal configurations of the problem variables in this class of hierarchical modular interdependency systems. The behavior of SEAM is entirely insensitive to the ordering of genes on the chromosome. Thus I show that the algorithmic advantage of compositional mechanisms in this class of problem is not dependent on assumptions of favorable gene ordering.

In summary, the abstract models of sexual recombination and symbiotic encapsulation illustrate sufficient sets of conditions under which the adaptive capacity of compositional mechanisms is fundamentally different from that of gradual mechanisms. Specifically, I show that these mechanisms are able to exploit modular interdependency structure and provide efficient adaptation in cases where gradual mechanisms are not able to do so. The models used illustrate that the adaptive potential of sexual crossover is sensitive to gene ordering on the chromosome, but this is not a principled limitation of compositional mechanisms since a model based on symbiotic encapsulation is insensitive to gene ordering.

Simulation results from these models and algebraic analysis provide an existence proof for the central claim: certain kinds of complex systems, considered unevolvable under the gradualist framework of evolution, are easily evolvable under compositional mechanisms. More formally, chapter 8 shows that although the expected time for a gradual mechanism to evolve systems with modular interdependency is exponential in the size of the system, the expected time for the compositional mechanisms is polynomial. This is a formal way of saying that systems of this kind quickly become unevolvable to gradual mechanisms when they are of any significant size, but that even large systems are easily evolvable via compositional mechanisms.

1.5 The Impact on Gradualism

These models and results significantly affect the kinds of systems we consider to be evolvable and unevolvable. For example, systems of many complex interdependent parts can appear unevolvable—especially when any small change in the system causes the system to cease functioning (Behe 1996). In general, when faced with the existence of a particular complex system in nature, the normal approach to explain how it may have evolved is to show that there exists a succession of protosystems that are gradually increasing in function where each one is a small modification of the last. Accordingly, a straightforward approach to explain the plausible evolution of a system where it is proposed that any small change causes it to cease functioning is to show that this is not in fact the case—that there does after all exist a succession of gradually changing protosystems approaching the system in question (Dawkins 1996).

More generally, we are interested in affirming the existence of a linear succession of protosystems where each one is a plausible random genetic change from the last—this tends to imply that changes will be small, but in principle, they may be changes of any size so long as they are random. If such a succession can be found, or reasonable hypotheses about the plausible existence of such a path can be upheld, then all well and good. But the adherence to this framework, the linear accumulation of random genetic changes, derives from assumptions about the underlying algorithmic principles.

Specifically, the simulations and analyses show that the existence of a succession of gradually changing protosystems is not, in principle, essential to explain the evolution of a complex adaptation. Although some intuitions to this effect have been in circulation, this book enables us to clarify the fundamental algorithmic distinction between compositional and gradual mechanisms; to define a class of complex systems that distinguishes their capabilities; to analyze the properties of such systems that make them problematic for gradual evolution; and to provide a sufficient set of circumstances under which they are easily evolvable via compositional mechanisms. The contribution of these results to evolutionary biology is not, of course, to merely point out that compositional variation mechanisms exist, but rather that compositional evolution belongs in a different algorithmic paradigm from gradual evolution, and that accordingly it can evolve things that gradual evolution cannot.

In chapter 8, I provide formal analyses of what "can evolve" and "cannot evolve" mean in a rigorous sense. This depends on showing that one process cannot be guaranteed to find high fitness points in less than time exponential in the size of the system, and that another is guaranteed to find high fitness points in time that is at worst a polynomial function of the size of the system. Basically these match with a biologist's intuitions: if a fitness improvement requires many genetic sites to be changed simultaneously to a specific new configuration, then the expected waiting time for this when the changes are made randomly is exponential in the number of sites that need to be changed. It just is not plausible for more than a small number of sites. In chapter 8 I provide formal analyses of the compositional models to see how long they take to make such changes, and show that (given some necessary assumptions) there is always a relatively easy genetic change available to find fitness improvements in these compositional models.

In chapter 9, I connect the features of the compositional models back to the hierarchical structure of the modularity and discuss the mechanisms and principles necessary for an evolutionary process to "scale up" evolution. Whereas mutational processes start out and end up manipulating individual nucleotide sites, compositional mechanisms begin this way but, through evolutionary time, scale up the variational mechanism to manipulate larger, more meaningful components: genes, suites of genes, and so on. This enables compositional processes to escape from the inherent tension of variability and heritability that is inevitable in random-mutation-based processes, for example.

I have introduced several important conceptual distinctions in the previous discussion, so let me recap. The grandest distinction is between exponential complexity and nonexponential complexity; in evolution these correspond to not-evolvable and evolvable, respectively. Included within nonexponential complexity is linear complexity and polynomial complexity. When applicable, hill-climbing is linear complexity and divide-and-conquer problem decomposition is polynomial complexity; so both of these are nonexponential. Gradual evolution is analogous to hill-climbing and compositional evolution is analogous to divide-and-conquer, so both of these make the evolution of large systems feasible when applicable. However, the types of system to which they can be applied are different and some types of systems that are feasible with compositional evolution (e.g., modular ones) are infeasible with gradual evolution. Gradual evolution can be further divided into strict gradualism (small changes only) and nonstrict, which may include large changes in principle. And finally, compositional evolution can be implemented with different mechanisms including sexual recombination and symbiotic encapsulation. These can both evolve systems that gradual evolution cannot, but again they have different capabilities and sexual recombination is limited in some ways that symbiotic encapsulation is not.

Is Gradualism Sufficient?

The possibility of large adaptive changes, and the possible contrast with gradualism, is already recognized in the evolutionary biology literature (see, e.g., *Symbiosis as a Source of Evolutionary Innovation,* Margulis and Fester 1991). However, there is disagreement about whether symbiotic encapsulation contradicts the supposed sufficiency of gradualism to explain evolutionary change.

Ridley (1985), having specifically mentioned symbiosis as a possible source of increases in complexity, states that "The Darwinian denies (as he must) that the complex co-adaptation arose in a single chance event" (p. 35)—and "in all these cases, including symbiosis, complex organs have been built up in small stages" (p. 41). So each adaptation "appears at first impossible to build up in a series of small but advantageous stages. But in fact they probably were" (p. 41). And thus Ridley concludes that "[c]omplex adaptations must have evolved by the natural selection of a large number of small mutations over a long period of time" (p. 42).

It is correct that the Darwinian must deny that a complex adaptation arose in a single *chance* event. But we must not therefore conclude that linear incremental improvement is sufficient to explain all adaptations. If Ridley is referring to the components that were assembled, then maybe (presumably) they evolved gradually (excluding the possibility of repeated endosymbiosis, for the moment). But the resultant system containing both the component parts did not evolve gradually. It did not evolve exclusively via the accumulation of a large number of small mutations because, in addition to this, there was a large inclusion of nonrandom genetic material that was preadapted in a different lineage. And this means, as figure 1.1 shows, that the resultant system is not derived from an unbroken line of small genetic changes. But does this contradict Darwinian gradualism or not?

On the subject of the apparent contradiction with Darwinian change, Maynard Smith (1991) states: "Symbiosis may give rise rather suddenly to evolutionary novelty; it is therefore seen as presenting a challenge to Darwinian gradualism. I think this is to misunderstand the reason why Darwin was a gradualist: essentially, it was because the origin of a complex adaptation would be miraculous." This does not really support the idea that Darwinian gradualism is correct; in fact, it says that Darwinian gradualism is incorrect, but that something deeper is still correct. Specifically, the deeper thing that is correct is the theory of evolution by natural selection—but this needs to be separated from gradualism.

Maynard Smith then suggests that in light of mechanisms that exchange genetic material across lineages, we see that a complex adaptation acquired in such a manner is not "miraculous," and—"There is, therefore, no contradiction between Darwin's belief that complex adaptations arise by the natural selection of numerous intermediates, and the possibility that new evolutionary potentialities may arise suddenly if genetic material that has been programmed by selection in different ancestral lineages is brought together by symbiosis" (ibid., p. 37).

Although it is easy to see that there is nothing miraculous, we should be careful with what we conclude from this. Of course, if a complex adaptation arises by symbiosis it does not come out of thin air but arises from the assembly of "intermediates." But if we assume that intermediates must form a single, unbroken, linear succession of small changes, then the possibility that a complex adaptation arises suddenly by symbiosis *does* present a contradiction to this. We could give Maynard Smith the benefit of the doubt here, but I think it would be fair to say that his statement strongly suggests that it is fine to carry on as though compositional events do not change anything important in our understanding of evolution, and that he has overlooked the possibility that intermediates from parallel lineages may provide different affordances than intermediates in a single lineage.

So, why is it important to make these seemingly nitpicky distinctions? We are all agreed that evolution by natural selection explains these observations. Nothing miraculous has occurred. There are no large random mutations that are beneficial. So what point is there in emphasizing that there is no linear succession of small random changes that connects the result of a symbiotic event to its ancestral lineages? The point is that by adhering to the framework of linear incremental improvement, we miss the fact that compositional events radically alter the underlying algorithmic principles and thereby the space of systems that can evolve. Compositional evolution enables the evolution of systems that would be otherwise unevolvable, and if we adhere to linear gradual evolution thinking, we make incorrect assumptions about which kind of system is evolvable and which is unevolvable.

What does this say about the necessity and sufficiency of gradualism in evolutionary change? Although there are no *miraculous* large changes, there *are* large changes. And moreover, it is not possible to see where these (nonmiraculous) large beneficial changes come from if we view evolution as a linear hill-climbing process. If the *components* that are brought together in a compositional event evolved gradually then gradualism is necessary in order to explain the evolution of the new entity. But it should be clear that even if the components evolved gradually, *the new entity* was not evolved gradually. Specifically, there is no path of small changes of monotonically increasing fitness approaching the configuration of features exhibited in this new entity. Thus the evolution of this entity is not accommodated by the model of linear incremental improvement.

A more fundamental question then arises from these considerations: if some entity AB was created by the composition of entities A and B, each of which evolved gradually, does it follow that AB *could* have evolved gradually (even if it did not in this particular historical scenario)? I will show that this does not necessarily follow. Specifically, I will show that it may be the case that although A and B are each independently evolvable gradually, AB is not evolvable gradually as a whole—nor are the two entities evolvable one after the other in a single individual. This will be the case when A and B correspond to *interdependent modules* in the sense that I define in chapter 4. As I will show, in systems with modular interdependency, each module is independently evolvable but the two modules cannot evolve together gradually because of dependencies acting between the modules.[2] Put simply, when there are interdependencies between A and B, it may be possible for A to evolve by linear incremental improvement, but if it does it becomes essentially impossible for B to evolve without causing dramatic fitness decreases by disrupting dependencies with A, and vice versa. Nonetheless, if A and B each evolve in parallel in different individuals then, even though not all variants of A work well with all variants of B (because of the dependencies between them), searching combinations of different variants is a relatively easy evolutionary process through compositional mechanisms.

As stated, the strongest evidence supporting the claim that it *does* matter whether genetic adaptations are accumulated linearly, or in parallel and then composed together, is that it changes our perception of what is evolvable and what is not. This is why I am able to show that a complex system that has all the characteristics usually associated with evolutionary difficulty (an exponential number of local fitness peaks, wide fitness saddles separating a local peak from the nearest point of higher fitness, configurations that are irreducibly complex, and fitness optima that cannot be reached through a linear succession of incremental improvements) is nonetheless easily evolvable through compositional mechanisms. In the course of this book, I will explain why this is possible by showing that compositional evolution belongs to a different algorithmic class from simple mutation hill climbing.

1.6 Some Related Issues

There are numerous related issues in both evolutionary biology and evolutionary computation that are raised by these models and results. In this section I briefly acknowledge a few important ones.

Noncompositional Mechanisms

I need to distinguish compositional mechanisms from a few mechanisms that may look similar superficially. Gould's concept of *punctuated equilibria* (Gould and Eldredge 1977) does not concern large genetic changes but merely the rate (the unevenness of the rate) at which small changes accumulate—compositional mechanisms concern large genetic changes. The notion of evolutionary jumps known as "saltations" (Goldschmidt 1940) concerns large genetic mutations (see also *Mutation Theory*, DeVries 1909) but these are undirected random mutations, whereas the point of the compositional models is to show that composition affords directed genetic changes that cannot be achieved with a higher mutation rate, for example. Mechanisms such as genetic inversions and gene duplication (Ohno 1970) provide large genetic mutations that introduce nonrandom genetic material that is considerably less likely to be disruptive than a random genetic change of the same scale (because they are a copy of genetic material that has already been subject to selection)—but this genetic material has been subject to selection in the *same* individual as the rest of the genetic material of the organism, rather than preadapted in a different genetic context as it is in compositional mechanisms. Such duplications of existing genetic material do not provide an increase in complexity in the same way that compositional mechanisms do (Ridley 2001, p. 43). These mechanisms potentially exploit a different kind of modularity, the repeated structures kind of modularity (like the fingers of a hand, or cells of a tissue), rather than the functional independence kind of modularity (like metabolizing nutrients and detecting toxins) addressed in this book.

This also leads us to mention small genetic changes that can produce large phenotypic changes (such as homeotic genes, Lewis 1978). Such changes potentially enable large changes in phenotype that are better than random but this is a different issue from the large *genetic* changes addressed here.

Selection on Groups of Genes

Sewell Wright's shifting balance theory, which describes evolutionary mechanisms whereby a population may escape local optima on a fitness landscape, is related to some of the models presented in this book. The models share some of the underlying motives and thinking but there are significant differences in the mechanisms (see section 9.1). For example, genetic drift does not feature in my models for escaping local optima.

The idea of compositional evolution based on symbiotic encapsulation is basically the idea that subsets of genetic material that have evolved semi-independently become part of a single individual at a new level of organization. This might sound similar to group selection, where individuals are selected for their utility to the benefit of the group rather than to themselves. And since this principle is applied recursively through subsequent hierarchical levels, it might further appear to be a model of hierarchical selection (Keller 1999; Gould 1982a, 2002). But this is not the case. Here we are careful to consider the selfish interests of the parties involved in a symbiotic encapsulation, as required by a microscopic, "selfish-gene"-style model (Dawkins 1976).

Nonetheless, the notion of hierarchical selection makes good sense from an algorithmic point of view. The principle that affords efficient adaptation in these models is that first searching combinations of small numbers of variables finds good small modules, then searching combinations of modules finds bigger modules, and so on. If the search were conducted solely at the lower level then suboptimal solutions would result. And if the search were conducted solely at the higher level then the combinatorics of the search space would be prohibitive. But by implicitly moving incrementally from lower levels to higher levels we gain the algorithmic advantage of a divide-and-conquer approach and the opportunity, in appropriate problem domains, to find good global solutions efficiently. (See discussion section 9.1.)

Modularity

An important concept of modularity in the genetic algorithm literature is Holland's notion of "building blocks" (1975). This is closely related to the notion of modules we define in chapter 4, but it is distinct in several important respects. The modules that the modified GA processes in the compositional model of chapter 6 are indeed building blocks (but not necessarily small ones). In contrast, the modules used by symbiotic encapsulation in chapter 7 are not building blocks: They are represented by subsets of variables but there is no dependence between the position of genes on the chromosome and the ability of this method to exploit modularity. Additionally, it should not be assumed that the notion of modules implies a problem that can be decomposed into *separable* subproblems. This is a mistake that has caused widespread confusion in the controversy around the building-block hypothesis and the operation of the GA. There may be strong nonlinear interactions between modules—that is, modularity does not imply that a problem is separable.

The notions of hierarchical modularity, and hierarchical decomposability, relate strongly to Herbert Simon's (1969) ideas and the wealth of design-engineering and social systems he refers to. However, chapter 4 shows that a system of hierarchical modular interdependency does not depend on the idea of modules with weak inter-module dependencies.

Finally, one of the best-known models of genetic dependencies is Kauffman's "NK landscapes" (1993). When the number of variables involved in each dependency K is large, they produce rugged landscapes that are very difficult for gradual evolution. However, these landscapes have no structural modularity and are therefore also difficult for compositional evolution. We will see that two landscapes with the same number of dependencies can be very different in difficulty because of differences in the structure of those dependencies.

"No Free Lunch" and the Building-Block Hypothesis

The "no free lunch" theorem (Wolpert and Macready 1997) basically says that "you cannot get something for nothing"—specifically, you cannot have an algorithm that is better than random search unless you also restrict the class of problems to which it is applied. One of the primary evolutionary computation aims of this book is to clarify whether the EA can in some circumstances provide an algorithmic advantage akin to divide-and-conquer problem decomposition as the intuition of the building-block hypothesis suggests. As Wolpert and Macready rightly point out, for any algorithm, the algorithmic advantage of the method is dependent on the class of problem to which it is applied. Accordingly, it is not my intent to show that a GA, standard or otherwise, is advantageous in all problem classes. On the contrary, I invest a good deal of this book identifying and illustrating the properties of a particular problem domain—specifically, the class of problems with modular interdependency. Thus, any failure of the building-block hypothesis to explain the operation of the "simple GA" in other problem domains is simply not relevant to my conclusions. But having said this, I find the intuition of the building-block hypothesis to be quite instructive. In contrast, the "schema" theorem does not turn out to be useful in these models. The schema theorem (Holland 1975) concerns the increase in copies of schemata with above-average fitness in a population, and historically, it is considered responsible for the supply of building blocks for the building-block hypothesis. In the models developed in this book, the notion of schemata, and schema combination, is very useful, but we have no need to invoke or defend the schema theorem since the selection schemes are quite different.

1.7 Contributions

The main motives and goals of this book are: to foster and capitalize on two-way interdisciplinary exchange between evolutionary biology and evolutionary computation, to provide a conceptual framework that incorporates a broader view of evolutionary mechanisms than the gradualist framework, to understand the adaptive role (if any) of symbiosis and symbiogenesis, and to better understand the competence of genetic algorithms, and in particular the utility (if any) of crossover and the building-block hypothesis.

The specific contributions for evolutionary computation include: 1. Clarifying the structure of dependencies between variables in modular problem domains, in particular, hierarchically modular problems. (These are related to, but resolve important limitations of, building-block problems in GA theory.) 2. Demonstrating the conceptual contrast of hill climbing and divide-and-conquer problem decomposition mechanisms in evolutionary algorithms. (This is related to, but more general than, the notions of the building-block hypothesis.) 3. Providing a concrete illustration of mechanisms that permit automatic module acquisition and assembly in evolutionary algorithms. This provides a conceptual framework that accommodates cooperative coevolution and function optimization, addressing fundamental issues such as representational recoding and open-ended scalability in evolutionary search. 4. Providing specific models for algorithmic methods such as methods for maintaining appropriate schema diversity, and the use of partially specified genotypes to represent functional or fitness dependencies.

The specific contributions for evolutionary biology closely parallel these: 1. Clarifying the structure of functional or fitness dependencies that produce different kinds of evolutionary difficulty. 2. Demonstrating the conceptual contrasts of gradual evolution and compositional evolution, thereby broadening our interpretation of evolutionary processes. 3. Providing a conceptual framework for evolution that begins to accommodate adaptive roles for symbiosis and symbiogenesis. 4. Providing specific models for evolutionary processes and the role of issues such as the genetic map, population-ecosystem diversity, population subdivision, and shifting balance theory.

The models themselves are quite simple: the fitness landscape can be defined in a simple equation, and each algorithm can be defined in a few lines of pseudocode. However, since the purpose of the models is an illustration of deeper conceptual issues, they require a fair amount of setup in order to convey why the models are the way they are, and what the results do and do not mean.

It is important to be clear about the scope and boundaries of this book and these claims. I provide these models as an illustration of the important potential that these mechanisms afford *in principle*, and to encourage analysis of evolutionary processes such as these that go beyond the usual gradualist conception of evolutionary change. This follows a style of cross-disciplinary research such as, for example, connectionism, which did not claim to necessarily be an accurate model of the way that the cortex worked in a detailed sense, but was nonetheless informative by demonstrating an alternate possibility that presented a challenge to established cognitive science. Moreover, the mechanisms I explore are not arbitrary excursions into possible biologies. First, abstract computational models such as these are relevant to natural evolution at least in the sense that we demonstrate that it is possible for nonteleological adaptive processes, that is, processes based only on fitness feedback, to behave in this manner. Second, mechanisms of sexual recombination, horizontal gene transfer, and symbiogenesis, for example, are a biological fact. Third, some of the other concepts that are explored have a rich, albeit controversial, background in biological thought—and throughout the book effort is made to draw the relevant connections to the biological literature and provide appropriate biological interpretations of models and results.

Similarly, the computational contributions of this book are theoretic and conceptual. The studies provide proof of concept for the algorithmic techniques and address issues of principle, not empirical observations about engineering domains or processes. But likewise, the computational models build on an established set of research questions, algorithms, and conceptual ideas. Highly abstract models like those presented here require further work to connect properly with detailed biological knowledge and validate the many assumptions theoretical models require. But in the meantime the fundamental algorithmic distinctions of the models prompt us to expand the way we think about natural and artificial evolution to include new possibilities.

2 Gradual Evolution

In this chapter I describe the gradualist framework of evolution and corresponding notions of evolutionary difficulty, in both the evolutionary biology and evolutionary computation literature. This includes an overview of simple evolutionary algorithms such as the genetic algorithm.

2.1 The Gradualist Framework of Evolution

Evolution by natural selection has been associated with the notion of accumulating slight modifications from the beginning: "If it could be demonstrated that any complex organ existed which could not possibly have been formed by numerous, successive, slight modifications, my theory would absolutely break down" (Darwin 1859). In fact, this statement is "clearly invalid" (Gould 1982a, p. 84), because if large changes that are beneficial (or not appreciably deleterious) are somehow available then natural selection can act on them. Nonetheless, the supposed necessity of small changes remains quite pervasive.

The notion of the necessity of slight modifications perhaps originates from observing character variation under artificial selection (animal breeding and plant breeding), and by observing the spectrum of quantitative variation in natural organisms. Of course, variation observed during relatively infinitesimal timescales might not be representative of evolutionary changes in general, and even if it were, this does not categorically exclude the possibility of large changes. But there is a more fundamental reason to support this notion of exclusively small variations. Specifically, the idea that evolution must proceed by successive slight modifications follows from the idea that changes are random and unguided. That is, large, random, unguided changes are generally considered unlikely to be beneficial (a position I agree with). This probably follows from the idea that a small change from an adaptive peak will likely remain somewhere on the adaptive peak, whereas a large change will probably not (Fisher 1930); then, given that high fitness points are rare, a large change is more likely to arrive at a lower fitness configuration than the peak we started on. Accordingly, we arrive at the conclusion that beneficial changes are more likely to be small than large. In fact, we should be careful not to equate the probability that large changes are beneficial with the probability that beneficial changes are large (consider the probability that tables are four-legged and the probability that four-legged things are tables), but the expectation that large changes will *nearly always* be catastrophic does suggest that large changes will be very unlikely to feature in successful evolutionary trajectories.

When the genetic basis of variation is understood, the idea of successive slight modifications is further reinforced. If genetic mutations are the source of variation, and these are small and few in number, then successive slight modification seems to be the only option. It is clear that we should separate genotypic variation from phenotypic variation—a small change in genotype does not necessarily mean a small change in phenotype. Still the general concept of changes being unguided suggests that large genetic mutations are unlikely to be beneficial; more to the point, they are less likely to be adaptive than small genetic changes. In short, large changes would have to rely on "hopeful monsters" (Goldschmidt 1940; Gould 1982b).

In summary, "strict gradualism," evolution via the linear accumulation of genetic modifications that are exclusively *small*, is supported both by the observation that organismic variation in phenotypic characters (both that occurring naturally and that occurring under artificial breeding) is generally observed to be slight, and by the knowledge of mechanistic sources of small variations, that is, spontaneous point mutations produced by DNA replication errors. Additionally, although it is accepted that large genetic changes could be selected for if they were beneficial, the supposition of small changes is supported by considering the *prima facie* likelihood of large random variations being beneficial. This is a core assumption of the gradualist framework of evolution. But the definition I want to work with is that this framework asserts that evolution occurs via the sequential linear accumulation of random genetic variations, of whatever size. This does not require that genetic changes are small in principle, but it is a natural assumption that this is likely.

I should emphasize that the *gradualist framework of evolution* and *evolution by natural selection*, though they were both supplied by Darwin at the same time, are different things. Compositional evolution does not challenge the principle of evolution by natural selection. Both the gradualist framework of evolution and compositional evolution depend on the principle that variants that reproduce more effectively increase in number more quickly than those that reproduce less effectively, and thereby come to replace them. The principles of heritable variation and differential reproduction are not in question. But compositional evolution does cause us to separate evolution by natural selection from the gradualist framework—not only from strict gradualism but from any linear process of accumulating random variations of any size.

The notion of gradual evolution has become embedded in evolutionary thinking in many different ways. For example, as population genetics took shape (with Fisher, Haldane, and Wright in the 1930s), the assumption of evolution by successive slight modifications became entrenched. Goldschmidt's theory of saltations[1] was rejected, and evolution by small changes was also supported in more subtle ways. Specifically, if we assume that evolutionary change involves only small modifications then the only fitness effects that matter are those that can be accounted for by individual small changes. So, although the fitness effect of a large change might not be equal to the sum of fitness effects from the small changes of which it is composed, we need not consider the influence of this possibility on evolutionary trajectories. The upshot of this is that population genetics models sometimes ignore this possibility altogether, and often model loci individually (see the section on epistasis, p. 37).

This leads us to the main impact of gradualism on evolutionary thinking that I want to discuss—the impact of gradualist models on notions of evolutionary difficulty. But first I introduce the basic evolutionary computation model of the gradualist framework.

2.2 Evolutionary Algorithms

Evolutionary Algorithm Basics

Evolutionary computation is, in general, the field encompassing computational techniques based on, or inspired by, evolution. In practice, the term is essentially synonymous with the class of problem solving, optimization, and design techniques known as "evolutionary algorithms" (EAs) (see De Jong 2002 for an overview). Any attempt to briefly describe the components of an EA that are common to all varieties will not do justice to all emphases. But, without being specific about procedural details, an EA generally has the components shown in table 2.1.

The basic form of the algorithm uses repeated cycles of *evaluation*, *selection*, and *reproduction with variation* to shape a population of candidate solutions for some

Table 2.1
Components of an evolutionary algorithm (EA).

The components of a simple EA	The biological metaphor/inspiration
An EA maintains a (large) number of candidate solutions or designs for a problem.	A population of individuals.
All candidate solutions are evaluated with respect to some quality or performance criterion.	Every individual has a "fitness."
Those candidate solutions that are higher quality are used for generating new solutions with higher probability than those that are low quality. Low-quality solutions may be discarded.	Differential reproduction. Differential survival.
New candidate solutions are created by random variations of the existing candidate solutions. And those variations may propagate to future candidate solutions.	Descent with modification. Heritable variation.

problem. A number of random candidate solutions, individuals, are generated to initialize the population. Evaluation is the process of assessing the value or quality of a candidate solution with respect to some objective measure of quality or performance. Selection is applied to (probabilistically) focus search around those solutions that are superior. Reproduction produces new candidate solutions by random variation of selected individuals. Successive repetitions of evaluation, selection, and reproduction (with variation) change the composition of the population by promoting candidate solutions that are superior, and by exploring the space of possible solutions in the vicinity of superior solutions.

The principle of an EA is that by making successive random variations of candidate solutions that are good so far, the algorithm is able to bias the exploration of solution space (with respect to random search) to invest more exploration in those parts that are most promising. If, by virtue of the fact that "offspring" may inherit some of the desirable characteristics of their "parents" (i.e., fit individuals have a better chance of producing fit variants than unfit individuals do), then repeated selection and variation should exploit this bias appropriately and accumulate successive adaptive modifications. Accordingly, an EA is often considered to proceed something like a hill-climbing[2] process (Muhlenbein 1992), discussed below, except that an EA is usually based on a population of solutions rather than a single solution.

The Simple Genetic Algorithm

Evolutionary algorithms (EAs) come in many flavors, for example: genetic algorithms (Holland 1975; Goldberg 1989), evolutionary strategies (Back, Hoffmeister, and Schwefel 1991), evolutionary programming (Fogel, Owens, and Walsh 1966), and genetic programming (Koza 1992). The differences between these methods largely depend on the default choice of representation (e.g., bit strings, real-valued vectors, finite-state machines), the choice of variation operator (e.g., mutation and/or crossover), and the default selection method (e.g., fitness-proportionate selection or truncation selection).

For most of the work that follows in this book, the genetic algorithm, GA, is the best archetype (see Mitchell 1996). A GA usually uses a binary encoding over large linear chromosomes (fixed-length bit strings), a large population (on the order of 100 to 1,000), both point mutation and crossover for variation, and fitness-proportionate selection by default. The overall operation is often "generational," meaning that the entire population of individuals is evaluated, selected, and reproduced as a batch before the next cycle commences. Something like this is what is meant when referring to the "simple GA." A procedural outline of the simple GA (SGA) is given below (figure 2.1).

Initialize population with random individuals, i.e., random bit strings.

1. Repeat until stopping criterion (e.g., threshold quality reached, or population no longer changing significantly).
    a. Evaluate the fitness of all individuals in population using an "objective fitness function" giving the quality of each string.
    b. With selection probability of each individual proportionate to their fitness, select (with replacement) individuals from population to be "parents."
    c. For each parent, p1, generate an "offspring" individual by:
        i. Picking another parent to be p2, and creating a new string that has some bits from p1 and some bits from p2. (This is referred to as "crossover" or "recombination.")
        ii. Randomly changing some of the bits in the string, i.e., applying point mutation with low per-locus probability.
    d. Replace original population with new population of offspring.

Figure 2.1
A procedural outline for a generational simple genetic algorithm (SGA). Step (i) may be omitted for a mutation-only version, in which case step (ii) mutates a copy of the parent. There are a few implementation details that are not spelled out in this description; I will give more precise descriptions for the algorithms that are implemented in the simulation studies.

`10101000101001010 0` – parent.

1010**0**000101**11**10100 – offspring with point mutations (bold).

Figure 2.2
Point mutations on a bit-string individual.

This description includes mutation (figure 2.2) and crossover (figure 3.7) as variation operators. However, some kinds of EA do not include crossover, and the basic intuition for many (but by no means all) researchers about how EAs work considers crossover to be optional. Further, some researchers consider the operation of crossover to be useless or, at least, nothing more than a "macromutation" equivalent to a large number of point mutations (Jones 1995). Whether or not this is necessarily true is one of the research questions I want to answer. Accordingly, I will start by considering the operation of the GA without crossover, that is, a mutation-only GA. The later sections will discuss the impact of crossover in detail.

There are many varieties of GA (as there are of other types of EA). For example, there are varieties that use different selection methods, different variation operators, different representations, and all sorts of sophisticated add-ons such as diversity maintenance techniques. There are also parametric choices to be made: the size of the population, whether or not to use crossover (or for what proportion of offspring to use crossover and what recombination rate to use), how much mutation to use, and so forth. These differences make it very difficult to make thorough comparisons between one type of GA and another. In this book I am not going to try to make comprehensive comparisons. The particular variants of algorithms that I define, and the experiments that are performed, are provided for illustration. But we will see from analytic argument that different kinds of algorithm have profound differences in their behavior and in the kind of problems they can solve in principle.

Evolutionary Algorithms as Evolutionary Models

Evolutionary algorithms in computer science are inspired by natural processes, but are not generally intended to be accurate models of biological evolution. EAs, as noted, are an optimization and design technique, and most researchers feel free to introduce new features as required to address computational needs. Having said that, it is common to see researchers taking inspiration from evolutionary biology to enhance performance, for example, island models to promote diversity (Starkweather, Whitley, and Mathias 1991), and also to see researchers appealing to biological plausibility as a guide for making choices in certain design decisions (usually in cases where computational preference is undecided).

Although evolutionary algorithms are generally not obliged to follow biological models closely, the basic framework of the EA outlined above adheres to some quite strong assumptions in common with early population genetic models—for example, the preoccupation with the genetic change of a single population (i.e., the coevolution of multiple species is often handled simplistically as purely adversarial interactions and generally does not involve genetic exchange between populations), and the assumption of a single fixed niche (i.e., all individuals are evaluated with a single given fitness function).

The usual assumptions restrict the kind of dynamics that may occur. In particular, we start with the assumption that we are modeling the adaptation of a single species in a single niche. That is, all individuals in the population are candidate solutions for the same problem. This has several important consequences: first, all individuals are in a competitive relationship—superior solutions are promoted by competitively excluding inferior solutions from the population. In the absence of any additional measures to the contrary, this introduces an inherent pressure for the population to converge to a single type—around the current best solution. Second, it is therefore not possible that some subset of the population may diversify into a different niche and coexist without competing with the remainder of the population. Third, it follows that there is no possibility for different types to specialize diversely in parallel, or coexist, let alone enter into collective behaviors or cooperative relationships. Although there are a few notable exceptions and qualifications (e.g., fitness sharing and cooperative coevolution) that I will detail later, these limitations are true of the simple GA (SGA) and underlie the assumptions of EAs in general.

Some assumptions in the basic EA framework include:

- The model is based on the adaptation of a single population in a fixed niche: all individuals are assessed with respect to the same criteria—the same fitness function.
- Every individual has an identifiable fitness (objective performance metric) and all individuals can be ranked in this single dimension of quality.
- The only type of dynamic between variants is competitive exclusion: all individuals are in the same niche and compete to be members of the next generation.
- There is no change in the mechanisms of selection, variation, reproduction, or evaluation over evolutionary time.
- At least in SGAs without crossover, the unit of selection, the individual, is considered to be unambiguous. The compositional phenomena we address in this book require that we expand our models and relax our assumptions in both evolutionary computation and evolutionary biology (as discussed in section 3.4).

2.3 Concepts of Evolutionary Difficulty

The basic intuition of optimization for an EA is the same as the basic intuition of adaptation for natural evolution: by accumulating small random variations that incrementally improve fitness we can arrive at progressively fit adaptations. Accordingly,

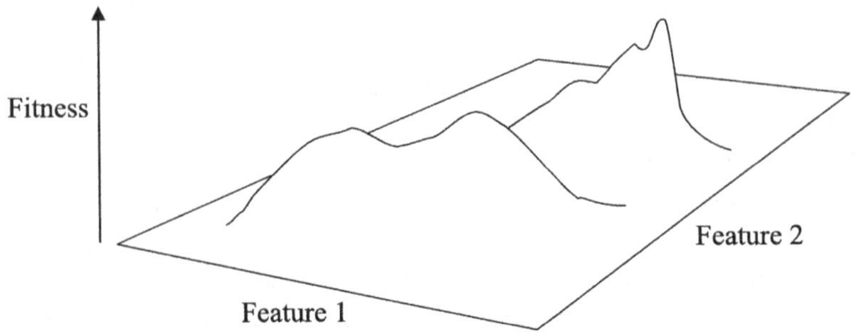

Figure 2.3
A fitness landscape.

many of the same notions of evolutionary difficulty are common for both artificial and natural evolution.

Fitness Landscapes

Wright (1967) introduced a tool which has become highly pervasive for thinking about evolutionary processes, the *fitness landscape*. A fitness landscape (figure 2.3) is a surface where the vertical position at each point is given by the fitness of a corresponding genotype, and the neighborhood of points on the surface is given by the neighborhood of corresponding genotypes under genetic variation. That is, genotypes that are adjacent in genetic sequence space correspond to adjacent points in the fitness landscape, and the height of each point is given by the fitness of the corresponding genotype.

In principle, the fitness landscape can be defined the same way regardless of the genetic operators involved (Jones 1995). For example, we could define adjacent points in the landscape using k-point mutation instead of single-point mutation. In general, for the fitness landscape to be intuitive we want it to be the case that the closer two points are to each other in the landscape, the higher the probability of transitioning between them under genetic variation. This is natural and intuitive when the distance metric is mutational distance, that is, *Hamming distance*—the sum of differences in all dimensions of change, which for binary genotypes just means counting the number of bits that are different. I will discuss nonmutational neighborhood metrics later, but the metric of small modifications (genetic or phenotypic) is intuitive and by far the most pervasive.

Armed with the fitness landscape, we can now understand an evolutionary process as a hill-climbing process. That is, evolutionary change can be seen to ascend local gradients in the fitness landscape by making small changes in the neighborhood of

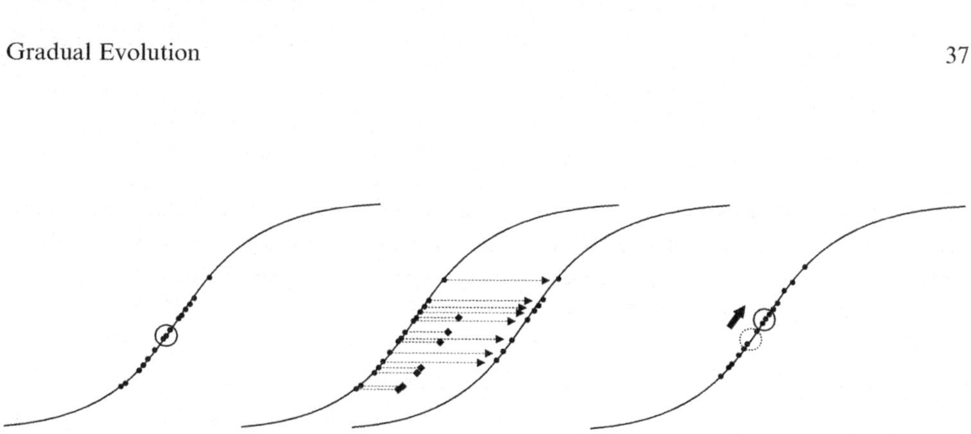
(a) (b) (c)

Figure 2.4
Population mean climbing a local fitness gradient. The curve represents the local fitness landscape, the points represent individuals of a population, and the circle represents the approximate population-mean position on the landscape. (a) A population of individuals is represented by its mean; (b) selection removes less fit individuals but allows more fit individuals to pass through; and (c) the remaining individuals have a new population mean, as does the next generation of new individuals generated from them. In the process, the population mean in (c) has climbed the local fitness gradient with respect to its position in (a).

the population mean, and moving toward, or selecting for, variants that are fitter or "higher." Then, since evolutionary change allows movement to only local points on the landscape, evolution must ascend local gradients to arrive at local optima, local peaks in the landscape. This process is depicted in figure 2.4.

Epistasis, Ruggedness, Local Optima, and Fitness Saddles

Put simply, *epistasis* is interdependency between genes. It means that the effect of one allele depends on what other alleles are present. Two mutations are epistatic if the effect of having both mutations together is not equal to the effects from the two mutations added together.[3] Epistasis is widespread in natural systems both in physiological interactions and in interactions among fitness effects (Wolf, Brodie, and Wade 2000). If a particular allele has different fitness effects over a number of different genetic backgrounds in a population (and therefore exhibits epistasis) we may describe the fitness effect of that allele by decomposing it into its additive component and an epistatic component (describing how much it deviates from additivity). For reasons that we will discuss, it is additive fitness effects, or the additive component of fitness effects, (among the variation in a population) that most population genetic models are concerned with (Phillips, Otto, and Whitlock 2000). But it is with the epistatic, nonadditive, fitness effects where fitness landscapes become interesting. If genetic changes have epistatic interactions then the corresponding fitness landscape is nonplanar. In computational terms, difficulty in a combinatorial optimization problem is largely created by the frustration of problem variables. One variable is said to be dependent on another when the effect of changing the variable is dependent on the state of the other. Following the biological terminology, this is also often referred to as epistasis. For a discussion on types of epistasis see Phillips 1998; Weinreich, Watson, and Chao 2005.

Intuitively, the *ruggedness* of a surface is the extent to which it deviates from a flat plane. Evolutionarily, one problem with ruggedness is that it may create *local adaptive peaks*. A local adaptive peak is a point in the adaptive landscape where no neighboring points have higher fitness. This corresponds to a configuration of the system where there is no small change in the system that can produce a higher fitness configuration. In computational terms, a *local optimum* is similarly a point in the landscape that corresponds to a candidate solution that cannot be improved by any small change, that is, a mutation (in some contexts, the term excludes solutions that are globally optimal).

A fitness landscape with many optima can prevent a gradual mechanism from finding high-fitness configurations. This is one of the predominant notions of evolutionary difficulty:

> the central problem of evolution . . . is that of a trial and error mechanism by which the locus of a population may be carried across a saddle from one peak to another and perhaps higher one. (Wright 1935, p. 264)

Thus, the idea that evolution proceeds by the accumulation of slight modifications gives rise to the intuitive notion of a population climbing a local fitness gradient in a fitness landscape. And from here, the idea that the population might become trapped in a local optimum, a point that has no neighbors of higher fitness, creates a powerful notion of evolutionary difficulty. Specifically, we must explain how evolution is able to cross a fitness saddle, the region of depressed fitness between one local optimum and another (figure 2.5). An important concept of evolutionary difficulty thus concerns the width of fitness saddles, that is, the distance between a configura-

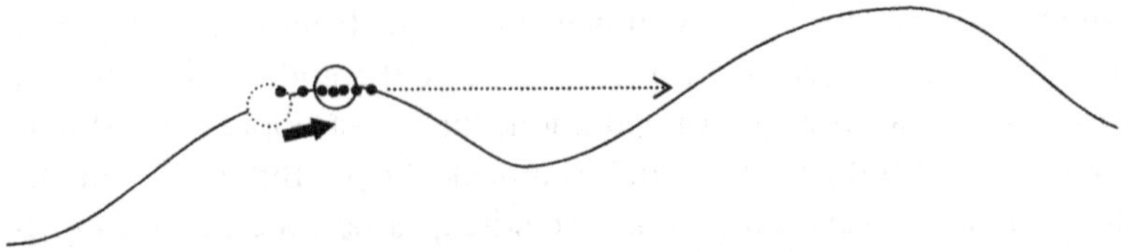

Figure 2.5
A fitness saddle. Wright characterizes evolutionary difficulty as the problem of crossing a fitness saddle, i.e., a population climbs a local gradient to the local fitness peak but is unable to traverse to higher fitness points on other fitness peaks.

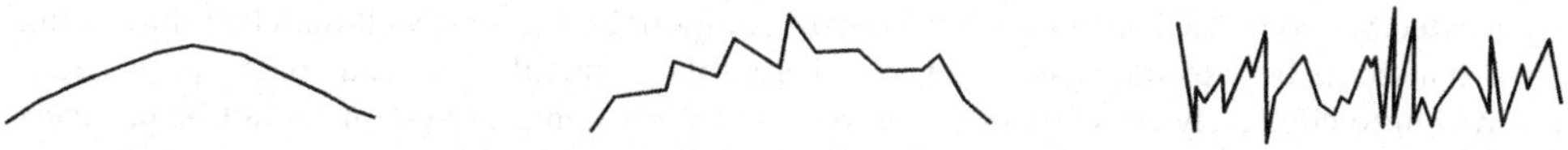

Figure 2.6
Smoothness and local optima. (a) A smooth unimodal landscape with no local optima—considered easy for evolution. (b) A landscape with some ruggedness. (c) A highly rugged landscape with many local optima.

tion and the nearest configuration with equal or higher fitness. For gradual mechanisms we may measure distance in terms of the number of variables or loci that need to be changed "in one go"—this is the Hamming distance, for binary variables.

Note that there are several alternative scenarios that could enable successful adaptation in problematic cases. One possibility is that large amounts of genetic material may accumulate without being expressed in the phenotype, thus allowing *neutral evolution* (Kimura 1983) and permitting variants to travel along neutral pathways (Huynen, Stadler, and Fontana 1996; Reidys, Stadler, and Schuster 1997) that "tunnel" their way to fitter parts of feature space (Van Nimwegen and Crutchfield 2000). This possibility enables a valley crossing by utilizing large amounts of random mutation that is unguided by selection; but unlike the hopeful monster this need not occur in a single mutational event (see section 5.3).

Although GAs generally operate in a high-dimensional binary space, it is still popular to visualize fitness landscapes as two-, or sometimes one-dimensional, metric spaces. Intuitively, these are often imagined as a "walk" through adjacent points in the high-dimensional space—that is, adjacent points in the one-dimensional landscape are adjacent points in the high-dimensional space. The ruggedness of this landscape is then taken to indicate the correlation among the fitness of mutational neighbors in the search space. Figure 2.6 shows some landscapes of increasing ruggedness, and an increasing number of local optima, that are taken to indicate a spectrum of evolutionary difficulty (see "NK landscapes," Kauffman 1993). In the simple GA one common explanation for failure is *premature convergence*, where the population loses diversity and becomes genetically similar before finding the global optimum. Thus it becomes stuck on a local optimum.

Irreducible Complexity

Another emotive notion of evolutionary difficulty is also based on violating the assumption of accumulating small changes. "Irreducible complexity" is defined by Behe as follows:

By irreducibly complex I mean a single system composed of several well-matched, interacting parts that contribute to the basic function, wherein the removal of any one of the parts causes the system to effectively cease functioning. An irreducibly complex system cannot be produced directly (that is, by continuously improving the initial function, which continues to work by the same mechanism) by slight, successive modifications of a precursor system, because any precursor to an irreducibly complex system that is missing a part is by definition nonfunctional. An irreducibly complex biological system, if there is such a thing, would be a powerful challenge to Darwinian evolution. (1996, p. 39)

A simple illustration of an irreducibly complex system is depicted in figure 2.7.

Behe indicates that many biological systems are irreducibly complex at the molecular level. The notion of an irreducibly complex system sounds a lot like the notion of a designed system, such as the infamous watch of Paley from almost two hundred years earlier (1802). But Behe incorporates the anti-Darwinian notion that not only is the system complex and specific in its structure, but that it also cannot be formed by accumulating small modifications. However, given the possibility of an indirect process where a part evolved for some function is exapted for some other function, or a dynamic evolutionary environment changing the effect of part removal and part addition over time, or atrophication of one part making a remaining part irremovable, for example, it is doubtful that irreducible complexity implies that there is no path of small changes approaching the adaptation in question. But even if we included the absence of a gradual path in the definition of an irreducibly complex system—irreducible complexity would only be a challenge for evolution *if* we assume that evolution proceeds via a gradual path of monotonically increasing fitness.

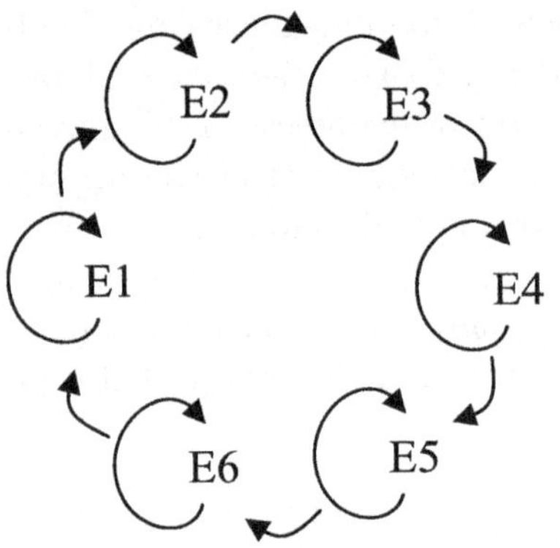

Figure 2.7
A hypothetical irreducibly complex system. A system of autocatalytic enzymes forms a hypercycle, and if any enzyme is removed the whole cycle is broken.

A Path of Monotonically Increasing Fitness

The notions of local optima, landscape ruggedness, Wright's "central problem of evolution" (1931), and Behe's notion of "irreducible complexity" (1996) are intended to characterize systems which are problematic for evolution because they do not admit evolution by accumulation of small modifications. In general the evolvability of a solution for an evolutionary algorithm, as in natural evolution, is understood to be connected to the presence of a path of monotonically increasing fitness to that solution.[4] In general, in nontrivial problems, we do not expect there to be such paths from most points to the global optimum of a landscape.

Nonetheless, following the assumption that gradual evolution is the only possibility for evolution by natural selection, there has been, in the near century and a half since Darwin, a great deal of research effort spent hypothesizing about plausible fine-scale paths of monotonically increasing fitness approaching problematic adaptations, and in identifying "missing links"—intermediate precursors of a complex adaptation (e.g., Dawkins 1996). (And similarly, a good deal of effort has been spent identifying systems that do not appear to have smooth paths of approach as typified by Behe.)

This effort is expended with good cause. If there are paths of small changes approaching all adaptations in nature then there is no evolutionary difficulty in achieving these adaptations. However, note that the perceived need for such paths arises from the assumption that evolution must work via the linear accumulation of successive slight modifications, via incremental improvement. We will see that operators like crossover and other compositional mechanisms require us to revise our notions of evolutionary difficulty, and that these classical notions of evolutionary difficulty are dependent on the underlying assumption of gradual change.

Summary of Concepts of Evolutionary Difficulty

The following assumptions are pervasive in our understanding of evolutionary difficulty in both natural systems and computational problem solving:

- There must always be some path of successive slight modifications conferring monotonically increasing fitness approaching any evolvable feature or adaptation.
- There is a meaningful neighborhood metric on which a fitness landscape may be based, giving a meaningful notion of local adaptation and local hill climbing for evolutionary change.
- Ruggedness in a fitness landscape, and the existence of local optima, corresponds to evolutionary difficulty.

- A population will, for the most part, be more or less converged around a local fitness peak, i.e., stuck on a local fitness optimum.
- A system where the removal of any one part causes nonfunction (irreducibility) is difficult for evolution.
- Although epistasis is not necessarily absent, natural selection will act primarily on the additive effects of gene substitutions.
- Large adaptive changes should be relegated to "hopeful monsters."

All of these assumptions and notions of evolutionary change and evolutionary difficulty are based, directly or indirectly, on the assumption of gradual change. We know that in principle genetic changes do not have to be small and that if large genetic changes were beneficial they would be selected for. But these concepts of difficulty all depend on the assumption that changes will be small (which is reasonable if we are working on the assumption that they are random and undirected—which is the case unless they are directed by prior selection as in the case of compositional mechanisms). If genetic changes do not have to be small, then hill climbing is not a comprehensive model of evolutionary change. Without hill climbing, the concept of the local optimum would not make sense, and, following from this, landscape ruggedness, the width of fitness saddles, the absence of smooth paths to an adaptation, and irreducible complexity each lose their power to determine whether a system is unevolvable. For sure, a lot of evolution is gradual, and to the extent that it is, these concepts of evolutionary difficulty remain useful. But if large genetic changes that are beneficial are plausible, then these concepts do not have the power to veto the evolvability of an adaptation.

In chapter 4 I identify a class of complex systems exhibiting all these notions of evolutionary difficulty: high degrees of epistasis, significant landscape ruggedness, wide fitness saddles, high-fitness configurations that appear to be irreducibly complex, and therefore, of course, no gradual path of monotonically increasing fitness

Table 2.2
Analogous issues in both evolutionary biology terms and evolutionary computation terms.

Evolutionary biology concept	Evolutionary computation concept
Gradual evolution	Hill-climbing optimization
Adaptive surface, adaptive peaks, fitness saddles	Fitness landscape, local optima, fitness saddles
Epistatic dependencies between alleles/genes	Frustration of variables
Irreducible complexity	Problems with strong/numerous interdependencies

to reach high-fitness points in the landscape. Nonetheless, I will show that this type of system is easily evolvable.

2.4 Summary

This chapter has introduced the gradualist framework of evolution. I have discussed the traditional (gradualist) notions of evolutionary difficulty and their dependence on the assumption of small variations.

Note that there are significant parallels between the issues and phenomena discussed in evolutionary biology and evolutionary computation. Some concepts are the same in both disciplines: fitness landscape, ruggedness, smooth paths of adaptation, local optima, convergence, and diversity. Other concepts have close analogues in each discipline. Table 2.2 summarizes some terminological analogues between the concepts and issues in evolutionary biology and evolutionary computation.

3 Compositional Evolution

In this chapter I survey a spectrum of mechanisms, both in evolutionary biology and evolutionary computation, that step outside the gradualist evolutionary framework. The mechanisms I want to address are compositional mechanisms that produce large genetic changes by bringing together genetic material from different individuals.[1] Where they are available, I highlight corresponding notions of what might be easy or difficult for evolution under these mechanisms.

3.1 Compositional Mechanisms

There are many mechanisms that manipulate subsets of preadapted genetic material in nature (figure 3.1). All of these mechanisms manipulate preadapted gene complexes between individuals and sometimes between species. This list begins to emphasize a spectrum of mechanisms: specifically, the mechanisms near the beginning of this list reuse complexes that are preadapted in similar organisms (same species), whereas the mechanisms toward the end of the list may manipulate genetic material preadapted in relatively unrelated parallel lineages (different species).

The two mechanisms I examine in this book are taken from either end of this spectrum. The first is sexual recombination. Although sexual recombination (usually) occurs among individuals of the same population, it manipulates feature complexes by exchanging them between *different* individuals. Indeed, to the extent that organisms are similar, sexual recombination between them has no effect, so it is the diversity of lineages in a population that makes sexual recombination productive (if it is). The second mechanism I will examine is one that can combine gene complexes from unrelated parallel lineages, that is, entirely different species. Specifically, I examine a mechanism of interspecific genetic integration based on endosymbiosis/symbiogenesis, which I will call *symbiotic encapsulation*. Margulis (1993a) suggests that sexual recombination and endosymbiosis can be thought of as forms of the same process but with different degrees of relatedness between the entities involved: "symbiosis and meiotic sexuality entail the formation of new individuals that carry genes from more than a single parent. In organisms that develop from sexual fusion of cells from two parents, these parents share very recent common ancestors; partners in symbioses have more distant ancestors" (p. 169). The following sections survey these mechanisms and discuss the relevant concepts in population genetics and evolutionary computation.

Sexual Recombination

The genetic material of organisms is packaged into chromosomes, each containing (typically) thousands of genes. Sexual organisms are diploid, having two sets of

- Sexual recombination combines genetic material from members of the same species.
- Natural hybridization may occur between related species (Harrison 1990; Arnold 1997; Rieseberg et al. 2003).
- Allopolyploidy (having chromosome sets from different species) (Werth, Guttman, and Eshbaugh 1985) generally occurs between related species.
- Horizontal or lateral gene transfer (Mazodier and Davies 1991; Smith, Feng, and Doolittle 1992; Davies 1996; Ochman, Lawrence, and Greisman 2000; Lawrence and Ochman 1998; Li and Graur 1991; Campbell 2004; Lindell et al. 2004) can occur between both similar and dissimilar organisms.
- Endosymbiosis can encapsulate the genetic material of wholly unrelated microbial species leading to symbiogenesis, the genesis of a new species through symbiosis (Margulis 1993a).

Figure 3.1
Mechanisms of genetic composition.

chromosomes (carrying almost the same genetic information), each set being derived from one of its parents. We can refer to them as the "paternal" copy and the "maternal" copy (although the genetics of sexual reproduction does not require any differentiation of the sexes). During meiosis haploid cells are produced, the gametes, having only one set of chromosomes. When the haploid gametes from different individuals join ("syngamy"), a new diploid cell is produced. In figure 3.2 I have drawn diploid organisms having only one chromosome, that is, one *pair* of chromosomes each.[2]

Sexual reproduction thus creates new genotypes having new combinations of haploid chromosomes from the parents, but it does not *necessarily* produce new haplotypes. To create new haplotypes we need *sexual recombination*. Sexual recombination occurs during the production of the haploid cells (not during syngamy). It can occur in two ways: (1) by the reassortment of chromosomes; and (2) by the reassortment of parts of chromosomes through crossover. The reassortment of chromosomes occurs because when the haploid cells are produced, although they always have a complete set of chromosomes, this set may comprise some maternal chromosomes and some paternal chromosomes. This can only occur in organisms that have more than one chromosome (which most do). Figure 3.3 shows organisms with two (pairs of) chromosomes undergoing sexual reproduction with sexual recombination occurring from chromosomal reassortment.

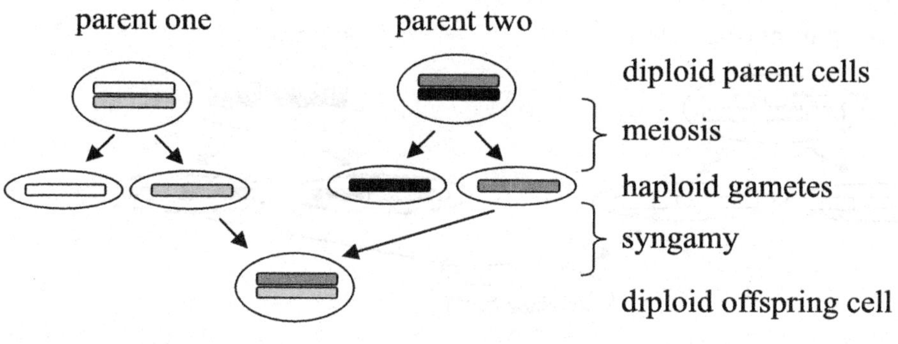

Figure 3.2
Sexual reproduction.

Crossover is a different mechanism acting within individual chromosomes that produces new haploid chromosomes by taking parts of a paternal chromosome and complementary parts from the homologous maternal chromosome (the other member of a chromosome pair, with corresponding gene sequence). Figure 3.4 illustrates the production of recombinant haploids by crossover in parent 2, producing an offspring diploid with one recombinant chromosome. In general, some of the gametes produced by meiosis may be recombinant and others may not. Here I have drawn only recombinant haploids for parent 2, and only nonrecombinant haploids for parent 1.

Figure 3.4 illustrates recombination of single-chromosome cells to emphasize that reassortment of chromosomes (figure 3.3) is a different mechanism from crossover. Both the assortment of chromosomes and crossover produce new haplotypes (technically known as "amphimixis," see Kondrashov 1993). In general, organisms have many chromosomes and also exhibit crossover, so both mechanisms act in the production of recombinant haplotypes. For some purposes the distinction between these two mechanisms is not important. However, one distinction that can be important is that of differences in the expected recombination rate. The recombination rate for genes on different chromosomes (chromosomal reassortment) is 0.5; since chromosomes assort randomly, there is a 0.5 probability of a given pair of genes appearing together in the haploid cell. But for genes on the same chromosome (crossover), the recombination rate is between 0 and 0.5, depending approximately on the rate of crossing over in general for that organism (often on the order of one crossover per chromosome) and the genetic distance (number of loci) between the genes. Assumptions about the recombination rate can have a dramatic affect on the results of sexual recombination and will feature significantly in the models that follow.

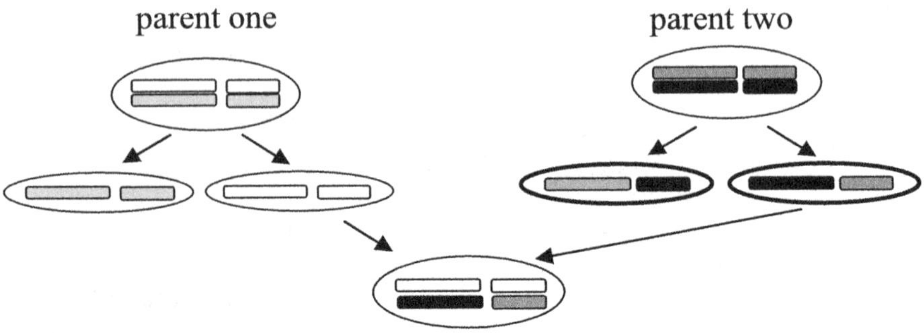

Figure 3.3
Sexual recombination through the reassortment of chromosomes. The haploid gametes may take chromosomes from either the paternal or maternal copy of each chromosome producing recombinant haplotypes of complementary types—shown with bold outlines—or in some cases they may take chromosomes from the same copy, although this becomes rarer as the number of chromosomes increases.

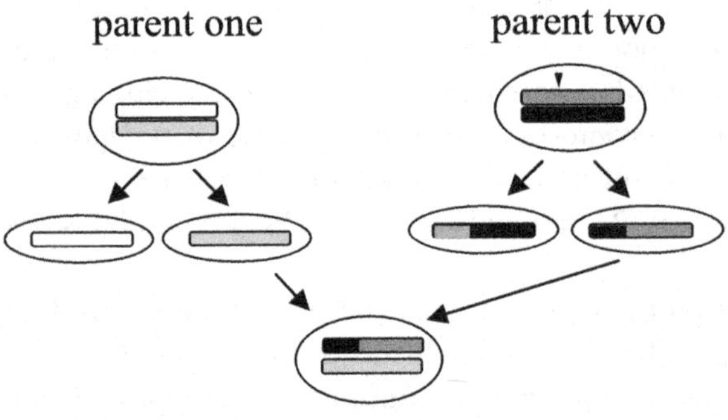

Figure 3.4
Sexual recombination by crossing over.

Genetic algorithms normally consider only haploid chromosomes. Haploid organisms in nature do not reproduce sexually and therefore generally produce new haplotypes only by mutation. An exception is bacterial sex involving bacterial conjugation (see the "microbial GA"—for an abstraction of this, Harvey 1996, 2001). Accordingly, sexual recombination in a GA is somewhat anomalous; we may perhaps imagine the individuals of a GA as the haploid gametes of diploid sexual organisms, although this would mean that selection is applied to the gametes rather than to the diploid individuals. Nonetheless, for the purposes of examining the ability of recombination to discover fit haplotypes, a haploid representation is sufficient.

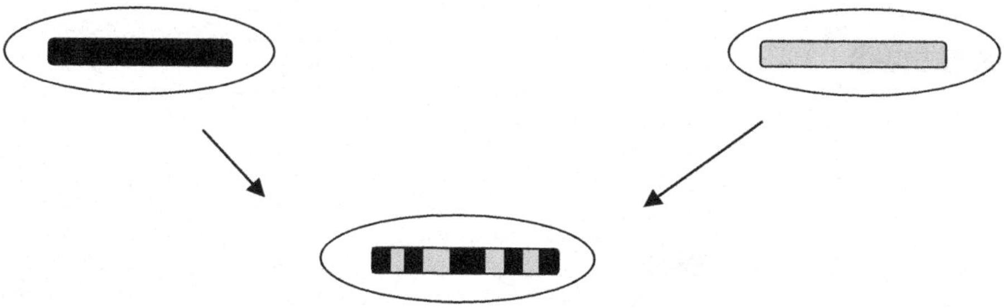

Figure 3.5
Uniform crossover or "free recombination."

Furthermore, in a genetic algorithm "sexual recombination" is generally taken to be synonymous with "crossover." Figure 3.5 shows *uniform crossover* where individual alleles are taken from either parent with equal probability. This is really closer to chromosomal reassortment of alleles that are all on different chromosomes in the sense that each pair of alleles recombines with probability 0.5 regardless of genetic distance.[3] This is called "free recombination" in the biological literature. Figure 3.6 shows *one-point crossover*, a more accurate model of crossing sections of chromosomes under crossover.

On the detailed level, crossover in the genetic algorithm creates an offspring individual by taking some genes (bits) from parent 1 and some genes from parent 2. Three types of crossover commonly used in GAs are shown in figure 3.7.

In one-point crossover, a crossover point is chosen, and all alleles on the left of this point are taken from parent 1, all alleles on the right are taken from parent 2, or vice versa. In two-point, or more generally n-point crossover, contiguous blocks of alleles between n randomly positioned crossover points are taken from each parent, swapping donors at each crossover point, as shown. We can see that one-point crossover is the same as two-point crossover where one of the two points is always positioned before the first (or after the last) locus. Accordingly, one-point crossover treats the end points of the string as special points, whereas two-point crossover (or n-point crossover where n is even) does not.

Under uniform crossover (Syswerda 1989), alleles (bits) are taken from either parent with equal probability on an independent per-locus basis. The most obvious difference between uniform crossover and n-point crossover is that under uniform crossover there is no correlation between adjacency on the chromosome and the

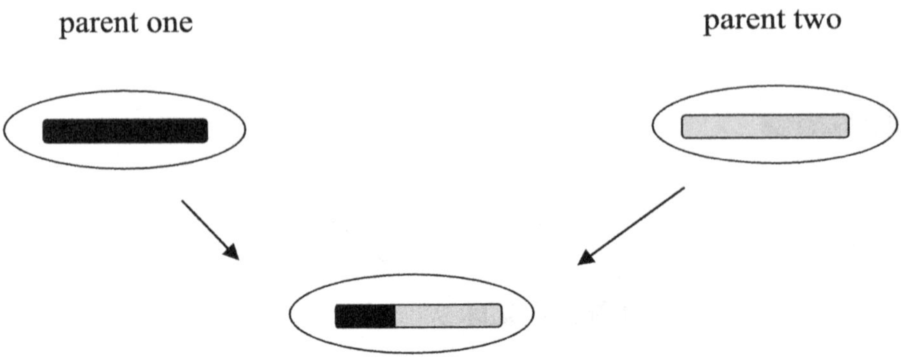

Figure 3.6
One-point crossover.

	One-point crossover	Two-point crossover	Uniform crossover
Parent 1	**101010010010100**	**101010010010100**	**101010010010100**
Parent 2	100101010011110	100101010011110	100101010011110
Offspring	**1010100100**11110	**10101**1010011**100**	**1**0**11**0**0**0**1**0**0**1**0**1**1**0

Figure 3.7
Crossover operations on bit-string individuals. Crossover points are indicated by the short vertical tick marks. Possible crossover points for uniform crossover are indicated by the dotted marks.

probability of genes being transferred to the offspring. Put another way, the combinations of $p1$ and $p2$ genes that end up in the offspring are the same (statistically) regardless of how they are ordered or positioned on the chromosome. In the terminology of population genetics, it would be said that there is no *physical linkage* between genes under uniform crossover, but there is for one- and two-point crossover (discussed below). In biological terms, uniform crossover corresponds to a case where all the genes of interest reside on different chromosomes, or cases where there is a very high number of crossovers per reproduction, or cases where several (one-point) recombinative events occur before selection has an appreciable effect on its results.

Finally, note that for binary strings, uniform crossover has the same effect as producing an offspring with alleles the same as the parents' alleles at loci where the alleles of the parents agree, and randomly assigned alleles at all other loci (Watson and Pollack 2000b). From this it is easy to see why uniform crossover, in particular, is considered to be nothing more than a macromutation (albeit one that preserves similar parts of the parents—see Chen 1999).

Sexual recombination produces new combinations of genetic material within a species (although, compositional evolution via sexual recombination will require that the genetic material that is brought together has been subject to different selective pressures, such as in subdivided populations). In nature there are also mechanisms that produce new combinations of genetic material by exchanging material between species.

Horizontal Gene Transfer

The exchange of genetic material between members of different species is more widespread than might be imagined given the normal definition of species. Recent nucleotide sequencing indicates that processes of interspecific genetic transfer account for the origin of significant amounts of both cytoplasmic and nuclear DNA in microorganisms:

> The most reasonable explanation ... *[for anomalies in the phylogenetic tree]* is that the pattern of evolution is not as linear and treelike as Darwin imagined it. Although genes are passed vertically from generation to generation, this vertical inheritance is not the only important process that has affected the evolution of cells. Rampant operation of a different process—lateral, or horizontal, gene transfer—has also affected the course of that evolution profoundly. Such transfer involves the delivery of single genes, or whole suites of them, not from parent to offspring but across species barriers. (Doolittle 2000, p. 93; see also Doolittle 1980)

There is also evidence that lateral gene transfer is possible between multicellular organisms: "DNA elements have been observed transferring into and between higher organisms, such as plants, fungi and metazoans, including humans" (Syvanen and Kado 1998). The importance of transferred genes in adaptation is seen in cases such as anti-biotic resistance (Davies 1996; Ochman, Lawrence, and Groisman 1998). Generally it is clear that in such cases it is "easier" for an organism to acquire such an adaptation by transfer from another organism that already has it than it is to evolve the adaptation for itself. And its clear that, as Doolittle points out, horizontal gene transfer is not accommodated by a tree-shaped ancestral graph. But it is generally not appreciated that these events change the underlying algorithmic principle of the evolutionary process.

Lateral transfer may involve a gene or a suite of genes, but there are occasionally more radical processes of interspecific genetic integration, as follows.

Endosymbiosis and Symbiogenesis

Endosymbiosis (Hoffmeister and Martin 2003) is the symbiosis (living together; De Bary 1887) of two organisms where one lives inside the other. In some cases of endosymbiosis, it is very difficult to establish the independent status of the parties involved (see the work of Frank, e.g., 1997, for models of this process). Indeed, the endosymbiosis of prokaryotes (nonnucleated bacteria) with one another has in some cases become effectively irreversible, that is, the parties involved have subsequently become dependent on one another and cannot live independently. Such endosymbiosis is involved in the origin of various organelles, for example, mitochondria and chloroplasts in eukaryote cells. And there is some evidence to suggest that other organelles, such as flagella, also resulted from the physical inclusion of symbiotic bacteria (Margulis 1993b).

In some cases, the symbiotic entities remain as physiologically distinct organelles within the larger host cell—for example, plastids such as mitochondria and chloroplasts (figure 3.8). But there are also mechanisms, such as transposons, that can transfer genetic material from mitochondria (for example) to the nucleus or vice

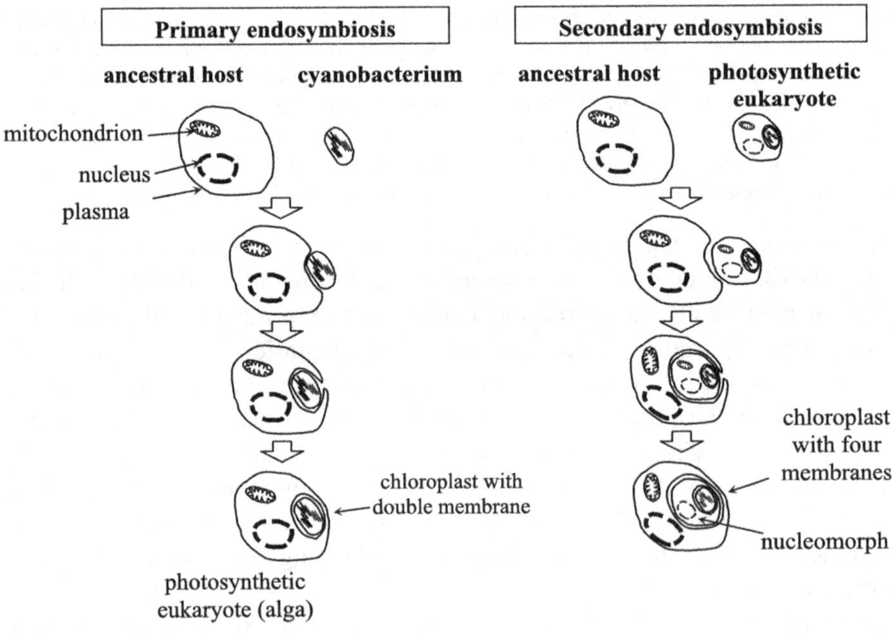

Figure 3.8
Endosymbiosis. (Adapted from artwork of Daniel L. Nickrent, Southern Illinois University.)

versa, implying that symbiotic origins may account for nuclear DNA as well as cytoplasmic DNA, as Doolittle's data concord. Such evidence suggests a more general process—*symbiogenesis*, the origin of new species from the integration of symbionts. In this view, endosymbiosis is not simply responsible for the origin of eukaryote organelles, but for the origin of the eukaryotes themselves (including all plants and animals). The idea that new organisms could be created in such a manner was introduced as early as 1890:

> Complex organisms might arise "through the unification of elementary organisms into colonies, and the transformation of the aggregate of them into an entity of a higher order. . . ." (Famintsyn; translated in Khakhina 1992, p. 33)

The symbiotic origin of organisms was further developed by Merehzkovsky (1909), through studying lichens, algae, and fungi, and by Kozo-Polyansky (1921) (see Khakhina 1992). Meanwhile, in Western biological thought, Wallin (e.g., 1927) had similar thoughts about the origin of mitochondria, but at that time the idea was ridiculed and dismissed. The symbiogenic origin of eukaryote organelles now accepted, the concept of symbiogenesis is most well known in modern Western science through the work of Margulis starting in the 1970s.

Margulis describes the process as follows:

> [D]ifferent bacteria form consortia that, under ecological pressures, associate and undergo metabolic and genetic change such that their tightly integrated communities result in individuality at a more complex level of organization. (Margulis 1995, p. 136)

(See also López-Garcia and Moreira 1999.) Moreover, evidence suggests that secondary endosymbiosis has also taken place; that is, endosymbiosis involving the inclusion of an endosymbiont. Figure 3.8 depicts primary endosymbiosis involving a host cell and a photosynthetic cyanobacterium resulting in a photosynthetic eukaryote (left), and secondary endosymbiosis involving a host cell and a eukaryote (right). (See also Saffo 1990.)

The process of creating new species from symbiotic relationships—symbiogenesis—is the basis of serial endosymbiosis theory (Margulis 1970, 1993a). This theory proposes that endosymbiosis has been a recurring source of innovation in the evolution of complex cells. Accordingly, though its action may be rare in evolutionary history, the impact of symbiogenesis has been profound (eukaryotes include all plants and animals). Certainly, the genetic impact of symbiogenesis is, to say the least, unconventional. Symbiogenesis involves the encapsulation of genetic material from parallel lineages into a new whole—a new entity replicating as an individual. Certainly, from the point of view of either entity involved, it affords large nonrandom jumps in genotype (and phenotype) that introduce large amounts of preadapted DNA. And moreover, the idea that the organisms involved were symbionts before they were encapsulated, even if their relationship was not mutually beneficial, supports the idea that the combinations of organisms so created are favorably biased by prior coadaptation.

The adaptive utility of symbiogenesis is underresearched and poorly understood, and its potential to produce large adaptive jumps is of primary interest in this book. Moreover, the notions of serial endosymbiosis suggest an idea of repeated inclusion and hierarchical encapsulation, the consequences of which are even less well understood. Hierarchical encapsulation is one of the features of the major evolutionary transitions.

The Major Transitions in Evolution

The major evolutionary transitions (Buss 1987; Maynard Smith and Szathmary 1995; Michod 1999) involve the creation of new higher-level complexes of simpler entities. Summarized by Michod, for example, they include the transitions "from individual genes to networks of genes, from gene networks to bacteria-like cells, from bacteria-like cells to eukaryotic cells with organelles, from cells to multicellular organisms, and from solitary organisms to societies" (1999, p. 7). There are many reasons to be interested in the evolutionary transitions: they challenge our notions of the individual as the unit of selection, they involve the adoption of new modes of transmitting information, and they address fundamental questions about individuality, cooperation, fitness, and not least, the origins of life (Buss 1987; Maynard Smith and Szathmary 1995; Michod 1999).

In several of the transitions, "entities that were capable of independent replication before the transition can replicate only as part of a larger whole after it" (Maynard Smith and Szathmary 1995). Although Maynard Smith and Szathmary identify several transitions that do not fit what they describe as "symbiosis followed by compartmentation and synchronised replication,"[4] several of the transitions, including the origin of eukaryotes from prokaryotes (Margulis 1993a,b) and the origin of chromosomes from independent genes (Maynard Smith and Szathmary 1993), do involve the quite literal union of previously free-living entities into a new whole.

This form of change has some obvious contrasts with how we normally understand the mechanisms of Darwinian evolution. The ordinary (nontransitional) view of evolutionary change involves the accumulation of random genetic variations within an entity, whereas innovation by composition involves the union of two different entities, each contributing relatively large amounts of genetic material to the new composite entity. Moreover, the result is quite different from a random variation applied to either donor entity since each contributes highly nonrandom genetic material by virtue of being independently preadapted as an entity in its own right, if not in its symbiotic role.

I propose that all the mechanisms listed above (in figure 3.1) can be viewed as a spectrum of compositional mechanisms. As mentioned, I will focus on the first and last of these, sexual recombination and interspecific integration, because they represent the extremes of a spectrum: the exchange of genetic material between very similar organisms (within a species) and the exchange of genetic material between potentially unrelated species. In the latter mechanism, I will use the idea that entities at one level of organization are encapsulated into a new individual at a higher level of organization. I shall refer to this mechanism as "symbiotic encapsulation," meaning the union of previously free-living and semi-independently adapted entities into a new whole. Symbiotic encapsulation might be seen as a transitional change in the sense of the major evolutionary transitions, whereas sexual recombination is an intratransitional form of composition.

3.2 Models of Composition

Sexual Recombination

There are many different theories addressing the origin (Maynard Smith 1978; Michod and Levin 1988), maintenance (Doncaster, Pound, and Cox 2000), and benefit of sexual recombination (Kondrashov 1993; Otto, Feldman, and Christiansen 1994) in natural evolution; for a comprehensive review see Birdsell and Wills 2003. Here we are interested in models for the benefit of sex. Population genetics models for the benefit of sex have many flavors also: single locus models, rapid adaptation to a changing or oscillating environment (especially parasite coevolution—see Hamilton, Axelrod, and Tanese 1990), and DNA repair. So, to be more specific, here we want to focus on models for the benefit of sexual recombination—the creation of new haplotypes through the combination of genetic material from different individuals.

Theories for the benefit of sexual recombination can be further divided into models of the adaptive benefit to the sex-promoting allele, and the adaptive benefit to the population. Ideally, a full account of the adaptive benefit of sex would show a benefit for the sex-promoting allele, that is, it would show conditions where the frequency of a sexual variant will rise in the population. But here I am going to focus on what it is that a sexual population can evolve (that an asexual population cannot) *given* that it is sexual. The question of how the population came to be sexual is a separate question and requires a different style of model (see, e.g., Otto and Barton 1997).

To answer the question of when sex provides a benefit, we start by assessing what sex does. In population genetic terms, sex reduces *linkage disequilibrium* (Felsenstein 1974). Linkage disequilibrium is a measure of how far the frequencies of allele combinations in the population differ from those expected given the frequencies of the individual alleles in the population. If the frequency of the allele combination AB, for example, is equal to the frequency of A multiplied by the frequency of B, then those alleles are said to be at linkage equilibrium; otherwise those alleles exhibit linkage disequilibrium. Linkage disequilibrium is said to be positive if extreme genetotypes (AB and ab) are overrepresented with respect to intermediate genotypes (Ab and aB). (This is sensitive to the labeling of the alleles, of course, but it is meaningful if we assume some consistency in the labeling of the two alleles—for example, that beneficial alleles are both uppercase for both loci.)

There are several reasons why a population may exhibit linkage disequilibrium. It may be that individuals carrying both A and B have a fitness that is greater (or lesser) than expected given the average fitness of individuals carrying A and the average fitness of individuals carrying B. In other words, there is an epistatic interaction between A and B that makes AB extra fit, for example, so that individuals carrying this combination increase in frequency in the population. Alternatively, in a finite population, it might be that a new B mutation happened to arrive in an individual that was already carrying an A and though this individual carrying both A and B reproduces, individuals carrying B without A are absent.

In any case, whatever the causes, linkage disequilibrium is reduced by sexual recombination. In a sexual population, even if AB is much fitter than would be expected from the fitness of A and B individually, the AB combination will be broken up by recombination returning the population closer to linkage equilibrium. Similarly, even if a B mutation happens to arrive in an individual already carrying an A, sexual recombination will create individuals having B but not A.

The effectiveness with which sexual recombination reduces linkage disequilibrium depends on the amount of *physical linkage* between the alleles in question. If the alleles are very close to one another on the same chromosome, then recombination events that separate them will be uncommon—this is *strong physical linkage*. On the other hand, if the alleles are very far apart on the same chromosome or on different chromosomes, they have weak or no physical linkage. Thus the mechanism of physical linkage is closely related to the measure of linkage disequilibrium although they are in fact different concepts. Physical linkage refers to the tendency of alleles of different genes to be inherited together by virtue of their physical proximity on the chromosome, whereas linkage disequilibrium is the deviation of joint frequencies from the frequencies expected from the product of marginal frequencies. The two concepts are often conflated, especially in the evolutionary computation literature. An additional complication in GAs is that the term "tight linkage" is generally tied to the idea that it is *beneficial* to have a set of alleles physically linked (and in linkage disequilibrium) because they constitute a useful building block. This depends on the correspondence of physical linkage with epistatic dependencies (epistasis) and we will see that this is critical in the models of sexual recombination in chapter 6.

It is interesting to note a distinction in emphasis. To an optimistic adaptationist (as is common among evolutionary computation practitioners), sexual recombination offers the possibility that it might take the good parts from two parent individuals and bring them together in the offspring. Sexual recombination does have the potential to make new combinations of alleles by bringing together genes from two different donor individuals. However, population genetics models tend to focus more on the action of sexual recombination in breaking up combinations of alleles that were resident in either parent. The notion of reducing linkage disequilibrium is quite useful in getting a formal grasp of this issue. For example, if AB is overrepresented in the population then sexual recombination will break it up more quickly than it produces it; if AB is underrepresented in the population then sexual recombination will create it more quickly than it breaks it up. But in either case, sexual recombination is moving the allele frequencies closer to linkage equilibrium. In other words, sex always reduces overrepresented combinations—when AB is *under*represented, sexual recombination may create it, but at the same time Ab and aB are necessarily *over*represented and sexual recombination reduces their frequencies. Conversely, sex always increases underrepresented combinations—when AB is *over*represented, sexual recombination will reduce it, but at the same time Ab and aB are necessarily *under*represented and sexual recombination increases their frequencies. Accordingly, these two sides of the same coin can be accommodated by simply acknowledging that sexual recombination returns allele frequencies to linkage equilibrium.

So, working within the framework that sexual recombination reduces linkage disequilibrium, to show a benefit for sex we need (1) a reason for a population to have linkage disequilibrium, and (2) a fitness benefit to reducing it. I will assess the following models for the benefit of sexual recombination in terms of how they provide these two things.

Fisher–Muller model One of the most well-known models for the benefit of sexual recombination is the Fisher–Muller model, described by Fisher as follows: "For, unless advantageous mutations occur so seldom that each has had time to become predominant before the next appears, they can only come to be simultaneously in the

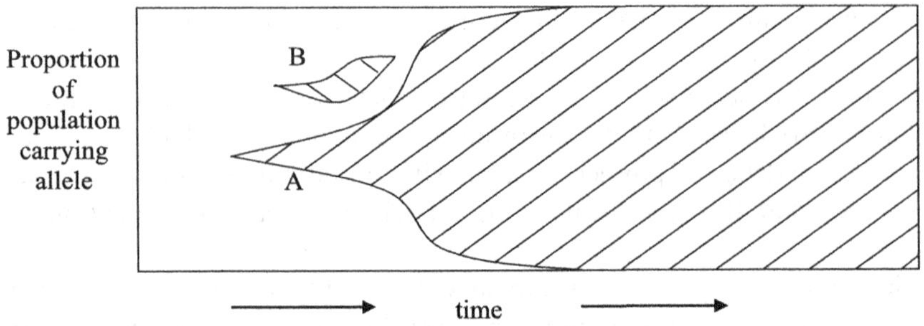

Figure 3.9
Frequency of alleles in an asexual population.

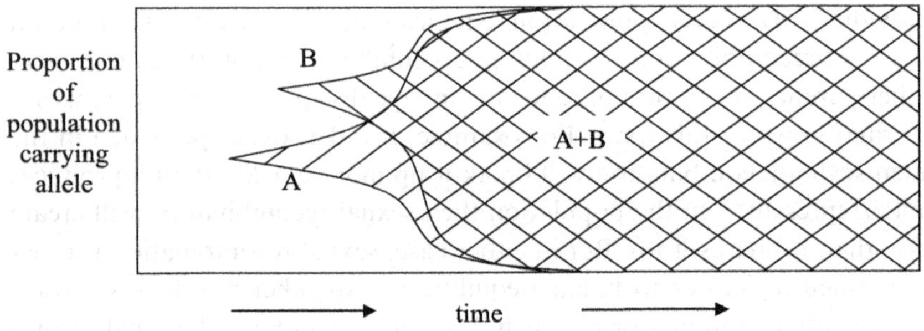

Figure 3.10
Frequency of alleles in a sexual population.

same gamete by means of recombination" (1958, p. 118). This is the basic idea of sex bringing together beneficial alleles.

Figure 3.9 illustrates the frequencies of alleles in an asexual population as two beneficial mutations are introduced into the population by mutation. The first to occur, A, begins to increase in frequency, but before it has reached fixation (frequency of 100% in the population) another beneficial mutation, B, occurs, and it happens that it does not occur in an individual that already had A. In an asexual population there is no way for the A allele to get into an individual that has the B allele, or the B allele to get into an individual that has the A allele. Accordingly, it cannot be the case that both A and B rise to fixation, and the clones of the two types of individuals compete to determine who survives and who is lost from the population.

In contrast, figure 3.10 shows the same two mutations occurring in a sexual population. Now we may think of the A allele and the B allele coming together to create the AB individual, or alternatively, we can just think of the A allele and B allele increasing in frequency independently—each one rising in frequency to fixation because it is unlinked to the other. This enables the sexual population, but not the asexual population, to make use of both beneficial mutations. Fisher's comment above also points out that if the A allele had already risen in frequency sufficiently before the B allele occurred, then the B allele would occur in an individual that already had the A allele and there would be no need to create the AB individual by sexual recombination.

Accordingly, the advantage of sex is sensitive to the likelihood of simultaneously segregating alleles (alleles that are not yet fixed in the population but at intermediate frequencies). This in turn depends on the likelihood of beneficial mutations occurring and how quickly they fix. And how quickly they fix depends on how beneficial they are and the size of the population. Thus this benefit of sex is not seen (or is reduced) in cases where beneficial mutations are rare, in cases where the fitness advantage of beneficial mutations is large, or in small populations.

In this model, linkage disequilibrium is created by the stochastic occurrence of new mutations (Ohta 1968). And a fitness benefit of reducing linkage disequilibrium is derived from the assumption that the mutations involved are beneficial and one must necessarily be lost if linkage disequilibrium is not restored—or equivalently, the benefit is derived from the fact that reducing linkage disequilibrium enables selection to act on the alleles independently, reducing competition between simultaneously segregating beneficial alleles. See also work on the "traffic problem," "clonal interference" (Orr 2000), and the "Hill and Robertson effect" (Hill and Robertson 1966; and Christiansen et al. 1998).

Muller's ratchet "Muller's ratchet" (Muller 1964) is a different but related model for the benefit of recombination in finite populations with mutation. The genotypes of a population may be classified by the number of deleterious mutations they carry. Suppose the fittest genotype class has no deleterious mutations. This genotype class can be lost from the population if either (1) through the stochastic effects of sampling in small populations, none of the fittest members of the population gets to contribute offspring to the next generation, or (2) every offspring of this class that does reproduce acquires one or more deleterious mutations. Now the fittest class has at least one deleterious mutation and subsequent mutation may result in this class being lost. The ratchet metaphor indicates that this is a one-way process; the stochastic effects of mutation and sampling in a finite population may lose the fittest class but cannot re-create it. Selection holds the fitness of the population as high as it can in the meantime, but eventually, stochastic events will cause another click and selection alone cannot re-create the lost class of genotypes.

In contrast, a sexual population can cross two half-unmutated individuals to recover an unmutated individual. This is the logical complement of the Fisher–Muller hypothesis where two beneficially mutated individuals are crossed to create a doubly beneficial individual. One describes the combination of good nonmutant genes and the other describes the combination of good mutant genes. The difference between the two models really lies in the starting frequencies of these good alleles and what is reasonable to assume about the frequencies of their occurrence. Specifically, in the Fisher–Muller model the good (mutated) alleles arise with low frequency (and not in the same individual) whereas in Muller's ratchet, the good (unmutated) alleles arise initially with high frequency (although not both in any one individual).

An important advantage that Muller's ratchet model has over the Fisher–Muller model is that it is generally considered reasonable to assume that deleterious mutations are much more common than beneficial ones. Accordingly, a model that deals with the purging of deleterious mutations seems much more relevant and powerful to a biologist than a model that depends on beneficial alleles. One important problem with the model is that the loss of the fittest genotype through stochastic sampling in a finite population relies on small populations; for large populations, the rate of losing the fittest genotype class can be very slow (Gordo and Charlesworth 2000). Another problem is the assumption that no beneficial mutations are available (Poon and Otto 2000; Rouzine, Wakeley, and Coffin 2003). In the ratchet model linkage disequilibrium is created by stochastic sampling and mutation. And, like the Fisher–Muller model, the benefit of reducing linkage disequilibrium is that it allows selection on individual alleles thus allowing beneficial nonmutant alleles to rise in frequency without competing.

The deterministic mutation hypothesis One of the most popular models for the benefit of sexual recombination in modern population genetics is the deterministic mutation hypothesis of Kondrashov (1988). This model also addresses the purging of deleterious alleles (rather than the promotion of beneficial alleles) and thus enjoys the wider applicability of the ratchet model. However, whereas the ratchet model and the Fisher–Muller model depend on stochastic mutation and sampling in finite populations to create linkage disequilibrium, the deterministic mutation hypothesis supposes that linkage disequilibrium is created by epistatic selection. This means that the creation of linkage disequilibrium applies even in infinite populations—in principle, where there are no stochastic effects of sampling as in finite populations—hence the *deterministic* mutation hypothesis.

The deterministic mutation hypothesis depends on the observation that the effectiveness of selection is greater when the variance of the character being selected is

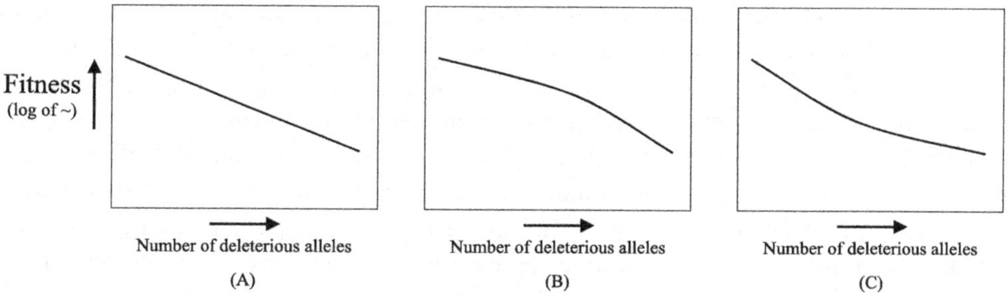

Figure 3.11
Three possible shapes of epistatic fitness effects. (A) No fitness interactions—each additional deleterious mutation affects fitness by the same factor (producing a straight line in the log of fitness). (B) Each additional deleterious mutation has an increasingly deleterious effect on fitness—this is known as "negative epistasis" because the curvature (i.e., the second derivative of log of fitness with number of mutations) is negative. (C) Each additional deleterious mutation has a decreasingly deleterious effect on fitness—i.e., "positive epistasis."

greater (Fisher 1958). Here the character we are interested in is the number of deleterious mutations a genotype carries. Shnol and Kondrashov (1993) showed that different forms of epistasis among mutations create populations with greater or lesser variance in the number of mutations the population carries. If the epistatic interactions between deleterious mutations are such that individuals with an intermediate number of mutations are overrepresented, then the variance in mutation number is decreased and the efficacy of selection to remove these deleterious mutations is reduced in an asexual population. In a sexual population, the reduction in linkage disequilibrium evens out the distribution of mutations in the population, increasing the relative abundance of individuals with extreme (rather than intermediate) numbers of mutations, thus increasing the variance in the number of deleterious mutations carried, hence increasing the efficacy of selection to remove the deleterious mutations from the population.

Different types of epistasis (figure 3.11) effect the distribution of mutation number differently: specifically, *negative epistasis* decreases the variance in mutation number and *positive epistasis* increases the variance in mutation number (Kondrashov 1982). For example, consider individuals that either have zero, one, or two deleterious mutations for simplicity. Negative epistasis creates an overrepresentation of individuals with just one mutation because selection removes double mutants from the population extra quickly (because they are more than twice as bad as single mutants). In contrast, positive mutation removes deleterious mutations from the population in double mutants a little slowly (because double mutants are a little less than twice as bad). This also creates linkage disequilibrium, but this time via an underrepresentation of single mutants (a relative overrepresentation of zero and double mutants).

In the model of the deterministic mutation hypothesis, linkage disequilibrium is created by epistatic selection. And reducing linkage disequilibrium is advantageous when it increases the variance in mutation number (hence increasing the effectiveness of selection to remove deleterious mutations). Hence sexual recombination is beneficial only under negative epistasis. In contrast, positive epistasis creates positive linkage disequilibrium, that is, an overrepresentation of genotypes with extreme mutation number (e.g., zero or two); reducing this with sexual recombination reduces the efficacy of selection to remove deleterious alleles and thus produces a disadvantage for a sexual population.

The deterministic mutation hypothesis (like Muller's ratchet) has the appeal of being relevant to the interaction of deleterious rather than beneficial mutations, and it applies to infinite populations. But it depends on the presence of negative epistasis. Empirical investigations are underway to measure the fitness of single and double mutants to see if negative epistasis is any more prevalent than positive epistasis (West, Peters, and Barton 1998; Elena and Lenski 1997; Elena 1999).

In comparing these three models, note that they all provide a benefit for recombination not just by reducing linkage disequilibrium but, more specifically, by reducing *negative* linkage disequilibrium. In the Fisher–Muller model, when two beneficial mutations are simultaneously segregating but there are no double-beneficial mutants, intermediate genotypes are overrepresented. In Muller's ratchet, when two beneficial nonmutant alleles exist in some member of the population but not together in any one individual, this is also an overrepresentation of intermediate genotypes. So in all three models it is a reduction in negative linkage disequilibrium—increasing the variance in mutation number—that provides a benefit for sexual recombination. But the three models differ in their assumptions about how this negative linkage disequilibrium is created. In particular, the first two models make no use of epistasis whereas the deterministic mutation hypothesis supposes that negative linkage disequilibrium is created by negative epistasis.

We can understand the advantage of sex in all cases as being derived from enabling selection to act on individual alleles. When selection acts on combinations of alleles in the Fisher–Muller model (i.e., in asexual populations) it promotes Ab and aB instead of promoting A and B separately. When selection acts on combinations of alleles in Muller's ratchet it maintains Ab and aB instead of promoting A and B separately. When selection acts on combinations of alleles with negative epistasis in the deterministic mutation hypothesis it promotes an overrepresentation of single mutants reducing the efficacy of selection relative to the case where selection acts on individual alleles. So according to this view, reducing linkage disequilibrium, and allowing selection to act on individual alleles, is where recombination derives its advantage.

The trouble with this view, from a computational perspective, is that if selection on individual alleles is preferred then a hill climber would be sufficient to attain whatever is being evolved. If selection on individual alleles is ideal, this must mean that there are no local optima in the fitness landscape, and if there are no local optima in the fitness landscape then a hill climber can climb the fitness gradient trivially. This would be disappointing from an algorithmic perspective: if this were the exclusive effect of sex, then sex would not be able to evolve anything that categorically could not be evolved by gradual incremental improvement. If there were another effect of sex that enabled something that a hill climber could not do, it would be interesting not only algorithmically but also biologically because it would require us to move beyond the gradualist framework. So, this reasoning suggests that if there is some compositional effect of sex, it is not a result of the fact that sex enables selection to act on individual alleles.

Recombination and the genetic map The view that sexual recombination can be fully understood as a mechanism that (merely) reduces linkage disequilibrium works well enough when applied to two-locus systems. Note that all the above models have two-locus exemplars. But when we are talking about multilocus systems, the way in which sexual recombination reduces the linkage disequilibrium between alleles is difficult to understand as independently reducing the linkage disequilibrium between many pairs of alleles. Specifically, the particular ordering of genes on the chromosome—the genetic map—restricts the particular haplotypes that can be produced by low recombination rates. For example, when crossing ABC with abc it is not possible to create AbC with one-point crossover in one generation. Indeed, the restrictions on combinations of alleles produced under sexual recombination are what determine the genetic map in real organisms. It is curious, then, that the genetic map does not feature in any of the popular models for the benefit of sexual recombination in the biological literature.

The population genetics models for the benefit of sex focus on the benefit of reducing linkage disequilibrium, and in the limit, allowing selection to act on individual alleles independently. A more general point of view is the view that sexual recombination *defines* the unit of selection. For example, the observation that allele combinations are not stable, not reliably reproducible, under sexual recombination is the motivating tenet of the "selfish gene" (Dawkins 1976), following from the work by Williams (1966). Specifically, if gene complexes cannot be reliably reproduced because they are broken up by sexual crossover, then the only units remaining that are reliably reproduced are short sections of chromosome—on the order of individual genes. On the basis of this, it is concluded that all adaptive change in sexual populations is driven by the selfish interests of genes, not individuals—because evolution is driven by the "selfish" interests of whatever unit of reproduction is in operation.[5]

The breakup of allele combinations by sexual reproduction places focus on the additive effects of alleles. In a large panmictic[6] polymorphic[7] population "combinations [of alleles] are broken-up too rapidly to permit effective selection among interaction systems[8] (unless the loci are so closely linked that alleles at different loci behave almost as if alleles of each other)"—and thus selection is "restricted to the net effects of alleles" (Wright 1977, p. 470). So, another way to look at the action of sexual recombination is that it introduces units of reproduction smaller than the whole chromosome. These units may be as small as the individual gene, in which case we need only consider the additive effects of alleles. In general this will depend on the recombination rate and the remaining physical linkage between alleles.

So the idea that sex forces selection to act on individual alleles in fact promotes the use of models that disregard epistasis (Wagner 2000), and without epistasis there are no local optima. It is not really the case that population genetics practitioners think that there is no epistasis in fitness landscapes; rather, the thought is that selection cannot act on combinations of alleles (in a sexual population) and so it cannot act on anything but the additive effects of alleles (Wagner, Laubichler, and Bagheri-Chaichian 1998). Thus in this view it seems prudent to focus most of one's attention on models of the additive effects of alleles. Whether this is a mistake or not is a question that I will develop in section 9.1.

In evolutionary computation, sexual recombination, rather than being seen as a mechanism that *prevents* selection on combinations of alleles that are *not* physically linked, is more generally seen as a mechanism that *enables* selection on combinations of alleles that *are* physically linked. In particular, the building-block hypothesis (BBH), discussed below, focuses on the ability of sex to process blocks of alleles rather than individual alleles. These are really just two different scales for the unit of selection, as defined by the recombination rate.

Before addressing the BBH, note that the potential of sexual recombination to manipulate gene complexes (blocks) effectively will be dependent on appropriate physical linkage coming from the genetic map. In a two-locus model the genetic map is degenerate in the sense that there is only one possible ordering of loci. Since all of the population genetic models use two-locus exemplars (also Barton 1995) they cannot address effects that depend on the genetic map. I have only provided a sample of the popular population genetic models for the benefit of recombination, but note that the effects exhibited in chapter 6 cannot be provided by any model that assumes no epistatic effects between genes or simplified forms of epistasis that do not introduce local optima, nor by any model that can be explained with a two-locus exemplar where the genetic map is degenerate.

Lying somewhere between the population genetics models using two-locus exemplars and models like the BBH discussed below, some other models show, without using a building-block structure, capabilities of a sexual population that are not available to asexual populations or hill climbers. Shapiro and Prügel-Bennet (1997) show that in a scenario where many loci must be changed simultaneously to escape a local optimum, mutational variation is ineffective because "[u]nlike crossover it has no knowledge of which parts of the strings are shared by many population members and thus disrupts parts of the string which are beneficial to fitness" (Rogers and Prügel-Bennett 2001; see also Chen 1999). Jansen and Wegener (1999, 2001) describe a similar effect.

These models demonstrate the advantage of focusing variation on an appropriate subset of loci, by using free recombination to search combinations of alleles at those loci. Since free recombination can produce any combination of the alleles segregating in the population, the expected time to make the jump off the local optimum to a point of higher fitness is exponential in the number of loci that need to be changed. But this is quite favorable to an expected time that is exponential in the size of the genotype, as would be the case under mutational variation (being unable to limit variation to an appropriate subset of loci). Jansen and Wegener also describe a variant landscape where the restricted subset of variants produced by low recombination rates is especially favorable. This advantage for sex depends on the correspondence of the epistatic fitness interactions and the ordering of loci in the genetic map. Using this correspondence the expected time to escape the local optimum is only a polynomial function of the number of loci that must be changed simultaneously. This problem has no obvious building-block structure, or flavor of problem decomposition, that was evident in the earlier intuitions of the BBH discussed below; but it does use the specifics of the physical linkage dependent on the genetic map to bias genetic variation, and this will feature significantly in the models that are developed.

The building-block hypothesis (BBH) There has been a long-standing battle in GA theory about the adaptive utility of crossover. For some researchers, crossover is considered to behave at best like a macromutation, merely producing large random changes, no more likely to be adaptive than a large number of point mutations (see, e.g., Jones 1995). If crossover does behave like a macromutation, then the same ideas about evolutionary difficulty hold for GAs *with* crossover as for the GAs *without* crossover. The question of whether there are circumstances where crossover cannot be accurately characterized as merely a source of large undirected mutations relates directly to a compositional interpretation of crossover in the GA.

For other researchers, the utility of the GA in general is intimately related to the idea that crossover can manipulate blocks of genes. Following the notions outlined by Holland (1975), Goldberg (1989) says the following about the operation of the GA under the heading "The building block hypothesis":

> Short, low-order, and highly fit schemata are sampled, recombined, and resampled to form strings of potentially higher fitness. In a way, by working with these particular schemata (the building blocks), we have reduced the complexity of our problem; instead of building high-performance strings by trying every conceivable combination, we construct better and better strings from the best partial solutions of past samplings. (1989, p. 41)

Forrest and Mitchell (1993a) restate these ideas as follows:

> The *building-block* hypothesis states that the GA works well when short, low-order, highly-fit schemas recombine to form even more highly fit higher-order schemas. (1993a, p. 109)

More recently, Holland (2000) says the following:

> The "building block thesis" holds that most of what we know about the world pivots on descriptions and mechanisms constructed from elementary building blocks.... Once a computer scientist starts thinking about building blocks as a source of innovation, the next obvious step is to look for algorithms that can discover and exploit building blocks. It is my claim that genetic algorithms (GA's) are particularly qualified for this task.... What purpose does crossover serve then? As is well known to most practitioners it serves two purposes: First of all, it recombines building blocks residing on separate strings into combination on a single string. The second effect is more subtle. Crossover uncovers new building blocks by placing alleles in new contexts. Moreover ... building blocks are often combinations of more elementary building blocks, so recombination works at this level too. (2000, p. 373)

Put simply, the BBH suggests that the GA will perform well when short sections of chromosome that confer above-average fitness contributions (building blocks) can be recombined to discover longer sections of chromosome that are even fitter.[9] The intuition is that different members of the population will discover different building blocks, and that sexual recombination will then search combinations of small building blocks to find larger building blocks, and so on. The similarity with the basic idea of the Fisher–Muller model should be clear—except that here we are talking about blocks of alleles rather than individual alleles.

```
(a) ***1**10*******0*0*

(b) ***11*10*0*********

(c) 1**0010100*01010000
```

Figure 3.12
Schemata of various orders and defining lengths. (a) A low-order schema (order 5, length 15). (b) A short, low-order schema (order 5, length 7). (c) A high-order schema (order 16, length 19).

Goldberg (1989) describes building blocks as "short, low-order, and highly fit schemata." A schema is a partial specification of the problem variables, or the set of all candidate solutions containing that subset of values. The set of strings in a schema is often depicted as a single tertiary string as in figure 3.12, where "*" can be read as "any allele can go here," or "this gene is not specified by the schema." The *order* of a schema is the number of specified genes, and so a *low-order* schema is one with a small number of specified genes. Finally, the *length* of a schema, or *defining length,* is the number of loci between the first and last specified loci (inclusive).

Underlying the claim of the BBH is the idea that the GA promotes copies of short, low-order schemata of high fitness in the population. This claim is based on what is known as the "*schema theorem*," which says "short, low-order, above-average [above-average fitness] schemata receive an exponentially increasing number of trials in subsequent generations" (ibid., p. 33; see also Altenberg 1995). This is intuitive enough; individuals containing above-average fitness schemata will tend to be above-average fitness individuals; these individuals will produce more offspring than other individuals under fitness-proportionate selection; and when the schemata have short defining length, there is a good chance that they will appear intact in their offspring. However, whether the schema theorem has anything to do with explaining the operation of the GA is questionable (Vose 1999).

One reason for this is because it is difficult to believe that selection in the GA can accurately respond to "schema fitness." Schema fitness is the average fitness of points in the hypervolume of the schema (the set of all strings in the schema), and is supposed to indicate the fitness contribution coming from that schema.

However, in practice, the GA can only at best assess the fitness of individuals in the population, which provide a very impoverished sample of the schema hypervolume. For example, consider a schema of low order, k. This schema contains $2^{(N-k)}$ different strings, where N is the number of bits in an individual. The members of the population can hardly be expected to give a reasonable sampling of the schema fitness when the set of strings in the schema is large; that is, when k is small and N is large. And even if the population did give a reasonable sampling the schema needs to be evaluated in a reasonable number of them before it is itself disrupted by recombination. So it is likely to be the individuals that get promoted (which will contain fit schemata but also some unfit schemata, or "hitchhikers"), not the schemata per se. A possible exception to this might be a case where the dependencies between loci in the schema with loci outside the schema are weak, low, or limited in some sense. In this case, accurate schema fitness could conceivably be assessed from a small number of individuals.

For now, let us suspend disbelief and go along with the idea that GAs process building blocks. When would this be algorithmically advantageous?

Algorithmic principles: Divide-and-conquer problem decomposition The population genetics models suggested that there would be an advantage in enabling selection to act on individual alleles—but the BBH suggests that selection should act on building blocks. Which of these is the most useful depends on the assumptions we make about the dependencies of the problem variables.

Algorithms for combinatorial optimization can be divided into different classes depending on the different assumptions they entail about the nature and structure of interdependencies in a problem domain. At one extreme we might assume that the interdependencies of the variables are arbitrarily difficult or random. In this case, the appropriate class of optimization methods are those that make no assumptions about the structure of the fitness landscape. These include exhaustive search, which explores the space of possibilities in its entirety, and random search, which explores the space of possibilities with uniform probability. These are impractical in all but the smallest of problems since the number of possibilities is subject to combinatorial explosion as the number of problem variables increases.

At the other extreme, we might suppose that the interdependencies between variables are weak or few. In this case, the appropriate class of algorithms uses this assumption to sample points nonuniformly, directed by prior samplings using the heuristic that effects of variables are approximately additive. These include "greedy" hill-climbing algorithms, which accept small variations to a candidate solution if they are superior, and gradient ascent methods. The effectiveness of this class depends on the implicit assumption of low interdependency between the variables in the problem, because its effectiveness requires that locally beneficial variations accumulate without mutual interference. (Horn, Goldberg, and Deb's "Long path problems" [1994] provide an interesting exception.)

These two classes represent the naive extremes of algorithmic possibilities: whereas exhaustive algorithms can deal with the arbitrarily difficult interdependency of problem variables, hill-climbing algorithms are guaranteed to be optimal only when the interdependency of the variables is weak or unimportant. In between these two extremes are many other possibilities. One possibility is the class of divide-and-conquer algorithms (see, e.g., Cormen, Leiserson, and Rivest 1991), which broadly includes algorithms that utilize modular structure in the interdependency of problem variables. Divide-and-conquer techniques exploit decomposable problems by dividing them into manageable subproblems. Their appropriateness depends on the assumption that the problem variables are neither close to independent (as for hill climbers) nor arbitrarily interdependent (as for exhaustive methods) but that the problem variables have some intermediate modular structure of semi-independent subsets. (These three cases were illustrated in table 1.1.)

There are several divide-and-conquer methods. In design and engineering domains, top-down functional decomposition of a problem into semi-independent subproblems is familiar and intuitive. In combinatorial optimization, dynamic programming methods are an important class of divide-and-conquer technique that utilize structured dependency bottom up by caching all partial solutions, without *a priori* knowledge of how to decompose the problem. Either top-down or bottom-up, divide-and-conquer strategies are fundamentally important because they exploit modular structure in a problem by exploiting semi-independent subproblems and thereby avoid the combinatorial explosion associated with high-dimensional problem spaces. The combinatorics involved in these three scenarios is outlined below by considering the optimization of a function, f, over a set of N variables, that is, optimize $f(n_1, n_2, \ldots, n_N)$.

1. Random search. If we make no assumptions about the interdependencies of these variables, then the size of the search space that must be covered to find the optimal solution is (at most) $S_R = k^N$ (where k is the *arity* of the variables, i.e., the number of values each variable can take).

2. Hill climbing. If the variables are individually separable, that is, if the contribution of one variable is unaffected by the values of other variables, then f can be described using the summation of N functions over one variable each. I.e., the function $f(n_1, n_2, \ldots, n_N) = f_1(n_1) + f_2(n_2) + \cdots + f_N(n_N)$. In this case, the size of the search space that must be covered to optimize f is at most $S_{HC} = kN$.

These are the two naive extremes: no assumptions about interdependency yields a search space of k^N; the assumption that all variables are independent of one another yields a search space of kN. The former is intractable for all but very small N, and the latter gives a problem that is trivially easy.

3. Divide-and-conquer problem decomposition. In between random search and hill climbing, there are many possibilities. Consider a case where the variables have some interdependency but their interdependencies are formed over two disjoint subsets of the variables: $f(n_1, n_2, \ldots, n_N) = g(f_1(n_1, n_2, \ldots, n_{N/2}), f_2(n_{N/2+1}, n_{N/2+2}, \ldots, n_N))$. Here, we may be able to exploit this modular structure to get some algorithmic advantage. For example, if the function g is a linear function like summation then the problem can be treated as two independent subproblems, and we can maximize the function f by maximizing the function f_1 and the function f_2 separately. So, if this decomposition is known, then the total search space that must be covered is at most $S_{DC} = 2k^{N/2}$. In general, of course, the decomposition is not known and discovering the decomposition adds some overhead to the method. Nonetheless, $2k^{N/2} \ll k^N$ for large N, and this forms the basis of the divide-and-conquer algorithmic advantage—when the overhead of finding the decomposition is low and g is a simple function. Conceivably, a problem could be divisible into many small subproblems, and/or each subproblem may be further divisible into sub-subproblems, and so on. In this case the overall time complexity of a divide-and-conquer method can be reduced to a polynomial function of N.

In human design and engineering problems divide-and-conquer is a familiar and intuitive approach. For example, we might divide the problem of designing a vehicle into the problems of drive power, steering and control, load bearing, and so forth. Or we may divide the problem of time-tabling a rail network into the many subtimetables within each region. Biologically, such a situation might apply if there are several biological subfunctions that can be adapted independently, but each subfunction may have complex internal interdependencies.

Royal Road functions Following the intuition that the GA with crossover should be good at "schema processing," Mitchell, Forrest, and Holland (1992) devised the Royal Road functions to exemplify when the genetic algorithm should perform well. The Royal Road functions define a strict building-block structure. Specifically, a function over 64 binary variables is defined as a sum of subfunctions over eight blocks of variables with eight variables each: that is,

$$f(n_1, n_2, \ldots, n_{64}) = \sum_{i=0}^{7} f_1(n_{8i+1}, n_{8i+2}, \ldots, n_{8i+8}).$$

f_1 rewards a block of variables if all the bits it contains are set to 1, and returns no fitness contribution otherwise. The idea was that this function defined short low-order schema of above-average fitness; and, if the BBH is right, this would be ideal to show the advantages of the GA with crossover. The variables within each subfunction cannot be optimized independently because they confer a fitness advantage only when they are *all* set to 1, but the function as a whole can be decomposed into blocks that can be optimized independently.

However, although the GA with crossover did better than the GA without crossover, a form of hill climber did better than both (Forrest and Mitchell 1993b). Clearly there is a fundamental problem somewhere in this model: if a hill climber performs better, then the Royal Road functions do not exemplify the value of the GA.

The concatenated trap functions The concatenated trap functions (Deb and Goldberg 1993) have the same basic building-block structure as the Royal Road functions (although they may use a different number of bits in a block and a different number of blocks). However, they use a different subfunction f_1. Specifically, a "trap function" rewards a block for having an increasing number of 0s, but in fact all 1s is still the fittest configuration for the bits of a block. A hill climber cannot solve this because it gets misled by the fitness rewards of 0s, but a GA can find blocks and put them together.

However, again a different kind of hill climber outperforms the GA. Jones (1995) showed that the macromutation hill climber, a random mutation hill climber that mutates blocks of consecutive bits at high mutation rates, instead of all bits at low mutation rates, solves the concatenated trap functions faster than the GA. So clearly there is still a fundamental problem somewhere in this model. Subsequent work in this direction defeated the macromutation hill climber by randomizing the genetic map so that the bits of a block were not consecutive (Goldberg, Korb, and Deb 1989), but of course, this also defeats the ability of crossover in the standard GA to manipulate building blocks.

So far, it seems we have not really gained anything by thinking about the block instead of the individual allele as the unit of selection, as in the population genetics models. The population genetics models suggested that reducing linkage disequilibrium and allowing selection to act on individual alleles would provide an advantage under some circumstances, but if this is true then a simple hill climber is sufficient. The building-block models suggested that reducing linkage disequilibrium *between* blocks of alleles but not *within* blocks of alleles would enable selection to act on blocks and provide an advantage, but this does not really change anything except a sense of scale. If selection on some individual unit, be it bits or blocks, is sufficient, then a hill climber can acquire units of that type and acquire all of them linearly (see also figure 4.9).

"Frequency thinking" versus "search thinking" Returning to the descriptions of the BBH above, there is an aspect of that intuition that has not yet been captured by these building-block models. Specifically, in those descriptions there is not simply the idea that the GA processes blocks instead of bits, but also an implication of a construction process—a process of putting things together to create new things. This relates to a deeper issue distinguishing the style of model that is normal in population genetics and the style of model that we look for in evolutionary computation. That is, population genetics models are often concerned with the state of a population at equilibrium. In this view most of the genetic material of interest is already in the population and we are just interested in the frequencies with which it occurs. This view is represented clearly in Muller's ratchet and the deterministic mutation hypothesis where the fittest genotype is present in the population at the outset.

In contrast, evolutionary computation models are more likely to view evolution as a search process where the population takes a trajectory from some low-fitness start position through previously unvisited regions of genotype space in an attempt to discover some fit genotypes we did not have at the start of the process. From a combinatorial optimization point of view, it does not make sense to look for a benefit of some mechanism by starting with the assumption that you began with the fittest genotype possible.

Accordingly, it is natural that the population genetic models view recombination merely as a process that balances the frequencies of allele combinations—increasing the frequencies of underrepresented combinations. In contrast, an evolutionary computation model is more interested in a process that makes a new allele combination, not merely increasing the frequency of an underrepresented allele combination, but, more specifically, changing its frequency from zero to some nonzero frequency. There is an aspect of this in the Fisher–Muller model. And there is clearly an appeal to this in the above passages about the BBH referring to putting blocks together in new combinations.

Nonetheless, something is missing from the building-block models for the benefit of recombination that we have seen thus far. I suggest that the feature missing from the Royal Road and concatenated trap functions is that there is no need to search combinations of building blocks to find good combinations of blocks. This omission is surprising given that this feature is clear in the passages about the BBH above. Goldberg, for example, suggests that the search space is reduced to a process of searching combinations of schemata rather than searching combinations of the original problem variables (see also Stephens and Waelbroeck 1999). Additionally, this process should continue through combinations of modules of successively larger scale. But the Royal Road models and the concatenated trap functions have separable building blocks—and thus there is no need to search combinations of blocks to find the best genotypes. If blocks are separable, all that needs to be done is increase the frequency of good schemata, in the manner suggested by the schema theorem. But if blocks are not separable then a building block that is best in one context may not be best in another—so merely increasing the frequency of the good schemata is insufficient. In the above discussion about problem decomposition I represented such a decomposable function as below and suggested that g was a linear function, in keeping with the Royal Road and the concatenated trap functions:

$$f(n_1, n_2, \ldots, n_N) = g(f_1(n_1, n_2, \ldots, n_{N/2}), f_2(n_{N/2+1}, n_{N/2+2}, \ldots, n_N)).$$

This is the mistake that the Royal Road and the concatenated trap functions make: by following the intuition of the schema theorem—that selection should act on blocks rather than bits—they miss the significance of the interactions between blocks. Divide-and-conquer problem decomposition, in contrast, does not require that subproblems be separable.

Although the idea of problem decomposition is intuitive and widely applicable in design and engineering, we are cognizant of the fact that the subproblems are almost never completely independent. For example, in the design of an automobile, the details of the power system, such as the weight of the engine, place constraints on the design of both the control system and the load-bearing system. Similarly, trains do travel between regions as well as within regions, so the timetable of one region is not independent of that in other regions. Thus the division of a problem into separable subfunctions depicted above is unrealistic. I will discuss this further in chapter 4 and define the notion of a *decomposable* function in contrast to this kind of *separable* function. However, despite subproblem interdependencies, design problems are often fruitfully approached by working on the subproblems, finding some reasonable solutions for the subproblems, and then resolving the interdependencies between alternate subsolutions.

If the intuitions of the BBH could be made to work—if GAs could do problem decomposition on problems that were not completely independent—then maybe GAs could do something that could not be done by any kind of hill climber. This is the intuition that is pursued in chapter 4 on modularity and chapter 6 on the benefit of sexual recombination. But most models we have seen thus far for the benefit of recombination have not shown any such ability for sexual populations and accordingly have not shown anything that a sexual population can evolve that an asexual population cannot evolve by linear incremental improvement based on random variations.

Beyond Sex

The action of crossover in GAs concerns the exchange of genetic material among members of the same species. We now look at the biological mechanisms of interspecific genetic integration (Hoffmeister and Martin 2003). The algorithmic mechanisms surveyed here follow the same intuitions of problem decomposition and searching combinations of modules that are indicated for sexual recombination. However, these mechanisms use the idea of encapsulating subsets of variables for reuse more explicitly, rather than merely relying on blocks defined by physical genetic linkage. They begin to move away from the metaphor of sexual recombination and can be seen as loose analogues of some of the interspecific compositional mechanisms.

There are two main concepts involved in the idea of compositional evolution: dividing a problem into subproblems, and putting parts together into wholes. These are complementary; problem decomposition is solution composition. With respect to the latter, one of the ideas I want to pursue is the idea that an evolutionary process can apply a compositional operator repeatedly, encapsulating small groups of entities into larger entities through several hierarchical levels of organization. This corresponds algorithmically to the idea of hierarchical problem decomposition. These concepts depend on exploiting modularity.

There are many evolutionary computation approaches that relate to these issues. Modularity is addressed implicitly by the use of variable-length, moving-locus, nonlinear, and generative encodings—for example, messy GA (Goldberg, Korb, and Deb 1989), linkage-learning GA (Harik and Goldberg 1996), genetic programming (Koza 1992), and cellular encoding (Gruau 1994). And modularity is addressed explicitly in mechanisms that encapsulate subsets of features for subsequent reuse during the search process—for example, "automatic module acquisition" (Angeline and Pollack 1993), "automatically defined functions" (Koza 1994), and "adaptive representation" (Rosca 1997). The advantage of these explicit methods is that "the modularization of representational components and their protection from mutation [internal variation] can be viewed as removing unnecessary dimension[s] from the search space ..." (Angeline and Pollack 1993, p. 162). Methods explicitly addressing problem decomposition and notions of selection on parts include learning classifier systems (Holland and Reitman 1978), cooperative coevolution (Potter 1997), evolutionary divide-and-conquer (Rosca 1997), modular inductive learning (MIL) (Juillé 1999), "arbiters" (Husbands 1993), "multi-level cooperative search" (Valenzuela and Jones 1994), and symbiotic adaptive neuro evolution (SANE) (Moriarty 1997), as well as the techniques embedded in the modularity methods listed above.

To highlight these two main concepts I will focus on one of these methods that starts out with small entities and uses a composition operator to put them together (the messy GA), and another that uses explicit problem decomposition (cooperative coevolution). Together these two methods cover a lot of the necessary concepts that I want to introduce.

The messy GA (Goldberg, Korb, and Deb 1989) is an evolutionary algorithm with some extra features: individuals are represented as partially specified strings with a moving-locus representation, recombination uses a "splice operator" to join partially specified strings together, and evaluation uses a "template" to fill in for unspecified loci. Later sections (mostly 3.3) will address each of these features in detail. But the basic idea is that each individual, instead of having a whole set of genes, has only a small set of genes. This subset of genes will, if all goes well, correspond to a subproblem in the overall problem (the exemplar is the concatenated trap function). Then when these have been subject to selection individually and good subsolutions have been found, a composition operator joins these small entities together into pairs, and so on, until an individual eventually represents a full set of the problem parameters. The intuition is that by optimizing small individuals first, this method can exploit the decomposition of the problem. But more important, it also illustrates the idea of assembling these subsolutions together, explicitly creating composite entities that can subsequently undergo further joins. The useful difference between the GA and the messy GA is that because individuals explicitly represent subsets of variables that correspond to subsolutions there is no reliance on physical linkage to enable subsets of variables to be manipulated effectively. This is useful when the subset of variables in each subfunction are not contiguous on the chromosome—an issue that will be important in distinguishing the ability of sex and symbiotic encapsulation.

However, in the messy GA, the two main aspects of the method, optimizing the parts and putting them together, are executed in separate phases. In the first phase, the solutions to the parts are uniquely identified—which is possible because the subproblems are separable. In the second phase, joining any two individuals together is acceptable because there are no dependencies between individuals that need to be resolved. Again, there is no need to search combinations of blocks in this problem (the fact that the blocks are distributed on the chromosome and their locations are unknown is a different issue from the possibility of epistatic interactions between blocks that might need to be resolved). However, the messy GA does illustrate the use of partially specified individuals to explicitly represent subsolutions, and the subset of variables that each individual optimizes does not have to be specified in advance. This feature of the messy GA is designed to overcome the problem that the bits of a subfunction are not next to each other in the genetic map and overcomes the limitations of the building-block notion that depends on physical linkage to represent subsolutions implicitly. This is a feature that we will use later in chapter 7 to great effect.

Cooperative coevolution presents an explicit divide-and-conquer approach to evolutionary algorithms (Potter 1997; Potter and De Jong 2000). In this method individual specialists coevolve to collectively solve a problem, and the notions of divide-and-conquer problem decomposition are very explicit. The basic idea is to have several evolving populations, each one responsible for evolving solutions to one subpart of the problem. Fit representatives from each of these populations are evaluated together, thus forming a candidate solution to the whole problem.

In earlier work (Potter 1997), there are explicit fixed roles for the individuals; later methods (Potter and De Jong 2000) show some ability for individual species to adaptively cover the problem domain and vary in the number of specialist species required. Potter also explicitly uses the idea of restricting competition to act only between specialists of the same type—specialists of different types cannot competitively exclude one another because they are held in different populations.

The way that specialists are used in some examples of the method is conceptually similar to the partially specified individuals of the messy GA—specifically, each specialist covers an explicit subset of the problem parameters. However, there is no general automatic method to determine how to decompose the complete set of variables into appropriate subsets in cooperative coevolution. Also, there is no notion in cooperative coevolution of assembling specialists together in a hierarchical fashion. Representatives of specialist species are evaluated together in a group but a successful group is never encapsulated so that we can form metagroups. Thus, alternate assemblies of specialists cannot be maintained and selected for, and the problem decomposition is necessarily only a single level of decomposition.

So, cooperative coevolution does not have a composition operator or other means of assembling specialists into composites recursively; but this method explicitly uses the notion of divide-and-conquer problem decomposition in many different substrates including string-based function optimization, the notion that competition should occur only within a group of specialists for a particular subproblem, and that specialists on different subproblems should be allowed to coexist and collectively cover the problem domain. These are also features that will be useful in chapter 7.

Symbiosis and symbiogenesis models in evolutionary computation Although Potter does not describe cooperative coevolution as a symbiosis model, the idea of cooperative coevolution is clearly analogous to the symbiotic evolution of coadapting populations—the subdivision part of compositional evolution. And although Goldberg et al. do not describe the messy GA as a symbiogenesis model (it is presented as a logical extension of sexual recombination to overcome a poor genetic map), the idea of explicitly joining small entities together into larger entities provides an analogue for symbiotic encapsulation—the genetic integration part of compositional evolution. These two methods provide most of what we need, but there are numerous other evolutionary computation models that are explicitly intended as models of symbiosis and/or symbiogenesis as surveyed below.

Bull and Fogarty (1995; Bull, Fogarty, and Pipe 1995) present a computational model of "artificial endosymbiosis." This, and other models that these authors present, has an emphasis more on the conditions under which endosymbiotic relationships will occur rather than an examination of when such mechanisms can provide superior optimization. The authors provide two possibilities for evolving entities—(a) a specification for the evolving genes is provided by two independently evolved half-specifications, and (b) a specification for the evolving genes is evolved as a whole. Pairs of individuals from the first case may be composed together to form individuals of the second case. The problem domain is a two-component NKC landscape (Kauffman and Johnsen 1989), and it is shown that when the dependency between the two clusters of variables in the problem is low, case (a) predominates, and when it is high, case (b) predominates. The roles for each of the entities involved is predetermined (each individual is assigned one of the clusters of variables in the problem). This work illustrates the idea of problem decomposition and the composition of subsolutions, and it also carefully examines the conditions of the problem domain that induce different results. However, the problem domain has only two modules and no hierarchical structure, so there is no possibility of repeated composition of entities. There is also no mechanism for automatically identifying the subdomains in the problem. Later work (Bull and Fogarty 1996) examines the alternatives of individuals that are either (a) a sexual host plus an endosymbiont, or (b) as before. That work explicitly refers to the parallels of sexual recombination and symbiosis. However, it does not use a composition operator, and has the same limitations with respect to the number and identity of specialists' roles. Bull (1997, 1999) applies similar ideas to other evolutionary transitions. Bull (1999), interestingly, mentions the possible involvement of the Baldwin effect, which relates to some ideas developed in chapter 7 of this book.

Numaoka (1995) provides an "animat"-based model of "symbiosis and coevolution" in which the sensing ability of an agent is evolved. Evolved behavior, controlled by two eight-bit parameters of the sensors, is applied to a foraging task called the "blind hunger problem." There is no explicit partial specification—specialization of different individuals to different subparts of the problem domain—or concatenation of partial solutions into a whole. The genetic operator is more like horizontal gene transfer ("microbial GA," Harvey 1996, 2001; also in Watson, Ficici, and Pollack 2002) than symbiotic encapsulation.

Kvasnicka 2000, "An Evolutionary Model of Symbiosis" (inspired by Watson and Pollack 1999d), includes explicit divide-and-conquer problem decomposition (in the style of Bull and Fogarty), and a concatenation operator that assembles partial solutions together. However, the problem domain is a concatenation of several nonoverlapping NK landscapes, which makes subproblems that are entirely separable; thus this problem would be amenable to a macromutation hill climber (Jones 1995). Kvasnicka uses an ad hoc method to limit string bloat: only when a certain fitness threshold is reached is the composition operator applied. In general, there is no means to know where this threshold should be placed on an unknown problem. The roles of independent symbionts are predefined, and tight genetic linkage (see section 6.4) is assumed.

Hirasawa et al.'s "genetic symbiosis algorithm" (2001) is the same as the simple GA but with the addition of some "symbiosis parameters" that modify fitness. These parameters for a pair of entities are derived from the Euclidean distance between genotypes and the fitness difference of individuals and define a matrix of association relations that control competition, exploitation, and mutual benefit. There is no composition operator, and no hierarchy in variation or in the problem domain. The method essentially provides an interesting form of fitness sharing for diversity maintenance. Mao et al. (2001) use similar ideas to handle interaction among objectives.

Tsujimura, Mafune, and Gen (2001) present a "symbiotic genetic algorithm" that is specific to the domain of job-shop scheduling. It applies selection based on two objectives (make span and idle time) in a manner similar to implicit fitness sharing. A third objective (total job-waiting time) is applied to promote diversity. The algorithm has no composition operator and no hierarchy.

I might mention in passing that immune systems (Hofmeyr and Forrest 1999) and ant algorithms (Dorigo, Di Caro, and Gambardella 1999) also gain their basic intuition from the algorithmic advantage of problem decomposition by selecting for individual antigens and individual ants that collectively provide solutions to a protection problem or graph-routing problem, respectively.

In all these methods there are ideas about problem decomposition and subsolution assembly, but none employs a composition operator that encapsulates specialist entities together into a new composite entity over multiple levels (as opposed to one level of decomposition).

Hierarchical models Barricelli (1957) presented a paper entitled "Symbiogenetic Evolution Processes Realised by Artificial Methods," where he sets out to model symbiogenesis and to use computer simulations to investigate the dynamics of symbiotic processes. This predates some of the work often cited as the foundation of work in genetic algorithms (e.g., Holland 1975) and it is remarkable how many of the ideas we are discussing here are present in Barricelli's work. For example, the idea of compositional mechanisms and their combinatorial advantage, the potential for open-ended evolution under compositional mechanisms and its superiority to monolithic approaches, and the close relationship of sexual recombination and symbiogenesis can all be found in this paper. Additionally, Barricelli uses a substrate where the boundaries of organisms are flexible and allow for the possibility of encapsulation. He also discusses horizontal gene transfer and the tendency of populations to converge without diversity maintenance mechanisms.

However, this work is performed in one-dimensional and two-dimensional cellular automata (Ilachinski 2001) with fairly ad hoc transition rules. This is an interesting substrate, and the implicit boundaries of replicating patterns in the automata are a potentially powerful means to develop complex composition results; but the method is entirely impenetrable to analytic treatment. It is also very difficult to see how results in this domain affect our understanding of (what have now become) the traditional GA and related hypotheses like the BBH. The main problem in this respect is that there is no explicit goal or function to be optimized in this system, which is fine as an artificial life experiment, but does not assist us in identifying the adaptive capacity of different mechanisms in a measurable way.

Dumeur (1996) presents a very interesting and unconventional style of GA in "Evolution through Cooperation: The Symbiotic Algorithm." The method uses a tree with leaves holding the values of problem parameters. The ordering of nodes and subnodes in the tree controls the likelihood of co-occurrence of problem parameters in a candidate solution. "Symbiotic associations" are represented by co-occurrence of parameters on a subtree. The only application tested is to cover the peaks of a multimodal function (a sinusoid)—it is not clear what the modular structure of this problem is in terms of the problem variables (i.e., in the binary variables that represent a candidate solution), if it has one. It may be that the mechanics of this approach are not all that different in spirit from those developed in chapter 7, but the approach is very different and accordingly it is difficult to see the parallels with this and other GA work clearly. In the representation that Dumeur uses it is very difficult to make associations with the BBH, to identify the class of problems that it is well suited for, or to ascertain its ability to maintain the diversity of competing schemata, for example.

Classifier systems provide an interesting spectrum of divide-and-conquer optimization at different scales. "Michigan-style" classifiers (Holland and Reitman 1978) optimize only at the small scale (selection is for individual rules). This is efficient when rule interdependencies are simple, but may produce suboptimal results in other cases. In contrast, the "Pitt" approach to classifiers (De Jong 1988) can in principle find optimal configurations of rules by selecting for whole rule sets, but in general it suffers from the combinatorics introduced by the much larger search space this defines. Hierarchical classifiers (see Barry 1996) potentially offer the advantage of both approaches. Some of the mechanisms developed in this book, for selecting for complementary sets of schemata and for identifying when a collection of schemata makes a valuable composite, may be useful in classifier domains.

Following ideas introduced by Wilson and Goldberg (1989), Tomlinson and Bull (2001) examine the use of "symbiogenesis in learning classifier systems" where classifier rules are composed into sets of rules that are chained together. Rules that are composed together reproduce together as a group. They also utilize the notion of "encapsulating" a set of rules with respect to their "behavior"—that is, the opportunity for rule firing when multiple rules can be applied at a given time is resolved with reference to set membership. This work provides the opportunity for hierarchical compositions (implicitly), and the role of a rule is flexible, not predetermined. Such work embodies many of the concepts examined in this book but in the domain of classifier systems rather than straightforward function optimization.

Rosca (1997) develops techniques covering a lot of the fundamental ideas we are pursuing under a heading of adaptive representation and hierarchical learning. Specifically, the work explicitly addresses divide-and-conquer problem decomposition where individuals specify for a subdomain of a function, and Rosca explicitly pursues the hierarchical assembly of specialists into complete solutions. Individual specialists are evaluated collectively. Diversity is maintained by techniques similar to restricted mating, where mating is restricted to individuals in the same subdomain cluster. The role of an individual in the collective task is specified by the "subdomain" part of an individual, and the behavior of the individual is specified by a function within that subdomain (analogous to the "condition" and "output" parts of individual classifier rules). The subdivision of the problem domain is not given *a priori* (see also Juillé and Pollack 1996). The substrate is genetic-programming *s*-expressions and the problem domain is symbolic regression. Crossover of *s*-expressions can enable composition. The main limitation in this work is that although (1) there are diverse specialists covering the problem space, (2) there is a combination operator (genetic-programming crossover) that could put specialists together into a generalist; in fact, the crossover operator cannot put diverse specialists together into a composite because the only way they were maintained as diverse specialists in the first place is by restricted mating. So, in fact, there is no clear hierarchical assembly of coadapted specialists into composites. Additionally, since this work is in the genetic-programming domain we cannot connect it to the BBH and string-based crossover. Also, when applied to arbitrary symbolic-regression problems that may or may not be amenable to decomposition, it is difficult to assess exactly how it works when it does and analyze its behavior. Nevertheless, this work suggests a lot of potential to bring the ideas developed in this book into the genetic-programming domain.

All of these models show some form of problem decomposition at multiple levels. However, they use various substrates—cellular automata, tree representations, classifier systems, genetic programming—none of them using the simple string representation of the GA. Thus it is difficult to see how to incorporate these models in a unified framework and to transfer intuitions from these models to biological evolution operating on linear chromosomes. If we could extract the underlying divide-and-conquer principles—the coevolution of semi-independent specialist entities and the encapsulation of entities through successive hierarchical levels—and illustrate them in a simple string-based representation like the genetic algorithm, this would be progress. We would be able to see how these methods relate to one another and to sexual recombination. It would also be preferable if we could apply these methods to a straightforward function-optimization problem where the underlying modular structure that was being exploited was clear and formal analyses were possible. Although none of the existing methods provides all of these things, many of them provide important parts of the feature set I develop for the models in this book.

3.3 Some Issues in the Use of Compositional Mechanisms

In this section I survey some of the underlying issues that arise in the implementation of EAs using compositional mechanisms. This will help us understand what features are important in the existing methods. I begin to synthesize the features that should be retained for the models used in later chapters.

Building-Block Processing under Recombination

Two practical difficulties with building-block crossover in GAs come from a lack of diversity in the population and "disruption." That is, when fitness-proportionate selection is applied to a panmictic population it tends to become genetically converged very quickly and thus sexual recombination has no effect. And the problem of disruption of a building block in crossover refers to the fact that the stability of a building block, that is, its likelihood of being recombined with other building blocks appropriately, is dependent on the colocation of constituent genes on the chromosome, that is, "tight" genetic linkage. Considerable research effort to improve the performance of EAs has been directed at issues of diversity maintenance and robust representations of functional subcomponents that would allow the appropriate manipulation of building blocks when discovered.

Genetic Linkage and Partial Specification

A long defining length (see figure 3.12) increases the probability that a useful schema in a parent will be disrupted in reproduction with crossover. If disruption of schemata by crossover is high then even if a schema has a fitness that is above average it may not receive an exponentially increasing number of trials in subsequent generations. Initial disruption analysis by Holland (1975) has been developed further by many others (e.g., De Jong 1975; De Jong and Spears 1990). The selection schemes that I use in the compositional models are quite different from those where such an analysis is important, and in these cases the likelihood of schema creation is more important. However, issues of favorable genetic linkage, which have a strong effect on schema disruption, are also relevant to schema creation, as discussed below and in section 6.4.

Figure 3.13 shows the possibility of combining two schemata under one-point crossover assuming tight physical linkage—that is, an arrangement of the genetic map that provides favorable physical linkage. However, it also illustrates the difficulty of combining two schemata in cases of poor linkage. In general, in cases with a random genetic map an arbitrary number of crossover points must be placed at appropriate positions in order to guarantee that good schemata from each parent can be brought together in the offspring. Accordingly, we see that one of the weaknesses of crossover is that the modules that we wish to manipulate are represented only *implicitly*, by virtue of the collocation of their genes on the chromosome. It should be clear at this stage that the notion of what bits *should* travel together in crossover events—because they are epistatically dependent on one another and correspond to useful schemata—is quite different from the notion of which bits are in reality likely

tight linkage	poor linkage
10**1010**010100100	10**1**01001**0**010**10**0
10010101101**1110**	**1**00**1**0**1**010**0**11110
10**1010**01001**1110** ↑	?

Figure 3.13
Building-block combination and disruption. Left: Combining two low-order schemata using one-point crossover is possible when physical linkage is tight, i.e., defining length is short (see figure 3.12). Right: When linkage is poor because the ordering of epistatically related genes is random, one-point crossover cannot create an offspring with both schemata.

to travel together under regular crossover because they are close to each other on the chromosome. I will refer to the former as "dependency" or "epistatic dependency," and to the latter as "physical linkage."

One way to rectify the problem of poor linkage is to reorder the genes so that interdependent genes are close together—so that genetic linkage corresponds with epistatic dependency. Accordingly, several variants of the GA have proposed moving-locus schemes, for example, the GA with an inversion operator, messy GAs (Goldberg, Korb, and Deb 1989), and linkage-learning GAs (Harik 1997). Despite the validity of these approaches, it is important to remember that the need to rearrange genes is a result of using a recombination operator that is sensitive to gene positions. And it should also be noted that genetic linkage based on gene ordering on linear chromosomes cannot in principle represent epistatic dependencies that cannot be linearized.

Unfortunately, the notions of epistatic dependency and physical linkage are sometimes conflated. The term "linkage learning" is a case in point. Linkage learning in some cases (e.g., Harik 1997) refers to the process of discovering and representing the epistatic dependency of variables in a problem by moving them around so that they are next to each other on the chromosome. In other cases, for example, Kargupta 1997, linkage learning is used to mean simply the discovery and representation of epistatic dependency by whatever means, and not necessarily by the use of rearranging physical linkage. More recently, explicit probabilistic models of epistatic dependencies between genes have been based on Bayesian nets (Pelikan, Goldberg, and Cantú-Paz 1999).

A different method proposed to overcome the weaknesses of crossover is the use of "crossover masks"—additional binary vectors, specified along with each

0**1**010**0**1**1**	– GA.
((2,1), (6,0), (8,1))	– Messy GA, moving-locus.
-1---0-1	– fixed-locus, partial-specification.

Figure 3.14
Representation of genomes/schemata for the GA, messy GA, and partial specification.

chromosome—that specify which bits of the chromosome should travel together in a crossover event (Louis and Rawlins 1991). Other methods use a real-valued vector that represents the probability that each bit will be transferred to the offspring. In these approaches there are various methods required to regulate how the values in the mask vectors are updated (e.g., see Vekaria and Clack 1998). Similar to the notion of crossover masks is the use of "partially specified representations": methods where each individual may represent a variable number of genes and may therefore leave some alleles for some genes unspecified. The messy GA combines the use of partial specifications with moving-locus representations (Goldberg 1989).

Figure 3.14 compares the notion of a desirable schema within an individual in the simple GA (bold genes) with the representation of a schema-individual in the messy GA that uses a moving-locus representation for genomes. In the messy GA each gene is represented by a locus–allele pair. The desirable schema in the GA representation is transferred to an example messy GA representation in the second line of the figure. Moving the genes together in this way allows the messy GA to transfer the schema intact during recombination. This figure also shows how the schema can be represented using a fixed-locus, partial-specification representation. One useful interpretation of the use of partial specification is that whereas under regular crossover it is problematic to determine which subset of genes in each parent should be inherited in the offspring, when combining together partially specified individuals, the individuals themselves are already explicitly representing the desirable subset of genes. Previous work has discussed the relationship between the use of partial specifications and moving-locus representations, and the other properties of the messy GA (Watson and Pollack 1999c).

Recombination in the messy GA is represented in figure 3.15. Two parents, A and B, represent partially specified strings using locus-allele pairs. The offspring, C, is simply the union of specified genes from both parents. This is the "splice operation" of the messy GA (Goldberg, Korb, and Deb 1989). It should be noted that when the two parents involved in a splice operation are not overlapping in the genes that they

A: ((2,1), (6,0), (8,1))

B: ((1,1), (3,0), (5,0))

C: ((2,1), (6,0), (8,1), (1,1), (3,0) (5,0))

Figure 3.15
Splice recombination in the messy GA.

```
A: -1---0-1

B: 1-0-0---
__________

C: 110-00-1
```

Figure 3.16
An alternate representation of the splice operation in figure 3.15.

specify, this operation is in fact insensitive to the ordering of genes in the chromosome and accordingly may just as well be represented by the fixed-locus but partially specified representation shown in figure 3.16. Here unspecified genes, or "don't cares," are represented by a dash and the offspring is created by taking specified genes from either parent where available. This provides a fixed-locus but partial-specification representation of individuals that effectively represents schemata explicitly. The representation of individuals and the combination operation shown in figure 3.16, inspired by the splice operation of the messy GA, is the basis of the combination operator that will be detailed in chapter 7.

Figure 3.16 conveniently avoids the issue of what happens when there are conflicts in the specified alleles of partially specified individuals. Suppose, for the sake of argument, that we arrive at some method that can successfully evolve different useful schemata in different individuals, and moreover that we have some means to represent where the schemata are in each individual so that they can be transferred as a coherent whole into the offspring. Even then we still have the issue of how to handle conflicting schemata. This is known, in general, as the "competing conventions" problem. To take a scenario from a different domain: if we are evolving neural networks to control a robot, and both networks work reasonably well but by different methods (different conventions), then if we take a subset of one network and a subset of another and put them together we are likely to end up with a network that does not function properly. If, on the other hand, both networks work by the same method but with only slight variations (same convention), then it might plausibly be valuable to try a combination of partial networks.

The intuition that recombination between radically dissimilar individuals will likely produce nonfunctioning offspring is in opposition with the intuition that recombination requires parents to be different in order to be worth doing at all—that is, to the extent that parents are similar, recombination between them has no effect, and to the extent that parents are dissimilar, recombination between them is likely to produce nonfunctioning offspring. However, this apparent conflict is alleviated when the parents have the possibility of being complementary—representing different roles within the problem as a whole—for example, by specifying for nonoverlapping subsets of genes using a partially specified representation. This possibility is explicitly utilized in cooperative coevolution (Potter 1997). However, when individuals specify for different roles or tasks, some extra machinery is required to evaluate and compare them.

Evaluation of Parts

In the messy GA, individuals are partially specified subsets of genes. Accordingly, an objective fitness function that expects a completely specified subset of genes presents a problem. In some problems, partially specified individuals may be evaluated naturally, or by filling in unspecified values with some kind of default value. In other cases, especially in cases where there are important interdependencies between genes, this is not possible or does not give a useful indication of the value of a schema.

What we really want to know when considering the utility of a particular schema in a compositional system is whether it is useful in creating larger schemata or fully specified strings. Accordingly, a schema should be evaluated in some context or "template" of the remaining values. "Templating" in the messy GA simply means superimposing the schema of interest onto some other fully specified string. In some versions of the messy GA, this template is created from the assembly of other individuals in previous rounds of evolution (Goldberg et al. 1993). In cooperative coevolution, an individual fulfilling one role within the problem as a whole is evaluated in a "shared domain model" along with representatives of individuals fulfilling complementary roles. These scenarios are reminiscent of the "rowers" analogy in Dawkins 1976 (pp. 38–39 in the 1989 edition)—specifically, a set of independently replicating entities may thus become coadapted by virtue of evaluation in a shared domain. In cooperative coevolution this scenario is set up explicitly, but cooperative coevolution does not have any subsequent method to explicitly combine coadapted individuals together. In the messy GA, where the template has also been evolved, this scenario is also apparent but the opportunity for coadaptation is less explicit.

One interpretation of these scenarios then, is that individuals that cover different parts of the problem domain may become coadapted to one another and complement one another's unspecified characteristics. This provides an explicit opportunity for divide-and-conquer problem decomposition (see also Rosca 1997) and, in some cases, potential relief from the competing conventions problem.

Selection on Parts: The Credit Assignment Problem

The next issue is as follows: if a partial solution must be evaluated in some context—for example, an assembly of other partial solutions (a template or shared domain model)—how do we apportion fitness to the modules involved? This is known as the "credit assignment problem." In genetic algorithms using crossover (where the implicit modules are sections of chromosome and the context is the individual) the credit assignment problem is manifest as "hitchhiking" (Forrest and Mitchell 1993b). In the messy GA, where the modules are partially specified individuals and the context comprises other spliced-on individuals and the template, the credit assignment problem is manifest as "parasites" (Goldberg, Korb, and Deb 1989). In cooperative coevolution the credit assignment problem is avoided because different individuals are not joined together and so cannot hitchhike on the credit of others.

In general, there is no principled solution to hitchhiking in the models we have seen. In the messy GA, parasites are handled by the use of a two-phase model. In the first phase, individuals are not recombined (or spliced together) and are not allowed to grow in size—thus eliminating the possibility of parasites. And when this is relaxed in the second phase, it is assumed that only good schemata remain in the population.

Thus the credit assignment problem for coevolving modules in compositional processes is an issue that will demand a more general solution in the models that follow.

Coevolution of Parts: Competitive Exclusion and Fitness Sharing

In general then, one way or another, compositional methods often involve the coevolution of complementary parts (and their assembly into wholes). In the simple GA with crossover, the parts are schemata and the wholes are individuals. In the messy GA, the parts are the size-limited individuals of the first phase, and the wholes are the templates and/or the fully specified individuals formed in the second phase. And in cooperative coevolution, the parts are represented by explicitly segregated species, and the wholes are represented in the shared domain model.

In a general framework of coevolving modules, it is necessary that we allow individuals covering different parts of the problem domain to coexist; otherwise, we will not be able to search different combinations of them. But maintaining such diversity in the cooperative coevolution of modules presents a problem. If we apply the usual kind of selection that we use in competitive evolution then, under repeated selection, the type that is best on average will sooner or later competitively exclude all other types. In biological models (e.g., Arthur 1987), competitive exclusion of one species by another, and one allele by another (pp. 17–48), is in some cases counteracted by "frequency-dependent fitness" effects (p. 52). That is, in principle, as the frequency of one type increases this may have consequences for the fitness function of the species/types involved, and in some cases, may apply negative feedback on the frequency of that type. Under certain conditions this may enable stable coexistence of more than one type. In artificial EAs, frequency-dependent fitness effects are known as "fitness sharing" (e.g., Goldberg and Richardson 1987). Fitness sharing comes in many varieties (e.g., "crowding," Cavicchio 1970 and De Jong 1975; "thresholding," Goldberg, Deb, and Korb 1990; "implicit fitness sharing," Smith, Forrest, and Perelson 1993; "niching," Deb and Goldberg 1989—see Mahfoud 1995 for an overview), but the basic idea common to all methods is that the value of being a particular type is depressed as a function of the number of other individuals of the same or similar type. Fitness-sharing methods can in principle then permit different types of entities to coexist, which is just what we need if we want to search combinations of them to find composite solutions.

However, the problematic aspect of fitness sharing is that it requires us to define the identity of types or at least the similarity of types—and it is generally not clear what metric of similarity (genotypic, phenotypic, behavioral) is appropriate. In cooperative coevolution, the types are predefined and selection is separated so that one type cannot exclude another. In templating (Goldberg, Korb, and Deb 1989), similarity is sometimes based on genotypic Hamming distance. In the general case, where we do not know the roles of individuals *a priori* or cannot assume that genotypic similarity is a good indication of performing the same functional role, we need a more general method of maintaining diversity.

Multidimensional Fitness and Pareto Coevolution

Previous work has investigated issues of diversity maintenance in coevolution in simple abstract games (Watson and Pollack 2001b). These investigations have led us to identify several concepts that will be raised again in our models. In coevolutionary games, it is often useful to consider a game as containing several different "aspects of play" (Bucci, Pollack, and De Jong 2004; De Jong and Pollack 2004). For example, in chess there is only one explicit objective—"play good chess"—but this may implicitly involve being good at endgames, being good at controlling the center of the board, being good at protecting the queen, and so on. Generally, an aspect of play that is good in one context (against one opponent) is not necessarily good in another context (against another opponent). In fact, in some cases, the gradient of the fitness landscape leading to fitter types within an aspect of play can even be reversed depending on the selection of opponents. For example, in tennis, a fast serve might be advantageous against most opponents, but against other opponents serving slowly might provide the advantage—perhaps to let you get to the net to receive the return. This induces a condition of "intransitive superiority," and is one cause of "cycling" and "forgetting" (revisiting the same parts of strategy space more than once) in coevolutionary dynamics (Watson and Pollack 2001b; De Jong 2004a; Bucci and Pollack 2003; Ficici 2004).

If there are many aspects of play, and different aspects have different importance against different players (especially if the effect of an aspect of play on fitness changes sign with different opponents), then the quality of a strategy in general should not be reduced to a single-dimensional value—a single fitness measure. For example, using the average fitness of a player over many different opponents loses significant valuable information about what that player is good at and what that player is not good at. This leads us to consider coevolution as a multidimensional optimization process. In this interpretation, each individual has a multidimensional fitness measure, each dimension corresponding to different aspects of play. However, we generally do not know *a priori* what those different aspects of play might be. But, we may imagine the quality of a player in *different aspects of play* to be represented loosely by the performance of the player *against different opponents.*

In two-player competitive games, we can treat each opponent as a representative of an aspect of play, and thus each individual in the population defines a value for one dimension in their multidimensional fitness (see Ficici and Pollack 2000; De Jong 2004a). We use the term "Pareto coevolution" (Watson and Pollack 2000a; Ficici and Pollack 2001) to refer to the application of multiobjective algorithms (e.g., Fonseca and Fleming 1995) to multidimensional measures coming from other coevolving players.

In the basic selection model of normal coevolution, an individual A may replace an individual B if it is on average better than B against a sample of other players. The basic selection model of Pareto coevolution is that an individual A may replace an individual B only if A gets a better or equal score than B does against each and every player in a sample of other players (and better against at least one). Thus Pareto coevolution is basically the idea that the evolving population should approximate the Pareto front of nondominated strategies and will thereby avoid the convergence of the population that is inherent in single-dimensional interpretations of fitness. The Pareto coevolution idea has been applied and developed further in subsequent work

(Ficici and Pollack 2001; Noble and Watson 2001; De Jong and Pollack 2002; Bucci and Pollack 2002; De Jong and Pollack 2004), with particular emphasis on ensuring monotonic improvement in coevolutionary processes (Ficici and Pollack 2003; De Jong 2004b). In chapter 7 I will describe the biological analogues of this idea which originated from niching and population subdivision.

In multiplayer (here meaning more than two players) cooperative games, we may use different *groups* of coevolving individuals to provide different contexts—and in principle, each group-context represents a dimension of play. The idea is that by using different groups of individuals to provide the context in which a partially specified individual is evaluated, we allow individuals to coevolve and coadapt to one another and provide a solution to the evaluation of parts since groups collectively cover the whole set of problem parameters (much like templates in the messy GA and the shared domain model in cooperative coevolution). But by using Pareto dominance as the selection criteria (instead of the usual best-on-average selection criteria) we permit different individuals covering the same subset of parameters to coexist if they are nondominated—which provides an appropriate regulation of competitive exclusion and helps prevents premature convergence to suboptimal subsolutions. I develop this further in section 7.3.

3.4 Some Conceptual Issues of Compositional Evolution

Large Changes within One Lineage: Contrast with Composition

Large phenotypic changes from small genotypic changes Ontogenic mechanisms, "translating" the genotype into the phenotype, may permit large nonrandom changes in more than one way. For example, a small genotypic change may cause a complex of features to be expressed more than once in the phenotype, as in an additional repetition of a body segment. They may also allow subsequent modifications in the genotype to produce changes in all phenotypic repeats of a body segment, for example. "Small changes early in embryology accumulate through growth to yield profound differences among adults" (Gould 1977). Assuming that ontogenic processes are, at least to some extent, themselves subject to adaptation (and not entirely the result of predetermined biological causation), favorable ontogenic processes would presumably be selected for, should they occur (Arthur 1997).

Other processes potentially involved in large nonrandom changes include *exaptation* (Gould and Vrba 1982). Exaptation refers to cases where a collection of features adapted for some purpose is coopted for some other purpose or function. With respect to the function of interest, a large set of phenotypic features is introduced simultaneously. And since this set of features has been subject to prior selection (albeit for a different function) it is a nonrandom set of features. The utility of this scenario requires that the feature of interest be variationally close to a structure that, although functionally different, is also well adapted for some purpose.

Mechanisms for large genetic changes within a lineage: Gene duplication Any genetic mechanism that reuses a subset of genetic material that has been preadapted by prior selection potentially enables a large nonrandom genetic change. Gene duplication (Ohno 1970) provides a case in point. Genetic errors in replication can produce repeated segments of genetic material. Such mechanisms are responsible for the observation that many genes appear to be derived from similar sequences, that is, they are duplicated and subsequently modified by mutation. The new section of chromosome so introduced is of course quite different from random genetic material because it contains sequences that have been arrived at through prior adaptation. Of course, it may cause some disruption, but it is easy to see that it may permit a large nonrandom change that has a higher likelihood of being nondeleterious than a random change would have.

Other genetic mechanisms manipulating sections of chromosome (see Altenberg 2005, p. 106) within a single chromosome include translocation and inversion. Also, polyploidy, the duplication of chromosomes, when resulting from the breeding of individuals in the same species, produces an effect similar in some respects to gene duplication, although on a larger scale. However, to the extent that the two sets of chromosomes are not identical, polyploidy may be seen as compositional, and allopolyploidy, the acquisition of an extra set of chromosomes through the breeding of distinct species, is clearly in the space of compositional mechanisms.

Within a lineage versus between parallel lineages Mechanisms like gene duplication have some further similarities with ontogenic mechanisms of large changes. That is, they both utilize biases coming from prior adaptation within a single lineage. It can also be seen that this bias is in the most part related to the repetition or duplication of feature complexes. This introduces a notion of repeated modules and the implication that the adaptive advantage of these mechanisms, if any, may depend on those modules being similar or at least being derived from similar beginnings. Put another way, this implies that these mechanisms will be useful when the adaptive domain is such that *self-similarity* in subsets of features is a useful heuristic.

In contrast the mechanisms that exchange subsets of genetic material *between parallel lineages* (described previously), do not necessarily involve the repetition or duplication of feature complexes, and do not invoke any implication that the newly introduced features are similar to existing features. Rather, from the point of view of each of the entities involved, the features introduced from a different lineage are not a rearrangement or duplication of something it already has, but something new.

In this book, I am focusing on mechanisms manipulating subsets of genetic material preadapted in parallel lineages. Accordingly, I will not pursue further mechanisms of ontogenic change or genetic duplication—mechanisms utilizing bias from repeated or duplicated structure. This choice is motivated by wanting to understand the possibility of large, adaptive genetic changes via sexual recombination and the major evolutionary transitions (neither of which involves duplicating sections of chromosome), and problem decomposition without the assumption of repeated subproblems.

Note that many natural complex systems do involve self-similar or repeated structure (Mandelbrot 1982), so this may be a very good heuristic for adaptive bias (e.g., Hornby 2003).

Directed Genetic Changes

I have asserted a few times that compositional mechanisms are capable of producing nonrandom changes that are directed by prior selection. It should be clear that the mechanisms I discussed above are capable of producing large modifications (in genotype). The important issue that we are moving toward, however, is whether such changes are likely to be adaptive. It is of course highly unlikely that they are adaptive—drawing together genetic material from different organisms, producing large changes in genotype, is highly unlikely to produce an adaptive change. But evolution is used to working with small probabilities. Random changes from mutation are also highly unlikely to be adaptive, especially large genetic changes. What we really want to know is: under what conditions are compositional genetic changes more likely to be adaptive than random genetic changes? Neither kind of change is *likely*, in an absolute sense, to produce fitness improvements, but that does not mean that one is not extraordinarily more likely to produce a fitness improvement than the other.

In order to talk about the possibility of nonrandom changes, we need to define what we mean by *random* changes. But before defining a random *change*, it is useful to choose a definition of a random *distribution* of strings (or configurations of variables). A common default definition is: a distribution of strings where all alleles at all loci are equally represented, and in fact all combinations of alleles at different loci are equally represented. This is a uniform distribution of strings in the space of possible strings based on the metric of Hamming distance.

A random *change* necessarily requires the notion of a point of origination. For our purposes, this is a parent string. Then a natural definition for a distribution of random changes is: a uniform distribution of strings in the Hamming space around the parent. We may then picture a random change as the addition of a vector (to the parent vector) drawn with uniform probability from a distribution of vectors that have no net directional component—more specifically, the set of possible offspring that may occur a given distance from the parent occur with equal probability (and are uniformly distributed in direction).

This notion of random changes matches exactly with our normal notion of mutational change[10]—specifically, a mechanism that introduces random genetic material to a string with a uniform distribution over the loci, and uniform distribution over the alleles of each locus. One-point, k-point, and per-locus methods of mutation are all valid examples—though they will have different distributions over the probable distances that an offspring may be from the parent.

Clearly, the changes produced by recombination (or composition) are not like this. Specifically, the genetic material of possible offspring is partly biased by the material of the first parent and partly biased by the material of the second parent. From the point of view of each parent, the new genetic material that is introduced into the chromosome of the offspring is not (necessarily) random. Specifically, in mutational change, genetic material is either inherited from one parent or is introduced stochastically; and in recombination, genetic material is inherited from two parents. Thus, in any case where the population from which the second parent is drawn is nonrandom, the changes between each parent and the offspring are also nonrandom. This is simply a consequence of defining a "change" as a movement from a single point of origination. Note that we could, if we wished, define a change with respect to two strings—for example, a random change might then be one drawn uniformly from the possible results of recombination between two parents—in which case, mutational change would be "nonrandom." The point is that whichever operation we use to define random change, mutational change and recombinative change are different and they cannot both be random in the same terms.

This is a trivial observation, but it is worth clarifying: nonrandom variation is not "unevolutionary" in any way. Immediately we must clarify that recombination produces a nonrandom distribution of variants only when the population from which the parents are drawn is nonrandom. Thus, in the absence of selection, neither repeated mutation nor repeated recombination produce consistently directed change. However, when selection *is* applied, this does not affect the distribution of changes produced by mutation—but it does affect the distribution of variants produced by recombination. Under recombination, it is not only the selection that acts on the (unbiased) variants produced at the current generation that directs evolutionary change, but also the biases in the distribution of variants produced—and this bias comes from prior selection on the population.

By the reasoning above, mechanisms that exchange subsets of genetic material between individuals are a source of large, nonrandom genetic changes biased by prior selection. The next obvious question is: under what circumstances is this kind of bias, coming from recombinative variation, better than the undirected variation of mutation?

This is not a new question, nor is it one that is easy to answer. But the above reasoning provides some intuition that may be useful. Specifically, we have been thinking about both mutational and recombinative variation in terms of a distribution of variants produced using inheritance from at least one parent. The difference between these mechanisms is that under recombinative change some of the new genetic material that arrives in the offspring (i.e., that which was not inherited from the first parent) comes from a second parent, whereas under mutation all the new genetic material in the offspring is random. Note that if both parents of a recombinative offspring have been subject to exactly the same selection, then the new genetic material introduced from the second parent is not likely to be significantly different in its adaptive affordances from that which is inherited from the first parent. In contrast, if the two parents have been subject to different selective pressures, the following notion arises:

> To the extent that preadapted genetic material, when relocated to a different genetic context (e.g., a different individual), is more likely to be adaptive than random genetic material placed in that context, mechanisms that exchange sections of genetic material from existing individuals will produce a distribution of offspring that are fitter on average than the distribution produced by random mutational changes.

If, on the other hand, genetic material adapted in one context is, when placed in some other context, no fitter on average than random genetic material, then mechanisms that exchange sections of genetic material from existing individuals will not be better than random mutational changes. The advantage of compositional mechanisms may thus be said to depend in part on the extent to which genetic material is context sensitive (or more to the point, context *in*sensitive).

It does not seem unreasonable in some cases to suppose that genetic material that is adaptive in one context—a protein-encoding gene, for example—will have a better chance of being adaptive in some other context than random genetic material. If the gene still translates into the same protein, then for sure the protein may be useful in some contexts and not in others, but in contrast, hardly any completely random sequences of genetic material translate to a functional protein at all. But ultimately, the context insensitivity of genetic material is an empirical matter.

In the next chapter, I will discuss and define adaptive landscapes with limited context sensitivity—which I call "modular interdependency." This will help us in understanding when such compositional genetic mechanisms do and do not provide variation that is fitter on average than mutational change.

Intra- and Interspecies Relationships/Genomic Dependencies

When approaching the task of modeling a system as complex as natural evolution it is necessary to make many simplifications. A common simplification is to examine the adaptation of a single species as though it were isolate—as though the adaptation of other species were a kind of backdrop merely defining the niche for the species of interest. Although changes in the biotic environment may affect the niche of the species in question, and may in some cases produce quite tightly coupled coadaptive dynamics, there is a deeply rooted assumption that interspecific relationships are not an integral part of evolutionary mechanisms—at least in the following sense. Changes in the genetic makeup of other populations may affect what is selected for in the given population, but they do not affect the genetic makeup of the given population directly. In other words, it seems reasonable to study the evolution of a population as though it were independent from other populations because the mechanisms of genetic variation—mutation and sexual recombination—act only within a population, not across populations.

What then are we to make of events that involve the integration of genetic material across populations? The existence of horizontal gene transfer, for example, means that modeling the evolution of a single species in isolation is not easily justified. But further, since several of the major evolutionary transitions involve the quite literal union of previously free-living entities into a new whole, clearly, evolutionary models addressing the adaptation of a single population are not capturing the whole process.

The phenomena I focus on in this book cannot be properly understood with a single-species single-niche model. By looking explicitly at multispecies multiniche models, many assumptions need to be revised. For example, competitive exclusion is not the only possible dynamic, and convergence of the population/ecosystem to a single type is not the only stable state.

When intraspecies and interspecies relationships become entangled, the need to consider intragenomic and intergenomic fitness interactions becomes apparent. We need to consider fitness interactions between one locus and another, and also between one organism and another. In short, we must develop a model that encompasses both intragenomic interactions and intergenomic interactions. But further, in models of symbiotic encapsulation it becomes clear that these categories will change.

That is, when two entities reside in parallel lineages, any fitness dependencies between them are intergenomic. But if those two entities should become encapsulated into a new organism then those same interactions are, for all intents and purposes, now intragenomic. Accordingly, it will be important that the model of genetic dependencies we develop be able to encompass both intra- and intergenomic dependencies in a unified fashion.

Fitness Landscapes and Compositional Mechanisms

As mentioned earlier, in principle, a fitness landscape could be defined using whatever neighborhood metric is given by the genetic variation operators (Jones 1995). One might argue, then, that in the new neighborhood metric given by compositional variation operators like sexual crossover, the evolutionary process may still be described as one that moves the population mean up the local fitness gradient—selecting among neighboring variants based on fitness—but where "neighbors" are defined using a different distance metric from that defined by mutation (Altenberg 2005). This is reasonable and useful in some circumstances. However, there are some problems with this interpretation. Specifically, the way in which a genotype can be changed under crossover is dependent on the composition of other members in the population. Since the makeup of the population is altered over evolutionary time, the neighborhood metric is not constant. Accordingly, the idea of moving around in a fitness landscape is confusing, and most of the intuition of the landscape metaphor is lost, because the proximity of points in the landscape is constantly changed due to the movement of the population.

An alternative is to discuss the movement of the population in the space of possible populations (e.g., Nix and Vose 1992; Wright and Rowe 2001). For a given operator, even a population-sensitive operator, the neighborhood metric is then constant. That is, the new population configurations that can be reached from a given population configuration is fixed. However, this is quite a radical departure from the intuitive notion of a fitness landscape. First, each point in the landscape now represents a population, not a genotype. Second, what should the height at each point now be? In other words, what is the fitness of a population? If the population is diverse (and to the extent that it is not diverse, the landscape of a population with sexual crossover degenerates to the mutational neighborhood) then taking an average of the fitnesses for the members of the population loses a lot of information. And besides, it is not clear that this appropriately describes the gradient that a population would follow.

Another possibility is to consider the neighborhood between pairs of individuals (Jones 1995; Gitchoff and Wagner 1996). Again, it is not clear what the fitness of a pair is or whether the movement of a population can be understood from the neighborhood of pairs to one another under crossover. However, in restricted circumstances, this approach can be very useful (see section 8.1). In the meantime, I suggest that the notion of a fitness landscape does not easily accommodate variation operators that are population sensitive such as sexual crossover.[11] Nevertheless, I suggest that the spatial intuition behind fitness landscapes is too powerful to discard completely and that the mutational neighborhood metric provides a natural default metric for the fitness landscape—at least for understanding the difficulty of the landscape for gradual mechanisms.

Finally, note that symbiotic encapsulation, by introducing the notion of symbiotic relationships, makes explicit the fact that the fitness of an organism is significantly dependent on the biotic (as well as abiotic) environment, and perhaps even undefined in isolation (Lewontin 1982, 1983). Thus the surface, as well as the neighborhood metric, of fitness landscapes must be interpreted with care (see p. 145).

3.5 Summary

I have discussed a spectrum of biological mechanisms including sexual recombination, hybridization, lateral gene transfer, allopolyploidy, and symbiotic encapsulation (endosymbiosis, symbiogenesis, and perhaps some other events in the major transitions in evolution), that I call compositional mechanisms. In the computational models in subsequent chapters I am going to focus on the beginning and end of this spectrum: sexual recombination and symbiotic encapsulation.

I suggest that these mechanisms are not just a different kind of gradual change but that they require us to revise important underlying assumptions about how evolution works and what kinds of system are evolvable and which are unevolvable.

In the EA literature, the gradualist framework of evolutionary change is common. But notions of compositional change based on sexual recombination or crossover are also well-known though controversial. The underlying intuition of the building-block hypothesis that is important here is the algorithmic concept of divide-and-conquer problem decomposition. But it has proved difficult to show a GA operating as the BBH suggests. However, if some form of GA could behave in this manner, in some class of problem, then the divide-and-conquer algorithmic advantage this provides would be significant. This has led to many varieties of GA utilizing modularity in more or less explicit manners including the messy GA, cooperative coevolution, and a collection of related work that is explicitly intended to model aspects of symbiosis and symbiogenesis.

In reviewing this work I paid particular attention to the use of a composition operator that joins entities together into a new whole through multiple hierarchical

Table 3.1
Analogous issues of composition in evolutionary biology and evolutionary computation.

Evolutionary biology concept	Evolutionary computation concept
Terminological analogues	
Compositional evolution	Divide-and-conquer problem decomposition
Free recombination/no physical genetic linkage, e.g., genes on different chromosomes	Uniform crossover
Strong physical genetic linkage: gene on same chromsome	One- or two-point crossover
Common compositional mechanism: sexual recombination	Common compositional mechanism: crossover
Compositional mechanisms based on encapsulation, e.g., endosymbiosis	Compositional mechanisms based on encapsulation, e.g., automatic module acquisition and reuse
Symbiosis as a source of evolutionary innovation	Developing methods in coevolution and automatic module acquisition
Natural hybridization is often nonviable	Competing conventions prevents successful crossover
Common simplifications/assumptions	
Default population genetics model is single species in single niche	Default EA is one population and single static fitness function
Inter- and intragenomic dependencies usually modeled separately: epistasis vs. species interaction	Inter- and intragenomic dependencies usually modeled separately: epistasis vs. coevolution. (*NKC* model is an exception)
Coevolution-related issues	
If organisms reside in the same fixed niche (without frequency-dependent fitness effects, e.g., resource dependence) then repeated selection inevitably results in competitive exclusion	If all individuals are evaluated against the same objective fitness function (without fitness sharing) then repeated selection inevitably results in population convergence
When individuals live in a group containing fit individuals, parasitic "freeloaders" may be promoted	When schemata are evaluated in an individual containing other fit schemata, then less useful, even detrimental, schemata may be promoted. (credit assignment problem, hitchhiker problem)
Different organisms are fit in different ways—not fit in an absolute sense, but they have a "goodness of fit" to a particular balance of environmental features.	In coevolution, different individuals are fit in different ways—not fit in an absolute sense, but they have a "goodness of fit" to a particular distribution of coevolving individuals.
In an ecosystem, different organisms may coexist because they have a different balance of adaptive traits from other organisms, and therefore reside in different niches (often mutually defined by other entities in the environment). However, *A* may competitively exclude *B* if there is no niche in which *B* is fitter than *A*.	In Pareto coevolution, different individuals coexist because they are not dominated by other individuals: They have a different balance of abilities with respect to different coevolving individuals. However, *A* may replace *B* in the case that there is no opponent against which *B* is better than *A* (or no group context in which *B* is better than *A*).

Table 3.1
(continued)

Evolutionary biology concept	Evolutionary computation concept
Some of the most controversial issues in each discipline	
Does sexual recombination offer adaptive advantage?	What is crossover good for?
Shifting balance theory: a means to enable the evolution of interaction systems and their assembly, rather than depend on the accumulation of individually useful mutations.	Building-block hypothesis: a means to enable the evolution of useful 'building blocks' and their recombination, rather than depend on the accumulation of individually useful mutations.
SBT assumes genetic linkage is weak, and in normal circumstances, alleles are selected for only their additive effects, but Wright notes that if linkage were strong then coadapted alleles could behave as if they were a single allele of a composite gene.	Building-block hypothesis assumes that genetic linkage is tight and therefore schemata can be transferred from one individual to another as a unit, but Holland notes that if linkage is poor, then schemata will be disrupted and promotion of schemata will fail.

levels, and whether the roles of symbiotic specialists (the subproblems to which they adapt) are predefined or are defined adaptively. These are features that I want to incorporate in a complete model to properly highlight the algorithmic potential of compositional evolution.

There are many difficulties that arise in the use of compositional mechanisms. Well-known problems for GAs using recombination include poor genetic linkage and premature convergence of the population. More generally, problematic issues include the representation, combination, evaluation, and coevolution of proposed modules. Some existing methods, in particular the messy GA and cooperative coevolution, provide important approaches and features that are useful in developing the models that follow—but new approaches (including the concept of Pareto coevolution) are also required.

In the next chapter I want to move toward an understanding of what kind of complex adaptations are evolvable in compositional evolution that are unevolvable under gradual mechanisms.

Note that there are significant parallels between the issues and phenomena discussed in evolutionary biology and evolutionary computation. Some concepts are the same in both disciplines, for example, sexual recombination. Other concepts have close analogues in each discipline. Table 3.1 summarizes some of the parallels between the concepts and issues in evolutionary biology and evolutionary computation that have been discussed.

4 Modularity

With this chapter we begin the second part of the book. Having introduced the ideas and background for the concepts of gradual and compositional evolution, I will now provide the computational simulation models that illustrate my argument and claims.

The purpose of this chapter is to define a class of complex system that is not easily evolvable under gradual mechanisms, but is easily evolvable under compositional mechanisms. Defining such a class will assist us in clarifying the different adaptive capacities of these alternate mechanisms. The system I define is built from a high degree of epistatic interaction between variables that produces significant ruggedness and numerous local optima in the resultant fitness landscape—this prevents the effective operation of gradual evolution. However, the epistatic interactions are highly structured, creating modules and submodules of interdependent variables. This modular structure makes the system, in principle, amenable to problem decomposition and the effective operation of compositional mechanisms, as I will show in subsequent chapters.

The discussion is divided as follows. First I distinguish between types of epistatic interactions that are easy and difficult for gradual mechanisms—this analysis starts with interactions between just two variables. The following subsection addresses how larger networks of epistatic interactions might be arranged so that they are strongly epistatic but modular. This follows the intuition that compositional mechanisms may be able to manipulate systems of variables with modular dependency more effectively than gradual mechanisms and that such a structure should therefore exemplify the adaptive potential of compositional mechanisms.

This structure is then expanded to define a system with a large number of variables that decompose into modules and submodules hierarchically. A specific example is defined, *hierarchical-if-and-only-if*, HIFF, which I will use for the simulation experiments in following chapters. In the discussion I indicate a more general construction for hierarchically modular systems, and review some contrasts and similarities of the HIFF problem with existing test problems/landscapes in the literature that have been proposed for discriminating the ability of the GA with and without crossover.

Note that "modularity" is a word attached to several distinct concepts (Callebaut 2005; Wagner, Mezey, and Callebretta 2005). Modularity may refer to the reusability of a subsystem in a repeated fashion (such as the segments of a segmented body), but it may also refer to the functional independence of one subsystem or behavior from another (such as the cardiovascular system and the nervous system, or metabolizing nutrients and detecting a toxin) (Lipson 2004). In the models in this book I am interested only in the second kind—modules in the sense of functionally semi-independent subsystems—because this is the type of modularity that can be exploited by compositional mechanisms. Repeated modularity is, of course, widespread and highly significant in evolutionary adaptability and may be exploited by mechanisms such as developmental processes or gene duplication—but that would be a different book.

Note also that the models in this chapter are concerned with modularity in the adaptive problem rather than modularity in the organism. However, modularity within an organism may be closely related to modularity in the adaptive problem at a number of different levels. The fitness interdependencies of different genes present an optimization problem with modular structure for nucleotide changes, the structural decoupling of biochemical pathways within a cell may reflect the availability of unrelated nutrients in the environment, or the functional decoupling of cortical functions may reflect the inherently modular nature of the computational tasks they perform. More directly, mechanisms such as symbiotic encapsulation are, I will show, suitable for adapting to modular problem domains, and clearly directly result in the physical modularity of the organism in such structures as organelles. More subtly, the reorganization of the genetic map resulting from implicit selective pressure to increase robustness to genetic variation may produce modular genetic structure reflecting the modular structure of the epistatic interactions between genes.

There are some philosophical provisos that should be highlighted in the assumption of a "problem for an evolving entity" (Gould and Lewontin 1979). It should be noted that the premise of a problem that organisms must solve, or a predefined fitness landscape on which organisms move, can be misleading in some circumstances. For example, in many cases it would be incorrect to assume that the niche in which an organism ultimately resides existed in a predefined sense before the organism concerned existed (Lewontin 2000; Levins and Lewontin 1985). Similarly, in many cases, the niche to which an organism is fitted is fundamentally affected (perhaps effected) by the biotic context of other evolving organisms and it would therefore be incorrect to assume that the fitness landscape has a static form that exists independently of the organisms that reside in it (Lewontin 1982, 1983).

These provisos should be taken into account. If, as seems likely the case, the relevant constraints on an adaptive species are predominantly the result of a biotic environment, then the fitness landscape presented to an organism at any one time is predominantly plastic and unconstrained in longer time scales, and does not preexist in any meaningful sense. Accordingly, if every aspect of the environment is plastic and somewhat intangible in this sense, then it is difficult to know how to accommodate the separation of organism and environment or proceed with adaptive explanations at all (Levins and Lewontin 1985).

At the end of this chapter I offer some comments on the compatibility of the adaptive landscape model that I define with these points of view. In the meantime, I suggest that the adaptational stance is one of those that is useful for understanding biological systems and phenomena, and in this book I find the problem-solution metaphor is a pragmatically useful one for exploring the issues I want to address.

4.1 Interdependency

I start the development of a new model of *hierarchical modular interdependency* by considering the interaction of just two variables.

Pairwise Interactions and Fitness Saddles

Sewell Wright (1931) stated that "the central problem of evolution ... is that of a trial and error mechanism by which the locus of a population may be carried across a saddle from one peak to another and perhaps higher one" (p. 264). This conception of evolutionary difficulty and the now-familiar concept of evolution as a combinatoric-optimization process on a rugged adaptive surface or fitness landscape (Wright 1967) are central to issues of evolvability, and the ability of adaptation to escape or otherwise avoid local optima—configurations of features where no small change in features will produce a fitter variant—is of central importance.

Ruggedness in a fitness landscape is introduced by the frustration of adaptive features, or epistasis when referring to the interdependency of genes. That is, it occurs when the selective value of one feature is dependent on the configuration of other features, or when the fitness effect of a mutation is dependent on genetic background.

Note that population genetics models often use very simplified forms of epistasis. For example, an epistatic model may suppose that the deleterious effect of a mutation may be increased or decreased when in combination with other mutations but it is often assumed that the mutation is always deleterious (or that its reversion is always beneficial). This is a condition that may be termed "magnitude epistasis" (Weinreich, Watson, and Chao 2005)—that is, the magnitude of the fitness effect of a mutation changes in the context of other mutations, but it never changes from being deleterious to beneficial, or vice versa, in different genetic backgrounds. Often epistatic models are simplified further so that the fitness of a genotype can be determined as a function of the number of mutations it carries (Kondrashov and Kondrashov 2001). Such models are easier to handle analytically because the unique combination of mutations carried by a genotype does not matter—only the number of mutations affects fitness. However, such models preclude the possibility of local optima in the fitness surface and the difficult issue that Wright describes. In part this emphasis is due to the fact that it is common to focus only on epistasis between alleles that are simultaneously segregating in the current population (sometimes called "statistical epistasis"), because only this epistasis will affect how natural selection alters the frequencies of those alleles. In this view, the fact that an allele that is individually deleterious may produce a dramatic fitness *increase* when in combination with some other allele is considered immaterial if this other allele is not present in the population, because if it is not present in the population then natural selection cannot be affected by this fitness interaction. Note that the measured statistical epistasis in natural populations is generally believed to be weak compared to the individual additive fitness effects of alleles.

In contrast in evolutionary computation, epistasis is usually not considered to be a property dependent on the current population but rather a property intrinsic to the space of possible genotypes. In this view, fitness interactions between alleles are responsible for creating features of the fitness landscape such as isolated fitness optima. The fact that a population may be stuck at one optimum, unable to sample the combination of alleles required to discover another optimum, is not a reason to ignore the other optimum but a problem worth studying. In this view, the fact that the measured statistical epistasis in a population may be small does not alter the fact that there are strong epsistatic effects in the landscape as a whole. How a population might come to sample other parts of the fitness landscape and how natural selection may be able to select on combinations of alleles are separate issues from the inherent epistatic structure of the genotypic space. Accordingly, in evolutionary computation, it is common to see epistatic models that are much more complex and introduce multiple local optima. This is not in contradiction with biological observations because the epistasis between simultaneously segregating alleles in a population at an instant in time is only a tiny window on the epistatic interactions inherent in the space of all possible genotypes. In order to address the evolvability of complex systems and the evolutionary trajectories of a population over extended evolutionary time, it is necessary that we take the broader view.

The particular feature of fitness landscapes that we need to model to understand evolutionary difficulty is the creation of fitness saddles. These can only be created when a mutation that is beneficial in one context is deleterious in another—a condition that may be termed "sign epistasis" (Weinreich, Watson, and Chao 2005). The simplest illustration is provided by a model of two features, *F1* and *F2*, each with two possible discrete states, *A*/*a* and *B*/*b* respectively, creating four possible configurations: *AB*, *Ab*, *aB*, and *ab*. Figure 4.1 shows three kinds of interaction between these two features. In each case we are interested in the effect on fitness of different combinations of feature values.

In case 1 the fitness effects of each variable are independent of the other. The corresponding fitness landscape is planar. In case 2 the preference of *b* over *B* is reversed

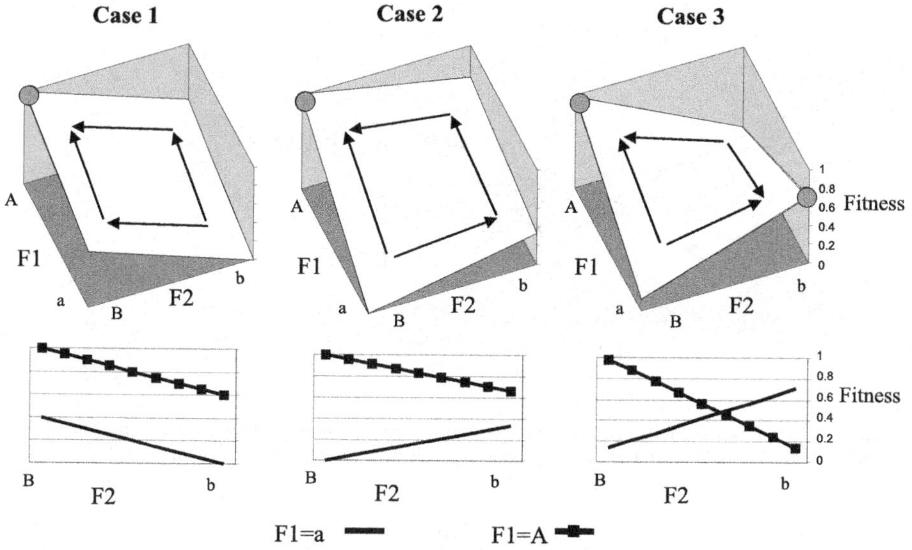

Figure 4.1
Different kinds of fitness interactions. Arrows overlayed on each fitness landscape show the paths of increasing fitness that can be followed by changing one feature at a time. The large dots indicate local optima. Case 1: No epistasis. Case 2: "Easy" Epistasis. Case 3: Difficult epistasis or "interdependency."

depending on the value of *F1*, but *A* is always preferred over *a*. In this case there is still only one optimum in this fitness landscape and therefore no fitness saddle. In case 3, the preference relation between *b* and *B* is reversed according to *F1*, and the preference relation between *a* and *A* is also reversed according to *F2*. This creates a fitness saddle in the corresponding fitness landscape and two local optima. That is, there is no path of increasing fitness from *ab* to *AB* for a mechanism that makes small changes to feature values. Escaping the local optimum at *ab* requires a jump switching both features at once (see figure 4.2).

Local optima occur only when the preferred value of *F1* switches according to the value of *F2*, and the preferred value of *F2* switches according to the value of *F1*—a condition that may be termed "reciprocal sign epistasis" (ibid.). Other kinds of epistasis are solvable by incremental accumulation of single-feature mutations. I define the *interdependency* of features to mean this problematic kind of epistasis, and adopt this as the basis of the models that follow. Using this kind of epistasis, rather than arbitrary or simplified epistasis (which may be either the easy kind or the difficult kind, in general) allows proper control of the consequences of these dependencies in terms of local optima, and the width of fitness saddles.

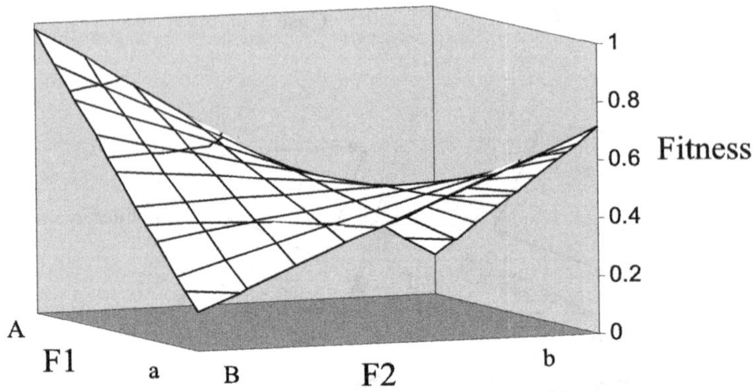

Figure 4.2
A fitness saddle created by the interdependency of two variables. A different view of case 3 in figure 4.1—this view shows the two local optima at AB and ab and the fitness saddle between them.

Biological cases show interdependency in natural systems also (e.g., Lewontin 2000, p. 84).

Defining "Interdependency"
Let us define the "*preference for a over A in the context of x*," for a two-feature system as above, to be $pref(a, A, x) \equiv f(a, x) - f(A, x)$, where $f(p, q)$ is the fitness of the two-variable system where *F1* takes value *p*, and *F2* takes value *q*.

If the preference for values of *F1* is the same for all contextual values provided by *F2* then there is no epistasis between these features and the fitness landscape is planar. That is:

$$no\text{-}epistasis(F1, F2)$$
$$\equiv (pref(a, A, b) = pref(a, A, B) \wedge pref(b, B, a) = pref(b, B, A)).$$

In other words, for two features *F1* and *F2* to have no epistasis means that the fitness difference between two values of *F1* is the same regardless of the value of *F2*, and vice versa. I now define "*F1 is dependent on F2*" as follows:

$$depends(F1, F2) \Leftrightarrow sign(pref(a, A, b)) \neq sign(pref(a, A, B)).$$

Note that *depends*$(F1, F2)$ does not imply *depends*$(F2, F1)$, and, if *F1* is dependent on *F2*, but *F2* is not dependent on *F1*, then there are no local optima in the system. However, "difficult epistasis" between *F1* and *F2* is defined as follows:

$$interdependent(F1, F2) \Leftrightarrow (depends(F1, F2) \wedge depends(F2, F1)).$$

Table 4.1
Fitness values based on if-and-only-if (IFF).

p	q	$f(p,q) = (p\ IFF\ q)$
0	0	1
0	1	0
1	0	0
1	1	1

If we let the two features in the system be represented by Boolean variables then the Boolean function *equality*, or *if-and-only-if*, IFF, (and its negation, *exclusive-or*, XOR), define interdependency between these variables. Other Boolean functions of two variables are not suitable since they either have only one solution, or solutions dependent on only one variable. I will be using the following function as the basis of discrete interdependency models in following subsections: $f(p,q) = (p \text{ IFF } q)$, where $f(\langle\text{true}\rangle) = 1$ and $f(\langle\text{false}\rangle) = 0$ as shown in table 4.1.

An example interdependent system of two *continuous* valued variables in the range $[0,1]$ is defined by $f(p,q) = pq + (1-p)(1-q)$. This is the function illustrated in figure 4.2.

Interdependency in Larger Systems

Having defined the basis for interdependency between a pair of features, the next step is to define a system of interdependencies over more than two variables. A problem becomes more and more difficult for a gradual mechanism like a hill climber to solve as the width of fitness saddles increases. The "width of a fitness saddle," for our purposes, is the separation of a local optimum to the nearest point of equal or higher fitness. In multidimensional discrete spaces, e.g., systems of many binary variables, this width is measured in the number of variables whose state must change (Hamming distance). So, if many variables need to change state all at once in order to get from a given configuration to a higher fitness configuration then this is difficult for gradual mechanisms.

Such a system can be created over a large number of variables by overlapping pairwise interactions of the kind above. For example, let the fitness of three variables, p, q, and r, be the sum of fitness contributions from two pairwise interactions as follows, $f(p,q,r) = f1(p,q) + f2(q,r)$, where each of $f1$ and $f2$ have the difficult dependency structure defined above. In this structure, p has a direct dependency with q and, through q, also has an indirect dependency with r. Accordingly, the pairwise fitness contributions can be arranged such that in some cases a fitness increase in the overall system requires changing all three variables at once.

For example: let p, q, and r be binary variables, and $f1$ be defined thus:

$f1(0,0) = 0.7, \quad f1(0,1) = 0.1, \quad f1(1,0) = 0.4, \quad f1(1,1) = 0.9$

and $f2$ be defined thus:

$f2(0,0) = 0.8, \quad f2(0,1) = 0.3, \quad f2(1,0) = 0.2, \quad f2(1,1) = 0.5.$

Then it so happens that the configuration $p = 1$, $q = 1$, $r = 1$ has the fitness $0.9 + 0.5 = 1.4$, and the only configuration with a fitness higher than this is $p = 0$, $q = 0$, $r = 0$ (with a fitness of $0.7 + 0.8 = 1.5$). The dependencies between the three variables can thus create situations where a fitness improvement requires changing all three variables simultaneously.

Let us extend this a little further. Equation 4.1 describes a system of N variables where every variable has pairwise dependencies with every other variable. In this system, for convenience, I define the interactions between all pairs to have the same pairwise fitness function:

Equation 4.1: The weighted sum of pairwise interactions

$$g(S_1, S_2, \ldots, S_N) = \sum_{i=1}^{N} \sum_{j=1}^{N} W_{ij} f(S_i, S_j)$$

where $S_1, S_2, \ldots S_N$ are the variables of the system, and $f(p,q)$ is the pairwise interaction of variables with states p and q. W_{ij} is the weighting of the interaction between variables i and j.

For illustration, let us define $f(p,q) = (p \text{ IFF } q)$, for binary variables p and q using our canonical base function IFF as shown in table 4.1 previously. For now, we will assume that the interaction of all variables has equal weighting, that is, $W_{ij} = 1$ for all i and j, but it will be useful to vary this later.

With a little consideration, it is easy to see that when the number of variables with state $= 0$ is greater than the number of variables with state $= 1$, the change of any variable to state $= 0$ will increase fitness, and vice versa. That is, the optimal state for any variable is to be in agreement with the majority, and any change in state that increases the size of the majority will increase the fitness of the system as a whole. Therefore the system has only two optima—that is, all 0s and all 1s. The width of the fitness saddle between these two points is N, that is, to jump from one to the other requires changing all variables at once. A hill climber can find either of these two configurations easily, and given uniformly random starting configurations, is equally likely to arrive at either optimum, but having been led to one optimum it is then very difficult for a hill climber to find the alternate optimum should that be required. If we make the fitness of 1s, say, slightly higher than that of 0s in the $f(p,q)$ function, then the all-0s optimum is a local optimum and escaping from this point to the global optimum at all 1s requires changing all variables simultaneously.

So, a construction of this kind, using many pairwise interactions, is sufficient to create broad fitness saddles and, in principle, local optima that are arbitrarily difficult (depending on the number of variables in the system) for a gradual mechanism to escape from. This example has a very uniform construction—more generally, if the interdependencies between variables are arbitrarily structured (in the style of NK landscapes for example; see Kauffman 1993), then they can create rugged landscapes with multiple local optima. Local optima will trap gradual evolution at a suboptimal local fitness peak, requiring simultaneous changes in many variables to provide a fitness improvement. Hence it is easy to see how interdependency between many variables may prevent continued adaptation by gradual mechanisms. But we have not yet discussed what properties of a system might make it easy for compositional mechanisms yet still be difficult for gradual mechanisms. In this respect it will be the structure of the interdependencies that will provide the properties required.

4.2 Modular Interdependency

The basic idea of compositional mechanisms that I want to elucidate is that they might be able to optimize and manipulate semi-independent subsystems in parallel and subsequently combine them together. This will require a form of modularity. But although modularity is an intuitive enough idea, it requires some care to define it appropriately.

The naive approach to defining a modular structure is to make subsets of variables independent of one another (e.g., Royal Road and concatenated trap functions, see section 3.2). In this case, the fitness of a system of variables can be described as the sum of fitness contributions coming from two or more nonoverlapping (disjoint) subsets of the variables in the system. For example,

$$f(s_1, s_2, \ldots, s_N) = f_1(s_1, s_2, \ldots, s_{N/2}) + f_2(s_{N/2+1}, s_{N/2+2}, \ldots, s_N).$$

This is the usual definition of *separability* (Whitley et al. 1995b) (and a function that is separable in this sense is also separable in the more particular sense I define below). However, using separable modules that can be solved independently of one another in this manner is an overly simplistic notion of modularity. For example, in biological systems, we are accustomed to thinking of the cell as a meaningful module of a multicellular organism in many respects, but we do not suppose that the molecular interactions, internal functioning, nor adaptedness of the cell is independent of other cells. In engineered systems such as a factory plant or a software program, we may naturally identify subprocesses or subprocedures that are meaningful modules, but they are, of course, not independent of the rest of the factory or program. So this separable kind of module does not fit with our natural intuitions about modular systems.

Moreover, this form of simplistic modularity is also a mistake when trying to define scalable problems that distinguish the ability of gradual and compositional mechanisms (as in distinguishing the ability of mutation and sexual recombination in prior genetic algorithm research). In a separable problem, the configuration of a module that is fittest in one context (individual) is fittest in all contexts. If an evolutionary process finds a fit configuration for a module this configuration is never "wrong"; it never needs to be undone or redone or changed when it is put together with other modules because it has no dependencies with other modules. The interesting ability of a compositional mechanism is its ability to manipulate modules as wholes—to swap out one configuration of a module and swap in another—enabling it to find good combinations of modules. In a separable modular system, any combination of good modules is fine because there are no intermodule dependencies that need to be resolved. Without a need to search combinations of modules, good modules can be accumulated serially (if they are not too large) and a compositional mechanism is redundant. The inadequacy of separable modules for our purposes will become clearer when I define an alternative for comparison. For now, suffice to say that only when there is some form of intermodule dependency is there a need to search combinations of modules.

The obvious progression from modules that are entirely separable is modules that have a little overlap—for example, consider two groups of variables as before with many intragroup dependencies and relatively few intergroup dependencies. This is provided by a model such as the NKC model (Kauffman and Johnsen 1989). Overlap introduces simple intermodule dependencies that need to be resolved to maximize fitness. But there seems to be an inherent tension here. If intermodule dependencies are weak or few then resolving them will be relatively unimportant, providing only a small improvement in fitness. If intermodule dependencies are too strong then the modules cease to be meaningful modules at all; they have no utility that is independent of other modules. This seems to create a problem for the supposed benefit of compositional mechanisms. How could a subset of variables be identified and usefully manipulated as a whole by a compositional mechanism if they are strongly interdependent on variables in other modules? And if they are not strongly interdependent on variables in other modules then it will not be so important to resolve these dependencies and a compositional mechanism will provide only a slight advantage over a gradual one. It seems at first that there is a direct trade-off here: to the extent that the fitness contributions of a module are independently identifiable, compositional mechanisms will be of little advantage, and to the extent that the fitness contributions of a module are not independently identifiable, compositional mechanisms will not work at all.

This apparent trade-off, I suggest, has prevented the prior formulation of clear problem structures that are amenable to compositional mechanisms and hard for gradual mechanisms, and the lack of clarity here is at the root of the confusion around the utility of operators like sexual crossover in the genetic algorithm. However, this apparent trade-off results from a concept of modularity that is again too simplistic. It is not the case that there is an unavoidable trade-off between strong intermodule dependencies that confer significant fitness changes but make modules difficult to identify, and weak intermodule dependencies that make modules easy to identify but confer insignificant fitness changes. It is possible for a modular system to have strong intermodule dependencies that confer significant fitness changes when resolved but nonetheless these modules are easily identifiable.

To work toward an understanding of how this can be the case, I introduce a way of counting configurations that enables us to quantify the interdependency of two modules. I then use this to examine a small example system that exhibits significant intermodule dependencies and yet has easily identifiable modules.

Consider a system of two modules, A and B. Let $C_A = \{a_1, a_2, \ldots, a_p\}$ be the set of possible configurations that module A may take and similarly, $C_B = \{b_1, b_2, \ldots, b_q\}$ be the set of possible configurations that module B may take, where p and q are the sizes of these configuration spaces, that is, $p = |C_A|$ and $q = |C_B|$. We want to know the configurations that have maximum fitness for each module. If there are no dependencies between modules then there is only one such configuration for each module regardless of the configuration of the other module. But if there are dependencies between modules then the maximum fitness configuration of A depends on the configuration of B and vice versa. Accordingly, we need to ask whether a given configuration of A is maximal in any context. Let us define a new set, M_A, to be the set of configurations of A that have some configuration of B for which they are maximal, and M_B similarly with respect to A. That is,

Equation 4.2: Set of maximal configurations

$$M_A = \{m_1, \ldots, m_r\}: (\forall m(m \in M_A): m \in C_A) \wedge (\forall x(x \in C_B)\ \exists m(m \in M_A)$$
$$\forall y((y \in C_A) \neq m): f(m,x) \geq f(y,x))$$

where { }: q is the smallest set for which q is true, and $f(s,t)$ is the fitness of the system when module A is in configuration s and module B is in configuration t.

This simply says that the members of M_A are configurations of A, and for all configurations of B there is some member of M_A, m, for which there is no other configuration of A that is fitter than m. I will call M_A the set of *maximal configurations*.

Now, if $|M_A| = |C_A|$, that is, every configuration of A is best for some configuration of B, then we have achieved nothing by proposing A as a module. But if $|M_A| < |C_A|$ then the possible configurations of A that might be maximal (depending on the context provided by B) is less than the total number of possible configurations for A, and we can reduce the number of possibilities we need to maintain in search even without knowing the state of B. Put another way, regardless of the configuration of B, the members of C_A that are not members of M_A cannot be optimal and may be discarded from further consideration. Thus, whenever $|M_A| < |C_A|$ there is some utility in considering A as a module separate from B even though there may be dependencies between A and B.

Naturally, the smaller the size of M_A the better (for optimization purposes), that is, the fewer configurations need to be maintained and considered. Indeed the special case where $|M_A| = 1$ is highly desirable in general because it means that the optimal configuration for A can be found independently of B and thus the problem can be decomposed into two separate subproblems. $|M_A| = 1$ is my definition of a *separable* submodule.

Note, however, that this definition is less strict than the simple notion that the fitness of the system can be described as the sum of fitness contributions from A and B. Specifically, it is possible that the fitness contribution of A changes with the changes in the context provided by B (thus the fitness of the system cannot be described by a linear sum of that from A and B), yet the maximal fitness configuration of A may nonetheless be the same under all configurations of B.[1] In other words, my definition of a separable module does not require that there be no epistatic interactions between it and the rest of the system, just that there be no interdependency (i.e., no dependencies like case 3 in figures 4.1 and 4.2). The rationale for this definition is that it is only when the maximally fit configuration of a module is sensitive to context that optimization is made difficult. Other types of nonlinear fitness contributions, where changes in one module do not require a change in configuration of another module, are relatively unimportant. Also, note that A may be separable from B and at the same time B may not be separable from A, that is, $|M_A| = 1$ does not imply that $|M_B| = 1$. But, like the contrast of case 2 in figure 4.1 it is only when both A and B cannot be solved independently that local optima and fitness saddles are created between modules.

Decomposable but Not Separable

So, the more general case, $1 < |M_A| < |C_A|$, is the case of interest. When $1 < |M_A| < |C_A|$ the number of configurations of A that might be optimal given all possible configurations of B is greater than 1 but less than the total number of configurations that A might take. When this is the case, we can *reduce* the number of configurations of A that need to be considered (though we cannot reduce this number to one), and when $1 < |M_A| < |C_A|$ and $1 < |M_B| < |C_B|$ we will say that A and B are *decomposable* from each other, but not *separable*—or alternatively, that the system has *interdependent modules*. This provides the intermodule equivalent of the relationship of interdependency between a pair of variables defined earlier.

Additionally, the Hamming distance between configurations in M_A from one another controls the width of fitness saddles in the landscape. The important difference between this definition of modular interdependency and the simpler idea of adding a little overlap in the sets of variables contributing to modules is that its not always clear what effect a little overlap of modules will have on the difficulty of search. It may be the case that modules with slightly overlapping sets of variables still have a unique maximally fit configuration. If interdependencies between modules created by slightly overlapping variables do create a maximal set of configurations bigger than 1, it is likely (though not necessarily the case) that these configurations are not far apart in Hamming space, making it easy to resolve intermodule dependencies by making a small change to a module.

In contrast, this definition of modular interdependency is independent of a construction method for creating the interdependencies. Two modules have interdependency if their maximal sets are both bigger than 1, and this definition imposes no restriction on how similar those configurations are to one another. In principle, a small maximal set should be exploitable by a compositional mechanism regardless of how different those configurations are. If we can define a modular system where members of a maximal set are very different from each other this will maximize how difficult it is for undirected mutations to change from one to another. But so long as the maximal set does not have too many members, a compositional mechanism should be able to exploit the modularity by swapping in and out different members of the maximal set discovered in different individuals.

Table 4.2
A modular interdependency matrix.

i\j	1	2	3	4
1	0	4	1	1
2	4	0	1	1
3	1	1	0	4
4	1	1	4	0

Table 4.3
Configurations for a four-variable system with their fitnesses.

Configuration	Fitness	Hamming
0000	24	4
0001	12	1
0010	12	1
0011	16	2
0100	12	1
0101	4	1
0110	4	1
0111	12	1
1000	12	1
1001	4	1
1010	4	1
1011	12	1
1100	16	2
1101	12	1
1110	12	1
1111	24	4

An Example of a Nonseparable but Decomposable System of Four Variables

To illustrate, consider a system of four variables organized into two pairs $(1,2)$ and $(3,4)$. I use equation 4.1 with $f(p,q) = (p \text{ IFF } q)$ as before, but this time W is a symmetric weight matrix indexed by i and j $(1 \le i \le 4,\ 1 \le j \le 4)$ as defined in table 4.2. For the purposes of illustration, table 4.3 enumerates the possible configurations of this system with their fitnesses (we will discuss the column headed "Hamming" shortly).

Now let us calculate the set M_A.

$$C_A = \{00, 01, 10, 11\}$$

$$C_B = \{00, 01, 10, 11\}$$

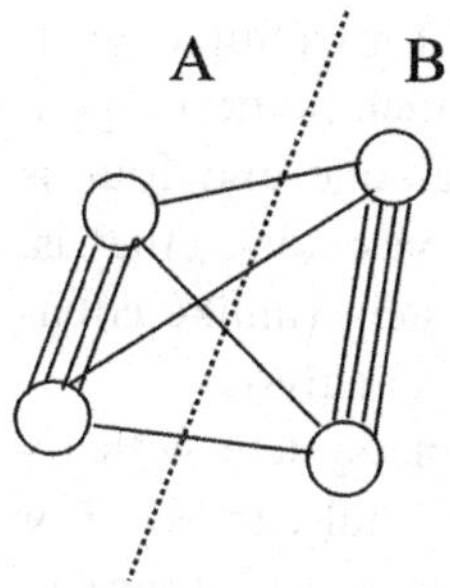

Figure 4.3
A dependency graph illustrating equation 4.1 with W as defined in table 4.2.

When $B = 00$, the configuration $A = 00$ is maximal.
When $B = 01$, the configuration $A = 00$ or $A = 11$ is (equally) maximal.
When $B = 10$, the configuration $A = 00$ or $A = 11$ is (equally) maximal.
When $B = 11$, the configuration $A = 11$ is maximal.
Thus, $M_A = \{00, 11\}$.

Note that therefore the configurations $A = 01$ and $A = 10$ are never maximal, regardless of the configuration of B, and may be discarded from further consideration. Thus, since $|M_A| < |C_A|$, A is decomposable from B. But note also that A and B are not separable because $|M_A| > 1$, that is, different configurations of B require different configurations of A to maximize fitness. In this example, the modules A and B are symmetric and therefore M_B also equals $\{00, 11\}$.

Thus equation 4.1 with W given by table 4.2 defines a system of four variables that, by the definition given above, is decomposable into two subsystems of two variables each, but these modules are interdependent and not separable. Inspection of the interdependency matrix W reveals why this is so. A couple of things are clear from this matrix: all variables have interactions with all variables, and; each pair of variables has stronger interactions per variable within its own pair than it does across pairs. This follows the same structure as that proposed by Simon (1969, pp. 197–199) for what he terms a "nearly decomposable system." Figure 4.3 depicts this system as a graph: nodes of the graph represent the four variables of the system, edges indicate an interdependency between two variables, and multiple lines indicate the strength of the interdependency, as per table 4.2. The dotted line indicates a decomposition of the system into two interdependent modules A and B.

Note that if this four-variable system is divided the other way, for example, variables one and four in module A, and two and three in module B, then no decomposability is evident at all. Each possible configuration of variables one and four is maximal for some configuration of variables two and three, and vice versa, that is, $|M_A| = |C_A|$, and $|M_B| = |C_B|$. The natural modularity of this system (unlike equation 4.1 with equal weights) is therefore quantifiably evident in this analysis.

The next issue then is to examine the properties of this example system with respect to the capacities of gradual mechanisms such as a mutation hill climber. For this purpose I included a column in table 4.3 showing the Hamming distance of each configuration to the nearest configuration with higher (or equal) fitness. Note that the fitness landscape has four optima for a single-bit mutation hill climber: that is, the points 0011, 1100, 0000, and 1111 have no points of higher fitness that may be reached by changing only one state variable. More precisely, 0011 and 1100 are local optima, and 0000 and 1111 are equally fit global optima. Further, the two global optima are maximally distant from one another in Hamming space, and the two local optima are maximally distant from these and each other.

Figure 4.4 shows a cross section through the fitness landscape of equation 4.1. This particular cross section through the fitness landscape is useful in indicating the relationship of local optima in the system. This section is a one-point mutation walk from one global optimum to the other, moving to (one of) the highest-fitness Hamming-distance-1 configurations available at each step, and without revisiting any point (see section 5.1). Specifically, this passes through a series of points with

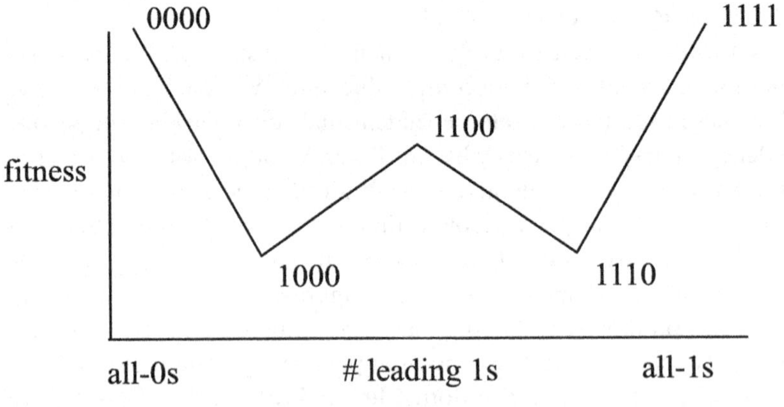

Figure 4.4
A particular cross section through the fitness landscape of equation 4.1 with W as per table 4.2.

an increasing number of leading 1s: 0000, 1000, 1100, 1110, and 1111. This cross section is useful in that it indicates the width of fitness saddles in the landscape—that is, the Hamming distance from a local optimum to the nearest point of higher (or equal) fitness. The global optima correspond to configurations where the two modules are in "agreement"—the local optimum in the middle is created by either configuration where the two modules are internally in agreement but incompatible with each other—that is, 0011 or 1100.

Note also that the members of M_A in this example, (00, 11), are distant from one another in Hamming space and therefore, despite the fact that this problem is decomposable (and, I will show, easy for compositional mechanisms), it is difficult for gradual mechanisms to optimize either module since small changes will not allow a module to switch between the solution that is compatible with one context to the solution that is compatible with another. After generalizing this model I will analyze its difficulty for gradual mechanisms in more detail in chapter 5.

4.3 Hierarchical Modular Interdependency

Aggregate Effects of Modules

In this section I aim to clarify what it is about the system above that gives it the properties it has, to better understand its structure, and define it over a larger set of variables. We will find that systems of this type have a more compact description when we use an explicit abstraction of hierarchical modularity.

Simon (1969) suggests two properties for a "nearly decomposable system" that provide a useful starting point (p. 100):

1. "the short-run behaviour of each of the component subsystems is approximately independent of the short-run behaviour of the other components";
2. "in the long run the behaviour of any one of the components depends in only an aggregate way on the behaviour of the other components."

This is a dynamic description of properties that can also be understood by a static analysis of the dependency matrix W above (table 4.2). The first property is implemented in the dependency matrix by virtue of the fact that intramodule weights are greater than intermodule weights. The second is more subtle but equally important, and relates directly to the notion of decomposability defined above. Specifically, this property relates to the condition that $|M_A| < |C_A|$.

When $|M_A| = |C_A|$, *every* configuration of A has sensitive dependencies with B. If this is the case then the module has no useful identity at the aggregate level.

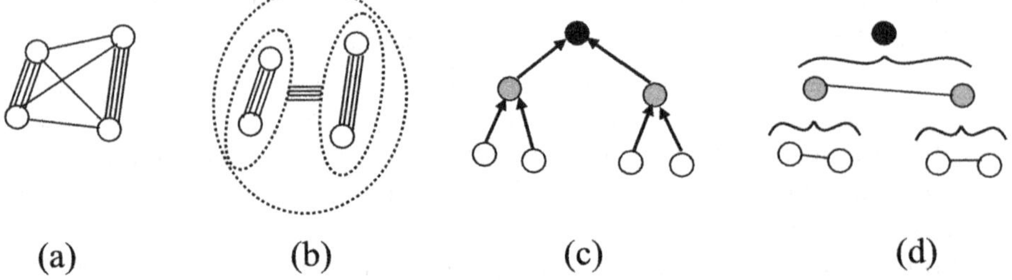

Figure 4.5
Abstracting the interaction between modules. (a) A four-variable modular system built from a network of pairwise dependencies. (b) This can be represented as a system composed of two interacting subsystems, each containing two variables. Intergroup dependences are abstracted into a single dependency of strength 4 acting between the aggregate states of the two modules. (c) The aggregate state of each module is represented by a new variable, which stands in for the aggregate effect of the variables that contribute to it. (d) Here gray nodes represent emergent phenotypic characters that depend on the effects of several genes, but are "more than the sum of the parts." This cannot be represented by a network of pairwise dependencies (see later discussion).

However, when $|M_A| < |C_A|$, we can describe the state of A as the state of a new aggregate variable (Simon and Ando 1961) related to the cumulative state of the primitive (i.e., the original, nonaggregate) variables in A. This new aggregate variable is sufficient to exactly describe the dependencies of A with the rest of the system.

Figure 4.5c indicates how intermodule interaction can be abstracted into the interaction of the aggregate states of the respective modules. For the particular example system introduced above, the abstraction can be implemented as follows. For every intermodule dependency, if the states of the variables involved in this edge of the graph agree with each other then the fitness of the system is higher than if they do not agree. Thus the fitness contribution of intermodule interaction can be calculated from counting the number of agreements between all the variables in A and all the variables in B. This in turn can be calculated as $1_A 1_B + 0_A 0_B$, where 1_A, 1_B, 0_A, and 0_B are the number of 1s and the number of 0s in modules A and B. And in fact, since, with binary variables, the number of 0s in a set S is $|S| - 1_s$, and vice versa, we need only count the number of 1s in each group.

Let us write the proportion of 1s in a set S as $[S]$, that is, $[S] = 1_s/|S|$, then the fitness contribution of the system coming from intergroup interaction may be written as $Wf'([A],[B])$ where $f'(p,q) = pq + (1-p)(1-q)$, and W is a weighting factor. The original pairwise fitness function of two primitive variables, $f(p,q) = (p \text{ IFF } q)$ is the same as $f'(p,q)$ when p and q are binary variables.

Then we may rewrite the system described in equation 4.1 as follows:

Equation 4.3: Modularity using aggregate variables

$$g(S_1, S_2, S_3, S_4) = W_1 f'(S_1, S_2) + W_1 f'(S_3, S_4) + W_2 f'([S_1, S_2], [S_3, S_4])$$

where $f'(p, q) = pq + (1 - p)(1 - q)$, $[S]$ is the proportion of 1s in the set S, and to match the weight matrix described in table 4.2, $W_1 = W_2 = 8$.

This formulation of the function makes it very obvious that the fitness of the system can be described as the sum of the two intramodule fitness contributions and the intermodule fitness contribution and, more significantly, that the intermodule fitness contributions can be described as a simple function over aggregate properties of each module. Thus, since the aggregate properties lose information about the module (i.e., the number of possible values that $[A]$ can take is less than $|C_A|$) it cannot be the case that every state of B requires a different configuration of A, and thus it cannot be the case that $|M_A| = |C_A|$. This makes it clear that Simon's notion, that is, that the long-term behavior (or in this case the long-range or intermodule dependency) of the system depends only in an aggregate way on other components, is closely analogous to our notion of decomposability based on the number of configurations that induce different maximal-fitness configurations in one another.

From these considerations, it is useful to summarize the properties of a system with decomposable modules by noting that, although the fitness dependencies between modules may be significantly difficult to resolve, the interface between the modules has a low dimensionality. By this I mean that the number of different interactions between modules (different with respect to their effect on maximum-fitness configurations) is at most $|M_A| \times |M_B| < |C_A| \times |C_B|$.

This matches aspects of our intuitions about modules in both natural and engineered systems. We understand a module to encapsulate its internal complexity, so that not all the details of the internal state are important on the outside, that is, in its functional interaction with the rest of the system. The functioning of a cell has a complex chemical network of interacting molecules but the chemical interface between cells has a much lower dimensionality than the configuration space of all the intracellular molecules. We understand the cell as a module because it encapsulates the internal details of the cell. In engineered systems, a subroutine in a program, for example, encapsulates the internal complexity of the routine leaving only a small interface with the remainder of the code.

The description of a modular system using aggregate terms effects a *dimensional reduction* (Stephens and Waelbroeck 1998; Altenberg 2005). The notion of dimensional reduction, the idea that the system can be redescribed more simply at a higher level of abstraction, is analogous to the methods of *renormalization groups* (Wilson

1979). Renormalization groups are integral in the analysis of complex physical systems, such as spin-glass systems, exhibiting complex dependencies and local optima in their energy functions.

The intuition I am pursuing here is that compositional mechanisms will be able to exploit this dimensional reduction of a system, when available, by exploring combinations of modules instead of exploring combinations of the original basic variables, as I shall illustrate.

Hierarchy and Scaling Up

The above abstraction of the intermodule interaction into aggregate terms provides a convenient tool for abstracting and generalizing the model system hierarchically. Thus far I have developed it from a system of two interdependent variables to a system of four interdependent variables (in two pairs). One way this can be extended further for increasing numbers of variables is by adding additional modules, or increasing the number of variables within each module (in Simon's terms, we may increase the "span" at either of these two hierarchical levels). Another way we may extend the system is through additional hierarchical levels.

To add a successive hierarchical level of modularity I define a system of eight variables composed of two interacting subsystems of four variables. This can be achieved appropriately with equation 4.1, where $f(p,q) = (p \text{ IFF } q)$ as before and W is the weight matrix specified in table 4.4.

Table 4.4
A hierarchically modular weight matrix.

i\j	1	2	3	4	5	6	7	8
1	0	16	4	4	1	1	1	1
2	16	0	4	4	1	1	1	1
3	4	4	0	16	1	1	1	1
4	4	4	16	0	1	1	1	1
5	1	1	1	1	0	16	4	4
6	1	1	1	1	16	0	4	4
7	1	1	1	1	4	4	0	16
8	1	1	1	1	4	4	16	0

Using the same method as described for the four-variable system above, we can rewrite this as follows:

Equation 4.4: Hierarchical modularity using aggregate variables

$$\begin{aligned} g(S_1, S_2, \ldots, S_N) = {} & W_1(f'(S_1, S_2) + f'(S_3, S_4) + f'(S_5, S_6) + f'(S_7, S_8)) \\ & + W_2(f'([S_1, S_2], [S_3, S_4]) + f'([S_5, S_6], [S_7, S_8])) \\ & + W_3 f'([S_1, S_2, S_3, S_4], [S_5, S_6, S_7, S_8]) \end{aligned}$$

where $[S]$ is the proportion of 1s in the set S, as before, $f'(p, q) = pq + (1-p)(1-q)$, and for the weight values in this specific matrix, $W_1 = W_2 = W_3 = 16$.

A system like equation 4.4 can be generalized into a recursive function that systematically divides a large set of variables into subsets, through several hierarchical levels, until we arrive at the "atomic" variables. It is also not necessary to restrict ourselves to systems where the number of submodules per module is two. Nor is it necessary that the modules are equal sized or to maintain any implication that the variables in a module are in some sense consecutive—their ordering is arbitrary—so a system may be divided into modules that depend on any disjoint (nonoverlaping) subset of the problem variables. I have called the resulting equation 4.5 the "continuous" version of HIFF (HIFF is defined below). This function could in fact be applied to continuous variables, but the reason I have called it this is that, even if it is applied to binary variables, the interaction between modules is not "all or nothing" but by degrees, as I will explain shortly.

Equation 4.5: Continuous version of HIFF

$$g(S) = \begin{cases} 0, & \text{if } N = 1 \\ f'([S^1], \ldots, [S^k]) + \sum_{i=1}^{k} g(S^i), & \text{otherwise} \end{cases}$$

where S^i is the ith disjoint subpartition of the variables in S, $[S]$ is the proportion of 1s in the set S, and, $f'(s_1, s_2, \ldots s_k) = \prod_{i=1}^{k} s_i + \prod_{i=1}^{k}(1 - s_i)$, and k is the number of submodules per module. N is the size of the system or subsystem S, and for the whole system, $N = k^H$ where $H \in \mathbb{Z}^+$ is the number of hierarchical levels in the system.

Equation 4.4 is then a special case of equation 4.5 where $N = 8$, $k = 2$, and the disjoint subpartitions are equal sized. When $k = 2$, f' can be simplified to $f'(p, q) = pq + (1-p)(1-q)$.

Emergent Effects of Modules

The form of this function is a natural extension of the four-variable system defined earlier, the only reason for drawing out the eight-variable system explicitly like this is to discuss the scaling of weight values that is not immediately evident in the two-level four-variable system. Specifically, notice that in equation 4.4 the fitness contributions of all the dependencies within a module taken together is equal to the fitness contributions of all the intermodule dependencies between two modules taken together. That is, although each intermodule dependency is weaker than each intramodule dependency there are more intermodule dependencies than intramodule dependencies by the same ratio. This makes the modularity of the system equally important at all scales. This is seen in the weight values of equation 4.4—that is, $W_1 = W_2 = W_3$. Although it is not essential that they be exactly equal as they are here, the balance of intra- and intermodule dependencies is important for meaningful modularity when all interdependencies are derived from pairwise interactions.

In particular, if intermodule dependencies are too strong then intramodule dependencies can be over powered and cease to create local optima. This can be illustrated with a cross section through the fitness landscape (figure 4.6). Like that shown for the four-variable system in figure 4.4, this cross section extends from one global optimum at all 0s to the other at all 1s visiting $N + 1$ points in total. Figure 4.6 shows a section through a 128-variable system defined with the continuous version of HIFF in equation 4.5.

Note that the points like the one indicated with the arrow in figure 4.6 are local optima with the weight values defined; but with a different weight scaling, if intramodule dependencies are not significantly stronger than intermodule dependencies, then this point will not be a local optimum and the basin of attraction for the global optimum will increase.

In general, in systems built from pairwise dependencies, if intermodule dependencies are too weak, then—although resolving them may be difficult—they become less important in terms of their fitness effect. In this example system, it is very difficult to jump from the second-highest fitness point on this curve at $1^{N/2}0^{N/2}$ to either of the two global optima, but the fitness increase from this jump is only small; and if the fitness of the global optima were increased, the points nearby (indicated with the arrow) would cease to be local optima. In this class of model, this region of weight parameters, where the modularity of the problem is scale invariant, is where the modularity of the system is most evident.

This kind of modularity might be present in natural and engineered systems, but it has not captured all of what we want to represent in modular systems. In the pre-

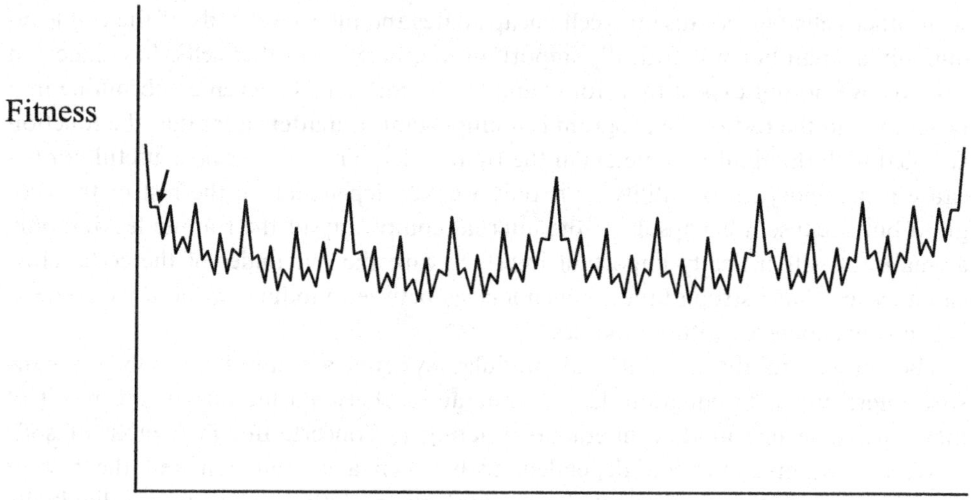

Figure 4.6
A cross section through continuous HIFF. This cross section extends from one global optimum at all 0s to the other at all 1s visiting $N+1$ points in total. Specifically, the kth point in the cross section, for $0 \leq k \leq N$, is the configuration $1^k 0^{N-k}$—i.e., a string with k 1s followed by $N-k$ 0s. The fractal nature of the fitness landscape, resulting from the recursive definition of modules and submodules, is clearly visible in this section. Consecutive points in this series are separated by Hamming distance 1, i.e., one-point mutations, and as discussed in the next chapter this particular cross section is one of the paths that satisfies a mutation walk (defined in figure 5.1) and reveals many interesting properties of the landscape.

vious arguments and in the above example system I have shown that it is possible for a system to have identifiable modules even though satisfying the dependencies between modules might require changing many variables at once. That is, a system can be meaningfully modular if it is decomposable even if the members of the maximal set for a module are very far apart in Hamming space. However, I have not yet shown an example where resolving difficult dependencies like these is really worth it in terms of fitness improvements. It seems that in natural systems, and certainly in engineered systems, getting the dependencies between functional modules resolved appropriately is critically important to the proper functioning of the system as a whole and should therefore confer significant fitness advantages.

The proper functioning of a cell, for example, is very strongly dependent on proper signaling with neighboring cells. Although the chemical interface between cells has a much lower dimensionality than the configuration space of all the intracellular molecules, this interface also matters a lot for the proper functioning of the cells. We understand the cell as a module not because it has weak or unimportant interactions with other cells but because the cell encapsulates the internal details of the cell leaving only a small but still critically important interface with other cells. In engineered systems, we do not expect that, for example, the interface between a subroutine in a program and the rest of the program is unimportant; it matters a lot that the function is called with the right parameters in the right order. The subroutine is useful not because it has independent utility or is only weakly dependent on the rest of the program but because it encapsulates the internal complexity of the routine leaving only a small but still critically important interface with the remainder of the code. How can a system have strong fitness dependencies between modules without overpowering the dependencies within modules?

The answer to this is that real modular systems are not built only on pairwise interactions. In equation 4.5, the interaction between modules is the result of many pairwise intermodule interactions acting in concert. But in a piece of software, for example, the interdependencies between a subfunction and the rest of the code is not the result of all the internal parts of the code acting individually with the code outside the function. The interdependencies between a subfunction and the rest of the program are explicitly low dimensional and act via the arguments of the function. In biological cells, the interaction of one protien with another does not result from the cumulative effect of many pairwise dependencies between all the amino acids of one protein with all the amino acids of the other. Although all the amino acids in each protein are involved in determining the three-dimensional structure of the molecule, it is the relatively low-dimensional features of the protein such as its shape, the relative position of resultant active domains, and the points of articulation in its shape, that determine its functional interface with other proteins.

Frame (d) of figure 4.5 attempts to represent something subtly different from frame (c). Frame (c) represents the aggregation of variables as used in equation 4.5, that is, $(S_1, S_2, \ldots S_N) \rightarrow [S]$, where this is merely a compact way of representing the cumulative effect of the underlying pairwise dependencies. In the following function, the aggregation of variables within a module will be only subtly different mathematically, but is better interpreted as a new higher-level feature of the system—a feature that emerges from the interaction of its constituent parts, but is more than the sum of its parts. These emergent properties, that mediate the interaction between modules, correspond to features such as the three-dimensional shape of a protein or the data transformations of a subproceedure. This means that it is necessary to introduce explicit higher-level interdependencies between modules in the system, as we see in the next section.

4.4 Hierarchical-If-and-Only-If (HIFF)

In this section I define a modification of equation 4.5 that introduces higher-order interdependencies between modules that enable us to make the intermodule interactions stronger than intramodule interactions without overpowering them and breaking down the modular structure of the system. In both equation 4.5 and the following modifications, the fitness of modules is maximal when all the variables within the module have the same state. The difference is that in equation 4.5 the interdependency between modules responds to a degree of agreement, but in hierarchical equality and hierarchical IFF below, the interdependency between modules will be "all or nothing." This can be interpreted as the interaction between two modules based on new emergent properties rather than merely the collective effect of the constituent variables in each module.

Specifically, in equation 4.5 the interaction between a pair of variables or modules is $f'(p,q) = pq + (1-p)(1-q)$. When variables are binary, $f'(p,q) = f(p,q) = (p \text{ IFF } q)$, and either function, f' or f, returns a fitness of 0 or 1. But for larger modules, where p and q take intermediate values, $f'(p,q)$ can return intermediate fitnesses. Hierarchical IFF uses a different definition for the interaction between two modules, specifically $f(p,q) = (p = q = 0 \vee p = q = 1)$, which is exactly the same as $(p \text{ IFF } q)$ and $f'(p,q)$ when p and q are binary variables but differs from $f'(p,q)$ when p and q take intermediate values. That is, when this subtly different version of $f(p,q) = (p = q = 0 \vee p = q = 1)$ is used, the interaction between large modules (where the proportion of 1s in each module may take intermediate values between 0 and 1), will still be "all or nothing." It will return a fitness bonus if all the variables in both modules are either *all* 1s or *all* 0s, but otherwise there is no bonus for the variables in two modules being in partial agreement. This is illustrated in figure 4.7.

More generally, we can define this all-or-nothing version of f over $k \geq 2$ variables in any discrete alphabet using configurations where all variables have equal values, as follows:

$f(p_1, \ldots p_k) = 1$ if $(\exists (s \in \Sigma)\ \forall i\colon p_i = s)$, and 0 otherwise, where Σ is the discrete set of allowable values for the problem variables, e.g., $\Sigma = \{0, 1\}$, for binary problems.

An all-or-nothing version of equation 4.5 can then be defined by substituting this definition of $f(p_1, \ldots p_k)$ for the previous definition of f'. But note that $f([S^1], \ldots, [S^k]) = f(S_1, \ldots, S_N)$; that is, checking that the proportion of 1s in all the modules is 0 or 1 is the same as checking whether all the variables inside all the modules are

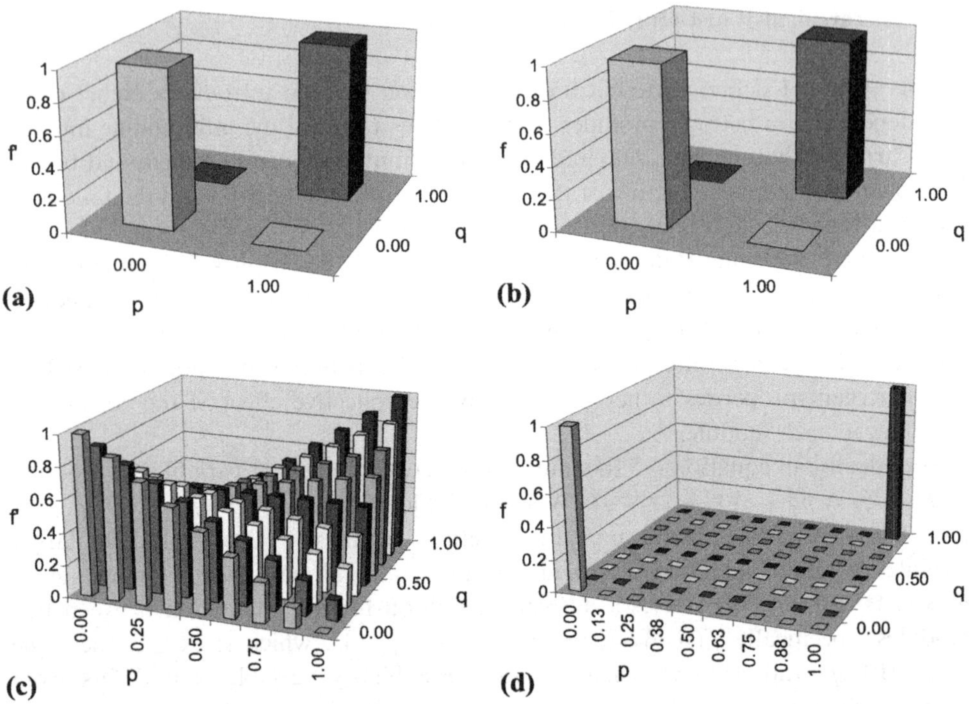

Figure 4.7
Continuous and discontinuous interactions. The left column (a and c) shows $f'(p,q) = pq + (1-p)(1-q)$. The right column (b and d) shows $f(p,q) = (p = q = 0 \vee p = q = 1)$. These are identical when p and q are binary variables, top row. But the functions differ for larger modules, when p and q take intermediate values, bottom row.

either 0 or 1. So, notationally, we can dispense with the proportion-of-ones function altogether and simplify as equation 4.6 below.

Equation 4.6: Hierarchical equality no-scaling

$$g(S_1, \ldots, S_N) = \begin{cases} 0, & \text{if } N = 1 \\ f(S_1, \ldots, S_N) + \sum_{i=1}^{k} g(S^i), & \text{otherwise} \end{cases}$$

where S_i is the ith variable of the configuration, S^i is the ith disjoint subpartition of the variables, $f(p_1, \ldots p_k) = 1$ if $(\exists(s \in \Sigma)\ \forall i\colon p_i = s)$, and 0 otherwise; where Σ is the discrete set of allowable values for the problem variables; and $N = k^H$, where

$H \in \mathbb{Z}^+$ is the number of hierarchical levels in the system or subsystem, and k is the number of submodules per module.

In equation 4.6, f is intrinsically discontinuous. Specifically, a module does not confer any fitness contribution unless all submodules are in agreement (have the same state). This is why I refer to the earlier system, equation 4.5, as the "continuous" version of this form of hierarchical modularity.

This all-or-nothing aspect of equation 4.6 means that the resultant intermodule dependencies cannot be described in terms of the sum of pairwise interactions, as in equation 4.1, and are instead made into explicit higher-order dependencies. This has the consequence that we can now change the relative importance of intra- and intermodule interdependencies without the risk of intramodule dependencies being overpowered as discussed earlier. It also has the fortuitous side effect that it makes analysis of the simulations much easier (see the generalization of the function discussed in section 4.5).

In previous work (Watson, Hornby, and Pollack 1998; Watson 2001; Watson and Pollack 1999a,c, 2000b, 2001a, 2003), and consequently, in the previous work of others (Knowles, Watson, and Corne 2001; Oates and Corne 2001; Van Hoyweghen, Goldberg, and Naudts 2001a; Van Hoyweghen and Naudts 2001; Jansen and Wegener 2001; Wiles, Tonkes, and Watson 2001; Pelikan and Goldberg 2000, 2001, 2003; Potter, Bassett, and De Jong 2003), a particular scaling of intermodule interaction was used. Specifically, in this variant, the fitness contribution of a module is scaled by the number of variables in the module. This function is known as "hierarchical-if-and-only-if," HIFF. I will continue to use HIFF in the models that follow in later chapters in order to align with the existing literature.

HIFF, and also a more general form, "hierarchical equality" (H-equal), are both defined by equation 4.7. The only difference in equation 4.7 when compared to equation 4.6 is that the fitness contribution for a module is multiplied by the size of the module, that is, N.

Equation 4.7: Hierarchical-if-and-only-if (HIFF) and hierarchical equality (H-equal)

$$g(s_1, \ldots, s_N) = \begin{cases} 1, & \text{if } N = 1 \\ Nf(S_1, \ldots, S_k) + \sum_{i=1}^{k} g(S^i), & \text{otherwise} \end{cases}$$

where S_i is the ith variable of the configuration, S^i is the ith disjoint subpartition of the variables, $f(p_1, \ldots p_k) = 1$ if $(\exists(s \in \Sigma)\ \forall i\colon p_i = s)$, and 0 otherwise; where Σ is the discrete set of allowable values for the problem variables; and $N = k^H$, where $H \in \mathbb{Z}^+$ is the number of hierarchical levels in the system or subsystem, and k is the number of submodules per module.

HIFF is the particular case for binary variables, that is, $\Sigma \in \{0, 1\}$ and where $k = 2$. H-equal is the general case allowing any number of submodules per module and any base for the constituent variables. HIFF and H-equal also assume, by default, that the subpartitions of the variables corresponding to the submodules are equal-sized consecutive blocks, that is, for "unshuffled"[2] HIFF with equal-sized submodules, $S^i = (s_{1+k(i-1)}, \ldots, s_{ki})$.

The HIFF function will be used in the simulation experiments that follow in chapters 5, 6, and 7. The scaling difference between equation 4.6 and equation 4.7 does not affect the decomposability of the system, the number of local optima, or the position of local optima. So HIFF is in all these important respects the same system as that defined by equation 4.6 or a system based on the weighted sum of pairwise interaction defined by equation 4.5 (or 4.1 with a dependency matrix like that shown in table 4.4). Since in most of the simulation results that follow I will show the size of the largest correct module discovered (i.e., the size of the biggest block of all 0s or all 1s) rather than the fitness of the system, the fitness scaling in equation 4.7 does not effect the appearance of these results curves either.

The remaining subtle difference between equation 4.5 and equation 4.7 is illustrated by comparing figure 4.8 and figure 4.6 showing cross sections that pass through the same set of points. The consequences of these resultant fitness landscapes for gradual evolution are discussed in the next chapter.

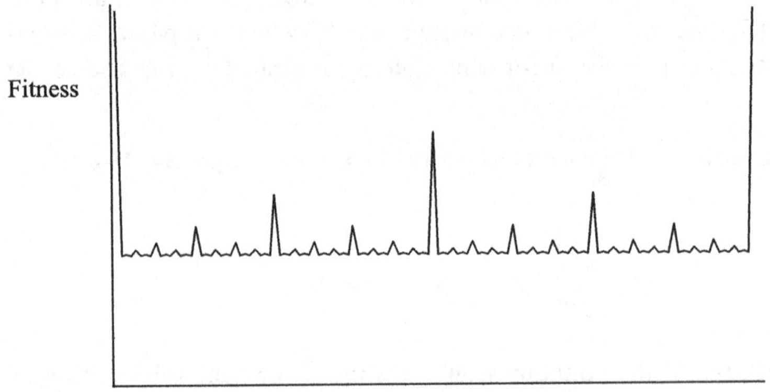

Figure 4.8
A particular cross section through the HIFF fitness landscape.

HIFF has a very regular and symmetric structure but this regularity is largely immaterial to the experiments that follow (see De Jong, Watson, and Thierens 2005a for generalizations). For example, none of the algorithms illustrated depend on translocational symmetries—that is, it is never assumed that the configuration that optimizes one module will be related to the configuration that optimizes another and that therefore, a schema discovered at one partition can be relocated to another partition. Accordingly, we may put candidate configurations through a random mapping, for example, an XOR with a predetermined random string, effectively randomizing the absolute locations of the optima, without affecting the results. For some results, it is also not important that the global optima (or the substrings they contain) are complementary strings (see Watson 2001). Features such as whether the submodules are equal in size (same "span" in each module), whether the hierarchical interdependency structure is "balanced" (same hierarchical depth of submodules in each module), and whether the modules at a given level have exactly the same fitness contributions, or whether the members of the maximal set for a given module have exactly the same fitness contributions, are also not the features of interest. (See De Jong, Watson, and Thierens 2005a.)

What should be retained is the property of *modular interdependency* and the property that different members of the maximal set are distant from one another in Hamming space. The particular instance of hierarchical modularity defined in HIFF is obviously too specific to be found in natural or engineered systems, but the underlying principle of modular interdependency is relatively general. This principle matches well with intuitive notions of modularity, incorporating the idea that modules are semi-independent but not completely independent; that modules afford a kind of encapsulation of internal complexity that reduces the dimensionality of a system, but that the remaining dependencies between modules are still important.

4.5 Discussion

Generalization

Equation 4.5 provides a starting point for generalizing this class of systems. To aggregate the effect of variables in large modules, equation 4.5 uses the proportion of 1s in each module, that is, $[S]$. The fitness interaction of two modules, A and B, is then given by $f'([A],[B])$. To generalize we can use different aggregation functions and different fitness functions. An aggregation function *transforms* a block of variables into a single variable (see figure 4.5, c). We can define the way that hierarchical modules produce dependencies by using general recursive functions F and T, below.

Then we may define base fitness functions and base aggregation functions, f and t, that provide different variations for this general hierarchically decomposable form.

Equation 4.8: Generalized form of hierarchically consistent modular interdependency

$$F(S) = \begin{cases} 0, & \text{if } |S| = 1 \\ f(T(S^1), T(S^2), \ldots T(S^k)) + \alpha \sum_{i=1}^{k} F(S^i), & \text{otherwise} \end{cases}$$

where S^i is the ith disjoint subpartition of the variables in S, k is the number of submodules per module, T is the general aggregation function defined below, f is the base fitness function, and α is a scaling factor; N is the size of the system or subsystem S, and for the whole system, $N = k^H$ where $H \in \mathbb{Z}^+$ is the number of hierarchical levels in the system.

$$T(S) = \begin{cases} S & \text{if } |S| = 1, \\ t(T(S^1), \ldots, T(S^k)) & \text{otherwise.} \end{cases}$$

Equation 4.5 is then a specific instance of equation 4.8, where

$$f(s_1, s_2, \ldots s_k) = \prod_{i=1}^{k} s_i + \prod_{i=1}^{k} (1 - s_i); \quad t(S) = [S]; \text{ and } \quad \alpha = 1.$$

Equation 4.6 can also be defined as a specific instance of equation 4.8, where $f(s_1, s_2, \ldots s_k) = 1$ if $(\exists (s \in \Sigma)\ \forall i\text{: } p_i = s)$, and 0 otherwise; $t(S_1, \ldots S_k) = x$ if $(\exists (x \in \Sigma)\ \forall i\text{: } s_i = x)$, and "null" otherwise; and $\alpha = 1$.

This modified transformation function, mimicking the discretization of the module interaction in figure 4.7, returns "null" if the states of all the variables are not in agreement with each other. And the slightly modified f function returns 0 if any of the modules are null.

HIFF (equation 4.7) can then be defined as $\text{HIFF}(S) = N \times F(S)$, with f and t as above, and $\alpha = 1/k$ (and by default, $k = 2$, $\Sigma = \{0, 1\}$, and subpartitions are equal-sized subblocks of the variables at each level). This equation 4.8 enables us to unify continuous HIFF and HIFF (both scaled and unscaled).

Conceptually, a transform function that not only reduces a set of variables to one variable but also restricts the possible range of values for this variable to be the same as the range of values for its input variables greatly assists analysis. In equation 4.5 the number of values that $[S]$ may take increases with the size of S and this means that the fitness interactions become more complex. But if $t(S)$ can only take the values 0 or 1 (excluding the invalid "null"), this keeps the dimensionality of the interactions exactly the same for any size modules.

This general recursive form of F and T allows us to describe a broader class of systems with hierarchical modular interdependency by substituting alternate base functions f and t, as illustrated above. Pelikan and Goldberg (2000, 2001) define a function with $k = 6$ that uses a "trap function" for f and $t(S) = 0$ if $[S] = 0$, 1 if $[S] = 1$, and null otherwise (see Watson, Hornby, and Pollack 1998). The resultant hierarchical trap function creates an interesting, difficult variety of hierarchical modular interdependency.

In all instances, it is important that f and t have at least the following properties:

1. f must incorporate interdependency between at least some of its variables if the overall problem is to have any local optima, and be difficult for gradual mechanisms.
2. t must be a function that reduces the dimensionality of the arguments it acts on in order that intermodule interaction can be described via aggregate effects.

The second condition asserts that the number of possible values that $t(S)$ may take must be less than the number of configurations that S may take. When $t(S) = [S]$, for example, the number of values that $t(S)$ can take is $k + 1$ where k is the number of variables in S, but the number of configurations that S can take is 2^k. Alternatively, if the variables are continuous, it may be sufficient to reduce more than one variable into one variable: that is, $t : \mathbb{R}^k \to \mathbb{R}$. A simple way to ensure appropriate reduction is to use a function t that is insensitive to the ordering of its arguments (like counting the number of 1s)—this ensures that $|M_s| < |C_s|$, since some configurations for s will be indistinguishable at the aggregate level. But a transformation function that reduces a set of symbols to a single symbol of the same alphabet ensures even greater hierarchical consistency: that is, $t : \Sigma^k \to \Sigma$.

There are additional constraints for f and t that must be satisfied in order that the resultant landscape is amenable to compositional mechanisms. For example, it must be the case that the high-fitness configurations within a module correspond to aggregate values that are involved in high-fitness values of intermodule interaction. As a counterexample, if we defined $t(p, q) = (p \text{ XOR } q)$ and $f(p, q) = (p \text{ IFF } q)$ then these functions would satisfy the properties listed above, and $|M_s| < |C_s|$, but the high-fitness single-module configurations would lead search to favor configurations that aggregate into low-fitness multimodule configurations.

The method of constructing a hierarchically decomposable system can be further relaxed to encompass a still broader range of systems with modular interdependency. For example, it is not necessary that f and t be defined uniformly over all modules at all levels, but it is not so easy to determine what the overall effect will be when different functions are combined. Pelikan and Goldberg (2000) give a problem definition including these relaxations (see also De Jong, Watson, and Thierens 2005a).

The recursive construction of equation 4.8, and the above guidelines for relaxing f and t, indicate a broad class of hierarchically decomposable systems that, as we will see, are difficult for gradual mechanisms and easy for compositional mechanisms. With some care, less restricted systems may be also be defined in the style of equation 4.1 with an appropriate dependency matrix.

Relationship of HIFF to Other Modular Systems

The building-block hypothesis appeals to the notion of problem decomposition and the assembly of solutions from subsolutions. Accordingly, there have been many varieties of GA test problems with a structure based on building blocks. It also describes the assembly of bits into blocks, blocks into bigger blocks, and so on to provide a complete solution—thus the hierarchical aspect of the process is clear to our intuition and hierarchical structure of a kind is incorporated in a few existing building-block problems. Some of these problems use difficult fitness functions to model interdependency between the bits within a block. However, very few have any model of interdependency between building blocks; those that do are not consistent in the type of interaction used both intrablock and interblock (summarized in figure 4.9 later).

Whitley et al. provide a review of test problems from the GA literature (1995b) and summarize (1995a), "most common test problems used in the past to evaluate genetic algorithms lack" the inclusion of "strong nonlinear dependencies between state variables." That is, although the contribution of a single variable to the overall evaluation may be nonlinear, there may be no nonlinear interactions *between* variables, and therefore the optimal value for each parameter can be determined independently of all other parameters.

There are several building-block-style functions—the Royal Road (RR) functions (Mitchell, Forrest, and Holland 1992; Forrest and Mitchell 1993a), revised Royal Road functions (Holland 1993; see also Jones 1995), concatenated trap functions (Deb and Goldberg 1992, 1993), and others, that clearly emphasize a gross-scale building-block structure. But, like the real-valued functions that Whitley investigated, these consist of concatenated blocks, each of which may be optimized independently in a cumulative fashion. The RR1 version of the Royal Road problem (Forrest and Mitchell 1993a), for example, can be imagined as a staircase-leading search in stepwise fashion in the correct direction (see figure 4.9). The RR2 function (Forrest and Mitchell 1993a) and the revised Royal Road functions make hierarchy explicit. However, the interactions between bits within the first-level blocks is still

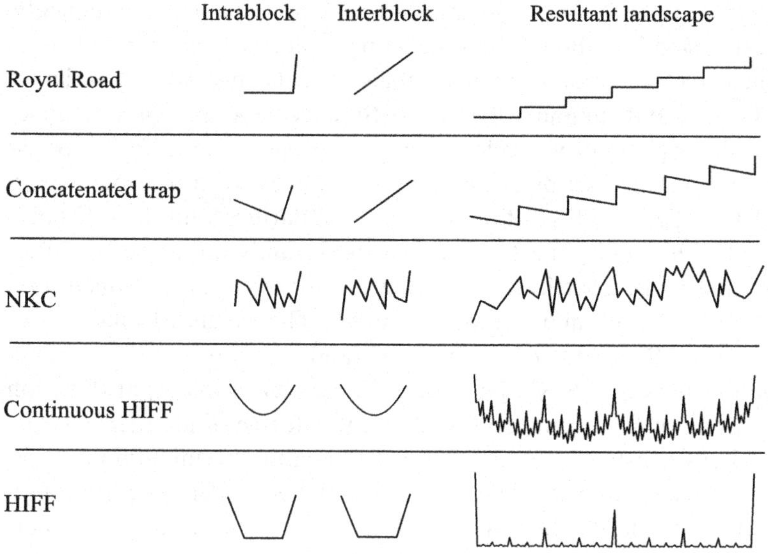

Figure 4.9
Comparing HIFF with other building-block functions. Showing the shape of intrablock dependencies with increasing number of 1s in a block from left to right, and interblock dependencies with increasing number of correct blocks from left to right, and a cross section through the resultant landscape when the intra- and interblock dependencies are combined.

very different from the interactions between blocks in subsequent levels. Although the fitness contributions of blocks accumulate nonlinearly because of "bonus" contributions from higher levels, the blocks are still separable in that the optimal bit setting for a block does not change.

Goldberg et al. (1993) acknowledge that they have "temporarily ignored the possibility of subfunction crosstalk." *Crosstalk* is defined by Kargupta (1995) as "a property of both the algorithm and the landscape" and appeals to the idea that the algorithm may be misled in identifying building blocks by changes in fitness contribution. Accordingly, Goldberg et al. suggest that noise in the fitness function may be an appropriate model for crosstalk. But this interpretation of crosstalk does not provide the same kind of interdependency between blocks as the interdependency between the variables within a block. A definition of building-block dependency as given in this chapter is not reliant on the algorithm being used—that is, the observation that the optimal bit setting for a block is different in one context than in another is algorithm independent.

Whitley et al. (1995b) argue for test problems that have nonseparable components, and propose an "expansion" method for constructing scaleable nonseparable functions from a nonlinear base function of two variables. By selecting pairs of variables in an overlapping fashion and summing the results they create a nonseparable function over an arbitrarily large set of variables. They also propose that using all possible pairs, rather than a minimal set of overlapping pairs, provides a method to vary the amount of interdependency. This notion has some similarities with the NK landscapes of Kauffman (1989, 1993). The NK landscapes certainly do model the interdependency of variables—the contribution of each of N variables is defined as a random lookup function of itself and K other variables. The expanded functions of Whitley are analogous to NK landscapes with $K = 2$ (and with a repeated base function instead of random lookup tables). This seems like a step in the right direction especially since the value of k, in some sense, defines the degree of interdependence. But this is still not wholly satisfying, for now we cannot identify meaningful modules. In the NK model (and the expanded function method) the dependencies form a uniform network without modularity. In HIFF we see that it is the structure of interdependencies, not just the number or order of dependencies, that is essential in understanding problem difficulty. Simply having a large number of random interdependencies and creating significant epistasis and local optima is not sufficient to distinguish gradual and compositional evolution.

Holland (2000) describes "hyperplane defined functions." One of the features of these is that high-order schemata that confer fitness contributions are built from pairs of lower-order schemata. This aspect of the construction technique is similar to previous work (Watson, Hornby, and Pollack 1998) that I developed in this chapter. Holland notes that the elementary schemata in the problem may overlap and may be conflicting but the importance of this point is not strongly emphasized. Specifically, if the elementary schemata are not overlapping and conflicting then they are separable—the solution to a building block is independent of context. In the example that Holland gives, there are only three loci that have any conflicts—which means that the problem may be solved by a simple hill climber. But more generally, by building the initial schemata out of random subsets of the variables and assigning random bit configurations, we are unable to ensure that the problem is difficult, or control how difficult it is. Accordingly, Holland is unable to give a time to solution for the GA or hill-climbing mechanisms on this class of problem. Also, Holland's notion of building blocks here assumes tight genetic linkage (short defining length of schemata) whereas the modular interdependency concept is independent of gene ordering and physical genetic linkage. Other building-block functions explicitly utilize the partial overlap of schemata to introduce a small amount of building-block interdependency (e.g., Wiegand, Liles, and De Jong 2001).

One other building-block problem of interest is provided by Louis and Rawlins (1991). They describe a problem where a global optimum at $0^{N/2}1^{N/2}$ can be arrived at by crossover from strings that correspond to local optima at all 0s and all 1s. Interestingly, they also discuss this problem in the context of multiobjective optimization, which will feature heavily in later models I develop in chapter 7. The interesting feature of this problem is that it rewards strongly competing schemata that are distant from the global optimum; the global optimum is an isolated needle and therefore difficult to find with a gradual mechanism, but crossover of the strings from the two local optima puts the global optimum within easy reach. The main restriction of this model is that the composition is only useful once—it is a two-module problem with no additional hierarchical levels.

Some extended NK models include "NKC" models (Kauffman and Johnsen 1989) intended to model two coupled semi-independent landscapes of two semi-independent species, and "NKCS" models corresponding to several coupled landscapes/species. An NKC landscape is an NKCS with number of species, $S = 2$. As in NK landscapes, the fitness contribution of each of N variables is dependent on its own state and the state of several other variables. But in NKCS models, the problem variables are divided into S-nonoverlapping (generally equal-sized) groups of variables, and for each variable, K of the epistatically dependent variables are drawn from the same group and C are drawn from other groups. In this manner we may imagine that each group of variables describes an NK landscape, but each landscape is epistatically coupled to S-other NK landscapes.

The idea here is that we may evolve one species on one landscape, and another species on another, but the movement of the first will influence the landscape of the second, and vice versa. For our purposes, we may also interpret this model as a single problem composed of interdependent modules, and the coevolving entities are coevolving modules specializing on different subproblems. This scenario clearly illustrates the opportunity to model intragenomic and intergenomic dependencies in a unified model, and NKC landscapes have strong parallels with the models developed in this chapter.

However, there are some inadequacies in NKC models. First, all NK models use random epistatic interactions between variables—but not all types of epistatic interactions are difficult for gradual methods. Second, the interdependency between modules is not a proper scaling up of the interdependency between the original variables. Specifically, it is the state of only a few individual variables that determines the epistatic fitness effects between modules, not the aggregate or emergent effects of the whole modules. Third, NKC models exhibit a single level of clustered dependencies or a two-level hierarchy. In order to understand repeated compositional operations we require a model that is scalable over many hierarchical levels.

I define a hierarchically consistent modular problem as one where the nature of the problem of finding modules at level h, given the solutions to modules at level $h - 1$, is the same for all levels. That is, searching combinations of good submodules, to find good solutions to modules, is the same kind of problem as searching combinations of good modules to find good solutions to metamodules. HIFF is hierarchically consistent.

Although none of these prior models exhibit strong intermodule dependencies in a hierarchically consistent fashion, this prior work has contributed a number of concepts embedded in the HIFF function. The general recursive structure of HIFF is inspired by the "expanded" functions (Whitley et al. 1995b), and the modularity of HIFF is clearly inspired by the building-block structure of the Royal Road functions (Mitchell, Forrest, and Holland 1992). The concept that makes HIFF difficult for hill climbers to solve, by introducing ruggedness in the landscape, is the concept of competing schemata in the same partition. This concept is used in the concatenated trap functions (Deb and Goldberg 1993) where both sets of 1s and sets of 0s are rewarded, and more generally it is similar to the difficult epistatic interactions created when fitness contributions are derived from overlapping schemata as in NK landscapes (Kauffman 1993). Together these concepts contribute significantly to the design of the HIFF function. The shuffled HIFF function (section 6.4) is additionally inspired by the issue of difficult genetic maps as used in randomized versions of the concatenated traps used to test the messy GA (Goldberg, Korb, and Deb 1989).

However, the differences between HIFF and prior models are important. HIFF extracts and unifies some of the important concepts of prior work to create a general hierarchically consistent function with quite extreme ruggedness and also extremely structured modularity. It also allows generalization in several different ways; by changing the base functions as discussed above and changing the degree of competition between competing schemata (as in "biased HIFF," Watson and Pollack 1999a,b). But the important difference is its ability to distinguish the capabilities of gradual and compositional evolution.

None of the NK landscapes, the Royal Roads, the concatenated traps, or the expanded functions properly distinguish the abilities of gradual and compositional evolution. The most important underlying conceptual issue is perhaps that previous models do not properly distinguish between separability and decomposability.

And this in turn prevents prior models from including appropriate intermodule dependencies.

Because the Royal Road functions have no interdependencies between modules and no local optima at all, there is no need to search combinations of modules to solve these problems and a random mutation hill climber can solve these problems faster than a genetic algorithm (Forrest and Mitchell 1993b). Jones (1995) showed that the concatenated trap functions fall victim to a different kind of hill climber (a "macromutation hill climber").

The ability of the macromutation hill climber (MMHC) to solve the concatenated trap functions (Jones 1995) relied on the heuristic of focusing mutations on contiguous loci (the MMHC picks two interlocal positions and assigns new random alleles to all loci between these positions). Accordingly, one method in the literature to defeat the MMHC is to use a random genetic map (e.g., Harik 1997). That is, the ordering of genes on the chromosome is randomized so that the bits of a block are not next to each other. Certainly, this makes the problem hard for MMHCs but it also makes the problem hard for the GA and crossover.

Specifically, a random genetic map prevents schema recombination under crossover. Conceptually, the problem of module interdependency is a different issue from the problem of not being able to assume that the genetic map contains useful information about epistatic interactions. In HIFF we will see that it is not possible for any form of mutation hill climber to solve intermodule dependencies even it it was able to use information from the genetic map to bias where mutations fall. This means that HIFF defeats all types of hill climbers but does not introduce a random genetic map that would also defeat the benefit of sexual recombination in the genetic algorithm.

Thus in HIFF with a natural genetic map, members of the maximal set for low-order modules are building blocks as Holland defined them. But, as argued in this chapter, modularity is meaningful and quantifiable in a manner that is independent of the ordering of variables in the genetic map.

So the failure of the Royal Road and concatenated trap functions to distinguish the ability of sexual recombination in the GA from the ability of a hill climber is due to the fact that in both cases, the blocks can be accumulated serially because there are no interblock dependencies and fitness responds monotonically with an increasing number of correct blocks. Without significant intermodule dependencies, hierarchically modular systems do not make sense—if there are going to be meta-modules at the next level up, then it has to be the case that some modules are more strongly interdependent than others. This cannot be so if there are no intermodule dependencies (Watson and Pollack 2005).

A comparison of intra- and intermodule dependencies in various functions is depicted in figure 4.9. In the Royal Road functions the intrablock dependencies produce an abrupt increase in fitness when a block is all 1s but has no gradient leading toward this configuration. In contrast, the interblock dependencies in the Royal Road functions provide a monotonic increase in fitness for each correct block. Accordingly, the resultant landscape exhibits a "staircase" with fitness increases for each correct block, leading the search monotonically to the fittest configuration of the system. In the concatenated trap function although the intrablock dependencies are more difficult than the Royal Road, with a deceptive optimum that leads search away from the fittest configuration of each block, the interblock dependencies are still linear. In the resultant landscape, although each tread on the stair is inclined in the wrong direction, this again creates a staircase that leads search in the right direction for any algorithm that is capable of discovering good blocks. In the NKC landscapes, the intermodule dependencies have the same form as the intramodule dependencies (i.e., all dependencies are random and arbitrarily rugged) but it is not clear what structure this creates, if any, in the landscape as a whole. In contrast, in the continuous version of HIFF (equation 4.5), and HIFF (equation 4.7), the intramodule and intermodule dependencies are consistent and create a hierarchically consistent modular problem (see section 4.3). The cross sections through the resultant fitness landscapes therefore show that there is no macroscale structure that makes the problem easy for mutation or macromutation hill climbers. Nonetheless, the recursive modularity of the system means that it exhibits decomposability and it is therefore amenable in principle to a process that can exploit modularity.

Deception and Bounded Difficulty

It has been suggested that in general it is reasonable to expect that there might be an upper bound on the highest-order nonlinearity in the type of problem we are interested in (Deb and Goldberg 1993). Presumably this derives from the intuition that if there were very high-order nonlinearities then the problem would be unsolvable. HIFF has order-N fitness interactions but I will show that it is easily solvable.

Furthermore, problems in the literature often equate order-k delineation with order-k separability (e.g., the Royal Road problems and concatenated trap functions). To see the distinction, note that equation 4.1 with table 4.4 defines a version of modular interdependency defined on pairwise (i.e., order-2 dependencies) and is therefore "order-2 delineable"—however, this problem is not separable into order-2 blocks because fitness contributions come from pairs of variables that overlap. The simulations that follow using HIFF show that there is no good reason to suppose that a problem needs to have separable submodules in order to be solvable by a genetic algorithm. HIFF is neither order-k delineable nor order-k separable—it involves interdependent modules and order-N fitness contributions. And the fact that the continuous version of HIFF is order-2 delineable but is just as difficult as HIFF for a hill climber shows that being delineable to a low order is not a guarantee that a problem is easy. Thus the order-k delineable and order-k separable concepts of GA easiness are not required to understand GA success, and do not capture all the properties that might be of interest in a problem.

"Deception" has been proposed as a concept of evolutionary difficulty (e.g., Deb and Goldberg 1992, 1993; see also Liepins and Vose 1991), and has been used extensively in building-block functions such as the concatenated trap functions. As Deb and Goldberg indicate, there are many different definitions of deception but the basic idea is that high-order schemata of high fitness (e.g., the global optimum) are not contained in low-order schemata of high fitness—in other words, if search focuses on high-fitness low-order schemata (as one supposes it will in the GA) then it will not by this means be reliably led to discover high-fitness high-order schemata.

One way to understand deception is as follows. In a deceptive problem there are different competing schemata in a partition—for example, the 0s kind and the 1s kind. Assembling together one kind of schemata leads to the global optimum, but assembling together the other kind does not. If the kind of low-order schemata that does not lead to the global optimum has a higher schema fitness than the kind that does lead to the global optimum, then we can understand why this would create difficulty for an algorithm that uses the heuristic of assembling together high-fitness low-order schemata.

Often the misleading schemata in deceptive problems are associated semantically with the idea of an arbitrary aberration in fitness contributions. Indeed, it seems unreasonable to suppose that the fitness contributions of low-order schemata will always be reliably informative of their potential to provide high-fitness high-order schemata. However, it would not make sense to entirely abandon the idea that the fitness contributions of schemata are genuinely informative—this is the necessary heuristic of fitness-guided search techniques. Accordingly, there must be some limit on the occurrence of arbitrarily misleading schemata in the problem; this leads to the idea of "bounded difficulty" where schemata up to a certain order k are deceptive but schemata above order k are not; and thus we arrive at the concatenated trap functions.

The ideas of problem difficulty in HIFF are related to these ideas of deception but are different in important respects. HIFF does include the idea of different competing schemata in a partition—specifically, the 0s kind and the 1s kind. However, in HIFF each kind of low-order schemata has the same fitness contribution and assembling together either kind of schemata leads to one of the global optima. In biased HIFF (Watson and Pollack 1999a), the fitness contribution of schemata built from 1s are higher fitness than those built from 0s and the problem therefore has only one global optimum at all 1s. In biased HIFF we might term the 0s schemata as deceptive. However, even in biased HIFF the "misleadingness" of low-order schemata is non-arbitrary in the sense that the fitness of low-order schemata accurately reflects the value of the high-order schemata that they contain. This follows directly from the hierarchical consistency of the construction functions used in HIFF. The idea of hierarchical consistency is intrinsically opposed to the idea of low-order fitness contributions being arbitrarily overruled by high-order fitness contributions as seen in "fully deceptive" problems (Deb and Goldberg 1993).

However, there is a more informative way to look at the misleadingness of low-order schemata in HIFF. Specifically, note that although modules built from 0s and modules built from 1s both confer fitness contributions, and that these always accurately reflect their potential for involvement in high-fitness higher-order schemata, the difficulty arises from the need to search for the correct combination of these modules. Thus, although for example, --00---- and 11------ both confer independent fitness contributions and both include one of the two global optima, the 1100---- schema does not include either of the global optima. Accordingly, we see that the difficulty coming from competing schemata in HIFF does not come from the fact that one kind of schema is "correct" and the other kind of schema is misleading—rather the difficulty comes from the incompatibility of some types of schemata with other types of schemata in the assembly of a complete solution.

In problems including arbitrarily deceptive fitness contributions, a problem is made up of a mixture of "correct" and "incorrect" fitness contributions. However, the idea of schema competition in HIFF is understood more precisely as a mixture of schemata types each of which are *correct in some contexts*. In this way we can acknowledge that when looking for a module to complete a solution it is not the case that any old above-average fitness module will be suitable, otherwise the problem would be trivial. But at the same time we have the idea that the fact that a module has above-average fitness is not accidental or arbitrarily deceptive, but rather is a result of its usefulness in other contexts.

Nearly Decomposable Systems

Herb Simon (1969) presented some important ideas on modularity, hierarchy, and the general structure of many different types of system. It may be valuable to clarify the distinction between Simon's ideas and those presented in this chapter. Simon's basic ideas about hierarchical modularity, interactions based on aggregate effects, and representing interdependency with an almost-diagonalizable matrix, are clearly present in the modular interdependency framework presented in this chapter. Taking a dynamical interpretation of HIFF (see below), Simon's description of the properties of "nearly decomposable systems" given earlier are true of both the continuous HIFF and HIFF. However, I have also built on and clarified some issues that were not so distinct in Simon's work (see also Watson and Pollack 2005).

Let us look at a concrete example of a nearly decomposable system that Simon (1969) provides: a system of heat exchange in a building with a number of rooms each containing a number of cubicles. The heat exchange between cubicles is more rapid than the heat exchange between rooms, and so forth, giving a heat exchange matrix much like the dependency matrix of table 4.4. Unfortunately, this dynamical system has only one attractor—eventually all the variables in the system approach the mean temperature of the initial condition. Let us see what this would mean if we interpret this system as a problem to be optimized. For example, let a candidate solution be a configuration of temperatures, and let the fitness of a configuration be its "stability" or the inverse of its internal heat disequilibrium—specifically, the fitness of a temperature configuration will be the sum of inverse absolute temperature differences between all areas. We may describe this system using the general form of modular interdependency described in equation 4.8, with $t(p,q) = (p+q)/2$ and $f(p,q) = 1/|p-q|$. A simple hill climber or annealer following the local gradients in this function will follow approximately the same trajectories through configuration space that the temperatures would in the physical system. However, the important property to note is that this function has no local optima—there is no configuration of temperatures for which there is no small change in temperature that reduces the energy of the system (increases the fitness of the system). In short, Simon has not described his class of systems in such a way as to distinguish between systems that have easy and difficult interdependencies.

Although Simon describes the interaction between modules as interaction which "depends in only an aggregate way on the behaviour of the other" modules—which is fine—he is not careful to clarify that this interaction may be strong and highly significant. Simon repeatedly refers to the idea that "interactions among the subsystems are weak but not negligible." For example, he refers to "a set of stable subsystems, each operating nearly independently of the detailed processes going on within the other subsystems" (ibid., p. 193) and states that "[i]ntracomponent linkages are generally stronger than intercomponent linkages" (p. 204). This interpretation of "decomposability," approaching what we have termed "separability," is unnecessary. In HIFF the interdependency between modules is strongly nonlinear and highly significant—the modules are not separable—yet they are still easily decomposable.

When decomposability is interpreted as nearly separable it confuses the strength of interactions for the structure of interactions. In short, Simon's concepts take us as far as the aggregate effects depicted in figure 4.5 (c) and used in continuous HIFF, but not as far as new emergent effects and higher-order nonlinearities that are more than the sum of the parts, as depicted in figure 4.5 (d) and used in HIFF.

Thus Simon contributed a significant number of valuable concepts for the ideas developed in this chapter. But the notion of "decomposable but not separable" systems and the concept of "modular interdependency" are more specific concepts than Simon's idea of "nearly decomposable" systems based on the assumption of weak subsystem interaction.

Modularity in Dynamical Systems (e.g., Ising Models)

Most of this chapter has treated a fitness dependency between genes as a static measure. A complementary notion of dependency may be formulated as a dynamic interpretation of state updates in a dynamical system (Variano, McCoy, and Lipson 2004). In this view, instead of interpreting an edge of the graphs like those depicted in figure 4.3, as a direct representation of fitness dependencies, we may for example, interpret an edge as a gene-expression interaction where one gene up-regulates or down-regulates the expression of another. This exactly parallels the relationship between the dynamics of random Boolean networks and the statics of NK landscapes (Kauffman 1993)—see Watson and Pollack 2005.

In the dynamic model, we are interested in the attractors of the system (expression patterns that will be common in the lifetime of the cell) and properties of the system such as the number of attractors in the system, the nature of the attractors (such as fixed point or cyclic), the stability of the attractors (stable or unstable), and the sensitivity of the attractors within the system to the external conditions of the cell's environment. In this analogy we can draw associations between the dynamic properties of the network and the static properties of a fitness landscape built from a similar structure of interdependencies. For example, if the stability of a configuration in the dynamical system is related to high fitness, then the attractors of a dynamical system are optima in the corresponding fitness landscape (Watson and Pollack 2005).

A question that follows from this interpretation is: what are the properties of a dynamical system built on a modular interdependency structure, and how does this relate to the fitness landscape defined on the same modular interdependency structure?

If we translate each edge in the dependency graphs to a state update rule (e.g., $[0,0 \rightarrow 0,0]$, $[1,1 \rightarrow 1,1]$, $[0,1 \rightarrow 0,0 \text{ or } 1,1]$, and $[1,0 \rightarrow 0,0 \text{ or } 1,1]$)[3] then the configurations with high fitness contributions are the stable configurations in the dynamical system, and vice versa. This particular state-update table is that used in Ising models (Cipra 1987). And the energy of a configuration (measuring the number of edges in the graph that connect nodes with unequal states) is a direct measurement of the likelihood of change, and is inversely related to the system's stability. Thus, the energy function of an Ising model with the connectivity structure of HIFF is structurally equivalent to the HIFF fitness function.[4] (See Van Hoyweghen and Naudts 2001 for a discussion of HIFF and Ising models.)

So, to answer the above question, there are strong associations between the dynamics of Ising models built on scale-invariant lattices, and the fitness landscape of systems with modular interdependency like that defined by HIFF. In particular, such a dynamic model has attractors corresponding to the same configurations of states as local optima in HIFF, and the size of the perturbation required to move the system to a more stable configuration is the same as the width of the fitness saddles for that configuration in HIFF. Thus the lowest energy, most stable, configuration of the dynamical model, and the highest fitness configurations of the static model are coincident—that is, all 1s and all 0s. Configurations of intermediate stability, such as where all large subdomains are internally in agreement but not in agreement across subdomains, correspond directly to configurations in HIFF where large modules are fully optimized internally, but intermodule dependencies are not resolved.

Recognizing this equivalence between what started as a hierarchical building-block function and a particular class of Ising models is interesting in itself, but significantly, it also provides access to an extensive repertoire of mathematical treatments and analysis, not least the renormalization group developed by Wilson (1979). The renormalization group is an analytical tool that explicitly abstracts the interdependency of low-level variables into the interdependency of higher-level variables. In scale-invariant lattices, this renormalization results in a higher-level system over aggregate states that is the same as that which described the interaction of the primitive states. And in fact this can be applied recursively. In regular lattices, the high-level model is only accurate when the "temperature" of the system (controlling the likelihood of state changes) is at a particular value—the critical temperature. At this temperature, even regular lattices exhibit interesting scale-invariant phenomena.

Renormalization groups have been enormously successful at describing many types of dynamical systems. The connections between modular interdependency of the type used in HIFF, the dynamics of simple dynamical systems like Ising models, and the ubiquity of systems that are amenable to renormalization group analysis, suggests, loosely, that the type of dynamical systems occurring in many physical systems may, under certain circumstances, exhibit characteristics in common with functions of modular interdependency like those we have defined here.

Finally, it is interesting to note that complex dynamical systems can exhibit modular interdependency in their dynamics when they are spatially distributed in a hierarchical manner and interdependencies are sensitive to distance. For example, consider a hierarchically clustered distribution of communicating agents such as voters in boroughs, cities, and counties. A quite simple tendency to synchronize voting preference with one's geographic neighbors will produce voting patterns with a modular interdependency structure. This follows from direct analogy with the model described by equation 4.5, or equation 4.1 and table 4.4.

Modular Interdependency as a Hierarchical Cooperation Problem

An alternative interpretation of the two-feature epistasis model in section 4.1 is obtained by viewing the two different features as two different players in a symmetrical two-player game, and the feature values as their possible strategies. In this view, the fitness contributions become the values of a pay-off matrix, and the salient characteristic of case 3, interdependency, is that the optimal strategy for player one is dependent on the behavior of player two and vice versa. The epistasis model we arrive at using (p IFF q) is analogous to the "mutual benefit" matrix from Maynard Smith and Szathmary (1995, p. 262), but here there is not yet any distinction between the two attractors of the system, that is, which of 1 or 0 is the "defect" strategy and which is the "cooperate" strategy, because we assign them equal value.

As we recursively reapply the two-feature model we apply the two-player matrix in a recursive fashion to define a four-player game (table 4.2). Note that now, in the context of (00), (11) is a "defect–defect" result for the other module, because it is in their selfish interest for each player not to change from this strategy, but if they both changed to (00), this would provide a higher payoff. Conversely, in the context of (11), (00) is "defect–defect" and (11) is "cooperate–cooperate." In other words, whether a strategy provides mutual benefit or not depends on the context in which the game is played.

Thus HIFF describes a hierarchical cooperate–defect game. The nature of the payoff values is such that maximizing the payoff for all (e.g., 128) players is achieved when two subgroups (of 64) players are compatible. Other attractors in the evolutionary game occur when particular subsets of players are compatible intragroup but not intergroup. Accordingly, optimizing HIFF requires the induction of hierarchical cooperation. The payoff values at every level of resolution help to identify good combinations of strategies—but, which of the two optima at every level is best does not become clear until the context of other players is stabilized. HIFF deliberately dissolves the distinction between epistasis (the interdependency of genes within

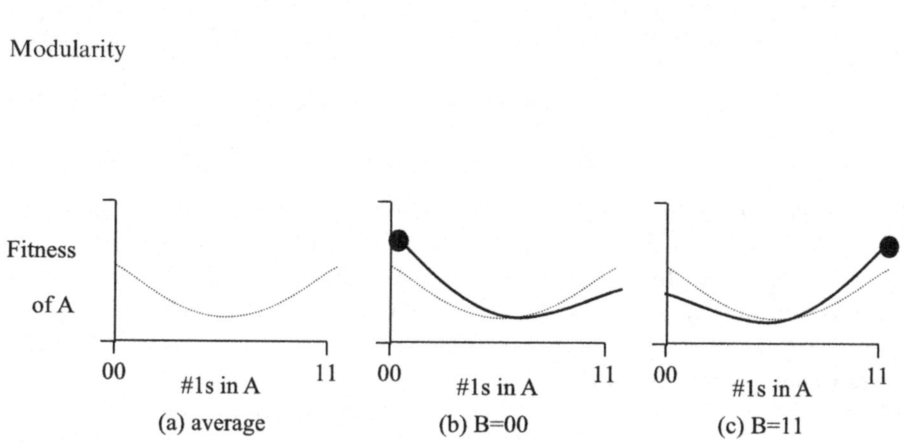

Figure 4.10
The fitness landscape of A, for different configurations of B.

an individual) and multiplayer evolutionary games (the interdependency of features of one entity with those of another) as is required from a model incorporating composition and the resultant changes in the unit of selection.

How Changes in One Module Affect the Fitness Landscape for Another

Returning to our four-variable, two-module example system (equation 4.1, table 4.2, fig. 4.3), let us consider the adaptation of the two modules, A and B, as though each module were being evolved semi-independently on separate but coupled fitness landscapes. The fitness of the system for different configurations of A, in the context of different configurations of B is shown in figure 4.10. Each figure shows the fitness for module A when in different configurations, specifically (00), (01)/(10), (11): (a) the fitness of A averaged over all configurations of B; (b) the fitness of A when $B = (00)$ is shown in the solid curve, and the optimal configuration of $A = (00)$ is indicated by the dot; and (c) the fitness of A when $B = (11)$ is shown in the solid curve—note that the optimal configuration of A has moved to (11).

This figure shows that the fitness landscape of A changes radically in some respects as B changes configuration—specifically, the optimal configuration of A when $B = (00)$ is the complete opposite of the optimal configuration of A when $B = (11)$. So, an entity evolving the values of A would find itself in a landscape that is radically dependent on the evolution of B. However, note that in other respects, A's fitness landscape is insensitive to the configuration of B—specifically, in respect of the configurations of A that are *not* optimal, that is, (01) and (10) are the same regardless of B. This is the property of modular interdependency that makes it amenable to dimensional reduction and thereby easy for a mechanism that can manipulate modules yet difficult for gradual mechanisms.

The notion of removing inferior configurations from further consideration is allied to the notion of focusing on "noninferior" configurations (Van Hoyweghen, Goldberg, and Naudts 2001a). But, as we see here, it is not the fact that (01) and (10) are not one of the equally good configurations that makes them undesirable, it is the fact that *there is no context* in which either (01) or (10) are the best configuration that makes them undesirable. Indeed, it is not necessary that (00) and (11) be assigned equal fitness contributions—see "biased HIFF" (Watson and Pollack 1999a).

Relation to Philosophical Provisos

Notice from the above observations that the fitness landscape resulting from modular interdependency is not wholly incompatible with the notion that an organism's fitness landscape is radically dependent on the state of its environment. In section 3.3 we introduced the perspective of compositional mechanisms as the coevolution of modules, and this is a view that we will be developing further in the compositional models that follow. In this perspective the particular adaptive landscape presented to an organism at any one point in time is some *subspace* of the landscape, and although the landscape as a whole is fixed, the subspace occupied by a particular entity is radically dependent on the state of other evolving entities at that time. Moreover, we will not predefine what roles or niches an entity is allocated—that is, we do not predetermine what subspace of the landscape an entity will reside in. Thus within the fixed constraints that the fitness function defines, niches are created and destroyed dynamically, and the shape and therefore properties of the niche for a given organism are not predefined.

4.6 Summary

The aim of this chapter has been to identify the properties of a system that make it difficult for gradual evolution and yet amenable to compositional evolution. I identified a class of system that has strong and difficult epistasis between variables, but also a highly modular structure that makes it in principle amenable to decomposition.

I reviewed some well-known test problems that have been used in the GA literature and suggested that, in large part, the inability to clearly demonstrate a GA performing composition of schemata is due to inadequacies in our understanding of modules.

Starting by examining the characteristics that are difficult for gradual change in pairwise interactions (systems of two variables) I defined the difficult type of epistasis as *interdependency*. I then distinguished the concepts of *separable* and *decomposable*, and crucially, showed that systems that are meaningfully modular do not need to have modules that are separable. Accordingly I can define an example system of four variables that is decomposable into two modules that are strongly interdependent and therefore not separable.

By scaling up this structure, in a hierarchically consistent fashion, I can create arbitrarily large systems of variables that form hierarchical modular interdependency. I defined one form of such a system several different ways so that we could see what was important about it—what features created difficulty for gradualism, and its relationship to concepts like aggregate effects and the nearly decomposable systems of Simon. I then defined a simple example of the class, hierarchical-if-and-only-if, HIFF, that will suffice for illustrating the class in the coming simulations. The property of scale invariance coming from the underlying hierarchical consistency in this function will be useful in simplifying formal analyses. The discussion highlighted that there are many features of this kind of system that resonate with existing work, especially in evolutionary computation, but also that there are important differences in all cases.

Physiological modularity, including hierarchical modularity, is a familiar and intuitive concept in biological systems: from proteins, to cells, to organs, to organisms (Raff 1996). However, the kind of modularity that is relevant for the arguments in this book is modularity in the structure of epistatic dependencies between different parts of the genetic material. Exactly how physiological structure and epistatic structure correspond is not well understood (see section 10.7)—and in general it is very difficult to measure the details of large-scale epistatic structure in biological systems. However, recent empirical studies suggest the presence of epistatic modularity and hierarchical epistatic modularity, and suggest that epistasis between (as well as within) complexes of genes is apparent (Segre et al. 2005; Hallinan 2004; Ravasz et al. 2002). It is also notable that genetic material is physically parceled into codons, exons, genes, and chromosomes, providing several hierarchical levels of modularity in physical linkage. In this chapter I have clearly not attempted to describe any specific biological system. Instead what I have given is a formal definition of a type of modularity that matches with intuitive concepts of modularity, and provided an idealized abstract example. This example is designed to exaggerate the distinction between the abilities of gradual and compositional evolution as clearly as possible—HIFF is as easy as possible for compositional evolution while being pathologically difficult for gradual evolution. This will serve to demonstrate that the gradualist framework of evolution is not comprehensive. Realistic biological modularity (see Callebaut and Rasskin-Gutman 2005) will of course be a lot messier, but so long as it has some level of modular interdependency, compositional mechanisms may be able to exploit this in a way that gradual mechanisms cannot. In the next three chapters I examine the ability of adaptive processes based on mutation, sexual recombination, and symbiotic encapsulation on this example system.

5 Mutation

In this chapter I assess the difficulty of evolving hierarchically modular complex systems using evolutionary processes based on variation from mutation. Specifically, I assess the properties of the hierarchical IFF system, defined in the previous chapter. In particular, I look at the fitness landscape characteristics that are generally deemed problematic for evolution—the number of local optima, the separation of local optima, or width of fitness saddles, and the irreducibility of high-fitness configurations—and assess the properties of HIFF with respect to these characteristics. I then show results for simulations of evolution using only mutation on HIFF to illustrate its adaptive difficulty for gradual evolution.

5.1 Examining the Fitness Landscape

In both HIFF (equation 4.7) and the continuous version of HIFF (equation 4.5), the maximum fitness configurations for the system, and for every module it contains, are those where the states of all the variables are equal—that is, for binary variables, the configurations with all 0s and all 1s. The second-best fitness configurations are those where all the biggest modules of the system are "correct" (i.e., either all 0s and all 1s) but where one of them does not agree with the other(s). For systems where the span, the number of submodules per module, is 2, these second-best configurations are half 0s followed by half 1s, or conversely, half 1s followed by half 0s. Similarly, lower-fitness configurations occur when $N/4$-sized modules are correct but one of them is incompatible with the others, and so on. The cross sections through the resultant fitness landscapes shown in figure 4.6 and figure 4.8 reveal the resultant fractal structure of the landscape.

A system having a large number of variables creates a fitness landscape that is multidimensional, but since these systems are highly regular and symmetric, a single cross section through the landscape, interpreted with some care, can give us a reasonable intuition about some of its important properties. The cross sections shown in these figures are carefully chosen to reveal salient properties of the landscape. Consecutive points in this series are separated by Hamming distance 1, that is, one-point mutations, and the section can be imagined as a particular one-point mutation walk across the fitness landscape from one global optima at all 0s to the other at all 1s, defined by the process in figure 5.1. There are exactly $N + 1$ points in this walk. For many of the points there are many others with equal fitness: for example, the first mutation will have an equal effect regardless of which locus it occurs at. Accordingly, the sequence defined by 1^k0^{N-k} for $k = 0$ to $k = N$ is only one of many possible walks that would traverse through points of exactly the same fitnesses.

1. Start at one global optimum.
2. Of all one-point mutations at bit positions that have not yet been mutated, mutate one (of those) that has highest fitness (even if it is lower in fitness than the current point).
3. Go to 2.

Figure 5.1
Ridge mutation walker.

One useful characteristic of this cross section is that it accurately portrays the Hamming distance from each point to the nearest points with equal or higher fitness. For example, the distance of one peak to the nearest equal or higher peak corresponds accurately to the values we calculated in the "Hamming" column of table 4.3. Thus this cross section gives us a clear intuition about the width of fitness saddles in the landscape, and some ideas about its ruggedness and the number of local optima. In particular, as is clear from the construction of the functions, at each hierarchical level of modules, the hamming distance to the next-best configuration doubles, that is, the number of state variables that must flip states simultaneously is equal to the size of the module, and this doubles at each hierarchical level. This is exactly the intent of the functions—to describe large systems of variables that are difficult for gradual mechanisms that can only accumulate random changes linearly.

The continuous landscape has the same number of local optima as HIFF at the same configurations as those in HIFF, and therefore the separation of local optima is also the same as HIFF. (However, the fitness values of different configurations are different.)

The cross sections in figure 4.6 and figure 4.8 are useful in developing an intuition for why these landscapes are difficult for gradual evolution, but below I analyze the characteristics of this landscape in more detail.

5.2 Difficulty of Modular Interdependency for Gradual Mechanisms

Here I examine the characteristics of systems with modular interdependency with respect to the concepts of evolutionary difficulty discussed earlier (section 2.3), specifically:

Ruggedness: The number of local optima.

Width of fitness saddles: The Hamming distance between a configuration and the nearest configuration with equal or higher fitness.

Irreducibility: Whether the system "ceases to function" under any small change.

These characteristics together tell us about whether there exists a path of monotonically increasing fitness from all points to the global optima, and more generally, the likelihood of finding such a path between a random configuration and a high-fitness configuration.

Figure 4.8 indicates the large number of local optima, the separation of the two global optima shown at opposite extremes of the curve, and the width of fitness saddles in general. It also shows that the high-fitness points are adjacent to low-fitness points such that any small change in these configurations is catastrophically deleterious. These properties are quantified below.

Ruggedness
The actual number of local optima in a landscape is intimately related to the number of variables that an algorithm can change in one go, as it were. To a single-bit mutation hill climber for example, HIFF will have more optima than for a two-bit mutation hill climber. In HIFF, a single-bit mutation hill climber (or any algorithm that can change at most one variable at a time) has $2^{N/2}$ local optima (where N is the size of the problem in bits), only two of which are globally optimal.

More generally, any string made by concatenating h-sized correct blocks requires a change of at least h bits to find a fitter configuration in HIFF. Such a string therefore cannot be improved by a k-bit mutation algorithm where $h > k$. There are $2^{(N/h)}$ possible strings of such concatenations. Thus a k-bit mutation hill climber will be faced with $2^{(N/h)}$ local optima, where h is the smallest integer power of 2 that is greater than k, that is, $h = 2^p > k$, $p \in \mathbb{Z}^+$. In short, HIFF has a number of local optima that is exponential in the size of the problem for any given mutation radius.

Width of Fitness Saddles
Since HIFF has many local optima it also has many fitness saddles, but to properly understand the difficulty of the problem we also need to know the widths of these fitness saddles. From our examination of local optima above we see that HIFF has $2^{N/2}$ saddles of width 2, and $2^{N/k}$ fitness saddles of width k. That is, there are $2^{N/k}$ configurations of the system for which the nearest configuration with equal or higher fitness differs in the setting of k variables. Put another way, there are $2^{N/k}$ configurations of the system for which all other configurations with equal or higher fitness differ in the setting of at least k variables. In short, the width of fitness saddle from a point to the nearest point of equal or higher fitness increases with the fitness of the point.

Another characteristic we may be interested in is the size of the "basin" for an optima. For example, for a k-bit mutation hill climber, how many different (starting) configurations are there from which this hill climber will be able to reach one of the global optima? For a 1-bit hill climber, the proportion of the space from which one of the global optima can be reached is $P_1 = 2N/2^N$ (there are N configurations 1 bit away from each global optimum, 2^N points in total in the space, and 2 global optima). In general, for increasing mutation rates, as the width of saddle that can be jumped increases, the size of the basin of the optima increases exponentially. However, note that for mutation, the expected time to make a specific jump of a given size also increases exponentially with the size of the jump.

It is essential to recognize that these restrictions apply not just to low mutation rates but to all mutation rates. In fact, they also apply to any method of undirected, random change; for example, genetic drift (Wright 1977), or neutral changes introduced by the addition of arbitrary neutral networks in the landscape. See Shackleton et al. 2000, Shipman et al. 2000, and Ebner, Shackleton, and Shipman 2001, for experiments on the addition of neutral mappings to functions including HIFF, and see Knowles and Watson 2002 for experiments showing that algorithmically this performance is no better than increased mutation. See also Knowles, Watson, and Corne 2001 for experiments using simulated annealing on HIFF. In previous work (Watson, Hornby, and Pollack 1998), we also showed that HIFF is not amenable to macromutation and passes the "headless chicken test" (Jones 1995), that is, using crossover but crossing one parent with a random string does not solve large HIFF problems efficiently.

Of course, a method that has some *a priori* bias, for example, one that tends to explore the complement of fit strings, may perform very well on HIFF (in fact, this particular bias is useful in later discussion). But, any method of increasing the exploration ability of an algorithm *arbitrarily* does not help in solving HIFF—that is, any method using a linear accumulation of random undirected variation is incapable of exploiting the decomposability of the landscape.

Irreducibility

According to Behe, a system is irreducibly complex if any small change in the configuration of the system causes it to "cease functioning." In HIFF, each module is "correct" only when all of the variables it contains are in mutual agreement (all 0s or all 1s). If we take a configuration at one of the global optima in HIFF and change the state of one variable, then we "break" the fitness contribution conferred by the agreement of the two largest modules, and the fitness contribution conferred by the agreement of the two largest modules within the half we changed, and within the quarter, and so on. In other words, we lose the fitness contribution from one module of each size at each level in the hierarchy. Arguably, this reasonably constitutes a cessation of function of the system as a whole. Certainly, the system does not degrade gracefully under small perturbations. Continuous HIFF differs from HIFF in this respect—because the interaction between large modules in continuous HIFF is by degrees and not "all or nothing," a small change in a module necessarily produces a smaller fitness change than it does in HIFF. This distinction in the effects on fitness derives from the distinction between, on the one hand, modular interdependency built from the aggregation of pairwise dependencies, and on the other, modular interdependency coming from the high-level interaction of new emergent properties.

A cessation of function should be quantifiably related to a decrease in fitness. The exact decrease in fitness will depend on the scaling of the weighted contributions from one level of module to another. In HIFF, each correct module has a fitness contribution equal to its size (the number of variables it contains) so a one-bit mutation from a global optimum results in a decrease in fitness of $N + N/2 + N/4 + N/8 + \cdots + 4 + 2 = 2N - 2$. Let us look at this decrease in fitness in comparison to the range of fitnesses in HIFF, and then compare the change in fitness to the size of the genetic change that produced it. The minimum fitness value in HIFF is:

N—e.g., coming from the string 010101....

The maximum fitness value in HIFF is:

$N(\log_2 N + 1)$—e.g., the fitness of the string 00000 ..., which has all modules at all levels correct, is $N + 2(N/2) + 4(N/4) + \cdots + N(N/N) = N(\log_2 N + 1)$.

Thus the range of fitness values in HIFF is:

$N(\log_2 N + 1) - N = N \log_2 N$.

Any one-bit mutation from a global optimum results in a decrease in fitness of:

$N + N/2 + N/4 + N/8 + \cdots + 4 + 2 = 2N - 2$.

The ratio of the change in fitness from any single-point mutation from a global optimum in HIFF is therefore:

$(2N - 2)/N\log_2 N \approx 2/\log_2 N$.[1]

I will call this the "relative change in fitness." (Notice that this measure is insensitive to a linear scaling of fitness values.)

The ratio of the change in *genotype* from a single-point mutation to the size of the genotype is:

$1/N$

I will call this the "relative change in genotype."

So, the relative change in fitness caused by a one-point mutation from a global optimum (or any fully correct module) is, $2/\log_2 N$, whereas the relative change in genotype is, $1/N$. For large N, the relative change in fitness is therefore very much greater than the relative change in genotype.

Thus, a small change from a high fitness point in HIFF "breaks" at least one module of all sizes, and by the above criteria, is significantly deleterious. Therefore we might conclude that by this criteria quantifying the magnitude of the fitness decrease with respect to the magnitude of the genotypic change that produced it, a high-fitness point in HIFF is indeed irreducibly complex. Nonetheless, a system that ceases to function under any small change is not necessarily unevolvable. And although HIFF is not reducible into small parts, it is reducible into large parts.

Sampling Epistasis

Although epistatic dependencies are observed in some biological systems, it is also observed that most of the fitness effects from allelic changes in biological systems can be accounted for by their independent, nonepistatic, components. Thus, it might seem that the emphasis on strong epistatic dependencies shown by the HIFF landscape is biologically unrealistic but, in fact, HIFF is compatible with these observations. When a set of genes is well optimized in HIFF, any single allelic change is catastrophically deleterious, as I analyzed above. Moreover, no pairwise interactions, no second single-point mutation, can recover any significant positive benefit relative to the deleterious effect of the first mutation. So, it might appear from these observations that HIFF has weak epistatic interactions because most of the change in fitness can be accounted for by the independent fitness effects of alleles.

However, this is not the case. In fact, the independent effects of genes account for none of the fitness changes—when averaged over *all* possible genetic contexts, every allele (at every locus) is equally valuable in HIFF (0s confer the same fitness contributions as 1s). The apparent weakness of epistatic dependencies results from measuring only pairwise (or small group) interactions on a configuration of genes that have been optimized to a high level—as may be the case for simultaneously segregating polymorphisms in a natural population at equilibrium. At this level, pairwise interactions are not sufficient to exhibit large fitness effects—but such epistatic effects are available through the interaction of large modules. Sampling combinations of arbitrary pairs of mutations cannot hope to accurately reflect the epistatic interactions inherent in the macroscale structure of a natural fitness landscape.

So, a well-optimized configuration of features in HIFF appears to be irreducibly complex because any small genetic change is catastrophic, causing the system to "fall off" its needle in the fitness landscape. However, although the adaptive problem cannot be reduced to the additive effects of individual genes, it can be decomposed into the large modular subsystems of which it is composed.

5.3 Expected Time to Solution for Gradual Mechanisms

The previous section indicates that HIFF has all the properties listed previously that are usually associated with evolutionary difficulty under the assumptions of the gradualist framework of evolution. In this section, I address the expected time to solution for gradual mechanisms. By the definition of a gradual evolutionary process used here, new genetic material that is introduced to produce an offspring genotype is not preadapted elsewhere and is therefore entirely random and undirected. An algorithmic analysis for this framework based on stochastic mutation hill climbing therefore provides a lower bound for gradual evolution. Other features of population-based stochastic search familiar in evolutionary models do not change these analyses. For example, using a population of candidate solutions instead of a single candidate solution, or fitness-proportionate selection rather than strict hill climbing, do not allow directed exploration that can take advantage of the landscape structure.

Using the notion of a path to solution and the expected time for steps on this path, we may reasonably say that an algorithm is *not* reliably successful on a problem if any of the following conditions are true:

- there is no guaranteed path to solution,
- the path to solution is exponentially long, or
- any step on the path takes exponential time.

For a single-bit mutation hill climber there is no guaranteed path on HIFF. HIFF has $2^{N/2}$ local optima under single-bit mutation (where N is the size of the problem in bits), only two of which are globally optimal. More generally, a k-bit mutation hill climber will be faced with $2^{(N/h)}$ local optima, where h is the smallest integer power of 2 which is greater than k, that is, $h = 2^p > k$. A random mutation hill climber (RMHC) (Forrest and Mitchell 1993a) mutates every bit with a given probability μ. In principle no problem can have a local optimum under this operator since the probability of moving from any point to any other point is nonzero. However, consider the case where the current string is $N/2$ 0s followed by $N/2$ 1s. The only string fitter is the global optimum at all 1s or all 0s. To achieve this jump, mutation must flip $N/2$ bits while keeping $N/2$ undisrupted. The best mutation rate to achieve this is $\mu = 0.5$ and this gives an expected time for the step that is 2^N—so search with RMHC cannot be guaranteed to find the optimum with probability better than random guessing.

A macromutation hill climber (MMHC) (Jones 1995) has the best chance of success of all mutation-based hill climbers. MMHC chooses two delimiting loci and randomizes the loci between them, thus concentrating mutations on a particular substring while leaving the remainder untouched. This algorithm has an advantage over other mechanisms because it explicitly uses the assumption of tight genetic linkage. Nonetheless, to escape from the next-best optima to either global optimum it must choose the correct delimiting loci—which has probability $1/N(N-1)$ (this allows macromutations both inside and outside the chosen points)—and it must also assign all 1s (or all 0s) to $N/2$ bits. This occurs in expected time $O(N^2 2^{N/2})$.[2] The critical feature of this function is that it includes a factor that is exponential in something proportional to N and thus quickly becomes infeasible for large N.

Thus we see that by these criteria, all these mutation-based hill climbers either have no guaranteed path to the optimum, or cannot be guaranteed to take a step on the path in less than exponential time. This gives a lower bound for the ability of gradual evolution to find high-fitness configurations in this system. In short, the time required for gradual evolution to find high-fitness configurations of this kind of complex system increases exponentially with the size of the system. A complexity analysis of this sort provides a quantifiable meaning for *unevolvability*—that is, if an evolutionary process cannot find high-fitness configurations of a system in time less than exponential in the number of system variables, then this system can be considered unevolvable. This fits nicely with our intuitive notions of evolutionary difficulty, since in this case, this kind of complex system exhibits all of the characteristics of evolutionary difficulty identified previously.

Preliminary Comparison with Compositional Mechanisms

I will not provide a detailed analysis of the expected time to solution for a compositional mechanism until after I have detailed a specific compositional mechanism. But for now, it is worth emphasizing that although HIFF is very difficult for gradual evolution, it is decomposable into a small number of more manageable problems and is thereby easily solvable *if* this decomposition is known or can be discovered, and *if* the search mechanism can manipulate modules as wholes.

Specifically, in HIFF, for any module A of any size, the maximal set of A will contain only configurations that are some combination of configurations from the maximal sets of the submodules it contains. That is, if A contains submodules B

and C, then all members of M_A will be some combination of members of M_B and M_C. Thus, finding M_A requires searching at most only $|M_B| \times |M_C|$ configurations. In HIFF, $|M| = 2$ for any module at any level in the hierarchy, so finding M_A given M_B and M_C requires testing only four configurations regardless of the size of the module. At the hth level in the hierarchy (where the level of primitive variables is the 0th level), there are $2^{(H-h)}$ modules where $H = \log_2 N$ and $0 < h < H$. The total number of modules to be found over all levels is thus $2(N - 1)$, and each of these can be found in four combinations of the modules from the previous level. The total number of combinations of submodules that need to be searched to find the solutions to all modules in the problem is thus $8(N - 1)$, and therefore, in principle, the maximum number of configurations that need to be tested to find a global optimum is only $8(N - 1)$.

In summary, if the decomposition of the problem is known and we have a mechanism that can identify the set M for a module, and swap in and swap out different members of M_B and M_C as whole units, then the number of configurations that needs to be searched in HIFF is less than $8N$. In contrast, as we have seen above, gradual mechanisms require the testing of a number of configurations exponential in N. Even if a gradual mechanism "knew" the decomposition of the system and could focus mutations on modules that were suboptimal, a gradual mechanism would still require $2^{N/2}$ guesses to find the solution to the largest submodules, since progress on sub-submodules cannot be used to inform mutational changes.

This illustrates the broad margin of difference that might be possible between gradual and compositional mechanisms. But in order to vindicate the adaptive capability of compositional mechanisms it will be necessary to show that a compositional mechanism can discover the problem structure and manipulate modules effectively. The model of evolution using sexual recombination in the next chapter shows that if the problem structure is given in the ordering of the genes then it can manipulate modules effectively, but otherwise it performs similarly to evolution with mutation. The model of evolution using symbiotic encapsulation in chapter 7 is not given any information about the location of modules in the problem and is able to discover modules automatically and manipulate them effectively. Before examining these compositional mechanisms, the remainder of this chapter examines the behavior of evolution using only mutation to illustrate the behavior of gradual evolution.

5.4 Simulation Results for Mutation

Random mutation hill climbing (RMHC) repeatedly applies mutation to the features of a single binary string (a fully specified feature set) and accepts a variant if

1. Initialize S to a random genotype, i.e., a random binary string of length N.
2. Generate S' by applying spontaneous point mutations at each locus, i.e., copy S into S', then for each bit position in S', with probability *mut*, replace this bit with a new random allele drawn with equal probability from $\{0,1\}$.
3. If *fitness* (S') $\geq$ *fitness* (S) then let $S = S'$ (otherwise discard S').
4. Go to 2.

Figure 5.2
Random mutation hill climber: a hill-climbing algorithm that seeks fitness improvements from random mutations applied to a single individual.

it is fitter (Forrest and Mitchell 1993a); see figure 5.2. This is also known as a "$(1+1)EA$"—that is, an evolutionary algorithm that selects the fittest individual from a set of one individual plus one mutant individual (Muhlenbein 1992).

The following simulation experiments were conducted with various mutation rates (that is, the probability of assigning a new random value $\{0,1\}$ to each bit)—specifically, $mut = 1/N, 2/N, 4/N, 6/N, 8/N, 12/N, 16/N, 24/N, 32/N$, and $40/N$. ($N = 128$.) $1/N$ is a fairly standard mutation rate for GAs—producing on average one mutation per individual per generation. (Note that since this is a mutation to a new random allele, rather than a bit-flip mutation, there is a 0.5 probability that a new random allele is different from the existing allele it replaces.) Although it is not quite random search ($mut = 1$), $mut = 40/N = 0.31$ is a ridiculously high mutation rate. However, the point here is to demonstrate that not even high mutation rates help.

Simulation results using the RMHC algorithm (figure 5.2) are shown in figure 5.3. Figure 5.4 shows the same experiments as figure 5.3, but curves show the size of the largest fully optimized module discovered (in the past 2000 evaluations) rather than fitnesses. Since the scaling of fitness values is rather arbitrary, the size of the largest module discovered is more informative for most purposes and I shall use this data to illustrate the results of simulations for all of the following simulation experiments.

Both figures show that a hill climber does not perform well in evolving this type of complex system. For comparison, the models in chapters 6 and 7 succeed in fully optimizing the largest possible module (128 bits) with a fitness of 1024 (the maximum possible). As per the intuitions drawn from the landscape cross sections (figure 4.8), the reasoning about the difficulty of systems with modular interdependency discussed in section 5.1, and the analysis in section 5.3, gradual evolution does not find high-fitness configurations, or large, properly optimized modules, regardless of the mutation rate used.

The highest and lowest mutation rates perform worst. Low mutation rates are obviously unable to get off the local optima in the fitness surface. High mutation

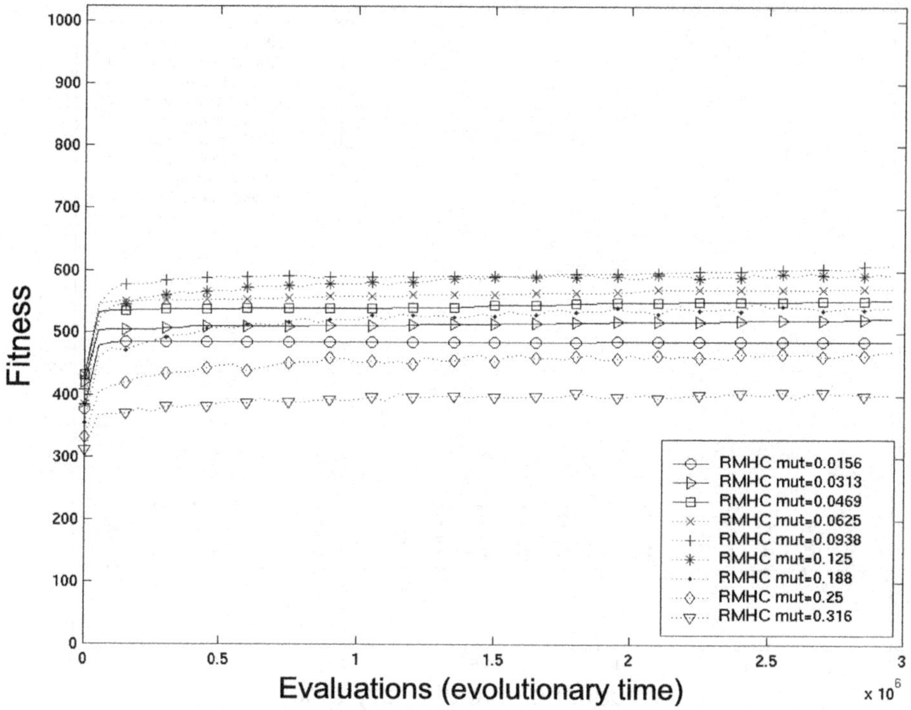

Figure 5.3
Results of mutation-based evolution on a decomposable system. Simulations using the random mutation hill climber, or the "$(1+1)$ evolutionary algorithm," applied to HIFF (equation 4.7). Curves show the average fitness of all individuals measured in the last 2,000 evaluations. Several curves are shown for different mutation rates as listed above. The maximum fitness value possible in this fitness landscape is 1,024. The maximum number of evaluations permitted (duration of simulation) is $3 \cdot 10^6$.

rates have a nonzero probability of discovering a genotype with higher fitness or even one of the global optima at any time, but high mutation rates are unable to make the jumps required because the specific genotype required for a fitness improvement is one of only a few in an exponentially large number of possible genotypes sampled by high mutation rates. Accordingly, the simulations show flat performance curves where, after the initial improvement, the expected waiting time for subsequent fitness improvements is exponential in N (section 5.3). The experiments show that a mutation rate in the middle of the range tested does best (although not well): $mut = 8/128 = 0.0938$ finds the biggest blocks. This reflects a trade-off between finding new mutations that are good and not messing up existing genetic material that is already good. The curve for this mutation rate is also shown in the summary figure

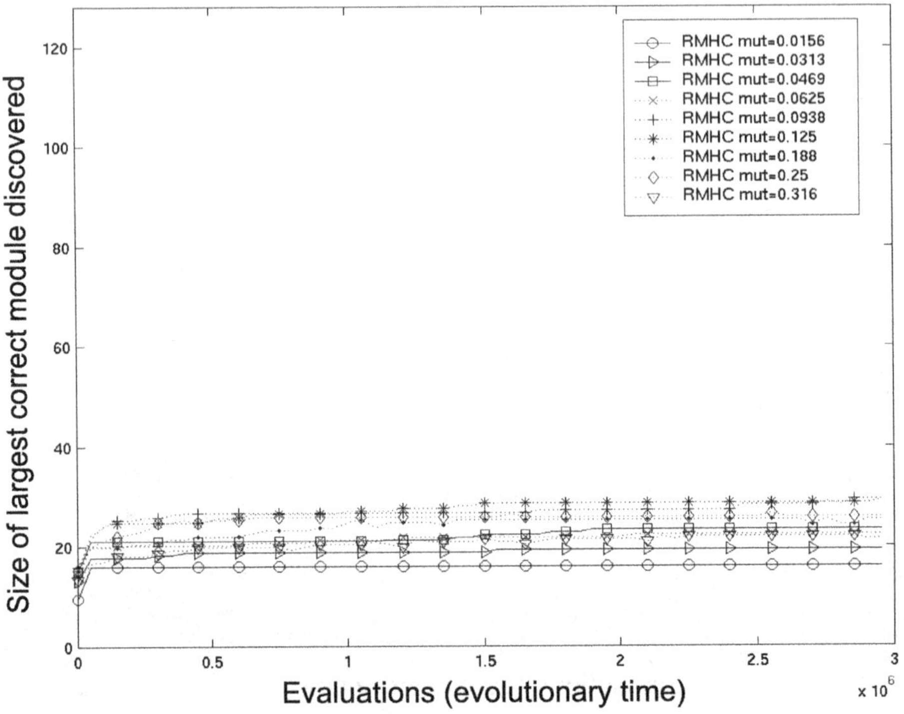

Figure 5.4
Results of mutation-based evolution on a decomposable system. The same simulation experiments as figure 5.3 but with curves showing the size of the largest fully optimized module discovered in the past 2,000 evaluations instead of fitness.

later (section 6.6). Oates and Corne (2001) provide an extensive investigation of the mutation landscape for HIFF, and the behavior of the GA on HIFF with small populations.

5.5 Summary

In this chapter we assessed the difficulty of HIFF for evolutionary processes based on mutation. I examined the properties of the landscape that are normally considered difficult for evolution coming from the assumptions of the gradualist framework. HIFF has the following properties:

- The number of local optima (for mutation-based algorithms) is exponential in N (N = number of variables in system).

- The width of fitness saddles is a linear function of N, i.e., fitness saddles of all sizes up to $N/2$ exist in the landscape. Therefore, no constant mutation radius is sufficient to solve HIFF in general.
- High-fitness configurations of the system appear to be irreducibly complex—i.e., any small change is catastrophically deleterious.
- There is no guaranteed path of small changes conferring monotonically increasing fitness that approaches the high-fitness optima in the landscape.

Accordingly, HIFF exhibits all these features of evolutionary difficulty.

A simple analytic examination shows that a mutation-based algorithm cannot be guaranteed to succeed in time less than exponential in N. This also holds for any algorithm using undirected exploration such as genetic drift (from stochastic sampling error), or neutral walks in redundant encodings. In other words, algorithms that linearly accumulate arbitrary variation cannot, by reasonable definitions, solve HIFF in less than exponential time.

Simulations of a simple mutational algorithm, RMHC, illustrate the performance of mutational mechanisms on HIFF. This provides an illustration of gradual evolution on this class of modular system. The simulations use a mutation hill climber rather than a population, but the point of these simulations is to show that if evolution is nothing more than a hill-climbing process it is unable to evolve modular systems of this type. If the variation generated in an evolving population is generated by spontaneous point mutation, then even if it could use any mutation rate, and even if this was coupled with some magical safeguard that prevented the fittest member of the population from being lost even under high mutation rates (as is the nature of a hill climber), an evolving population cannot be guaranteed to find high-fitness configurations of these modular systems in time less than exponential in the size of the system. Random variation is simply unable to make the specific large genetic changes that are required to escape from the many isolated fitness peaks in the landscape.

In short, this kind of modular system is unevolvable under the gradualist framework of evolution. In the next chapter we will investigate the operation of sexual recombination on HIFF and this will identify conditions where sex can provide compositional evolution and take us beyond the gradualist framework.

6 Sexual Recombination

In this chapter I examine the adaptive capabilities of an evolving population with sexual recombination on the class of modular interdependency systems defined previously. In particular, I use the hierarchical-if-and-only-if function, equation 4.7, to define the epistatic dependencies of genes and the corresponding adaptive landscape. From the prior analysis we know that this problem is difficult for mutation but we also know that it is, in principle, amenable to hierarchical decomposition. The question of this chapter then, is whether there are circumstances where an evolving population using variation by sexual recombination is able to exploit this decomposable structure by discovering and manipulating modules and submodules appropriately to assemble a high-fitness configuration for the system.

I use a simple computational simulation, the genetic algorithm (GA), to investigate this question. The GA models a population of individuals and each individual is represented by a single haploid chromosome. It should be noted that a haploid representation is used for simplicity but in nature sexual populations are diploid—having two sets of homologous chromosomes. For the purpose of the question addressed here—whether sexual recombination allows large nonrandom genetic changes that are adaptive in this problem class—a haploid representation is sufficient. If we want to interpret the simulations as a population of diploid individuals we may imagine that selection is applied only on the haploid part of the life cycle.

Each haploid chromosome is represented simply as a binary string of "genes"—that is, there are two alleles for each locus. Each gene represents the state of one variable in the HIFF problem. Thus each individual represents a complete state specification for the whole interdependent system of variables, or in engineering terms, a "candidate solution" for the "problem." The fitness of each individual is given by the HIFF function.

Our intuition, following that of previous GA researchers (see the discussion of the building-block hypothesis in section 3.2), is that different members of the population will discover different modules, and that recombination between individuals will be able to search combinations of modules to find larger modules, and so on. We find that with the use of HIFF we can clearly illustrate when this process is possible and when it fails. In particular, we find that appropriate diversity and appropriate gene ordering with strong genetic linkage, are required for effective recombination.

The following sections explore some different varieties of the GA that vary in the respects of the selection scheme and the variation operators. These different selection schemes will affect the diversity of the population: the basic form models a single panmictic (freely mixed) population; the more sophisticated form models a particular kind of population subdivision based on removing competition between dissimilar types. The variation mechanism of interest in this chapter is sexual recombination, often referred to simply as "crossover" in the GA literature. Different assumptions about the recombination mechanism have different effects on physical linkage. In particular, if we assume that linkage is weak (crossover points are numerous) then subsets of genes cannot be exchanged between individuals as wholes, that is, no particular subsets of genes from a parent are more likely to appear in the offspring than any other subset. And even if physical linkage is strong, the appropriateness of exchanging gene subsets between individuals depends on the correspondence between gene ordering (proximity on the chromosome) and epistatic dependency. In other words, weak linkage and/or poorly organized linkage are problematic for crossover. Crossover only works when physical linkage is "tight"—that is, strong and appropriately ordered.

The following simulations show that a population with the appropriate mechanisms to support diversity, and the appropriate assumptions about physical linkage, is able to solve HIFF easily. This demonstrates that under these circumstances, an evolving population with sexual recombination can compose modules to find successively larger subsystems of genes, and eventually find the globally optimal configurations for the genes. It is thus the first example of a compositional mechanism in these simulations. Chapter 8 provides an analysis, based on simplified conditions, that shows an expected time to solution that is polynomial in the size of the system.

However, these experiments equally show that there are conditions under which sexual recombination performs no better than mutation on this problem class. We can see that a single freely mixed population, or a recombination mechanism with weak linkage, or a linkage arrangement that does not correspond with epistatic dependencies, will each cause the compositional process to fail. In these cases the adaptation of individuals in the population is gradual—at best, only able to discover more fit configurations when they are available via small incremental changes. Accordingly, we will see that the effect of sexual recombination can be either gradual or compositional depending on circumstances and assumptions.

6.1 Overview of Models

In the following subsections I will briefly describe the simulation models and the corresponding experimental results for different assumptions.

- Basic model (section 6.2): Single freely mixed population, one-point crossover—GA with fitness-proportionate selection.
- Subdivided population model (section 6.3): GA with one-point crossover and deterministic crowding.

- Physical linkage models (section 6.4):
  - No physical linkage: uniform crossover.
  - Unfavorable physical linkage (random genetic map): HIFF with randomly re-ordered gene positions—"shuffled HIFF."

This chapter uses the GA and variants of the GA throughout because the issues of module discovery and manipulation under crossover are easily demonstrated with a simple linear bit-string representation and bit-string recombination. However, the issues of module discovery and manipulation under compositional mechanisms are relevant in other types of EAs also—the GA merely provides a simple illustration. The discussion on genetic linkage, however, is specific to the linear representation of chromosomes used in GAs—in chapter 7 I move outside the normal GA framework into a novel form of EA that is not dependent on the linear order of genes and could be applied in other substrates.

6.2 Results for a Single Panmictic Population—The Simple GA

In this section I investigate the adaptive capabilities of a population with sexual recombination using a simple model. The basic model will be the simple genetic algorithm (figure 2.1). The simple GA assumes a single freely mixed or unstructured (panmictic) population of individuals. In the following experiments I use a "generational" algorithm meaning that the reproductive cycles of the individuals in the population are synchronized (Syswerda 1990). The algorithm is described in figure 6.1. This model uses standard fitness-proportionate selection. This GA has no diversity maintenance and the population is unstructured, or panmictic—as is normal for a simple generational GA with fitness-proportionate selection.

In the stopping criterion, the duration of the experiment will be measured in evaluations of individuals (corresponding to lifetimes). This method, rather than counting generations, helps to avoid unfair comparisons of adaptive operators arising from different population sizes. For example, in principle, any variation operator (or no variation operator) can find the globally optimal configuration for the fitness landscape in one generation if the initial population is large enough (exponential in N).

Simulation Results

Figure 6.2 shows the simulation results for this model showing the size of the largest all-1s module in the population. A 128-bit HIFF (equation 4.7) defines the fitness landscape. The population size is 2,000. Preliminary investigations indicated that the reliability of the results in section 6.3 were improved with a large population

(1) Initialize population with random individuals, i.e., random bit strings.

(2) Repeat until stopping criterion (duration complete).

  (i) Evaluate the fitness of all individuals in population (using HIFF).

  (ii) Repeat p times (p = size of population).

    (1) With selection probability of each individual proportionate to their fitness, select (with replacement) two individuals from population to be parents.

    (2) Generate an offspring individual by:

      (a) Creating a new string by one-point crossover of parent strings (see figure 3.6).

      (b) Applying point-mutation with low per-locus probability.

    (3) Collect offspring in new population.

  (iii) Replace original population with new population.

Figure 6.1
A procedural outline for a simple (panmictic) GA.

size such as that used here. We use the same population size in all other experiments in this chapter to be sure that the result in section 6.3 is not merely the effect of a large population size. Some indication of the effect of different population sizes is given in Watson 2001.

Results measure the size of modules discovered in all individuals measured in the last 2,000 evaluations (new individuals). Several curves are shown for different mutation rates. Each curve is the average of 30 independent runs. The maximum module size possible in this fitness landscape is 128. The maximum number of evaluations permitted (duration) is $3 \cdot 10^6$.

We see that the population is not able to optimize large modules in this landscape. Figure 6.2 shows that the maximum-size submodule discovered in these runs is around 32 bits on average, only a little better than the results shown for a mutation hill climber.

Discussion

The simple GA with crossover did not do much better than the mutation hill climber of the previous chapter—crossover appears to make negligible difference in this problem. However, looking at the genetic makeup of the evolved populations in detail (data not shown) reveals that in this model the population very quickly becomes

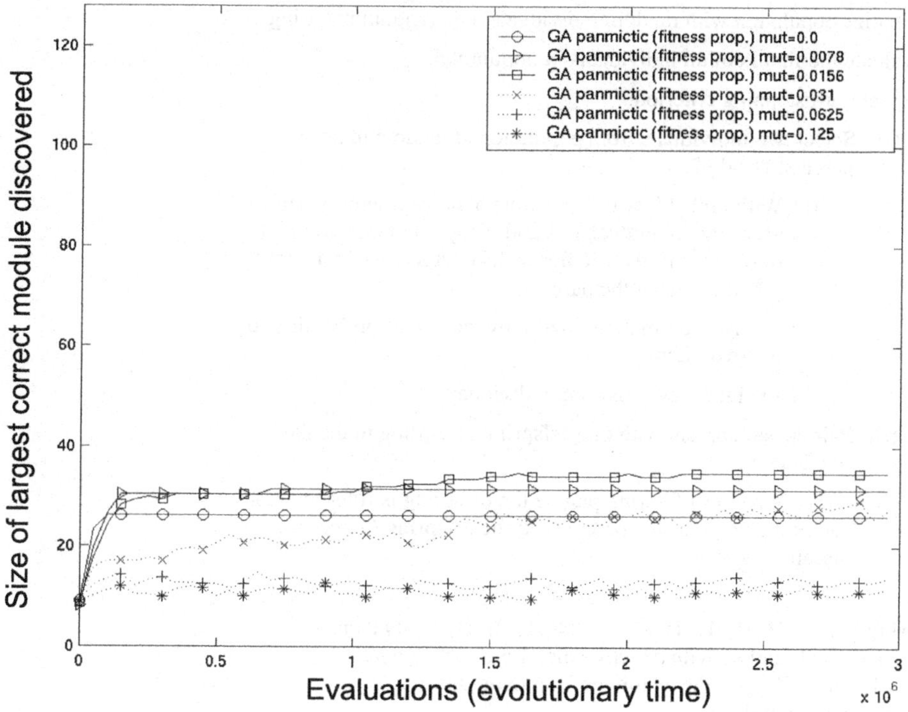

Figure 6.2
Results of a simple (panmictic) GA with one-point crossover on a 128-variable HIFF.

genetically converged. This is to be expected—when there is no pressure to do otherwise, the population will quickly converge to the most fit individual thus far discovered. If this happens before modules can be recombined between individuals then the string the population converges to will not be very fit (for more on "mixing" and trade-off with selection see Thierens and Goldberg 1993). To the extent that the population has converged, crossover between individuals results in little change between parents and offspring. Thus the only new variation in the population is supplied by mutation, and accordingly the results are not much better than previous mutation-only results.

6.3 Results for a Subdivided or Niched Population—GA with Crowding

Following from the previous experiment I now modify the selection scheme to model a process that may better preserve the initial diversity of the population. Specifically,

(1) Initialize population with random individuals, i.e., random bit strings.

(2) Evaluate the fitness of all individuals in population.

(3) Repeat until stopping criterion.

 (i) Select two individuals from population at random to be parents, 1 and $p2$.

  (a) With probability 0.7, generate a complementary pair of offspring individuals, $c1$ and $c2$ by one-point crossover of parent strings (see figure 3.7). Otherwise let the two offspring equal the parents.

  (b) Apply point mutation with low per-locus probability to the two offspring.

  (c) Evaluate new offspring individuals.

 (ii) Pair up each parent with one offspring according to the pairing rule below.

 (iii) For each parent-offspring pair, if the offspring is fitter than the parent then replace the parent with the offspring (otherwise discard offspring).

Pairing rule: if $\mathbf{H}(p1,c1)+\mathbf{H}(p2,c2) < \mathbf{H}(p1,c2)+\mathbf{H}(p2,c1)$ then pair $p1$ with $c1$, and $p2$ with $c2$, else pair $p1$ with $c2$, and $p2$ with $c1$, where **H** gives the genotypic Hamming distance between two individuals.

Figure 6.3
A procedural outline for a steady-state GA with deterministic crowding.

I use a GA with a diversity maintenance technique known as "deterministic crowding" (Mahfoud 1995). Crowding methods in general can be understood as a mechanism to focus competition in such a way that similar things compete but dissimilar things do not. In deterministic crowding (DC), this is achieved in two ways: first, individuals only compete with their own immediate ancestors (their parents); second, individuals of a "brood" (i.e., with the same parents) compete with the parent to whom they are most closely related. Pseudocode for a GA based on deterministic crowding is given in figure 6.3.

Some notes are necessary on the details of this algorithm. A "complementary pair" of offspring, $c1$ and $c2$, is created from two parents, $p1$ and $p2$, by using the same crossover point such that $c1 = p1 \times p2$ and $c2 = p2 \times p1$, where $a \times b$ is the result of crossover where genes are taken from parent-a on the left of the crossover point and from parent-b on the right of the crossover point (or vice versa). In other words, each gene of each parent will occur in either one offspring or the other. (In fact, the algorithm also performs well without the stipulation that both offspring are created with the same crossover point, but this feature makes analysis easier [see also figure 8.1 and discussion].)

Previous work suggested that 70 percent crossover performs better than 100 percent for some mutation rates—so I used 70 percent crossover throughout. (This is wasteful of evaluations when the mutation probability is zero: specifically, the offspring created without crossover remain identical to parents, and cannot produce a change in the state of the population—but such losses are not significant here.)

The important characteristic of this diversity maintenance method is that competition is restricted to similar individuals but breeding is not.[1] This model maintains diversity in the following manner. First note that individuals are selected to be parents at random, not according to their fitness. If fitness effects are introduced to select the parents, then this applies a global (population-wide) pressure to promote the better individuals found so far regardless of their similarity or diversity, which would cause the population to converge on the best adaptive peak found thus far. Instead, selection is applied at replacement (3-iii) where it is restricted to parent-offspring pairs. This isolated competition allows different subdivisions of the population to coexist temporally on different adaptive peaks in the landscape even if they are quite different in fitness. This effects an efficient form of niching where subpopulations climb local peaks but individuals on different peaks do not compete. However, if crossover should result in an individual that is fit in both subdomains it can take over both subpopulations. For example, if the genes of $p2$ are carried by $c1$, and $c1$ is fitter than $p1$ but $c2$ is not fitter than $p2$, then the genes of $p2$ remain in $p2$ *and* replace those of $p1$. Thus if a collection of genes are fit in more than one context they can replicate and spread in the population. This allows an appropriate balance of diversity maintenance and competitive exclusion.

Deterministic crowding was devised for pragmatic optimization purposes, and at first glance seems quite unnatural. However, there are several ways to interpret this model—for example, as a subdivided population or as a niching model.

In subdivided populations individuals compete strongly with other individuals in the same deme but not with individuals in different demes. Moreover, when migration between demes is low, individuals within a deme are generally genetically related. Accordingly, individuals compete most strongly with their own ancestors. When migration does occur, the resultant offspring also need to compete with the residents of the new niche. In this interpretation, instead of interpreting each DC individual as a literal individual, we may alternatively interpret each DC individual as a highly converged subpopulation. In this case, the particular configuration of features in the DC individual can represent the subpopulation "consensus" string. Then the reproduction of one DC individual with another is a model of interdeme migration and crossover.

Deterministic crowding may also be interpreted as a niching model. The general notion of allowing similar things to compete and dissimilar things to coexist is quite a normal interpretation of a multispecies ecosystem. The DC method can be interpreted as a specific implementation of this general model. In particular, if a given individual is assumed to compete most strongly with the other individual in the whole population to which they are most similar then this is likely to be one of their parents (see "preselection" in Cavicchio 1970, and Mahfoud 1995, p. 129). In this respect, DC is merely an implementational approximation to a model where individuals compete only with that other individual with whom they are most similar.

So there are perhaps biologically plausible interpretations of this crowding model. Other results not shown indicate that more standard population genetic models of population subdivision have an equally advantageous affect on population diversity. However, the biological plausibility of deterministic crowding and the particulars of the DC algorithm are not the central point. We merely want to show that if appropriate diversity is maintained in the population, by whatever means, then crossover is able to assemble modules effectively.

A completely different diversity maintenance method, based on competition over shared resources, is also able to maintain diversity appropriately (Watson, Hornby, and Pollack 1998). This resource-based fitness-sharing model uses a resource for each module in the problem and depresses the value of solving a module in proportion to the number of individuals that already solve that module. See Horn, Nafpliotis, and Goldberg 1994 for an example of resource-based fitness sharing where each resource corresponds to a dimension in a multidimensional optimization problem. However, such a resource model uses more domain knowledge than the DC method used here.

Previous work in other domains indicated that, under certain conditions, competitive resource consumption in a continuous space of resources can result in diversification and cooperative displacement into complementary roles (Ebner, Watson, and Alexander 2000). This model turns out to be very similar to the idea of "resource utilisation functions" in a continuous space of resources (MacArthur 1968). Whereas, our previous work on fitness sharing in HIFF is more closely allied to a "niche as hypervolume" model (Hutchinson 1965).

The results of the deterministic crowding model (figure 6.3 above), are shown below in figure 6.4. HIFF (equation 4.7) defines the fitness landscape as before. The population size is 2,000. Results show the size of the largest all-1s module measured in the last 2,000 evaluations averaged over 30 runs. Several curves are shown for dif-

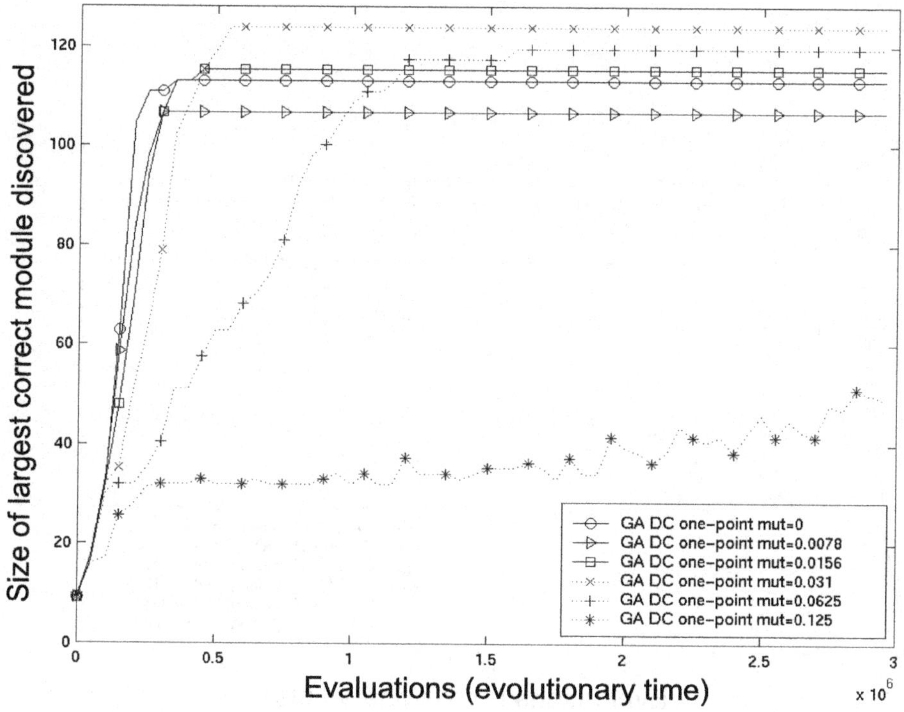

Figure 6.4
Results of the GA with deterministic crowding and one-point crossover on HIFF.

ferent mutation rates. The largest module that could be discovered in this fitness landscape is 128. The maximum number of evaluations permitted (duration) is $3 \cdot 10^6$.

We see that with the aid of the crowding mechanism the population is able to discover large modules in this landscape in all cases except when using very high mutation rates. In fact, with a mutation rate of 0.031 $(2/N)$ it finds *both* globally optimal configurations for the system—modules of 128 variables—in 28 out of 30 runs, by about 500,000 evaluations.

The DC model is an "off the shelf" diversity maintenance technique for GAs—so for the experiments on physical linkage in the remainder of this chapter I use the model as is. (The following chapter on symbiotic encapsulation does not use the DC model.) However, the exact form of the DC model can be relaxed in different ways. For example, the parent–offspring pairing in the pairing rule is not that important—the simulation results look similar though a little inferior without it (figure 6.5).

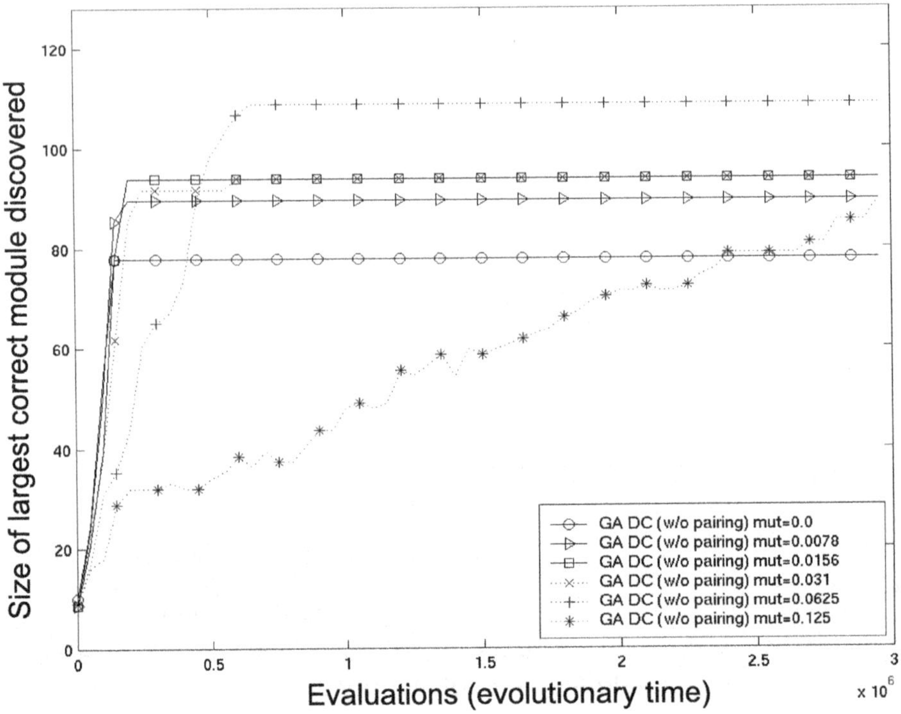

Figure 6.5
Results of the genetic algorithm DC—without pairing.

However, restricting the competition to similar individuals is required—if we pair up the offspring with two random individuals instead of the two parents then diversity is quickly lost and the algorithm fails (figure 6.6). In short, deterministic crowding works fairly well on this problem without using the pairing rule that makes offspring compete with the most similar parent. But it does not work well when offspring compete with two randomly selected individuals (instead of the parents). So it is the competition against parents (rather than the pairing rule) that is important in this algorithm.

Gradualism Is Neither Sufficient Nor Required

We also see (figure 6.4) that with no mutation the GA is still successful (at least 1 of the global optima is found in 23 out of 30 runs). Thus random variation is not necessary under these conditions where the population is initialized to random strings.

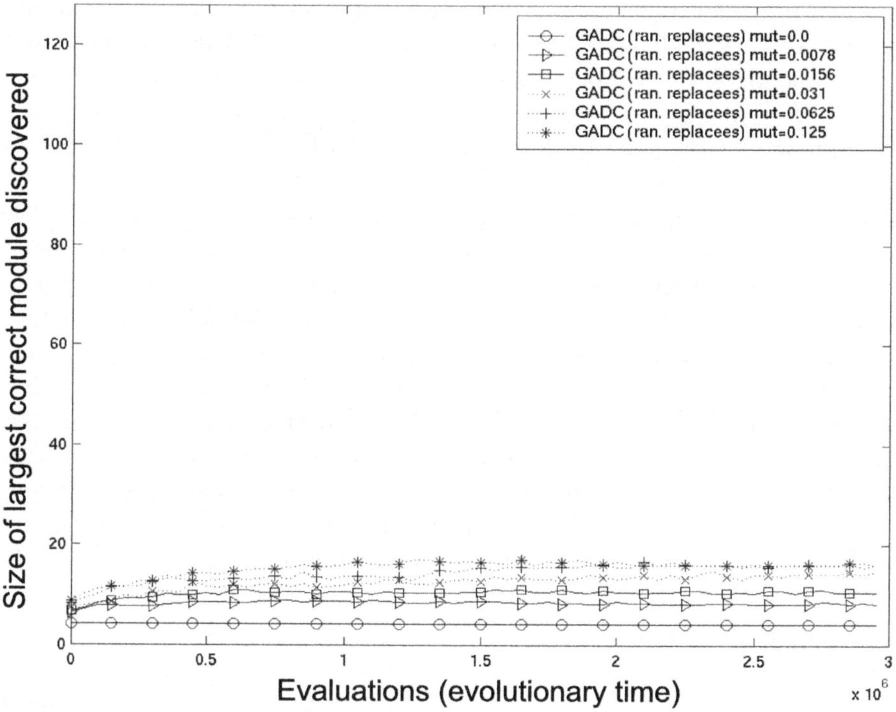

Figure 6.6
Results of the genetic algorithm DC—random replacees.

This is because the population of diverse genotypes, optimizing different modules in different individuals, is able to supply all the required variation to discover larger modules. Moreover, when individuals are already well adapted, random mutational variation is so much more likely to disrupt a large module than it is to discover a new one that it is better not to use it in this situation. (Alternatively, we may imagine crossover events between different individuals that introduce small numbers of genes as being effectively equivalent to small mutations—thus additional mutation is not required.)

It is noted that the random initialization of the population is required to cover all of the alleles at all of the loci. This is not so difficult when the number of alleles is small compared to the population size. But in other domains, for example where the variables of the system are continuous or take a very large number of possible values, it may not be plausible that the initial population covers the required alleles. In this case, or when the initial population is converged not random, a low mutation rate will presumably be valuable. Thus I do not suppose that this observation about mutation is general, however it does illustrate that there are conditions under which sexual recombination without mutation is sufficient, in principle. Other simulations (not shown) indicate that a GA with DC can solve HIFF with converged initialization if a suitable (not too high) mutation rate is used.

It should be noted, then, that the experiments of the previous chapter showed that on this class of problem gradual change is not sufficient to find fit configurations of the system. The simulations above now also show that mutation is not required to find fit configurations of the system. Thus under these conditions on this class of problem, gradualism is neither sufficient nor required.

I must quickly clarify however, that I do not intend to imply that gradualist models of change are not accurate models of some, almost certainly most, evolutionary change. I make these observations just to show that there are alternate scenarios for evolutionary change that are fundamentally different from, and independent of, gradualist models. (These claims are validated more strongly in the next chapter that shows 100% successful runs with no explicit mutation.)

6.4 The Dependence on Physical Linkage

In this model, it might look like sexual recombination has unequivocally provided robust adaptation in this class of adaptive landscapes. However, I have not yet discussed the assumptions about genetic linkage and these are, in fact, critical.

The experiments in the previous section used two important assumptions about physical linkage coming from the tendency of gene subsets to occur together during crossover events:

1. Physical linkage is significant in strength: that is, some subsets of genes are more likely to travel together during crossover events than others by virtue of their proximity on the chromosome.
2. Physical linkage is arranged or ordered favorably in the genetic map: for our purposes this means that epistatically dependent genes are close to each other on the chromosome so that those subsets that are likely to travel together during crossover correspond well with those subsets that form modules in the interdependency network of the genes.

These are strong assumptions so it is important that we examine what happens when they are relaxed.

No Physical Linkage: "Free Recombination" or "Uniform Crossover"

The previous experiments used one-point crossover. Clearly, whether two genes travel together from parent to offspring in a crossover event depends on whether they are on the same side of the crossover point. One-point crossover can be understood as an approximation to a crossover probability of $1/N$ per locus, where N is the number of genes. In multipoint crossover, the probability of two genes traveling together is equal to the probability that an even number of crossover points (possibly none) falls between their loci. This approaches 1 as the distance between genes approaches 0. But in general, as crossover probabilities increase, the distance between a pair of genes on the chromosome has progressively less effect in determining whether they appear together in the offspring with more than random chance (see discussion of genetic linkage in section 3.3).

The following simulation experiments use uniform crossover. This can be understood as an approximation to very high crossover probabilities where the proximity of genes to each other on the chromosome has no effect on their probability of co-occurring in the offspring. That is, it models sexual recombination with *no* physical linkage.

In natural systems, situations with no linkage, or very weak linkage, include:

- When all genes corresponding to variables in the system of interest reside in different chromosomes. In this case there is free recombination between the genes when an offspring is produced.
- When there are many crossover points per recombination.
- When an evolutionary system has low crossover rates, but selection pressure is low or applied only after several successive recombinations. In this case, offspring equivalent to those created from many crossover points may be produced.

Figure 6.7 shows simulation results for a GA with deterministic crowding using uniform crossover, that is, no physical linkage among loci, showing the size of the largest all-ones module in the population. As before, HIFF (equation 4.7) defines the fitness landscape. The population size is 2,000 individuals. Results measure the size of the largest modules discovered in the last 2,000 evaluations (births) averaged over 30 runs. Several curves are shown for different mutation rates. The maximum number of evaluations permitted (duration) is $3 \cdot 10^6$. (No mutation is best—see the discussion on convergence controlled variation below.)

It is clear from these results that the absence of physical linkage between the variables of the system in these circumstances prevents the population from finding fit adaptations. Most runs do not find modules greater than 32 bits, no runs find modules of 128 bits.

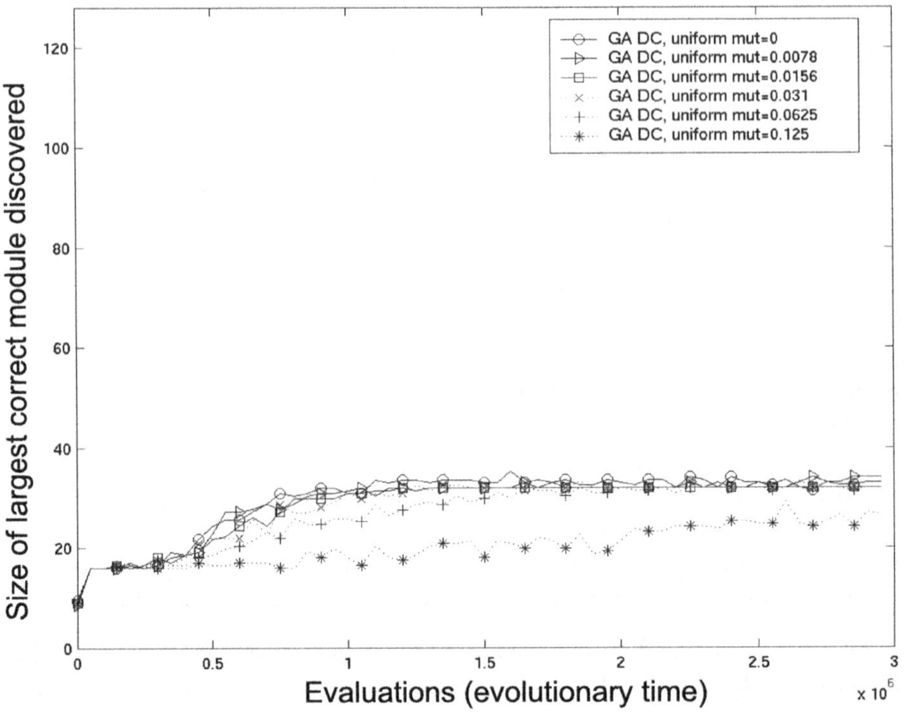

Figure 6.7
Results of the DC GA with uniform crossover on HIFF.

This failure can be understood by considering figure 6.8 below, which illustrates crossover between two individuals that happen to be well adapted to one module each but to different modules (left and right halves of the chromosome, shown underlined). A particular selection of possible crossover points are indicated by the short vertical tick marks: only one for one-point crossover; $N/2$, on average, for uniform crossover. Under one-point crossover there is a $1/N$ chance that the single crossover point may land in the correct position to enable these two modules to come together in one of the offspring.

However, under uniform crossover, where there are many crossover points, this is much less likely—the desirable modules will probably be broken up in crossover. In fact, to get the two all-0s modules into an offspring from the more extreme example strings, 00001111 and 11110000, has a probability exactly equal to randomly guessing the string 00000000 from scratch, that is, 2^{-N}. This also applies to "parameter-

	one-point crossover	**uniform crossover**
parent 1	**1010100100000000**	**1010100100000000**
parent 2	0000000010011110	0000000010011110
offspring 1	**10101001**10011110	1010000110000110
offspring 2	00000000**00000000**	0000100000011000

Figure 6.8
Crossover operations on bit-string individuals.

ized uniform crossover" (Spears and De Jong 1991) where the probability of taking a gene from parent-1 may be different from the probability of taking a gene from parent-2. In this example, any advantage an imbalanced transmission probability might have through increasing the likelihood of transferring one of the modules to the offspring is lost through the decreased likelihood of transferring the other module to the offspring.

In general, the probability of getting two modules together into an offspring is related to the number of per-locus disagreements that the parents exhibit over the loci of the modules. For example in figure 6.8 above, parent 1 disagrees with parent 2 on the allele values for four loci on the left-half module, and five loci on the right-half module (in this example, the two modules cover the entire chromosome, but they need not in general). All loci where the parents agree, or loci that are outside the modules, have no effect on this probability. But for all loci where the parents disagree, the allele that appears in the offspring must come from the correct parent. This probability is 0.5 for each locus independently under uniform crossover. Therefore the probability of both modules appearing together correctly in the offspring is 2^{-d} where d is the number of disagreements, in this case 2^{-9}.

So, it should be clear from these considerations that regardless of the arrangement of genes, sexual recombination without physical linkage (e.g., sex with uniform crossover) cannot recombine conflicting modules with a probability better than random mutation. This shows that the compositional advantage of sexual recombination is dependent at least on there being significant physical linkage. However, this is not

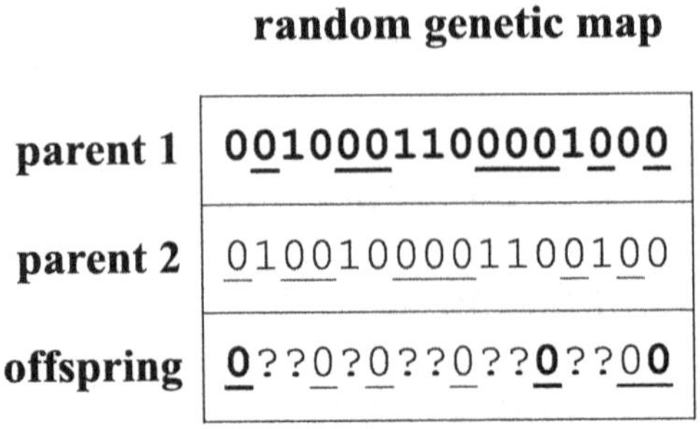

Figure 6.9
Crossover operations with a random genetic map—i.e., shuffled gene ordering.

the whole story—the advantage of sexual recombination with strong physical linkage (e.g., sex with one-point crossover) is further dependent on the arrangement of genes.

Reordered Linkage: Shuffled Gene Positions; a Random Genetic Map

In the example of figure 6.8, the successful transference of both modules to one of the offspring under one-point crossover is simply not possible unless the crossover point can be positioned such that all of the loci for one module are on one side of the crossover point, and all of the loci for the other module are on the other side of the crossover point. If the positions of genes within one module extended over the range of genes containing the other module then this would not be possible.

Figure 6.9 above illustrates a reordering of the genes for the individuals in figure 6.8. The genes for complementary all-0s modules are shown underlined in each parent. The question is, how to choose crossover points so as to get both these modules into an offspring. (See also figure 6.10.)

Figure 6.9 illustrates crossover between two individuals that each have one well-adapted module but the genes of these modules are distributed along the chromosome making their combination difficult. Conceivably, uniform crossover, or in this case eight-point crossover, could place crossover points in the exact positions that allow both modules to be transferred to one offspring. But in general, we need to allow an arbitrary number of crossover points and we already know (from figure 6.8) that recombination without genetic linkage cannot combine two modules together with a probability higher than randomly guessing the resolution of all disagreeing alleles.

Accordingly, effective recombination of modules even in the presence of strong physical linkage also requires that physical linkage correspond well with epistatic dependencies—that is, epistatically dependent genes must be close together on the

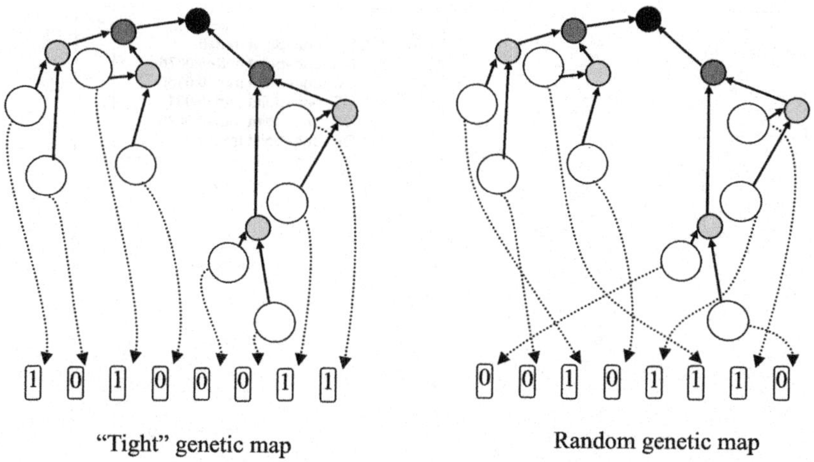

Figure 6.10
The correspondence (or not) of the genetic map with epistatic dependencies.

chromosome. We can test this reasoning by randomly reordering or shuffling the position of genes on the chromosome and repeating the previous experiments. There is no need to repeat the uniform crossover experiments since it is in all respects insensitive to the ordering of genes—so I repeat only the one-point crossover experiments.

The following experiments use "shuffled HIFF." That is, for each run, a different random ordering of the gene positions is chosen. The modules in the problem therefore do not, in general, have any structural correlation with the position of genes on the chromosome. This is illustrated in figure 6.10. This figure is, for variety, just another way of representing the concept depicted in figure 1.9—specifically, it uses the tree representation of dependencies introduced in figure 4.5c instead of the graph representation of dependencies introduced in figure 1.7. A number of genes (large circles) each contribute interdependently (solid arrows) to a number of aggregate effects (grey circles), and these contribute to higher-level features (dark circles), and so on.[2] This hierarchy pictorially represents the modular interdependency structure of the variables in HIFF. This system of genes must be mapped to positions on a chromosome. Left: tight physical linkage—ideally, genes that are epistatically related, that is, that contribute to the same features (solid arrows) will be next to each other on the chromosome. In this case, as in regular HIFF, sexual recombination with low crossover rates (strong physical linkage) will be able to recombine subsystems effectively. Right: random genetic map—without such a favorable situation,

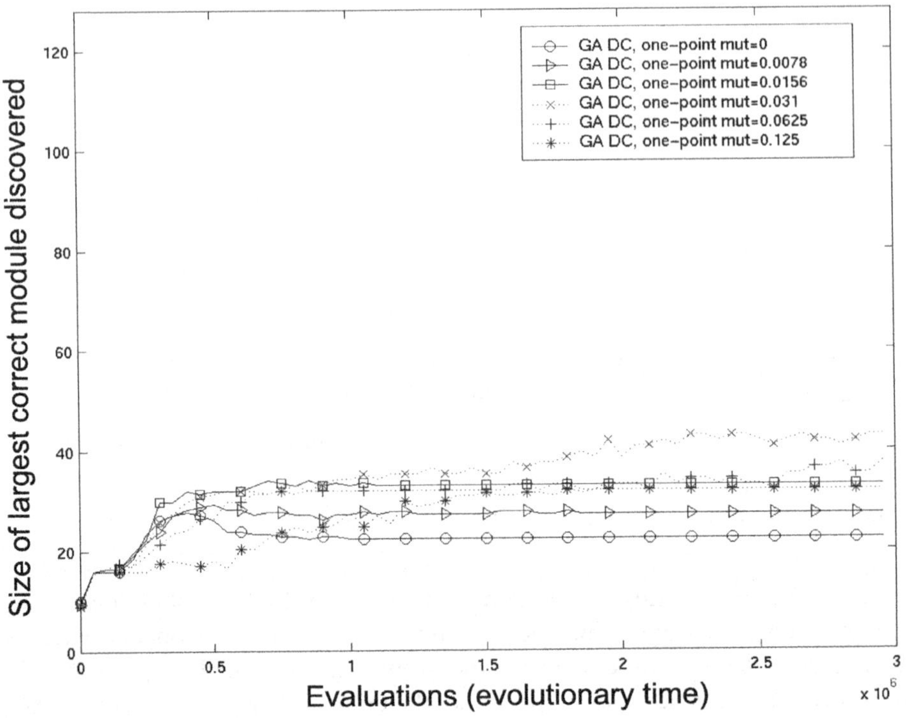

Figure 6.11
Results of the DC GA with one-point crossover on shuffled HIFF.

epistatically dependent subsets of genes may be arbitrarily positioned on the chromosome. In this case, as in shuffled HIFF, sexual recombination is unable to recombine subsystems effectively (regardless of the crossover rate).

Figure 6.11 shows the results for a GA with deterministic crowding showing the size of the largest all-1s module in the population (as per figure 6.3), but applied to shuffled HIFF rather than HIFF. Equation 4.7 with a random reordering of the genes defines the fitness landscape. Otherwise parameters are as before: the population size is 2,000 individuals. Several curves are shown for different mutation rates. The maximum number of evaluations permitted is $3 \cdot 10^6$.

These results, in comparison to figure 6.4, support the reasoning that the successful composition of modules via sexual recombination requires that epistatically dependent genes be physically linked through their proximity on the chromosome (and strongly linked through the use of low crossover rates).

Convergence-Controlled Variation

Interestingly, although uniform crossover does not perform well it does appear to do slightly better than mutation on HIFF (compare figures 6.7 and 5.4). This is because although the chances of transferring two different modules from parents into an offspring are minimal, the chances of not disrupting other modules that appear in both parents is better for uniform crossover (or one-point crossover) than it is for mutation. For example, consider two parent strings A and B that agree with one another on, say, two out of four modules, but do not agree on the other two—for example, 00001100 and 00000011. Then the probability of getting from this pair of strings to either global optimum by uniform crossover is 2^{-d}, where d is the number of disagreements between parents ($d = 4$ in this case). However, the probability via mutation is much lower because it requires that the good modules of all 0s are not changed while the incorrect modules are mutated as necessary. For example, the best mutation rate to change half the bits and not change the other half is 100 percent mutation (assignment of new random alleles). Thus, we see that the variation applied by uniform crossover is much like that of one hundred percent mutation only for the modules that disagree, but no mutation at all on modules where the parents already agree. In other words, variation from uniform crossover is focused on modules where the population has not yet converged providing an interesting form of "convergence-controlled variation" (Eshelman, Mathias, and Schaffer 1996). Since, in some circumstances, this is a reasonable heuristic for focusing mutation (Chen 1999) it may perform better than ordinary unfocused mutation.

However, previous work has shown that the fact that all types of crossover preserve those parts of the chromosome where the parents agree, is not sufficient to explain the success of one-point crossover on HIFF. It is in fact possible to use a crossover operator that deliberately disrupts all loci where the parents agree and applies one-point crossover on the parts that disagree. Since this still succeeds (Watson and Pollack 2000b), preserving similarity is not a required feature of a crossover operator in these circumstances. This also serves to illustrate that our selection schemes make traditional disruption analysis quite ineffective at predicting GA success under these conditions. Interestingly, this operator does not require the use of deterministic crowding or other diversity maintenance techniques since the operator itself prevents the population from converging. It should be noted however, that this result, though it proves the desired point that preserving the agreeing loci of the parents is not required, is dependent on the properties of HIFF (specifically the fact that competing solutions to modules are the exact complement of one another). It therefore does not offer a general problem-solving mechanism, and neither does it have a biological analogue that I can think of.

It should also be noted that although uniform crossover does better than regular mutation, the chances of innovation (i.e., the acquisition of a new module) by uniform crossover decrease exponentially as fitness saddles become wider and jumps require changing more loci at once. In other words, uniform crossover is not able to exploit the decomposition available in the problem and compose new modules from submodules.

Also, one-point crossover performs better than uniform crossover in shuffled HIFF—perhaps because for small schemata that happen to have short defining length there is less disruption than there is with uniform crossover.

Linkage Learning

In biological systems, the position of genes might be adaptively reordered by variation mechanisms, such as inversion and translocation, that reorder the position of genes on the chromosome. In engineering domains, favorable linkage cannot generally be assumed. Accordingly, many moving-locus (e.g., messy GA, Goldberg, Korb, and Deb 1989, see p. 75) and linkage-learning schemes have been proposed (see p. 83). The shuffled HIFF problem provides a good test problem for these methods and for biologically plausible models of gene reordering.

However, gene reordering mechanisms ultimately rely on a linear ordering representation of the dependencies of genes. This works well in HIFF, where there is a natural linearization of the treelike dependency structure (like the flattening of a hierarchical document structure into the linear order of pages in a book). But this is an approximation to the ideal linkage structure. For example, under HIFF, it should *not* be the case that the fourth and fifth genes in this string 00001111 are any more likely to travel together than the first and last, but of course they are when their linkage is dependent purely on linear separation. Similarly, if the span of the hierarchy is wider (i.e., the number of submodules per module is greater) this problem is more acute, since for example we cannot arrange three modules on a string so that all modules are equally close to each other. Moreover, it is not necessarily the case that all dependency structures can be appropriately linearized even approximately. This may mean that composition via sexual recombination has limitations even when combined with the action of reordering mechanisms.

Other linkage-learning methods do not rely on gene reordering. In the evolutionary computation literature, the generic term "linkage" is used to refer to both physical linkage (coming from the proximity of genes on the chromosome), and "epistatic linkage," meaning epistatic dependency. These two concepts are often conflated in the evolutionary computation literature since it is assumed that "good linkage" means a tight correspondence between gene positions and epistatic dependency. In fact, the structure of epistatic dependency is quite a different issue from physical linkage—as is clear from the fact that in shuffled HIFF we retain the same hierarchically modular structure of epistatic dependencies while randomly reordering the positions of genes (see previous discussion on genetic linkage, p. 82, and figure 6.10).

One class of linkage-learning algorithms that do not depend on gene ordering is distribution-estimation algorithms, like the Bayesian optimization algorithm (BOA) (Pelikan, Goldberg, and Cantu-Paz 1999). dBOA, a variety of BOA, works extremely well on shuffled HIFF (Pelikan and Goldberg 2000). However, although dBOA performs very well in terms of fitness evaluations, it also introduces a large computational overhead in systematically analyzing the fitness correlations of co-occurring gene subsets over all the strings in the population. Additionally, dBOA requires a diversity maintenance method based on Hamming distance that happens to be very appropriate for HIFF. In the next chapter we will show a method that solves shuffled HIFF without using the assumption that genetic dissimilarity (Hamming distance) is a good indicator of functional dissimilarity.

Interestingly, the operation of the BOA can be seen to be analogous to an incremental assembly of small dependency structures into larger dependency structures (as conditional probabilities are incrementally added to an initially empty Bayesian network) and it is, in this respect, a statistical method for implementing a form of compositional variation. This makes it quite different in operation from regular genetic algorithms (with or without crossover) and a very interesting direction for future modeling.

6.5 The Impact for GA Theory

A significant amount of prior work in the evolutionary computation literature has been directed, quite rightly, at attempting to answer the question "what is the genetic algorithm good for?," and in particular, "what is sexual recombination (crossover) in the GA good for?"

The important realization here is that if the genetic algorithm behaves more or less like a hill climber then it is not an interesting algorithmic class for computer scientists. If this is the case then we may as well use other stochastic optimization techniques such as a stochastic hill climber or simulated annealing.

By showing a clear distinction between gradual and compositional evolution, and showing that they map to the algorithmic classes of hill climbing and divide-and-conquer problem decomposition respectively, I have also shown that under some circumstances the GA (with crossover) can do something that a hill climber cannot do. This is an important result for evolutionary computation. Some of the intuitions used in this result are derived from intuitions of existing work in the evolutionary computation literature. The following subsections clarify the relationship of this result to some existing genetic algorithm theory and in particular the characteristics that make a problem easy or difficult for the genetic algorithm.

The Building-Block Hypothesis and the Schema Theorem

As stated, the building-block hypothesis (BBH) suggests that the GA will perform well when short sections of chromosome that confer above-average fitness contributions (building blocks) can be recombined to discover longer sections of chromosome that are yet fitter. The intuition is that different members of the population will discover different building blocks, and that sexual recombination will then search combinations of small building blocks to find larger building blocks, and so on (see section 3.2).

Given that the BBH is a statement about the simple GA, and is supposed to describe when it will work well in general, I cannot support the general form of the BBH. However, I have shown that a form of GA on a particular class of problem can assemble modules in a manner similar to the intuition of the BBH. Of course, under "no free lunch" (Wolpert and Macready 1997), we cannot expect any kind of GA to perform well in general; instead we must work at identifying what it is that the GA is good for, and I have already spent a chapter on defining a particular class of modularity for this purpose. But note that HIFF has a very structured modular construction and even here the simple GA failed to find high-fitness configurations (section 6.4). The addition of a diversity maintenance method (in this case deterministic crowding) was critical in enabling the GA to do the kind of module assembly that the BBH describes.

It should be clear that since this does not use fitness-proportionate selection or any other method that allows inferior schemata to be replicated, we are therefore not interested in schema *disruption* except in so much as it suggests a lower rate of schema *creation*. Similarly, we do not require useful schemata to be duplicated in the population. Thus, we are not interested in generating multiple copies of fit schemata, or in assessing the average value of a schema. Therefore the schema theorem is simply not relevant to the kind of GA that we are examining. And thus the validity of the schema theorem is not required for the supply of building blocks for recombination in this type of algorithm. Accordingly, the validity of the schema theorem for GAs in general must be separated from the intuition of building-block assembly that is described in the BBH.

The simulation experiments show that crossover cannot and should not be approximated as a source of random variation. The multiple-inheritance feature of crossover (see section 10.2 and previous discussion on directed genetic changes, p. 92) and the assembly of higher-order building blocks from low-order building blocks (as Holland originally suggested) is intrinsically unavailable in linear (single-inheritance) methods like hill climbing, the GA without crossover, or the GA with strongly converged populations (i.e., the GA without a diversity maintenance mechanism).

This places GAs using crossover and appropriate diversity maintenance in a fundamentally different class of algorithms from mutation-only algorithms (Culberson 1995), and shows that crossover provides more than large random changes or "macromutations" (Jones 1995).

6.6 Summary

Figure 6.12 and figure 6.13 summarize the simulation results thus far. Figure 6.12 uses a 128-bit HIFF. Figure 6.13 use a 128-bit shuffled HIFF. Best mutation rates (of those sampled earlier) are used for each method. RMHC—random mutation hill climber ($mut = 0.0938$). "GA panmictic"—genetic algorithm without any diversity maintenance, using fitness-proportionate selection, and one-point crossover ($mut = 0.0078$). "GA DC uniform"—GA with deterministic crowding diversity maintenance method, and no genetic linkage (i.e., uniform crossover) ($mut = 0$). "GA DC one-point (TIGHT)"—GA with deterministic crowding, and strong and favorably ordered physical linkage (i.e., one-point crossover with tight genetic map) ($mut = 0.031$). "GA DC one-point (RAN)"—GA with deterministic crowding, one-point crossover, and random genetic map ($mut = 0.031$). Error bars show plus-and-minus-one standard deviation of the mean from 30 runs.

In figure 6.12, the results on HIFF clearly show that, as expected, the GA with appropriate diversity maintenance and a tight genetic map succeeds easily (i.e., finds the biggest modules possible in 28 out of 30 runs), and all other algorithms examined so far fail (do not find either global optimum in any runs), on this problem under these conditions. In figure 6.13 the results on shuffled HIFF clearly show that all the methods we have seen so far, including the GA with deterministic crowding, are not able to discover and manipulate modules effectively on this problem under these conditions.

Accordingly, we have seen that there are some circumstances where sexual recombination is able to compose together modules to find larger modules. And we have

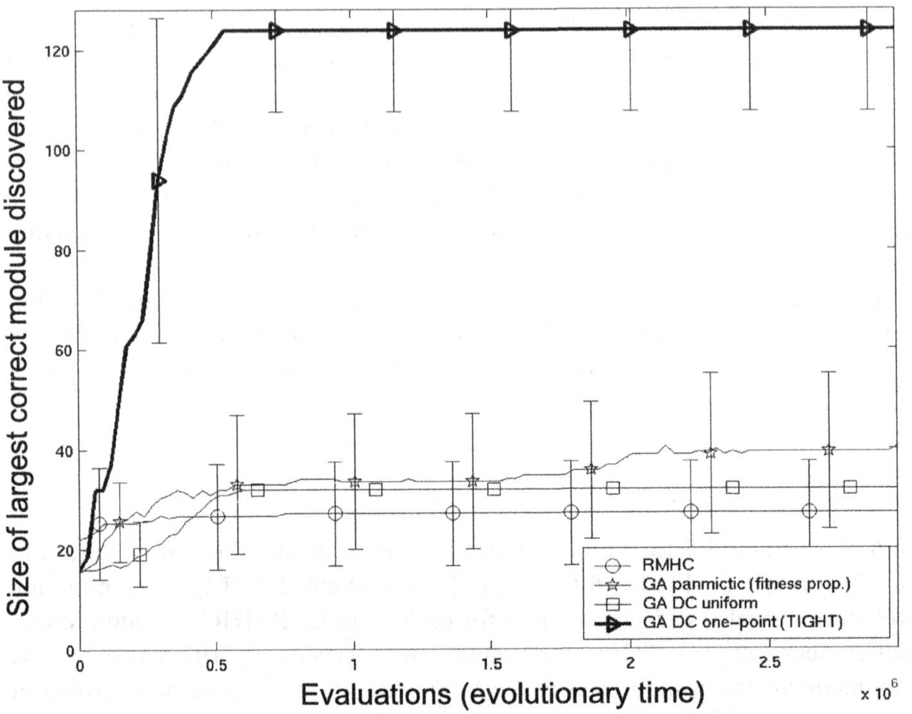

Figure 6.12
Summary of simulation experiments 1a: RMHC and GA methods on HIFF. The genetic algorithm models a sexual population; when it has diversity maintenance (GA DC) and uses physical linkage (one-point, rather than free-recombination/uniform crossover), it is able to evolve this type of system easily. The random mutation hill climber models gradual evolution; it cannot evolve this type of system under any conditions. This provides our first example of a type of complex system that is unevolvable under gradual evolution (RMHC) but easily evolvable under compositional evolution.

seen previously that this process is not available to gradual mechanisms such as mutation in this class of adaptive system. The conditions for this successful manipulation of modules include:

· Appropriate modular interdependency structure (e.g., a decomposable structure like that illustrated by HIFF). Reasoning in the previous chapter suggests that the structure of HIFF exemplifies the difference in adaptive capacities of gradual and compositional mechanisms. I previously suggested that HIFF is amenable to a divide-and-conquer problem decomposition in principle, and the operation of sexual recombination in these experiments illustrates exactly this process in operation.

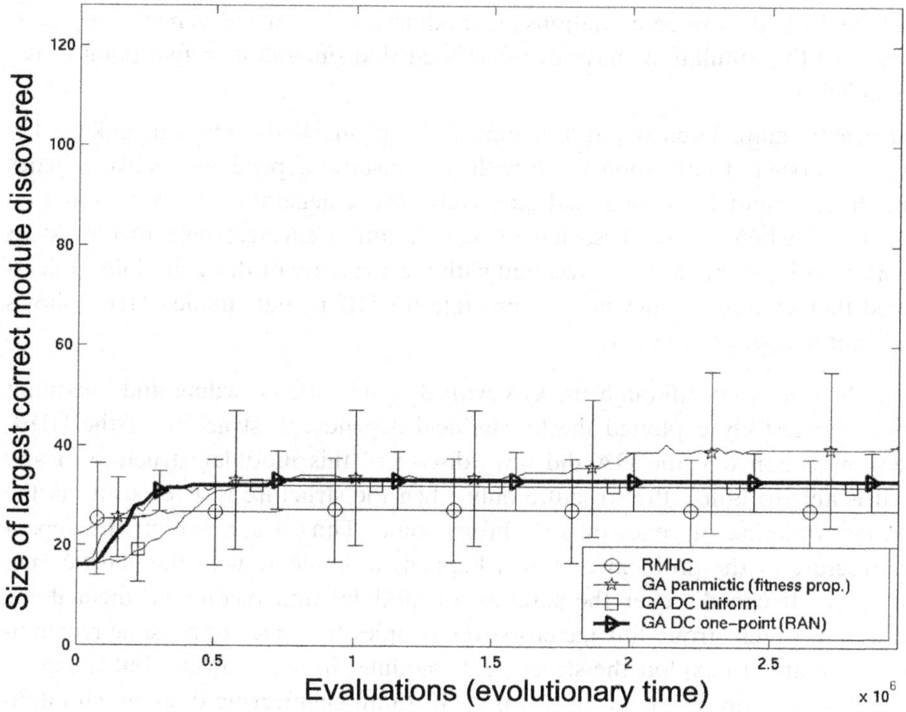

Figure 6.13
Summary of simulation experiments 1b: RMHC and GA methods on shuffled HIFF. The genetic algorithm models a sexual population; even when it has diversity maintenance (GA DC) and uses physical linkage (one-point, rather than free-recombination/uniform crossover), it is unable to evolve this type of system because the genetic map is random. The random mutation hill climber models gradual evolution; it cannot evolve this type of system under any conditions. Thus the advantage of compositional evolution by sexual recombination seen in figure 6.12 is dependent on the ordering of genes in the genetic map.

• Population diversity. If different members of the population are not able to maintain competing solutions to modules (different members of M_A for a module A, see section 4.2), at least as long as is required to test different combinations of modules and resolve their interdependencies (i.e., to test $M_A \times M_B$ for two modules A and B), then the performance of sexual recombination will degrade to approach that of mutation. Thus appropriate diversity in the population is required. I have demonstrated that the diversity provided by the deterministic crowding model of population subdivision is sufficient.

• Strong physical genetic linkage. If physical linkage is weak or absent, as modeled by uniform crossover, then the genes of a module cannot be transferred to an offspring as a whole to find new combinations of modules. Thus strong genetic linkage is required, and the simulations have demonstrated that one-point or two-point crossover is sufficient.

• Tight genetic map. Even if physical linkage is strong, if the physical linkage between genes does not correspond well with the epistatic dependency between genes then modules cannot be recombined effectively. More generally, the recombination of modules as wholes through sexual recombination is effective only to the extent that gene ordering happens to correspond with the structure of those modules. I demonstrated that such an arrangement is possible for HIFF, but shuffled HIFF shows that it is not necessarily the case.

It should be clear that although the GA with deterministic crowding and one-point crossover successfully exploited the hierarchical dependency structure of the HIFF problem in section 6.3, the GA did not "discover" this modular structure in any sense. It is able to utilize the structure only when the structure is given to it via the appropriate ordering of genes on the chromosome. Thus it can exploit the dependency structure of the problem only if it happens to coincide with the genetic map that is given. It can discover the solution to modules and recombine them if the biased way in which strong-linkage crossover samples the space of possible recombinations is suitable to exploit the structure of modules in the problem, but it cannot discover this structure in the problem for itself. In an engineering domain with difficult dependencies between variables where we do not have *a priori* knowledge of the dependency structure, we are not able to order genes appropriately on the chromosome and thus sexual recombination is not likely to provide the algorithmic advantage of compositional evolution. This means that unless we use some form of linkage learning mechanism to reorder the genetic map, the compositional advantage of sexual recombination will not be useful in most engineering applications of the genetic algorithm. Nonetheless this result is still important for genetic algorithm theory because prior attempts, even those assuming tight physical linkage, failed to show a principled advantage to sex in the GA. Whether biological systems naturally have appropriate physical linkage of modules is empirically difficult to test, but it does not seem wholly implausible that the physical linkage of nucleotides packaged into genes is to some extent correlated with functional and epistatic dependencies (see section 10.7). Given this assumption, sexual recombination can provide compositional advantage in biological systems.

In the following chapter I investigate the operation of symbiotic encapsulation. The simulations will show that this is a mechanism of composition that is not sensitive to the ordering of genes in the problem as given, or put another way, it is a mechanism that is able to dynamically discover and explicitly use the learned dependency structure of the genes. From an engineering point of view, this model is interesting because it is not subject to the same restrictions as sexual recombination in the genetic algorithm. Similarly, from a biological point of view it shows that compositional evolution can be provided without making any assumptions about the genetic map. Chapters 6 and 7 each illustrate sufficient conditions for compositional evolution, but together they also help us to better understand how sex and symbiotic encapsulation differ in their adaptive capabilities.

7 Symbiotic Encapsulation

In this chapter[1] I introduce a novel compositional model based on symbiotic encapsulation—the joining of entities from different reproductive lineages into a new reproductive whole. This model is based on compositional change in the major evolutionary transitions whereby "entities that were capable of independent replication before the transition can replicate only as part of a larger whole after it" (Maynard Smith and Szathmary 1995). And more specifically, the model abstractly represents a mechanism of "symbiosis followed by compartmentation and synchronised replication" (ibid.).

The models in this chapter show that the adaptive capacity of composition is not dependent on *a priori* knowledge of which genes are dependent on which other genes, or the assumption that this information is implicitly provided by favorable gene ordering. Thereby, the models in this chapter also demonstrate an algorithmic difference in the adaptive capabilities of sexual recombination and symbiotic encapsulation. That is, all the mechanisms listed in the spectrum of compositional mechanisms can be understood under the divide-and-conquer algorithmic framework and are distinct from the hill-climbing framework of gradual evolution. But within the set of compositional mechanisms there are additional algorithmic distinctions to be made. Specifically, symbiotic encapsulation can provide divide-and-conquer adaptation in circumstances where sexual recombination cannot, as we will see in the model presented in this chapter.

In the following subsection I outline the basic framework of the symbiotic encapsulation model. In the subsequent subsections I detail the components of the encapsulation model and illustrate its adaptive capacities using simulations on HIFF. Since this model is quite different from the genetic algorithm and other previous evolutionary computation methods, section 7.6 spends some time discussing its various features and differences with respect to previous models to assist in placing this model in context.

7.1 An Overview of the Symbiotic Encapsulation Model

The composition model introduced in this chapter is called the "symbiogenic evolutionary adaptation model," or *SEAM*, to invoke the notion of symbiotic union or joining.

This model includes the idea of integrating the features adapted in different lineages into a new whole simply by encapsulating extant entities into a new higher-level entity—that is, symbiotic encapsulation—and this is the fundamental distinction from the model of sexual recombination. But this new integration model has implications for our selection model too. As a consequence, SEAM begins to look quite different from the model of sexual recombination in the previous chapter. But, in later discussion I will outline the similarities between the two models and show that in many respects they are not that different. Specifically, we will see that each can be seen as a model of evolution that acts at more than one level of selection: crudely, on modules and on assemblies of modules. In sexual recombination the modules are represented by tightly linked schemata and the assemblies are individuals. In SEAM, the modules are represented by individuals and the assemblies are made from the explicit joining of individuals. But in the meantime, by introducing SEAM in the manner shown below, I provide a stepping stone to a more general understanding that allows us to see the sexual recombination model in a new light.

The three main features of SEAM are:

- Variable-sized entities and a mechanism of creating new entities by joining extant entities.
- Evaluating entities in transient groups made from other entities.
- A selection scheme based on testing the stability of a proposed join in many environmental contexts.

Briefly, SEAM develops as follows. The ecosystem is initialized with many different small entities. Pairs of entities are then picked at random to see if they might form a stable symbiotic join. If the overall fitness of either entity alone could be, dependent on environmental contexts, greater than the fitness of the entity with the proposed symbiotic partner, then the composition is deemed "unstable" and the original entities are returned to the ecosystem. Otherwise the composition is deemed "stable" and the two entities will always co-occur in the future. The process of building and selecting compositions of entities is repeated, eventually building larger and larger composite entities.

Three main features of SEAM are depicted in figure 7.1. Frames (a) through (c) in the figure loosely correspond to variation, evaluation, and selection, respectively. In (a) new entities are created from the composition or joining of two randomly selected extant entities (see figure 7.3). In (b) the fitness of any entity (possibly the result of a previous join) has dependencies with its environmental context, that is, a random selection of other entities from the ecosystem (see figures 7.4 and 7.5). In (c) the new pairing is subject to many such contexts. If there is some environment of other entities in which either component of the join is fitter individually than when it is with its proposed partner, then the join is deemed unstable and is dismantled. This follows the assumption that the partnership must be in the "selfish" interest of the partners involved. In our implementation, the stability of a proposed join is tested in many

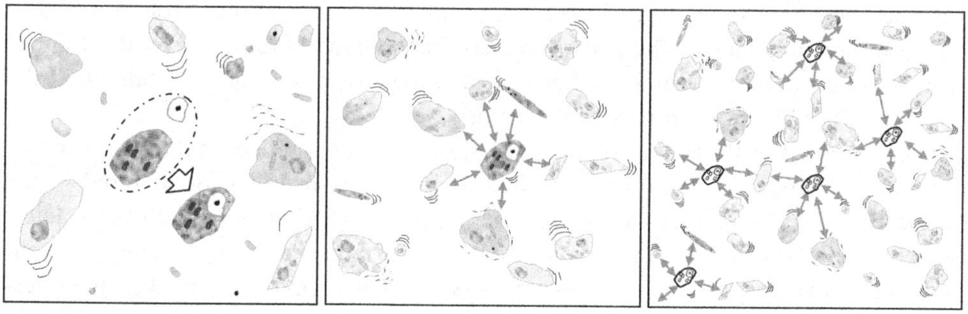

(a) (b) (c)

Figure 7.1
A caricature of processes in SEAM. (a) New entities are created by joining two existing entities together. (b) The fitness of an entity is dependent on its environmental context. (c) An entity is placed in many contexts to test the stability of a new join.

contexts and is immediately undone if found to be unstable. This models the assumption that competition between joined and nonjoined variants of an entity occurs rapidly such that only reliably successful joins persist long enough to be involved in a subsequent join (see section 7.3, equation 7.3). A join that persists through (c) is treated as a new entity that may participate in further joins as the cycle of the model repeats.

These processes are detailed in the following subsections.

7.2 Entities and Their Encapsulation

Mutually Exclusive Characters and the Overlap of Feature Sets

Section 3.1 listed a spectrum of compositional mechanisms with sexual recombination at one end and symbiotic encapsulation (e.g., endosymbiosis and symbiogenesis) at the other. Whereas the previous chapter modeled sexual recombination, this chapter is concerned with a model of composition based on symbiotic encapsulation at the other extreme of this spectrum.

The ordering of mechanisms in the spectrum that I emphasized in section 3.1 was based on the similarity or dissimilarity of the entities being composed: the entities involved in sexual recombination are of the same species, whereas symbiotic encapsulation can occur between individuals across species. A second distinction is found in the relationship between the genetic material provided by the donor entities and that appearing in the composite. Specifically, whereas sexual recombination involves alignment and crossover exchanging corresponding subparts of the chromosome, and taking on average half of the genetic material from each parent, the result of endosymbiosis approaches the union of genetic material from the donors—taking all the genetic material from both parties involved.

The alignment of these two trends in the spectrum of compositional mechanisms—similarity/dissimilarity of entities, and half-and-half/union of genetic material—may not be arbitrary. I illustrate with a hypothetical example. Consider a set of characteristics that can be subdivided into subsets where members within each subset are mutually exclusive but members across subsets are not. For example, the characters {TALL, ROUGH, SMOOTH, SHORT} can be subdivided into {TALL, SHORT} and {ROUGH, SMOOTH} by these criteria. For convenience, let us call each subset of mutually exclusive characters a *feature*: for example, the feature HEIGHT has two possible (but mutually exclusive) characters, namely TALL and SHORT. The features then are a dimensionalization of the possible character combinations. Now consider the result of combining an entity specifying for {SHORT} with an entity specifying for {TALL}; the result, by our characterization, cannot be both tall and short—it must be one or the other.

{TALL} + {SHORT} → {TALL **XOR** SHORT}

Biologically, a blending, resulting in medium height for example, is another reasonable possibility in some cases. But still there is no possibility that the result can be both fully tall and fully short, and on average, the characteristics of the donor entities can only be half-inherited in the offspring. Similarly, a mixture, resulting in some of the stalks of a plant being tall and the remainder being short, is also neither fully tall nor fully short, and on average, the characteristic of the donor entities can only be expressed in half the offspring.

In contrast, the result of combining an entity specifying for {SHORT} with an entity specifying for {SMOOTH}, by our characterization, could be an entity that is both short and smooth.

{SHORT} + {SMOOTH} → {SHORT **AND** SMOOTH}

A natural interpretation of mutually exclusive characters is that they reside on the same loci and are mutually exclusive in the haploid chromosome: that is, genes are *features*, and the alleles of a gene are mutually exclusive *characters* of the feature. But this is a particular instantiation of characters and features that presupposes a mechanism of meiosis that is not strictly necessary. That is, if by some circumstance, alignment and crossover failed and entire duplicate chromosomes resulted in the offspring, as in polyploidy events, then the conclusions about some characters being mutually exclusive and some being compatible would still hold even though all alleles of both parents were genetically represented in the offspring. Similarly, if two alleles of a gene are *not* intrinsically mutually exclusive then gene duplication prior to crossing could conceivably result in an entity expressing both characters.

In this scenario then, entities resulting from the combination of entities specifying variations of the same feature set will specify the same feature set themselves and will on average specify half the characters of each parent (assuming unbiased dominance effects, etc.). Whereas, entities resulting from the combination of entities specifying variations of different (nonoverlapping, i.e., not mutually exclusive) feature sets could conceivably specify the union of features from the donor entities. If we define entities specifying for the same (or largely overlapping) feature sets as *similar* (regardless of the values of these features) and entities specifying disjoint (or largely nonoverlapping) feature sets as *dissimilar* then the "similarity to dissimilarity" trend already noted for the spectrum of compositional mechanisms can be seen to logically coincide with the "half-and-half to union" trend in the genetic makeup of resulting entities already noted in the comparison of sexual recombination and symbiotic encapsulation.

From this point of view we see the mechanisms of sexual recombination and symbiotic encapsulation as specific types of a larger class of integrative mechanisms. That is, both mechanisms take the characters of two donor individuals and form a new entity from the combination of their characters. But in sexual recombination, the donor individuals are similar in the sense that their specified feature sets are largely overlapping, whereas in symbiotic encapsulation the donor entities may be dissimilar in the sense that their feature sets are largely nonoverlapping. This has the consequence that the result of sexual recombination events will express on average approximately half the characters of either donor, whereas the result of symbiotic encapsulation will express approximately the full union of characters from both donors. This expectation follows logically from the definition of features as sets of mutually exclusive characters, and the assumptions about the similarity of donors with respect to overlap in the set of features they possess, rather than from the nature of the genetic mechanisms involved.

Similarly, this general perspective is useful in understanding the expected results of other mechanisms in the compositional spectrum. Figure 7.2 illustrates the spectrum of mechanisms in a two-dimensional space representing the similarity of compositional entities to the two donor individuals from which they are created. Each axis represents the percentage of characters from each donor entity that is likely to be exhibited by the result of integration. The arrow indicates the spectrum of compositional mechanisms under discussion. The assumptions here are as follows: (1) asexual

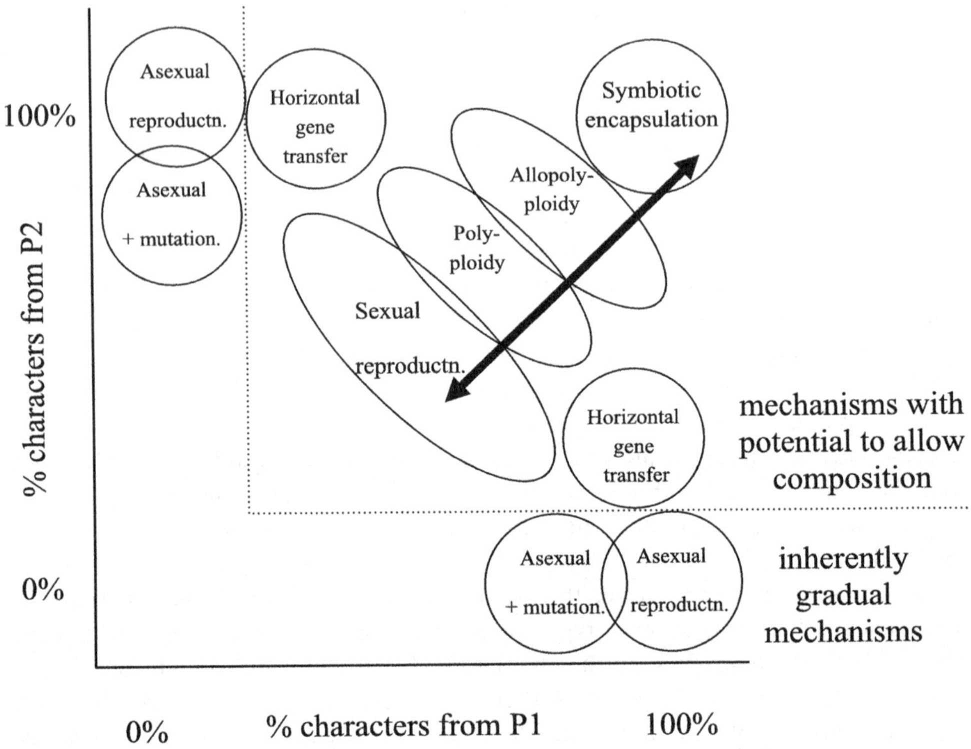

Figure 7.2
Mechanisms of integration from two donor individuals, P1 and P2.

reproduction maintains the characters of the first parent and does not involve characters from a second parent; (2) mutation reduces the heritability of characters from a parent; (3) sexual reproduction results in an offspring exhibiting on average half the characters of parent 1 and half from parent 2; (4) horizontal gene transfer introduces some of the characters from one "parent" into the other "parent" but, depending on how similar the parents are, some characters may also conflict and reduce the heritability of characters from the recipient individual; (5) polyploidy, in a manner similar to sexual recombination, will exhibit approximately half the characters from either parent on average, despite the fact that the offspring may contain the union of genetic material from either parent—but this depends on how similar–dissimilar the feature sets of the donors are; (6) as the feature sets become more different, involving chromosomes from different species (i.e., allopolyploidy), the characters of the parents will be less conflicting and offspring may involve on average more than half of the characters from both donor individuals; (7) symbiotic encapsulation, when occurring between wholly unrelated entities, may result in the union of characters from the donor entities. The figure shows the division where, on one side, mechanisms that take characters from only one donor individual are inherently gradual, and on the other, those that take characters from two donor individuals are potentially compositional.

For our purposes, it is not the genetic mechanisms themselves that are important in these different phenomena, so much as the expected overlap of features coming from the similarity or dissimilarity of the donor individuals. Following this framework, the symbiotic encapsulation mechanism I detail in this chapter is much like that of the sexual recombination mechanism detailed previously but I make different assumptions about the nature of the entities involved. Specifically, in the sexual recombination model I assumed (as is quite normal) that the sets of features exhibited by the donor individuals were fully overlapping. Accordingly, recombination of entities produced conflicts in characters (assuming the population was not fully converged) that needed to be resolved to create a new entity. Specifically, which of the mutually exclusive parental alleles was to be inherited by the offspring was resolved randomly under uniform recombination, and according to physical linkage under one-point crossover. In contrast, in the symbiotic encapsulation model detailed shortly, I assume that the entities are dissimilar from one another and generally nonoverlapping in the sets of features they specify. The next section details the representation of entities and their encapsulation.

A Model of Entities and Their Encapsulation

The focus of the model in this chapter is the notion of a mechanism that composes dissimilar entities—entities that are mostly nonoverlapping in the features they specify—producing resultant entities with the union of their characteristics. These entities may be interpreted as genes, bacterial cells, more complex cells, or any other higher level of organization—the intent is to model transitions between these levels in an integrated model of entities. I will use the word "species" to refer to types of entity at any level. Entities are represented only by their *feature values*, and for now, species are simply the set of entities with identical feature values. These features may be interpreted as genes, as phenotypic features corresponding to genes, or as higher-level features of an organism such as resource usage or a behavioral strategy. In general, they are the set of characteristics that affect the fitness of an entity and the fitness-sensitive interactions of the entity with its environment and other entities.

SEAM abstracts away all population dynamics within a species and therefore the ecosystem will incorporate only one representative entity of each species. An appropriate level of metaphor is that the set of entities represented in the model is an ecosystem of species (rather than a population of individuals).

The basis of SEAM will be that a composite is created from the joining of features from two different species of entity. Accordingly, it is necessary that different entities will specify different subsets of features (not just different values of the same set of features). To provide a simple example: let each feature take one of two values, 0 or 1, and let the features be identified by an index, F_n. Then one entity might specify features $F_3 = 0$, $F_7 = 0$, and $F_{12} = 1$, and a second species might specify $F_1 = 1$, $F_9 = 0$, $F_{10} = 1$, and $F_{15} = 0$. Then their join may create the new entity with features $F_1 = 1$, $F_3 = 0$, $F_7 = 0$, $F_9 = 0$, $F_{10} = 1$, $F_{12} = 1$, and $F_{15} = 0$. (See the messy GA "splice" operation, figure 3.15.)

I will use a large finite set of possible features for the sake of simplicity in the implementation of the model, but the maximum number of features could be flexible in alternate implementations. In this way it is simple to write the specification of an entity using a fixed-length string. Note that in the GA, individuals also generally use a finite set of binary features, genes, (but unlike the entities in SEAM) individuals in the GA must generally specify a value for every possible gene. This is natural for a model of evolution within a single lineage where every individual has basically the same features but varies in the values of these features.

For example, working in a sixteen-feature space, we may write the two entities given in the example above as A and B in the left of figure 7.3 below, and their composition may be written as $A + B$. The null features, "–", in this representation, are placeholders for features that are not (currently) specified by an entity.[2] I will refer to the "size" of an entity to mean the number of non-null features—for example, the entities used in the left of figure 7.3 have sizes 3, 4 and 7, respectively. Composition of two entities, A and B, produces a composite entity, $A + B$, that is twice the size of the donor entities and exhibits the union of their features. The composite is created by taking specified (i.e., non-null) features from either donor where available.

```
   A: --0---0----1----          A: ----1----00-1--
   B: 1-------01----0-          B: --1-0---0-1----
-----------------------     ----------------------
 A+B: 1-0---0-01-1--0-        A+B: --1-1---000-1--
```

Figure 7.3
Symbiotic encapsulation (an abstraction of figure 7.1a).

Figure 7.3 also illustrates how we will deal with conflicting specifications when they arise. Where conflicts in specified features occur we resolve all conflicts in favor of one donor, for example, the first.

Algebraically, we may define the composition of two entities A and B, as the superposition of A on B, below. $A = (A_1, A_2, \ldots, A_n)$ is the entity where feature F_i takes value A_i. $S(A, B)$ is the superposition of entity A on entity B, and $s(a, b)$ is the superposition of two individual feature values, as follows:

Equation 7.1: Composition of two entities

$$S(A,B) = S((A_1, A_2, \ldots, A_n), (B_1, B_2, \ldots, B_n)) = (s(A_1, B_1), s(A_2, B_2), \ldots, s(A_n, B_n)),$$

$$\text{where, } s(a,b) = \begin{cases} a, & \text{if } a \neq \text{null}, \\ b, & \text{otherwise.} \end{cases}$$

This composition will be the only mechanism of variation in SEAM. The intent is that the model will start from "primitive," that is, single-feature, entities and compose them into larger composites, and compose these together, and so on. When small entities are composed with relatively large entities, their effect is like that of single-feature mutations, but as entities become larger, their composition enables variations that scale up with their size.

Note that the way we use species in this model has no implication of restricting possible unions based on type—in principle, new entities may be created by the composition of any two existing entities regardless of their species, that is, regardless of the features they specify.

Consequences for Adaptation

The algorithmic intuition of this model is that different small entities (with a small number of specified features) will adapt to different simple subparts of the adaptive domain and that complex adaptations may subsequently be formed by composing them together. In this respect, the algorithmic intuition is largely the same as that for sexual recombination. However, since sexual recombination between entities with overlapping features sets must involve a half-and-half combination operator, sexual recombination has the problematic aspect that the extraction of appropriate subsets of characters from each parent is dependent on strong physical linkage and the favorable ordering of genes on the chromosome (i.e., a "tight" genetic map). That is, the combination operator needs to be biased to take subsets of features that correspond to coherent modules, because otherwise modules cannot be selected for and manipulated as wholes.

In contrast, the intuition here is that a mechanism of composition using entities with nonoverlapping characters will enable the entities themselves to represent modules (as distinct from the idea that a module may be represented by a subset of genes within an individual). If a whole entity represents a module, and entities can be combined to provide larger modules, then it is not necessary to extract subsets of genetic material from within a given entity. In other words, the appropriate subsets of genes are linked by virtue of being specified within some entity, rather than by virtue of being proximal to each other on the chromosome, and thus the position of genes along the chromosome within an entity becomes irrelevant. This is the key that releases symbiotic encapsulation from the limitations of sexual recombination—specifically, symbiotic encapsulation is not dependent on a favorable genetic map.

7.3 Evaluation and Selection

Having defined a variation operator that describes a join of two entities, the next feature of the model needs to determine whether such a join would be selected for. My basic assumption here is that the symbiotic relationship must be in the "selfish" interest of both the component entities involved. That is, if the fitness of either component entity is greater *without* the proposed partner than it is *with* the proposed partner then the composite will not be selected for. If, on the other hand, the fitness of both component entities is greater when they co-occur then the relationship is deemed stable and will persist.

However, in this model entities are only partial specifications of feature sets and I am assuming that the features of one entity have interdependencies with the features of another. In other words, the fitness of any entity is dependent on its environmental context; possibly, in one environment an entity may be fitter when co-occurring with the proposed symbiont, and in another context the symbiosis may depreciate its fitness. Thus whether a symbiotic relationship is preferred or not depends on what environmental contexts are available (i.e., the preference for a composite is interdependent with context—see p. 145).

Evaluating an Entity in Different Contexts

For our purposes, the set of possible environmental contexts is well-defined: an environmental context is a complete set of features. Such a context allows some partially specified entity (which may be the result of many joins) to be assessed by superimposing the partially specified entity into the context. (See figure 7.4.)

(a) `---0-11---110---` ***x***

(b) `0110101100010011` ***θ***

(c) `0110111100110011` ***S(x,θ)***

Figure 7.4
A partially specified entity must be assessed in a context. (a) An entity specifies a partial set of feature values. (b) An "environmental context" is a complete set of feature values. (c) The entity x superimposed on the context θ.

I assume that the overall fitness of the entity will be a sum of its fitness over different environmental contexts weighted by the frequency with which each environment is encountered. However, we would not generally suppose that the frequencies with which different environments are encountered by one type of entity would be the same as the frequencies relevant to a different type of entity. That is, we imagine that different species have different distributions over possible environments.

Let us assume that we have a measure of the "context-sensitive fitness," $csf(x, \theta)$, of an entity, x, in any given environmental context, θ, and that the overall fitness of the entity x, will be $F(x)$, which is the sum of its fitness over all environments weighted by the frequency of that environment for that species, as below.

Equation 7.2: Weighted sum of context-sensitive fitnesses

$$F(p) = \sum_{\theta \in Contexts} (\lambda_{(\theta,p)}\ csf(p, \theta))$$

where $\lambda_{(\theta,p)} \geq 0$ is the weighting of the environmental context θ, for entity p.

Now, whether a symbiotic relationship is preferred or not depends on the relative weighting of each context to each entity involved, and many factors could influence this. For example, a biased distribution over environmental contexts may be "inherited" by virtue of the collocation of parents and offspring in a subdivided population (or ecosystem subdivided into species), or affected by the behavioral migration of organisms during their lifetime, or the selective displacement of one species by another in short-term population dynamics. I do not wish to introduce such factors and accompanying assumptions into the model. However, neither do I wish to assume an equal weighting of environmental contexts. In fact, it turns out to be critically important that we take account of the context sensitivity of a modular solution in order to maintain diverse complementary modules (as anticipated in the discussion of multidimensional fitness, p. 88). A way out of this problem is provided by the use of a selection model based on Pareto dominance.

Pareto Dominance

The concept of *Pareto dominance* is specifically designed for application in cases where the relative importance of a number of factors is unknown (e.g., see Fonseca and Flemming 1995 for a recent discussion of the use of Pareto dominance in EAs). Put simply, this concept states intuitively that, even when the relative weighting of factors (or "dimensions") is not known, the overall superiority of one candidate with respect to another can be confirmed in the case that it is not worse in all dimensions and better in at least one. More exactly, "x Pareto dominates y" is written "$x \gg y$", and:

$$x \gg y \Leftrightarrow (\forall\theta\colon csf(x,\theta) \geq csf(y,\theta) \text{ AND } \exists\theta\colon csf(x,\theta) > csf(y,\theta)).$$

or equivalently, given that x and y are different in at least one dimension:

$$x \gg y \Leftrightarrow \nexists\theta\colon csf(y,\theta) > csf(x,\theta).$$

In cases where there is some θ such that $csf(x,\theta) > csf(y,\theta)$ and some other θ such that $csf(x,\theta) < csf(y,\theta)$, we say that x and y are *nonsorted.* And in cases where $\exists x\colon x \gg y$ we say that y is *dominated,* else y is *nondominated.* For our ecological domain, these simple rules are easily interpreted. In the case where x is better in some environments than y, and y is better in some environments than x, then we do not know which is fitter overall unless we know the relative weighting of the environments for each entity. But, if x is always fitter than (or at least as fit as) y, then regardless of the weightings of the environments for each entity, we know that the overall fitness of x is greater than that of y (assuming x and y are different in at least one dimension).

This pairwise comparison of two entities over a number of contexts will be used to determine whether a symbiotic join produces a stable composite. If we write the composition of entities a and b as $a+b$, then, using the notion of Pareto dominance, $a+b$ is stable iff $a+b \gg a$, and $a+b \gg b$. In other words, $a+b$ is unstable if there is any context in which either a or b is fitter than $a+b$.

$$stable(a+b,a,b) \equiv a+b \gg a \text{ AND } a+b \gg b,$$

$$unstable(a+b,a,b) \Leftrightarrow \exists\theta \in Contexts\colon (csf(a,\theta) > csf(a+b,\theta) \text{ OR } csf(b,\theta) > csf(a+b,\theta))$$

where *Contexts* is a set of complete feature specifications.

To put it simply, if there is any context where b would be better off without a then b will not make a stable composite entity with a, and vice versa.

I should note that there is a subtle distinction between "the fitness of an entity *in* an environment" and "the fitness of the entity *and* environment together," that is, $csf(x, \theta) \neq f(S(x, \theta))$. However, the method I am using here precludes the need to separate the former from the latter because the pairwise comparison of two entities in the same environmental context implicitly "differences away" the contribution of the environment. It is reasonable to imagine that the nonepistatic contributions of an environment are also "differenced away" in biological scenarios. Formally,

$$csf(x, \theta) > csf(y, \theta) \Leftrightarrow f(S(x, \theta)) > f(S(y, \theta)),$$

where $f(w)$ is the objective fitness of the complete feature set w as given by the fitness function. This assumes that although we can measure the fitness of only a complete feature specification (organism and environment together) we can determine the information we need by differencing away the fitness contributions coming from the environment by including them in both sides of the inequality.

Thus our condition of instability becomes:

Equation 7.3: Stability of $a + b$

$$unstable(a + b, a, b) \Leftrightarrow \exists \theta \in Contexts\colon (f(S(a, \theta)) > f(S(a + b, \theta)) \text{ OR } f(S(b, \theta)) > f(S(a + b, \theta)))$$

Equation 7.3 becomes our abstraction for figure 7.1 (c).

The following simulation tests the stability of a proposed join and immediately undoes it if it is unstable per the above criteria. This might seem a little like I am explicitly testing whether a variation is good before I make it. However, this is not the intent of the model. Rather, I am assuming that new associations are made randomly, but, if and only if the new entity is reliably fitter than both of the parties involved will the new entity survive in the ecosystem. In other words, if there is some niche where one of the two symbionts will outcompete the composite then the composite is competitively excluded. I abstract the process of random joining and competition into the stability test. This models the assumption that competition between joined and nonjoined variants of an entity occurs rapidly such that only reliably successful joins (by these criteria) persist long enough to be involved in a subsequent join. A join that persists through the stability test is treated as a new entity that may participate in further joins as the cycle of the model repeats.

Building Environmental Contexts: Group Evaluation

In SEAM, the environmental contexts, used in determining Pareto dominance and the stability of a proposed composition, will be formed entirely from other members of the ecosystem. The intent here is that the assessment of a new composition involves selecting between being in permanent association with some particular member of the ecosystem or being in transient association with members of the ecosystem. If we were to employ the naive alternative, that is, selecting between being in permanent association with some particular member of the ecosystem or remaining in entirely random environmental contexts, then it would be likely that many more proposed associations would be preferred. This would result in many suboptimal associations (as we will see in control experiments). Additionally, since entities are evaluated in transient groups of other entities there is the potential that they may become coadapted to one another, and thereby primed to make successful permanent joins by composition. Figure 7.5 illustrates how to build a context from a randomly selected set of entities. In this example, six entities *a* through *f*, are needed to complete a fully specified feature set of eight features. Where specified features conflict, the specifications of the topmost entity take precedence, as in figure 7.3. Figure 7.5 becomes our abstraction for figure 7.1 (b).

Algebraically, we define a context, using the recursive function S^*, from an ordered set of $n \geq 2$ entities $X_1, X_2, \ldots, X_n$, as follows:

```
                   a:  --0---1-
                   b:  01------
                   c:  -0---0--
                   d:  ----1-0-
                   e:  ------10
                   f:  ---0-00-
------------------------------------
  Resultant context:  01001010
```

Figure 7.5
Building a context from other entities.

Equation 7.4: Building a context

$$S^*(X_1, X_2, \ldots, X_n) = \begin{cases} S(X_1, S^*(X_2, \ldots, X_n)), & \text{if } n > 2, \\ S(X_1, X_2), & \text{otherwise.} \end{cases}$$

where $S(X_1, X_2)$ is the superposition of two entities as per equation 7.1 above.

Some contexts may require more or fewer entities to provide a fully specified feature set. In principle, we may use all entities of the ecosystem, in random order, to build a context—but, after the context is fully specified, additional entities will have no effect. This allows us to write a context as $S^*(E)$, where E is all members of the ecosystem in random order. Implementationally, we may simply add entities until a fully specified set is obtained.

7.4 The Symbiogenic Evolutionary Adaptation Model (SEAM)

We may now put together the components introduced above to provide a complete model. To summarize, the model includes the following features:

- Variable size entities and a variation operator based on composition.
- Building environmental contexts from other coadapting entities in the ecosystem.
- Testing the stability of compositions by testing for Pareto dominance of the composition over the component entities.

Although each of these features is conceptually somewhat involved, the overall simulation model is not that complicated. Figure 7.6 summarizes the operation of SEAM.

7.5 Simulation Results for Symbiotic Encapsulation

This section provides the simulation results of SEAM as applied to a 128-bit shuffled HIFF. My intent is to illustrate the qualitative difference in the way that composition operates in this landscape as compared to the operation of gradual evolutionary change and also as compared to compositional change under sexual recombination as demonstrated in the previous chapter. Accordingly, I contrast the operation of SEAM with the results of a mutation-only algorithm, random mutation hill climbing (RMHC), shown in section 5.4, and a GA using sexual recombination (see the summary of simulations in section 6.5).

The pseudocode for SEAM is given in figure 7.6. The parameters used for these experiments are: number of features, $N = 128$; alphabet of features, $\Sigma = \{0, 1\}$;

- Initialize ecosystem, E, to random, single-feature, entities.[(1)]
- Repeat until *stopping condition*:
  - Remove two entities at random from the ecosystem → ***a and b.***
  - Produce ***a+b=S(a,b)***, using composition (see equation 7.1).
  - If ***unstable(a+b, a, b)*** return ***a*** and ***b*** to ecosystem, else add ***a+b*** to ecosystem.

where ***unstable(a+b,a,b)*** ⇔

$\exists \theta \in$ ***Contexts***: $(f(S(a,\theta)) > f(S(a+b,\theta))$ OR $f(S(b,\theta)) > f(S(a+b,\theta)))$

where ***Contexts*** is a random set of contexts each built by composing together other members of the current ecosystem, E, using ***S****(E) (see equations 7.3 and 7.4).

[(1)] Initialization needs to completely cover the set of single-feature "primitives" so that all values for all features are available in the ecosystem.

Figure 7.6
Pseudocode for a simple implementation of SEAM.

initial ecosystem size, 256 single-feature entities covering all alleles at all loci; maximum number of contexts used for dominance test, $t = 200$ (empirically, less than 20 of these are required on average to reveal the instability of a proposed join). The stopping condition is for $3 \cdot 10^6$ calls to the fitness function to have been used. f, the fitness function, is provided by shuffled HIFF with 128 binary features.

Initialization is done systematically for practical purposes, but may in principle be done without knowledge of the encoding dimensions by "overgenerating" the initial population and then removing duplicates—more specifically, by removing entities that behave the same (produce identical fitness changes) over a sample of random contexts (see Watson and Pollack 2001b).

The ecosystem size in SEAM is determined by N—in fact, ecosystem size $= 2N$. SEAM uses no mutation. There is no sexual crossover in SEAM, but the encapsulation operator is applied in all matings. Thus there are almost no parameters to the SEAM model and there is only one curve to be plotted. The remaining parameter, the number of trials (i.e., the number of contexts sampled) to determine whether a join is stable, is set to $t = 200$—this value was arrived at through preliminary experimentation. The effect of a low t-value is that incorrect joins are passed as correct (see section 8.2 for related analysis), and an unnecessarily high t-value results in wasted evaluations.[3]

Control Experiments

Recall that the three main conceptual features of SEAM are: the use of variable size entities and a variation operator based on composition; testing the stability of compositions by testing for Pareto dominance of composition over the component entities; and, building environmental contexts from other coadapting entities in the ecosystem.

RMHC and the GA provide a control experiment for the use of partially specified individuals and composition versus full-sized entities and crossover. That is, they use a fully specified feature set for each entity–individual, and use mutation for variation. The GA with sexual recombination provides a control for symbiotic encapsulation. We have already seen that RMHC and the GA fail on shuffled HIFF.

To provide a control for the use of Pareto dominance I also test the operation of an algorithm that is the same as SEAM except that instead of using the Pareto dominance test it simply replaces a component (parent) with the composite (offspring) if the average fitness of the composite, over the set of equally weighted environmental contexts, is greater than the average fitness of that component.

To provide a control for the use of coadapted templates (group evaluation) I also test an algorithm that is the same as SEAM except that it uses random feature sets for the contexts instead of contexts built from other members of the ecosystem.

Simulation Results for SEAM and Control Experiments

Performance is measured by the size of the largest correct module discovered (in the preceding 2,000 evaluations) averaged over 30 runs for each algorithm. The strings evaluated are the groups of entities (i.e., an entity with its contextual environment) forming a complete feature specification. The problem size is 128 bits.

Figure 7.7 shows the performance of SEAM and the two control experiments described above. SEAM finds *both* global optima (correct modules of size 128) in *all* thirty runs.

We see that the performance of the first control, that is, performing replacement when offspring are better on average than the parent rather than replacement when offspring Pareto dominate the parents, is not successful. Performance is much like that of the GA DC with random replacees (figure 6.6). In this experiment, many suboptimal associations are made and the entities fill up, or "bloat," with suboptimal feature values. (This is a well-known problem in other variably sized EA representations such as LISP s-expressions in genetic programming (GP). Other work

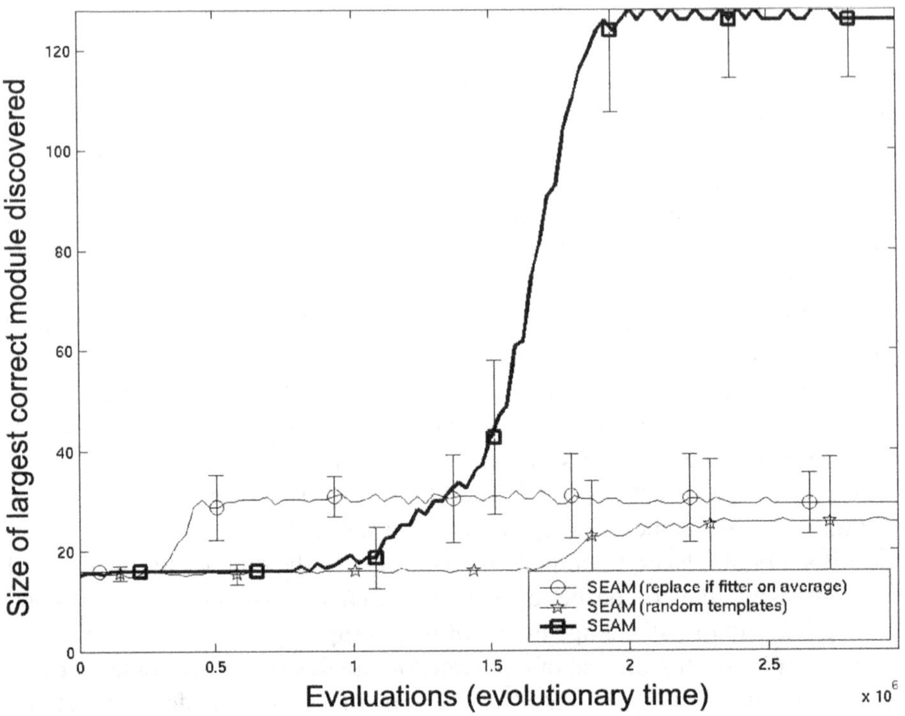

Figure 7.7
Simulation results for SEAM and control experiments.

addressed the use of multiobjective optimization techniques for reducing bloat in GP (De Jong, Watson, and Pollack 2001)—but the full SEAM method has not yet been applied to a GP problem.) This bloat defeats the composition operator (Watson and Pollack 1999c) because no compositions can be made if entities are already fully specified. Thus, the "greedy" selection for whatever configurations appear to be best on average causes the population to quickly converge on bloated suboptimal generalists, rather than properly exploring optimal specialists that cover the problem collectively. Although, as we can see in the figure, this is advantageous in the short term, the population is unable to find optimal configurations in the long term.

We also see that the other control using random templates/contexts to test the stability of a join is also unsuccessful. In this experiment, random templates are sufficient to distinguish suboptimal associations when making joins between small individuals. However, as modules become larger, random templates are insufficient to identify intermodule interdependencies correctly and suboptimal associations re-

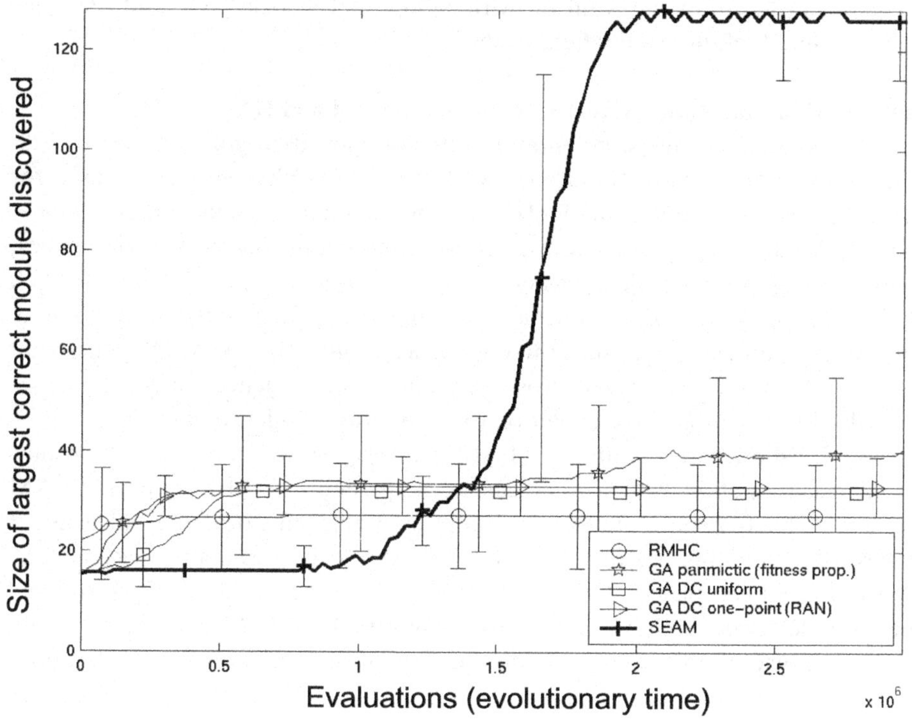

Figure 7.8
Summary of simulation experiments 2: SEAM and GA on shuffled HIFF. The symbiogenic evolutionary adaptation model provides an abstract representation of compositional evolution based on symbiotic encapsulation, showing the evolution of a complex modular system (shuffled HIFF). The genetic algorithm models a sexual population; even when it has diversity maintenance (GA DC) and uses physical linkage (one-point, rather than free-recombination/uniform crossover), it is unable to evolve this type of system because the genetic map is random. The random mutation hill climber models gradual evolution; it cannot evolve this type of system under any conditions. Thus the advantage of compositional evolution by symbiotic encapsulation (unlike the advantage of sexual recombination seen in figure 6.12) is not dependent on a favorable ordering of genes in the genetic map.

sult. Once again the individuals fill up with suboptimal associations, and the algorithm fails to find high-fitness configurations.

Summary of Main Simulation Experiments Using SEAM and GA

Figure 7.8 summarizes the simulation results for various algorithms on a 128-variable shuffled HIFF. Best mutation rates (of those sampled earlier) are used for each method that uses mutation. RMHC—random mutation hill climber ($mut = 0.0938$). "GA panmictic"—genetic algorithm without any diversity maintenance, using fitness-proportionate selection and one-point crossover ($mut = 0.0078$). "GA DC uniform"—GA with deterministic crowding diversity maintenance method, and no genetic linkage (i.e., uniform crossover) ($mut = 0$). "GA DC one-point RAN"—GA with DC, one-point crossover, and random genetic linkage ($mut = 0.031$). "SEAM"—symbiogenic evolutionary adaptation model ($mut = 0$).

As figure 7.8 shows, the results for SEAM are very successful as were the results for sexual recombination with a tight genetic map (figure 6.12). However, SEAM (since it is not able to exploit the assumption of favorable gene ordering) takes about four times longer for this size problem, $N = 128$. (SEAM takes about twice as long as GA DC to find complete solutions when $N = 64$.) But both these compositional methods are clearly different from the other algorithms. SEAM and the GA with deterministic crowding (given the assumption of tight linkage) find *both* global optima in at least 28 out of 30 runs. None of the other methods find *either* global optimum in *any* of the 30 runs.

Progress in the noncompositional mechanisms (i.e., mutation-only methods and the panmictic GA), and scenarios where composition is disrupted (e.g., the GA with random linkage), becomes increasingly more difficult in HIFF as the width of the fitness saddle to the next higher-fitness point becomes further away with each fitness increase. But in scenarios where composition is working effectively, that is, in the GA DC with tight linkage, and in SEAM, progress is not impeded in this landscape.

7.6 The Relationship of SEAM to Other Algorithmic Methods

A number of conceptual components used in the symbiogenic evolutionary adaptation model share features with some aspects of existing work. For example, the use of partially specified individuals and a combination operator that is insensitive to the genetic map is similar to the use of underspecified moving-locus presentations and the "splice" operator in the messy GA as developed in section 3.3. The concept of group evaluation, evaluating a partially specified individual in a context built from coevolved entities, is similar to "templating" in the messy GA but more explicitly related the use of the "shared domain model" in cooperative coevolution. Cooperative coevolution also contributes the idea that what we are really doing in generating coadapted schemata is a coevolutionary process. These ideas were also developed in section 3.3.

The relationship of SEAM to some issues raised earlier is worth emphasizing. Specifically, its relationship to: linkage-learning methods, methods of automatic module acquisition, the competing conventions problem, and the credit assignment problem.

SEAM shows equivalence between concepts of linkage learning and module acquisition. In other words, when SEAM solves shuffled HIFF with a random genetic map, it also discovers where the modules are in the problem. It represents these explicitly as (partially specified) individuals so that they can be composed together. The tree structure implicit in the sequence of joins that are made represents the tree structure of HIFF, and SEAM could easily be modified to output this explicitly. Representing epistatic dependencies using partially specified individuals avoids the limitations of representing dependencies in linear form (i.e., by their arrangement on the chromosome—e.g., Harik 1997; see also p. 182). By explicitly representing the interdependent variables as modules we are both learning the linkage in the problem and performing automatic module acquisition.

The results also show that the competing conventions issue is not necessarily problematic for crossover. HIFF has strongly competing (mutually exclusive) solutions to each module in every partition of the variables, but a GA can overcome the disruption caused by the recombination of incompatible subsolutions of different conventions if it has an effective means of selecting against poor offspring and for identifying valuable new schemata. Chapter 6 showed that the GA using deterministic crowding is sufficient for this purpose in this class of problem. And chapter 6 showed that the competing conventions issue is not an issue for SEAM even when a random genetic map is used.

SEAM shows that there are principled solutions to the credit assignment problem in this class of problem also. SEAM introduces methods for determining the value of a schema for the purposes of the future assembly of schemata. The method used is not based on schema fitness—the average fitness of strings included in that schema—instead, it is based on the influence that that schema has on groups of other schemata in group evaluation. A schema is selected because it is *nondominated* rather than because it is good on average (see p. 216, and the later discussion on identifying good modules, p. 261).

The key here is the use of Pareto coevolution which is an important new concept used in SEAM. This is, of course, inspired by Pareto-optimization techniques already in use in evolutionary approaches (Fonseca and Fleming 1995; Rosenberg 1967; Coello Coello 1999) and coevolution in general, but more specifically by the idea that different members of a coevolving population should cover different parts of the problem space. This basic idea is evident in one of the early well-known examples of coevolution for optimization purposes (where different individuals are expected to provide a diverse set of test cases) (Hillis 1992) and is developed extensively in other work (Juillé 1999).

Subsections below review briefly how the components of SEAM address the problems of using compositional operators that were listed in section 3.3 and also highlight some of the underlying concepts developed in Pareto coevolution. However, in chapter 9 I discuss the idea of "stochastic lookahead," which I think is a better way to understand how it is that evolution can do something smarter than just incremental improvement.

Recombining versus Combining

We saw in chapter 6 that when gene ordering is randomized, crossover is unable to exchange meaningful subsets of variables and recombine them in an offspring. As we have mentioned there are various different approaches that may be employed to overcome this problem, such as crossover masks, moving-locus representations, and other linkage-learning methods. The basic problem is the problem of determining which part of an individual constitutes a module—which part of an individual is a good part to transfer to the offspring. When gene ordering is random, the parts taken by one-point crossover, for example, do not correspond to meaningful modules.

The messy GA uses a combination of two features to address this problem. One is the use of partially specified individuals, the other is the use of a moving-locus representation (see p. 84). In previous work (Watson and Pollack 1999c) we showed that the moving-locus aspects of the messy GA are perhaps less important (at least, not essential) to enable successful recombination in a modular interdependency problem like HIFF. By using just the partial-specification features of the messy GA it is, in principle, possible to allow each individual to represent exactly one module explicitly (see figure 3.16). (This is in contrast to the regular GA where an individual is a fully specified feature set and therefore represents a collection of modules.) Using partially specified individuals in this manner there is no problem in extracting the appropriate parts from a parent in crossover because a parent *is* a part.[4] In this sense, we see a shift from *re*combination, where modules are moved from one assembly to another assembly, to *combination* where modules are put into an assembly explicitly for the first time.

Problems with Partial Evaluation, Bloat, and Diversity

However, the algorithm presented in previous work (Watson and Pollack 1999c) had some serious limitations. First, we needed to evaluate partially specified individuals; second, we needed a way to prevent suboptimal associations from being made; third, we needed an appropriate way to maintain diversity. These issues were handled in that work, but only in a limited manner.

It so happens that in HIFF, there is a natural interpretation of a partially specified string—we can simply fill in the unspecified loci with "nulls." But this may not be an available strategy in more realistic domains that require fully specified strings in order to perform an evaluation. With regard to the second limitation, we used a size penalty that prevented a premature increase in the size of strings until optimal joins had been formed. However, this penalty function required explicit knowledge of how the fitness of strings may grow with size. We have such knowledge in HIFF, of course, but again, in general, such knowledge will be unavailable. With respect to the third limitation, we used the resource-based fitness-sharing method as in earlier work (Watson, Hornby, and Pollack 1998). This works very well but again uses an explicit knowledge of the modules in the problem that is usually unavailable. It is not clear how the deterministic crowding method that we used to maintain diversity in chapter 6 should be adjusted to work on partially specified individuals (e.g., what is the distance between two individuals that are nonoverlapping in the features they specify?) and moreover, the deterministic crowding method assumes a genotypic similarity metric.

At this stage, our three problems were: evaluation of partially specified individuals, limiting exponential growth of strings (and premature commitment of unspecified variables to suboptimal values), and diversity maintenance.

Note that these limitations are not trivially solved in the messy GA or other methods either. In the messy GA, the growth of strings is limited to order k in the first phase of the algorithm—which assumes that there is a small k equal to the highest-order nonlinearity in the problem (which is not the case in HIFF), and it assumes that we have knowledge of this value. Goldberg, Korb, and Deb (1989) suggest the use of "thresholding" as a diversity maintenance technique (where individuals that are too dissimilar are not allowed to breed together). This method of diversity assumes that a distance metric is available to discern how similar two parents are. And, genotypic Hamming distance is not always an appropriate measure of functional dissimilarity.

However, there are some valuable clues available in previous work also. Goldberg, Korb, and Deb (1989) suggest the use of "templates" to permit partially specified individuals to be evaluated. These are fully specified strings used to fill in unspecified features of the individual being evaluated. In later versions of the messy GA, Goldberg et al. (1990, 1993) suggest that templates for one round of evaluation could be built from strings generated in previous rounds, hence reusing evolved blocks to make templates for subsequent evolution.

Meanwhile, in cooperative coevolution, Potter (1997) suggests the use of a shared domain model that enables the evaluation of an individual, fulfilling one particular role in a collective solution, to be evaluated in the context of other individuals co-adapted to fill in other roles in the collective solution. This is not so different from the idea of templates in the messy GA. Both use the idea of using coevolved individuals to build templates to evaluate subsequent individuals. However, cooperative coevolution does not use a join operator to explicitly make higher-level composites—it is a single-level decomposition of the problem domain. Since cooperative coevolution does not use a join operator, there is no problem of individuals growing in size. However, a single level of problem decomposition also means that the problem can only be optimized to the extent that the particular fitness interests of individuals in the different roles do not conflict with the optimal configuration for the group as a whole.

So, these methods suggest mechanisms that evaluate individuals in the context of other coevolving individuals. SEAM develops this idea: that is, it evaluates individuals in templates built from other coevolved individuals. SEAM evaluates partially specified individuals in groups that collectively cover the problem variables. Thus, we evaluate only fully specified feature sets and do not require the direct evaluation of partially specified individuals. However, we use the information from these group evaluations to evaluate the merit of a proposed individual in the group.

However, Goldberg et al. (1989) caution that the use of templating introduces the problem of "low signal-to-noise ratio" in the evaluation of individuals (i.e., noise in the evaluation coming from the fitness contribution of the templates is high relative to the signal coming from the fitness contribution of the individual being evaluated), and also that an arbitrary template may not reveal the necessary dependencies that a schema has with its genetic context.

Template Differencing

Our solution to the problem of low signal-to-noise ratio in SEAM involves something we might call "template differencing" that is allied to the method of evaluation in cooperative coevolution.

Naively, we might use the group evaluation proposed above and simply share out the fitness of the group to members of the group. However, this necessarily suffers from the problem of bloat where suboptimal feature specifications accumulate or "hitchhike" along with fit specifications. An alternative is to examine the fitness difference that an individual makes to a group when it is added or removed to or from the group, as in the shared domain model of cooperative coevolution.

So, the idea of template differencing is that we will measure the fitness of a group with and without the individual of interest and difference the two. This will give us an indication of how much the individual contributed to the group. However, because there are fitness dependencies between the individual and the group, using just one group will not give us a proper sample of an individual's possible contribution. Accordingly, we must test an individual in many groups. However, this does not solve the problem of how to prevent exponential string growth (see the credit assignment/hitchhiking problem, p. 87): that is, a suboptimal join is usually better than a random join and consequently individuals fill up with suboptimal feature specifications (even when we use template differencing to reduce noise).

The Pressure to Fill In Missing Features

In Watson, Reil, and Pollack 2000b we observed that when the missing features of a partially specified individual are "scaffolded" by the features of other coadapted individuals there is in some circumstances a tendency for individuals to be, we might say, complacent about whether or not they fill in for the missing abilities themselves. Briefly, if symbionts are reliably available in the ecosystem then there is no pressure for individuals to acquire the missing features for themselves (see Harvey 1993 for the equivalent phenomenon in the Baldwin effect). In a model of genetic assimilation of acquired characteristics this is a problem. But for our purposes, it offers an opportunity to alleviate the pressure for partially specified individuals to fill in with suboptimal features.

However, preliminary work using group evaluation (with or without template differencing) failed. If we took the average fitness an individual has in many groups, or the maximum (or, selected for minimizing detrimental effects to a group), individuals either never allowed additional features to be specified, or allowed too many additional features to be specified as before. At this stage we needed a principled way to determine when a join really created a good higher-level module rather than merely a collection of better-than-average modules. The solution in SEAM can be understood by two shifts in perspective. First, we use a more principled definition of what makes of a "good module"—what does it mean to be a good module and how would we find one? Second, rather than develop an evolutionary process that moves from poor solutions to good solutions, we developed an evolutionary method that moves from specialized solutions to general solutions. The ideas of stochastic lookahead (p. 261) and Pareto coevolution, respectively, were critical in addressing these issues.

Pareto Coevolution

I mentioned briefly on page 88 that coevolution can be regarded as a multiobjective optimization problem where each individual in a population represents a dimension to be optimized. Thus, desirable individuals are not those that do well on average against other individuals in the population, but are those that are nondominated. Specifically, if *A* can beat everybody that *B* can beat (and at least one player that *B* cannot beat) then *A dominates B*, and *B* may be discarded. But if *A* beats some opponents that *B* cannot beat, and *B* beats some opponents that *A* cannot beat, then *A* does not dominate *B*, and neither *B* (nor *A*) should be discarded on the basis of these comparisons. (See Ficici and Pollack 2000, 2001; Watson and Pollack 2000a; Noble and Watson 2001; De Jong and Pollack 2002; Bucci and Pollack 2002.)

The idea here is that a coevolving entity should be retained because it is "good for something" rather than merely "good on average." The intuition is that a selection scheme based on dominance will allow individuals to survive because they cover some part of the problem domain that other individuals do not. In contrast, selecting for individuals that are good on average is the greedy approach that will cause the population to converge on the best solution found so far. Such a selection scheme is conceptually similar to fitness-sharing methods, but here we abstract away all of the population dynamics inherent in fitness sharing. That is, rather than adjusting the fitness of individuals according to how many other individuals are similar and then allowing everybody to reproduce according to their adjusted fitness, we essentially transform fitness values into either 1 or 0—either an individual is nondominated and it survives, or it is dominated and it is discarded.[5] In this respect, our method is somewhat similar to implicit fitness sharing (Smith, Forrest, and Perelson 1993), except that in implicit fitness sharing it is assumed that the problem subdomains are given and in SEAM the problem subdomains are defined by other coevolving individuals. Further, Parteo coevolution and (genotypic) fitness-sharing methods are different in that the latter often require a similarity metric in order to ascertain who is similar and with whom fitness must be shared. In Pareto coevolution individuals are implicitly deemed similar if they perform similarly against different opponents.

The Pareto coevolution idea is useful for explicitly adversarial coevolutionary scenarios (Ficici and Pollack 2001; Noble and Watson 2001), but in SEAM we are concerned with something that, on the face of it, is not a coevolutionary problem. We are merely trying to optimize a single function, HIFF. However, via the use of partially specified individuals that represent partial feature specifications, and templates built from other coevolving individuals that build a complete feature specification, we have transformed an evolutionary problem into a coevolutionary problem. Moreover, by the use of Pareto coevolution, we have transformed a single-objective optimization problem into a multiobjective optimization problem.

If we apply the Pareto coevolution idea to the problem of finding good modules then the "dimensions" of the problem are each represented by a different group—that is, an individual is retained because there is some group it is good for. More exactly, a join between two individuals will be allowed if it creates a composite that dominates both parents. The SEAM model details the operation of this mechanism. This will work to find modules that cover the problem domain appropriately, and we will not have to specify where the modules are in the problem *a priori*, rather, the coevolution of modules will allow them to be discovered. Further, this means of promoting diversity does not rely on a genotypic similarity metric like Hamming distance. In essence, diverse modules are identified by virtue of having different performance profiles over a sample of groups. This is a purely behavioral metric of similarity that does not depend on knowing an *a priori* measure of similarity, nor does it assume any access to the properties of the genotype directly.

This is an interesting side point. In a purist frame of mind, the only information we have about a candidate solution is its fitness. However, many methods used in EAs also assume access to genotypic information for the purposes of fitness sharing/diversity maintenance, restricted breeding, and so on. This seems like a necessary evil perhaps—we would rather that we did not have to examine the genotype directly, but how else could we modify the fitness of an entity appropriately? In SEAM we present an alternative. We do not examine the genotype of any individuals directly, and the only measure of a combination of features that we will use is the objective fitness function. But nonetheless, we are able to ascertain important additional information about an individual and its characteristics. This is done not by an examination of the genotype but by examining its effect on fitness measures in a sample of different contexts.

7.7 Summary

In the previous chapter we saw that under some circumstances sexual recombination is able to provide the compositional change appropriate for adaptation on landscapes exhibiting modular interdependency like HIFF. However, we also saw that one of the provisos for this was that the ordering of genes on the chromosome must correspond well to the epistatic dependency structure of the adaptive domain.

Results of the previous chapters showed that mutation and sexual recombination are unable to exploit the decomposable structure of HIFF or otherwise overcome the large-scale fitness saddles in the landscape except when a tight genetic map is assumed for sexual recombination. The provisos for the successful action of sexual recombination were: appropriate modular interdependency structure, population diversity, strong genetic linkage, and favorable gene ordering on the chromosome (i.e., a tight genetic map).

In contrast, the variably sized entities in SEAM are able to identify and represent a correct assembly of compatible features forming a useful module for the next hierarchical level, regardless of gene ordering. Also the use of Pareto dominance in the selection scheme provides an appropriate tool for maintaining diversity that does not depend in any way on genotypic similarity measures. Thus only the first proviso remains for the successful operation of SEAM: appropriate modular interdependency structure.

Since SEAM has no gene-position-sensitive features, there is no difference in the operation of SEAM on HIFF and shuffled HIFF. Other variants of HIFF, such as biased HIFF (where 0s and 1s confer different fitness contributions), and H-XOR (based on exclusive-OR rather than IFF) (see Watson and Pollack 1999a,b), are also solved by SEAM.

These results using symbiotic encapsulation provide a second set of sufficient conditions under which complex systems of this kind are easily evolvable under compositional mechanisms. In particular, SEAM shows that a mechanism from the other end of the spectrum of compositional mechanisms given in figure 3.1 is not dependent on gene ordering in the way we saw for sexual recombination, or on any *a priori* knowledge of which genes are dependent on which others.

Taken together, chapters 4 through 7 illustrate the main claim of this book: compositional evolutionary mechanisms can provide adaptation akin to divide-and-conquer problem decomposition under certain circumstances, and therefore, certain kinds of complex systems, considered unevolvable under the gradualist framework of evolution, are easily evolvable under compositional mechanisms. Chapter 4 described an example complex system and discussed the general properties of the class that are important. Chapter 5 showed how this kind of system is unevolvable under the gradualist framework. And chapters 6 and 7 showed that this type of system is easily evolvable under two different compositional mechanisms, sex and symbiotic encapsulation, respectively.

The next chapter is a technical chapter that provides analytic proofs to support these simulation studies. These enable us to see whether the differences illustrated in these simulations really derive from a fundamental algorithmic distinction in the way that gradual and compositional evolution operate.

8 How Fast Is Fast?

The simulation experiments shown in chapters 6 and 7 show that compositional evolution can, under the given conditions, evolve complex systems exhibiting modular interdependency faster than mutation can. But, to a computer scientist, the proof of the pudding is the time complexity of an algorithm. It is all very well to show that some algorithm does better than some other algorithm on a particular size problem, but if it is really true that the algorithms are interestingly different then we will be able to see a fundamental distinction in how the algorithms scale with problem size. The simulation experiments shown in chapters 6 and 7 provide an illustration of the algorithms evolving a complex system of a particular size, but it is the formal analyses in this chapter that describe how these algorithms scale up to the larger complex systems of this class. Chapter 5 showed that no mutation-based mechanism of hill climbing, that is, gradual evolution, can be guaranteed to evolve this class of system in time less than exponential in the size of the system. Specifically, the best mutation-based approach would have a time complexity of $O(N^2 2^{N/2})$. If compositional algorithms really provide an algorithmic advantage from divide-and-conquer problem decomposition then they should scale polynomially with the size of the system.

This kind of fundamental distinction is interesting to the computer scientist because it means that for large systems, polynomial adjustments in the estimate of the time it takes to evolve the system will be insignificant. If the times are changed by a factor of two, for example, by using a different population size, or a different mutation rate, or whatever, it does not really amount to much because when the problem gets a little larger such distinctions will be drowned out by the exponential increase in the time required for the mutation-based approach. Getting a grasp of the fundamentally different time complexities of these different optimization principles helps us to see that compositional evolution is not just a slight modification to gradual evolution, but a fundamentally different algorithmic class.

In the following two subsections I provide proofs for the time complexity of the compositional mechanisms on HIFF and shuffled HIFF.

8.1 An Analysis of Sexual Recombination on HIFF

In this section[1] I provide some analytical results for various recombinative algorithms applied to HIFF. For these purposes I will not attend to the biological plausibility of each model because the intent here is only to understand the combinatorics involved in principle.

A nonseparable building-block problem such as HIFF is not amenable to some analytical approaches usually adopted in the literature. First, it is not possible to apply any analysis that assumes that the population as a whole converges incrementally on particular hyperplanes. In HIFF the operation of recombination may be defeated if the population is allowed to converge at just two loci that are incompatible. Second, most analyses assume separable problems, and, surprisingly often, focus on the extreme case where every bit is separable—the max-1s problem. However, Wright and Zhao (1999) provide an approach to analysis that, although directed at separable building-block problems, can be adapted for our purposes. Their approach is to prove that there is always a way to improve fitness, and then to give a solution time based on the product of the length of the path to the solution, and the time for each step on the path. Here I extend this work to use the same approach for a non-separable problem.

It can be quite straightforward to calculate an expected time to solution when there are no local optima in a problem—that is, when there is a path of monotonically increasing fitness from any point in the search space to the solution. In this case, the expected time is simply the product of the length of this path and the expected time for each step on the path. This is the approach that I will take in the following analyses. The interesting part will be to prove the existence of such a path under recombination despite the fact that there is no such path for a mutation-based algorithm. Ordinarily, such a straightforward approach would be defeated because both the existence of a path and the time required for a step are dependent on the state of the population when using recombination. However, to calculate an upper bound on the expected time it is sufficient to know certain properties, or invariants, of the population rather than its exact state. For example, Wright and Zhao (1999) provide an analysis of a recombinative algorithm on a separable building-block problem by using the property of the algorithm that prevents alleles from being lost. Under these conditions (detailed shortly) there is always some recombination operation that will improve the fitness of the best individual in the population.

Here I extend this idea to a nonseparable building-block problem, that is, HIFF. First, I analyze a *recombinative hill climber* that applies crossover repeatedly to just two strings. This simplification provides appropriate invariants that enable us to prove that there is always some choice of crossover points that will improve fitness, and to give an expected time to find such an improvement. Accordingly, this provides an analytical time to solution on this problem. These analyses are possible because of particular regularities in the standard form of the problem; when these regularities are removed the recombinative hill climber fails. Nevertheless, the principle of an algorithm that follows the recombination landscape is useful to us in less restricted cases. I show that a variant of the problem that is not solvable by the recombinative hill climber is solvable by a true GA—that is, a GA using a population. Though the analysis does not transfer directly to the true GA, a solution time

- Choose an initial population (see text).
- Repeat until satisfied:
  - Pick two parents at random from the population.
  - Produce a pair of offspring from these parents using crossover only.
  - If the fittest offspring is fitter than the fittest parent then replace the two parents with the pair of offspring.

Figure 8.1
A simple form of the gene invariant GA.

based on the assumption that the GA is exploiting the recombination landscape agrees with the empirical results.

Analysis on Separable Problems

The analysis provided by Wright and Zhao (ibid.), and the analyses that follow, feature the gene invariant GA (GIGA) (Culberson 1992). The variant of GIGA that best suits our purposes is described in figure 8.1.

There are several features to note about this algorithm. Competition is restricted to parents versus their offspring. The two offspring are created from the parents using the same crossover points and so each gene donated by the parents will be acquired by exactly one of the offspring. Given this and the fact that either both offspring are retained or both parents are retained (and there is no mutation) it follows that alleles are never lost from the population—hence, the "gene invariant" GA. Finally, note that the algorithm is elitist—the fittest member of the population cannot be replaced by an inferior individual.

Wright and Zhao add several other assumptions to this model: the problem is separable; a set of crossover masks is used that restrict crossover to operations that move exactly one block from one parent to the other; finally, the population is systematically initialized such that every possible bit combination within each block is present. This initialization gives a population size of c^k, where c is the size of the alphabet and k is the number of bits in a block.

These simplifying assumptions enable a useful property to follow: given the gene-invariance property of the algorithm and that crossover points are not permitted to move partial blocks, it is guaranteed that building blocks are never lost from the population; since all possible candidates for a block are present in the initial population and they can never be lost, there will always be some individual in the population that has any block that should be required. Thus, if the best individual in the population is not yet optimal then it must have some suboptimal block, and this block can be obtained from some member of the population using some crossover mask. This is the invariant property of the population that is required for the analysis. Although the exact structure of the population is not known, this property ensures that there is always some way to improve fitness using recombination.

To calculate an upper bound on the expected time, T, required for the population to find an individual that has reached the global optimum[2] Wright and Zhao focus attention on the fittest individual in the population. Their version of the algorithm asserts that one of the parents is the fittest individual (and the other parent is selected at random). The possible states that the algorithm may pass through in the course of search, that is, the possible populations, are then categorized into equivalence sets based on the fitness of the fittest individual. T is then given by the maximum possible number of fitness increases of this fittest individual, and the time expected for each increase. This yields $T = Br(D/d)$, where B is the number of blocks in the problem (equals the number of crossover masks), r is the size of the population, D is the difference in fitness between the global optimum and the worst possible string, and d is the difference in fitness between the global optimum and the next best string (i.e., the minimum fitness increase for finding a correct block).

Theorem 1 below modifies the proof provided by Wright and Zhao and uses the same assumptions about the problem, crossover masks, and initialization. However, Wright and Zhao categorize the state of the algorithm using the fitness of the fittest individual in the population and always use this individual as one of the parents. In contrast, I will categorize the state of the algorithm using the number of fully optimized blocks in a particular individual, which will always be used as one of the parents. But, this individual may not be the fittest individual in the population. Indeed, although the fittest individual possible (the global optimum) must have all blocks fully optimized, the fittest individual in the population at a given time does not necessarily have any blocks fully optimized.

In order to transform the theorem to work on the number of optimized blocks it is necessary to ensure that we never reduce the number of optimized blocks when we accept an offspring. We cannot directly measure the number of fully optimized blocks in an individual; neither can we infer the number of fully optimized blocks from a fitness measure. However, we can use the following observation: a fitness increase created by changing one block in an individual cannot reduce the number of fully optimized blocks in that individual. Figure 8.2 describes a modified algorithm that ensures this condition is applied.

The algorithm in figure 8.2 is almost the same as that in figure 8.1, but the replacement is more specific about which offspring is compared to which parent. Note that

- Choose an initial population (as before).
- Pick one parent at random from the population, $p1$.
- Repeat until satisfied:
  - Pick one parent at random from the population, $p2$.
  - Produce a pair of offspring from $p1$ and $p2$ using crossover only. Let $c1$ be the offspring that results from $p1$ plus one block from $p2$; let $c2$ result from $p2$ plus one block from $p1$.
  - If $c1$ is fitter than $p1$ then replace $p1$ with $c1$, and $p2$ with $c2$.

Figure 8.2
A modified gene invariant GA.

the algorithm selects only one new parent in each iteration, and evaluates only one of the new offspring. This means that maybe the second offspring, $c2$, was fitter than the one evaluated—and maybe we missed an opportunity to increase fitness. But for our purposes, it is more important that we know that $p1$ does not decrease in the number of optimized blocks. Although the algorithm in figure 8.2 explicitly makes reference to the fact that the partitions of blocks are known, and that the crossover masks swap only one block at a time, we are not adding any new assumptions to those used by Wright and Zhao. Significantly, note that the modified algorithm maintains the gene-invariant property, and the property that building blocks are never lost from the population.

THEOREM 1: An upper bound on the expected time for some individual in the population to find the globally optimal string, using the algorithm in figure 8.2, is given by $T \leq B^2 r$, where B is the number of blocks in the separable problem and r is the size of the population ($r = c^k$, where c is the alphabet size and k is the number of symbols in a block).

Proof:[3] Partition the set of possible algorithm states into categories based on the number of optimal blocks in $p1$. Category j, for $j = 0, 1, \ldots, B$, is the set of states where $p1$ has exactly j blocks fully optimized. Let Sj be the random variable that denotes the number of evaluations that the algorithm spends in category j. If the GA is in category j with $j < B$, then $p1$ has some block that is not at optimum, and there is a crossover operation that will swap in the optimal configuration of bits for that block from some other member of the population. This operation moves the algorithm state to a new category and has a probability of at least $1/(Br)$ since there are B crossover masks and r possible choices for the second parent. An upper bound for the expected time to leave any state is the inverse of a lower bound on the probability of leaving that state. Thus, the expected value of Sj, at $j < B$, is at most Br. The expected time to reach a population that contains the globally optimum string is at most the time it takes for the algorithm to reach category B, that is,

$$T \leq \sum_{j=1}^{B} S_j \leq B^2 r. \quad \blacksquare$$

The intuition behind this analysis is now very simple. T is given by the product of the number of blocks to be found, and the time to find a block in another individual and swap it in by crossover. The number of blocks is B, and getting a block into the best individual requires finding the right crossover mask (of which there are B), and picking the right donor individual (of which there are r)—hence $B^2 r$, or $B^2(c^k)$.

This expected time has the desirable property that it is not dependent on any measurement of fitness values in the problem. And the resultant upper bound for T is lower than that which Wright and Zhao provide, at least whenever $B < (D/d)$. Both analytic times assume that each crossover mask corresponds to exactly one block. However, Wright and Zhao's analysis could be modified to a more general set of masks, giving $T \leq Mr(D/d)$, where M is the number of crossover masks used. This set of masks may include masks that match with more than one block so long as they match only with whole blocks, and it must include the set of masks that correspond to the single fitness blocks, as before. In any case, an approach based on counting optimized blocks, rather than fitness improvements, is better suited to our needs in the following sections.

So far we have an upper bound on the expected time to solution for a recombinative algorithm on a separable building-block problem. However, we have to ask whether the simplified problems and algorithms involved in these analyses have captured the interesting properties of a GA. We have permitted modifications to the algorithm that do not violate the assumptions made about the problem—but notice that we are getting gradually closer to something much simpler than a GA. In fact, notice that using only the same assumptions about a problem as those used above (i.e., that the partitions of building blocks are known), a simple systematic hill-climbing technique would suffice. That is, in a separable problem with known partitions, each subset of interdependent parameters may be searched exhaustively—that is, each block may be processed systematically by testing every possible bit combination within that block and selecting the highest fitness configuration. While one block is being processed, we hold the setting of bits in other blocks constant to some arbitrary configuration. The particular configuration of bits used in other blocks does not matter since we know that the blocks are separable. Since systematic search within a block requires testing c^k bit configurations, and there are B blocks to be processed, this simple systematic search takes only $T \leq Bc^k$.

Further, for their analysis using GIGA, Wright and Zhao suggest that if the partitioning of blocks is not known then their analytic time can be multiplied by the number of possible partitionings. Since this can be applied to our simple systematic hill climber too, by this analysis, the simple method is still superior even if the partitioning is not known. I make this observation not to criticize the approach of Wright and Zhao, rather I present it as an illustration that separable problems do not justify the use of a population-based recombinative technique. Nonetheless, the above version of Wright and Zhao's analysis provides a good starting point for an analysis of GIGA on HIFF, which is not separable and, I shall argue, *does* require a recombinative algorithm.

Analyses on HIFF

The approach of Wright and Zhao provides an appropriate tool for analyzing the action of sexual recombination on HIFF. Their approach is quite intuitive: their algorithm (GIGA, figure 8.1) and their assumptions guarantee that there is always some choice of parents for which some crossover operation can produce an offspring that is the next step in a progression of individuals that increase in fitness. In other words, their approach is to prove that separable building-block problems have no local optima using their algorithm. I follow the same approach—but for non-separable building-block problems, and whereas the proof of Wright and Zhao is based on the fitness of an individual, the approach used in theorem 1 is based on the number of blocks that are fully optimized in an individual.

Condition 1: There is always some choice of parents for which some crossover operation can produce an offspring that is the next step in a progression of individuals that increases in the number of fully optimized building blocks. (Except when the progression has already arrived at a global optimum.)

This condition is central to the approach in this section. It refers to the ability of an algorithm to utilize the building-block structure of a problem. Or alternatively, to an invariant property of a population that enables an algorithm to utilize the building-block structure. Any algorithm that satisfies condition 1 and follows such a progression will take time $T \leq BS$, where B is the number of blocks to be found in a globally optimal string (i.e., equals the maximum number of steps in the progression), and S is the maximum expected time for each step in the progression. For a recombinative algorithm where condition 1 holds, $S \leq PM$, where P is the number of different ways of choosing parents, and M is the number of crossover masks, thus:

Equation 8.1: Expected time to solution in terms of steps on path to optimum

$T \leq BPM.$

Equation 8.1 will hold for any problem that can be described in terms of blocks in some way such that condition 1 holds. Proving that condition 1 holds (and that an algorithm follows this progression) will be more or less difficult depending on the assumptions made about the algorithm and the problem. In the separable problem addressed in theorem 1, condition 1 holds because all possible configurations for each block are given by initialization and cannot be lost by the variation operators that the algorithm uses. In theorem 1, $M = B$, and $P = r$, the size of the population. We cannot expect to prove condition 1 for a standard recombinative algorithm on a general nonseparable problem. However, HIFF is specifically designed to be easy for a recombinative algorithm and, GIGA is ideally suited for adaptation to our purposes.

Analyses for a Recombinative Hill Climber

For theorems 2 and 3 I reduce GIGA to a form of hill climber—by which I mean that I will not use a full population—just two strings. However, this will be a recombinative hill climber not a mutation-based hill climber (figure 8.3).

Höhn and Reeves (1996) call recombination like this "complementary crossover." Alternatively, one might call it a macromutation hill climber (Jones 1995) that uses bit-flip mutation (instead of the assignment of a new random value). Arguably, this is a degenerate form of recombination. Höhn and Reeves point out that a second parent is implementationally redundant. And I concede that the choice of com-

- Initialize a population of two random but complementary strings.
- Repeat until satisfied:
  - Using the two strings as parents create a pair of offspring by crossover only.
  - If the fittest offspring is fitter than the fittest parent then replace the parents with the pair of offspring.

Figure 8.3
Recombinative hill climber based on GIGA.

plementary parents is ideally suited to the complementary schemata rewarded in HIFF. Nonetheless, I maintain that it is more informative to regard the above algorithm as recombining two strings (that happen to be complementary) rather than bit flipping. Höhn and Reeves agree that there is a close relation between this operator and crossover, and suggest that the fitness landscape under this operator "reasonably approximates the crossover landscape." The purpose of using the algorithm here is to illustrate the concept of the crossover landscape as it is found in HIFF, and to provide a basis for understanding how a true GA might operate on this class of problem by avoiding the local optima inherent in the mutation landscape.

The following theorems do *not* assume that the algorithm is provided with a set of crossover masks corresponding to blocks in the problem. Ordinary crossover may be used with no restriction on where crossover points may fall.[4] Theorem 2 is based on two-point crossover, theorem 3 is based on one-point crossover—in the latter case it is a little more difficult to show that condition 1 holds. Note that these analyses are not restricted to the one problem instance defined in equation 4.7. HIFF has regular block sizes within a level, regular fitness contributions for blocks within a level, exactly two subblocks per block, and global optima that happen to be all 1s and all 0s. The analyses hold for the class of problem with any of these particulars relaxed, but for these analyses, the global optima must be complementary, and the fitness contribution of competing schemata in the same partition must be the same. In the next subsection we will discuss an extension to the class where building blocks are not necessarily complementary.

THEOREM 2: $T \leq \frac{1}{2}N^3$, where T is an upper bound on the expected time to find a global optimum in HIFF using the algorithm in figure 8.3 with two-point crossover, and N is the problem size in bits.

Proof: From equation 8.1, $T \leq BPM$ if condition 1 holds. For HIFF, B, the maximum number of blocks that need to be discovered in a globally optimal string, is:

$$\sum_{p=0}^{(\lg N)-1} 2^p = N - 1,$$

thus $B < N$. (Here, and henceforth, we use "lg" to mean logarithm base 2.) For two-point crossover, M, the number of possible pairs of crossover points, is $\frac{1}{2}N(N-1) < \frac{1}{2}N^2$. And for the algorithm given in figure 8.3, the number of different ways to choose parents, P, is just 1. Thus, $T \leq \frac{1}{2}N^3$ if condition 1 holds. Now prove that condition 1 holds: the two strings are complementary at initialization and since the gene-invariance property of the algorithm holds, the strings must always be complementary. This means that if a block is discovered in one individual the complementary block must necessarily be discovered in the other individual. Therefore any block not present in one individual can be swapped in from the other individual given the right crossover mask. Two-point crossover is a superset of the crossover masks required for this crossover to occur. The algorithm will detect such a successful crossover and follow this progression since it will always result in a fitter individual. So condition 1 holds. ■

THEOREM 3: $T \leq N^2$, where T is an upper bound on the expected time to find a global optimum in HIFF using the algorithm in figure 8.3 with one-point crossover, and N is the problem size.

Proof: Following the proof of theorem 2, the number of crossover masks for one-point crossover is $<N$, and thus, $T \leq N^2$ if condition 1 holds under one-point crossover. Now prove that condition 1 holds: if an individual is nonoptimal then it contains some block that either has both of its subblocks correct (but not matching) or has some subblock incorrect. This applies recursively. Consider the smallest incorrect block that has both of its subblocks correct (possibly just a pair of bits) and consider the crossover point between them. Since no fitness contribution can occur for a block that spans the crossover point (because it would include mismatched subblocks), the fitness of this individual is the sum of fitnesses of the substrings to the left and right of this point. The other individual used in the algorithm has the same fitness as the first, and its fitness is the same sum of fitnesses from the left and right substrings defined by the crossover point. Thus, if this crossover point is used, the fitness of the resulting offspring will have at least the same contributions from the two substrings and in addition, since the two individuals are complementary, the crossover will necessarily introduce matching subblocks that create a new correct block spanning the crossover point. Thus there is always some one-point crossover operation that will increase the number of correct blocks in the best individual, that is, condition 1 holds. ■

Figure 8.4 illustrates that the reasoning for condition 1 holds using a recombinative hill climber on HIFF with one-point crossover. Since there is always some crossover point that lies between correct but incompatible blocks, it is always possible to use this point to create a string that has higher fitness by using one-point crossover.

Thus far I have proved that condition 1 holds on HIFF for the algorithm in figure 8.3 using both one-point and two-point crossover. This shows that although a muta-

`11010001`	Consider an arbitrary string as an example. This size-8 string is suboptimal. It is composed of two incorrect size-4 blocks. So we recurse on either of the two incorrect size-4 blocks, for example, the left block.
`1101----`	This size-4 block is composed of a correct size-2 block (left), and an incorrect size-2 block (right). So we recurse on the incorrect block, i.e., right.
`--01----`	This size-2 block is suboptimal. But, it is composed of two correct size-1 blocks that are incompatible.
`110|10001`	So, we place the crossover point between the two size-1 blocks (bits) at this point. The fitness of the entire string can be expressed as the sum of *F_left*=*f*(`110------`) on the left-hand side of the crossover point, and *F_right*=*f*(`---10001`) on the right of the point.
`001|01110`	The other string used in the algorithm is the exact complement. And the left and right sides of the crossover point have the same fitnesses, i.e., *F_left* and *F_right*.
`110|01110`	The string created by combining the left of the first string and the right of the second string, still has at least the fitness of *F_left* + *F_right*.
`--0|0----`	But it now has an additional correct block here, created across the crossover point.

Figure 8.4
Illustrating that condition 1 holds.

tion hill climber finds a number of local optima that is exponential in N, HIFF has no local optima at all under recombination—there is always some way to increase the number of correct blocks, as condition 1 states. In this sense, HIFF exemplifies the transformation of a fitness landscape under different operators from a problem that is very difficult under mutation, into a problem that is easy under crossover. Having shown that there is always a path to an optimum, we can now focus on improving the estimate of the time to traverse this path.

We may improve on the upper bounds given in theorems 2 and 3 by returning to our original reasoning, $T \leq BS$, where B is the number of blocks to be found (i.e., steps on the path to the optimum) and S is the expected time to find a block (i.e., time to take a step). In the above theorems I prove condition 1 to assert that there is at least one crossover operation that will find a block given some choice of parents. So I used $S \leq PM$, and accordingly, $T \leq BPM$. But it should be clear that for this algorithm on HIFF there will be many opportunities to increase the number of correct blocks. For example, at the beginning of search there are many size-2 blocks to be found and many possible crossovers that may find one.

So, we can use an estimate of time to progress along the path to the optimum that takes account of the fact that the expected time for a step changes with each step, as the number of possible ways to find a block changes. The time to find one of q available blocks is PM/q, thus:

Equation 8.2: Expected time to solution in terms of steps on path to optimum

$$T \leq \sum_{b=1}^{B} \frac{PM}{q_b}$$

where B is the maximum number of steps in the path to the optimum, P is the number of choices of parents, M is the number of possible crossovers, and q_b is the number of ways that an additional block can be swapped in at the bth step. Thus, we may write:

Equation 8.3: Equation 8.2 simplified

$$T \leq PMu$$

where u is the sum of $1/q$ for all steps in the path to the optimum. Theorem 4 uses an upper bound on u to give an improved time to solution on HIFF.

THEOREM 4: $T \leq \frac{1}{2} M \lg^2 N$, where T is an upper bound on the expected time to find a global optimum in HIFF using the algorithm in figure 8.3, M is the number of crossover masks (i.e., $M = N - 1 < N$ for one-point crossover, $M = \frac{1}{2}N(N-1)$ for two-point), and N is the problem size in bits (for $N > 20$).

Proof: To use $T \leq PMu$ we must find u that is the sum of $1/q$ over all steps in the path, where q is the number of blocks that may be discovered at that step. At the first hierarchical level in HIFF there are $N/2$ size-2 blocks to be discovered (in the worst case, we may assume that the initial strings have none of their size-two blocks correct). By the reasoning of theorems 2 or 3, any one of these blocks may be discovered by one- or two-point crossover. Thus $q_1 = (N/2)$. There are now $N/2 - 1$ blocks remaining to be found at the first level, so $q_2 = (N/2 - 1)$. For the entire first level we require the sum of $1/q_1$ through $1/q_{(N/2)} = 1 + 1/2 + 1/3 + \cdots + 1/(N/2) \leq \ln(N/2) + 1$. The sum of $1/q$ for the pth level is $\leq \ln(N/2^p) + 1$. The overall sum of $1/q$ for all levels, u, is

$$
\begin{aligned}
u &= \sum_{p=1}^{\lg N} \sum_{k=1}^{N/2^p} \left(\frac{1}{k}\right) \\
&\leq \sum_{p=1}^{\lg N} \left(\ln\left(\frac{N}{2^p}\right) + 1 \right) \\
&= \sum_{p=1}^{\lg N} (\ln N - p \ln 2 + 1) \\
&= \lg N \left(\frac{\lg N}{\lg e} + 1 \right) - \frac{\ln 2}{2} (\lg N (\lg N + 1)) \\
&= \frac{\ln 2}{2} \lg^2 N + \left(1 - \frac{\ln 2}{2} \right) \lg N.
\end{aligned}
$$

For the algorithm in figure 8.3, $P = 1$. So,

$$T \leq Mu = M\left(\frac{\ln 2}{2} \lg^2 N + \left(1 - \frac{\ln 2}{2} \right) \lg N \right).$$

Thus T is $O(M \lg^2 N)$, and numerically, $T \leq \frac{1}{2} M \lg^2 N$, for $N > 20$. ■

In summary, theorem 4 reduces the upper bound on the expected time for the recombinative hill climber by a factor of at least N to $\lg^2 N$ in each case (table 8.1).

From a Recombinative Hill Climber to a Recombinative Population

Theorems 2 through 4 use the recombinative hill climber of figure 8.3, and in fact, demonstrate that a population greater than this degenerate case of two is not strictly necessary to solve the canonical form of HIFF. However, this is only the case because of biases in the algorithm that match particular properties of HIFF.

Table 8.1
Summary of theorems 2 to 4.

	one-point crossover	two-point crossover
theorem 2	N^2	
theorem 3		$\frac{1}{2} N^3$
theorem 4	$\frac{1}{2} N \lg^2 N$	$\frac{1}{2} N^2 \lg^2 N$

Specifically, GIGA is biased toward finding complementary individuals (a bias that becomes the rule when the population is of size 2), and HIFF has competing schemata that are exactly complementary. It is quite easy to break this non-population-based version of GIGA by making the global optima in HIFF noncomplementary. We can do this by choosing two random strings as the global optima and rewarding left and right substrings recursively. Alternatively, and without loss of generality, we can keep one of the optima at all 1s and randomize the other. Either way, the bits in the two global optima will agree in some loci and be complementary in others. This prevents the algorithm given in figure 8.3 from succeeding since the complement of a good block is no longer (necessarily) a good block. Equation 8.4 defines a variant of HIFF based on this idea, that I will refer to as HIFF2. $F(A)$ runs through the string twice using g and sums results; before the first pass the string is XORed with one global optimum, and before the second it is XORed with the second global optimum. $f'(A)$ now simply checks for blocks of all 0s.

The fitness of a string, A, under HIFF2 is given by:

Equation 8.4: HIFF with arbitrary global optima (HIFF2)

$$F(A) = g(A \otimes g1) + g(A \otimes g2),$$

$$g(S_1, \ldots, S_N) = \begin{cases} 1, & \text{if } N = 1 \\ Nf'(S_1, \ldots, S_N) + \sum_{i=1}^{k} g(S^i), & \text{otherwise} \end{cases}$$

where $p \otimes q$ is the bitwise exclusive OR of p with q, $g1$ and $g2$ are the two global optima, f' is the base fitness function defined below, and the other variables are as per equation 4.7: i.e. S_i is the ith variable of the configuration; S^i is the ith disjoint sub-partition of the variables (that is, for "unshuffled" HIFF, $S^i = (S_{1+k(i-1)}, \ldots, S_{ki})$); $N = k^H$, where $H \in \mathbb{Z}^+$ is the number of hierarchical levels in the system or subsystem, and k is the number of sub-modules per module.

$$f'(p_1, \ldots p_k) = 1 \quad \text{if } (\forall i\colon p_i = 0), \quad \text{and 0 otherwise.}$$

Note that f' is modified to accept only blocks of 0s as high-fitness configurations. Competing schemata are introduced by the fact that the two global optima are not identical. Note also that HIFF and H-equal are the special case where the two global optima, $g1$ and $g2$, are the string of all 0s and the string of all 1s.

Some experiments in Watson 2001 use the all-1s string as $g1$, and $g2 =$ "010101..." (i.e., loci with an odd index take the value 0, and the even loci take the value 1). Thus the two optima have exactly 50 percent bits in agreement and 50 percent complementary. The proofs of theorems 2 through 4 are not valid for the function in equation 8.4—it should be clear that the recombinative hill climber cannot succeed on this problem. However, if we reintroduce an adequate population we can recover a successful algorithm. Unfortunately, we are not able to prove a time to solution on this problem using a population. However, we will see that an estimate based on *assumed* invariants of the population gives reasonable times. Specifically, I use the rather heavy-handed assumption below. This assumption states explicitly that diversity is being maintained appropriately for recombination to work effectively. It supposes a levelwise discovery of blocks and that all members of the population progress together.

ASSUMPTION 1: When looking for a block at level p, all individuals in the population consist of complete blocks from at least level $p-1$, and these blocks will be a substring of either global optimum, g1 or g2, with equal probability.

THEOREM 5: $T \leq \frac{1}{2}N^2 \lg^2 N$, where T is an upper bound on the expected time to find a global optimum in HIFF or HIFF2 using a GA with two-point crossover, where assumption 1 holds, and $N > 20$ is the problem size.

Proof: Using $T \leq PMu$ (equation 8.3). Without the condition that every pair of parents are the exact complement of one another we cannot apply the reasoning of one-point crossover from theorem 3. But the reasoning for two-point crossover from theorem 2 applies with a slight modification. Since we do not assume that the parents are necessarily complementary but rather that they consist of correct subblocks of either type with equal probability, half of the blocks swapped in will make no improvement. The sum of $1/q$, where q is the number of ways to make an improvement at each step, is therefore twice the value of u calculated in theorem 4. Given that assumption 1 refers to all individuals in the population, the same opportunity for improvement is available for any choice of parents, so $P = 1$. The expected time to solution is therefore twice that of theorem 4, with $M = \frac{1}{2}N(N-1) < \frac{1}{2}N^2$ for two-point crossover. ■

This estimate of the expected time for a GA on HIFF takes no account of the population size, selection pressure, or any other aspect of the algorithm—all of these are embedded in assumption 1. Empirical illustrations of the analytic results for the recombinative hill climber with one-point crossover applied to HIFF (theorem 4), and a GA with two-point crossover applied to HIFF2 (theorem 5) can be found in Watson 2001. These results give times to solution that are under this estimated upper bound on expected time and, support the validity of the assumption for the experimental setup used.

Summary of Analysis for a GA on HIFF

This section has provided an analytic time to solution for a recombinative algorithm on a particular nonseparable building-block problem. The upper bound on expected time is based on proving a path to the optimum and the time for each step on the path. In the limited case of a population of two I proved that the expected time to solution is at most $O(N \lg^2 N)$, where N is the size of the problem in bits. For the more general population case I provide a time $O(N^2 \lg^2 N)$ based on the assumption that, at any time, the state of the population is such that the algorithm is able to provide recombination steps that follow the path described. Empirical results support that there is a population size for which the GA succeeds reliably and the analytic time to solution is an overestimate.

8.2 Analysis of SEAM on Shuffled HIFF

This section provides an analytic treatment of SEAM, and in so doing helps to explain how SEAM works on HIFF and under what conditions it would fail. The analytic treatment of SEAM on HIFF follows that developed for sexual recombination on HIFF given in section 8.1. Specifically, we calculate the expected time to solution from the product of the number of blocks to be found in a complete solution and the expected time to find each block.

Idealized SEAM

Let us define a join to be "correct" when two compatible entities, that are themselves fully optimized modules, are brought together to create a new higher-level fully optimized module of twice the size: for example, 00-- + --00 → 0000 is a correct join.

I start by proving that all the joins that SEAM makes will be correct if the stability of a proposed join is tested in all possible contexts. Although it is not the case that all possible contexts are tested in SEAM—a sample of contexts, built from other coevolving individuals, is used to test the stability of a join—this proof provides an appropriate stepping stone in coming to a more complete analysis of SEAM.

LEMMA 1: Only correct joins are made in SEAM if all possible contexts are used for testing stability, where "correct" means that the new entity created is a fully optimized module, and "all possible contexts" is the set of all strings collectively covering all possible configurations of features.

Proof: The set of all possible contexts includes the two global optima, that is, the strings of all 1s and all 0s, that we will call the "ideal contexts" for reasons that will become clear. An entity, A, entering into a join, is fully optimized internally; e.g., all 0s. Thus the fitness of the string created by superimposing entity A on one of the ideal contexts will be the maximum fitness possible (since the superposition of 0s on 0s, for example, will have no effect). Clearly, there is no pairing with any other entity, B, that could yield greater fitness. Moreover, any pairing with any compatible entity, that is, an entity of the same type (all 0s), will not depreciate the fitness of entity A in this context. That is, $f(\text{A} + \text{B} + \text{ideal\_context}) = f(\text{A} + \text{ideal\_context})$ when A, B, and the ideal context are each all 0s. However, any join of A with some other entity B that is incompatible (of the wrong type, i.e., all 1s, or internally incorrect) will decrease the fitness of A in the ideal context. The same reasoning applies for entities of all 1s. Thus, any compatible join will be deemed stable, and any incompatible join will be deemed unstable. Then, since SEAM is initialized with correct single-variable modules, all modules in the population at all times will be correct. ∎

It is clear from this reasoning that using only the two "ideal contexts" to test the stability of a proposed join is sufficient to ensure than only correct joins are made.[5] Intuitively, any join that could in some context be detrimental, will be detrimental in one of the ideal contexts. We can easily implement an "idealized" version of SEAM that can be used to illustrate this. The pseudocode is given below in figure 8.5; this algorithm is the same as that in figure 7.6 except that *Contexts* is the set of

- Initialize ecosystem, E, to random, single-feature, entities.[(1)]
- Repeat until *stopping condition*:
  - Remove two entities at random from the ecosystem → ***a and b.***
  - Produce ***a+b=S(a,b)***, using composition (see equation 7.1).
  - If ***unstable(a+b,a,b)*** return ***a*** and ***b*** to ecosystem, else add ***a+b*** to ecosystem.

where ***unstable(a+b,a,b)*** ⇔

$\exists\theta \in$ ***Contexts***: $(f(S(a,\theta)) > f(S(a+b,\theta))$ OR $f(S(b,\theta)) > f(S(a+b,\theta)))$

where ***Contexts*** is a set of exactly two strings, all 0s and all 1s. (see equation 7.3).

[(1)] Initialization needs to completely cover the set of single-feature "primitives" so that all values for all features are available in the ecosystem.

Figure 8.5
Pseudocode for idealized SEAM; as per SEAM figure 7.6, but using ideal contexts rather than contexts built from other members of the population.

two globally optimal strings rather than a sample set of contexts built from other coevolving entities.

Clearly, idealized SEAM is not algorithmically practical because it uses the two globally optimal strings as part of the algorithm. However, it is informative theoretically to consider the operation of idealized SEAM first. Following this, we consider the expected time for (the original) SEAM method to cover a *sufficient* number of contexts to reveal an incorrect join.

Note that any join that overwrites an entity at some loci with allele values that disagree will not be correct. If an entity A is joined with an entity B, and B is not fully compatible with A, then B will depreciate the fitness of A in one or other of the ideal contexts and the join will not be allowed. Thus it is never possible for a join to make a fully optimized block become suboptimal when ideal contexts are available. This, together with the knowledge that the initial population consists only of correct blocks, means that the population always consists of only correct blocks, and the number of correct blocks in the best individual in the population can never decrease.

Note also that since the only variation operator in SEAM is encapsulation, and in idealized SEAM an entity is never replaced by another entity unless it forms a correct join, this ensures that there can only be a monotonic increase in the number of correct modules in the population. Moreover, it is clear that since all primitive modules are available by initialization and all higher-level modules can be formed by some assembly of them, there is always a means to increase the number of correct modules given an appropriate selection of existing entities.

We now calculate an upper bound on the expected time to solution for idealized SEAM on HIFF using similar assumptions as we did previously, p. 225. Specifically, given the use of idealized contexts and the reasoning above, we know that at all times the entities in the population provide the necessary components for blocks at the next level in the hierarchy. This means that there is necessarily a change available in the population (a composition) that will increase the number of correct modules in the individual that has the greatest number of correct modules—up until the point that this individual is one of the globally optimal strings. (This is analogous to proving condition 1, p. 225.)

In the analysis of sexual recombination on HIFF, we used $T \leq BS$, where B is the number of blocks to be found (i.e., steps on the path to the optimum) and S is the expected time to find a block (i.e., time to take a step). In idealized SEAM we know that there is at least one join operation that will find a new module given some choice of donor entities from the current population. Unlike the conditions for sexual recombination we do not need to factor in the number of possible crossover masks, since given the correct donor individuals there is only one way to compose them (correct donor entities are not overlapping—so, $S(\mathrm{A}, \mathrm{B}) = S(\mathrm{B}, \mathrm{A})$) and this will necessarily produce the desired module as a result. So we could simply use $S = 3CP$, and accordingly, $T \leq 3CBP$, where P is the number of choices of parents/donor individuals, $C = 2$ is the number of contexts that need to be tested for each choice of parents (corresponding to the two ideal contexts in idealized SEAM), and the factor of three comes from the need to do three evaluations (A in c, B in c, and A + B in c), for each context c in C. However, as before, we can improve on this estimate by noticing that there is generally more than one encapsulation operation that will find a new module—at a given level (other than the top level) of the hierarchy there are many blocks to be found and many opportunities to increase the number of correct blocks (make a correct join). For example, at the beginning of search there are many size-2 blocks to be found and many possible encapsulations that may find a size-2 module given the initial population.

So, in a manner analogous to that used for the recombinative hill climber, we can use an estimate of time to progress along the path to the optimum that takes account of the fact that the expected time for a step changes with each step, as the number of possible ways to find a block changes. The expected time to find one of q available blocks is P/q, thus:

Equation 8.5: Expected time to solution for SEAM

$$T \leq \sum_{b=1}^{B} \frac{3CP_b}{q_b}$$

where B is the maximum number of steps in the path to the optimum, P_b is the number of choices of parents at the bth step, $C = 2$ is the number of contexts that need to be tested for each choice of parents, and q_b is the number of ways that a new block can be swapped in at the bth step.

Thus, we may write $T \leq 3Cr$, where r is the sum of P/q for all steps in the path to the optimum. Theorem 6 uses an upper bound on r to give a time to solution for idealized SEAM on HIFF.

THEOREM 6: $T = O(N^2 \ln N)$, where T is an upper bound on the expected time to find a global optimum in HIFF using the idealized SEAM algorithm in figure 8.5, and N is the problem size in bits.

Proof: To use $T \leq 3Cr$ we must find $r = r_1 + r_2 + \cdots + r_B$ where $r_b = P_b/q_b$, where q_b is the number of blocks that may be discovered at the bth step, and P_b is the number of choices of parents (or donor entities) at the bth step. We will count a step for each correct join the algorithm makes, which equals twice the total number of blocks in either globally optimal solution—that is, the total number of steps, $B = 2(N-1)$. At the first hierarchical level in HIFF there are $N/2$ size-2 blocks of each type (0 and 1) to be discovered (in the worst case, we may assume that the initial strings have none of their size-2 blocks correct). By the reasoning of lemma 1, any one of these blocks may be discovered by encapsulation of a particular pair of existing entities. So, $q_1 = 2N$ (because the order of selected parents does not matter so there are two ways to create each block). In the initial population in idealized SEAM there are $2N$ entities and thus $P_1 = 4N^2$ (assuming we do not bother to check that donor entities are different). Thus $r_1 = 4N^2/2N = 2N$. There are now $N-1$ blocks remaining to be found at the first level, and since the encapsulation of two entities into one reduces the population size by one, $P_2 = (2N-1)^2$. So $r_2 = (2N-1)^2/2(N-1)$. More generally, let the hierarchical levels in the problem be indexed with j from lg N to 1, and let the blocks that need to be discovered in that level be indexed with k from 2^j to 1, then for the kth block at the jth level $p = (2^j + k)^2$ and $q = 2k$. The overall sum of p/q for all blocks at all levels, r, is:

$$r = \sum_{j=1}^{\lg N} \sum_{k=1}^{2^j} \left(\frac{(2^j + k)^2}{2k} \right)$$

$$= \sum_{j=1}^{\lg N} \sum_{k=1}^{2^j} \left(\frac{2^{2j}}{2k} + 2^j + \frac{k}{2} \right)$$

$$\leq \sum_{j=1}^{\lg N} (2^{2j-1}(\ln 2^j + 1) + 2^{2j} + 2^{j-2}(2^j + 1))$$

$$r \leq O(2^{2\lg N - 1} \ln 2^{\lg N})$$

$$r \leq O(N^2 \ln N).$$

For the algorithm in figure 8.5, $C = 2$. So, from $T \leq 3Cr$,

$T \leq 6r$,

Thus, $T = O(N^2 \ln N)$. ■

From Idealized SEAM to SEAM

Idealized SEAM uses exactly the two ideal contexts for testing the stability of a join and is thereby able to ensure that only correct joins are made. In (ordinary, not-idealized) SEAM, a random sample of contexts is used where each context is built from an assembly of other entities in the population.

To expand the proof for idealized SEAM to SEAM we need to estimate the number of contexts required to correctly identify the correctness of a proposed join. Thus SEAM will make joins stable only if they are correct, as did idealized SEAM, but SEAM will require more evaluations to determine the correctness of the joins. The basic observation is that although idealized SEAM uses the global optima as contexts, it is not necessary that the contexts be globally optimal—only that they contain optimal submodules of about the same order as the individuals being tested, and since the contexts are built from other individuals of about the same order as the individuals being tested this condition is feasible for any size module as search progresses.

Lemma 2 provides the number of contexts we expect to need to test to determine the correctness or incorrectness of a proposed join. In SEAM a proposed join is tested in a number of contexts until the first occurrence of a context that reveals it to be incorrect. But when a join is correct, no such context occurs—in this case we must place a limit on the number of contexts we will test before being satisfied that the join is correct (i.e., t). This limit should be based on the allowable risk of accidentally accepting an incorrect join as stable.

LEMMA 2: $C = G\ln P/\ln(1-p) + (1-G)/p$ where C is the expected number of contexts required to determine the stability of a proposed join, G is the probability that the proposed join is a correct join, P is the acceptable risk (allowable probability) that an incorrect join is passed as stable-correct, and p is the probability that a single context will reveal an incorrect join to be unstable-incorrect.

Proof: $C = Ga + (1-G)b$ where a is the expected number of contexts required to determine that a correct join is correct, and b is the expected number of contexts required to determine that an incorrect join is incorrect. If the probability that a single context will reveal an incorrect join is p, then the expected number of contexts required to reveal an incorrect join is $b = 1/p$. The probability that an incorrect join will not be revealed to be incorrect in a single context is $1-p$. The probability that an incorrect join will not be revealed to be incorrect in k contexts is $(1-p)^k$. We want this probability to be P, thus $P = (1-p)^k$. So, $k = \log_{(1-p)} P$, thus $k = \ln P/\ln(1-p)$, where $k = a$ is the number of trials required to make the probability of an incorrect join passing as correct to be P. Thus $C = G\ln P/\ln(1-p) + (1-G)/p$. ∎

The intent in this analysis is to show that, with reasonable assumptions, there is a constant upper bound on C with respect to N, the size of the problem. This, in turn, will allow us to show a polynomial upper bound on the SEAM algorithm. Accordingly we need to bound G, P, and p appropriately. I address each term individually.

G, the probability of a proposed join being correct, changes as the algorithm progresses. In general, G is the ratio of the number of new blocks that could be created from a pair of existing blocks to the number of possible pairs of existing blocks. This ratio, and therefore G, cannot be greater than 1. P, the acceptable risk (allowable probability) that an incorrect join is passed as stable-correct should be low. Roughly, we want to make $O(N)$ joins without making any incorrect joins. In any case, $\ln(P)$, where P is a probability less than 1, will have a maximum which is negative.

Thus, given these bounds on G and P, if we can show that p, the probability that a single context will reveal an incorrect join to be incorrect, is constant, then we can show that C has a constant upper bound. Showing p to be constant is more complicated.

The probability that a context will reveal an incorrect join In SEAM, a join between two individuals A and B is incorrect if $f(\mathrm{A}+c) > f(\mathrm{A}+\mathrm{B}+c)$, or $f(\mathrm{B}+c) > f(\mathrm{A}+\mathrm{B}+c)$ for any c tested, where f is the fitness function and c is a context. To start with, let us consider only $f(\mathrm{A}+c) > f(\mathrm{A}+\mathrm{B}+c)$. It is easily seen that the join will be rejected if there is any context tested where the presence of B causes a decrease in the fitness of the string.[6]

Note that any alleles provided by B that are overlapped by A can play no part in these fitness evaluations. Thus any context that might possibly show $f(\mathrm{A}+c) > f(\mathrm{A}+\mathrm{B}+c)$ would also show $f(\mathrm{A}+c) > f(\mathrm{A}+\mathrm{B}'+c)$ where B' is the subpart of B that is not overlapping with A. Let D be the subpart of context c that is exactly covered by B'—that is, D is located in the same partition of the variables as B'. Let us also consider E, which is defined as the partition of variables that form the complementary block of B' (and therefore also form the complementary block of D), making a module at the next hierarchical level in the problem structure—that is, in HIFF this will be the block neighboring B' as defined in the hierarchical block structure; in shuffled HIFF, this will be the new randomized position of these same variables. Thus if B' and E are both internally correct and compatible (i.e., both 0s blocks, or both 1s blocks) then $\mathrm{B}'+\mathrm{E}$ forms a correct join. Similarly, since D is in the same partition as B', $\mathrm{D}+\mathrm{E}$ may or may not form a correct join.

As stated, we are interested in the probability of finding a context where the presence of B causes a decrease in fitness. In HIFF, a change in fitness resulting from the superposition of a module on a context can occur either because of the independent fitness contribution of that module (if it is a correct block or contains correct blocks), or from the fitness dependencies between that module and other modules in the context. If B is a correct block then its independent fitness contribution cannot be lower than that of D. However, if B is incompatible with E, but D is compatible with E, then B will cause a fitness decrease. In other words, if D + E is a correct block, and $B' \neq D$, then $f(A + c) > f(A + B + c)$. Thus the probability of revealing an incorrect join to be incorrect from a given context, c, is $p \geq q$ where q is the probability that c contains a correct block twice the size of B′ and located at the partition covered by B′ and its "neighboring" block, E. In this case, D + E makes a correct block, and the superposition of B breaks this block causing a fitness decrease. (Note that when A and B form a correct join, E is the same partition as A and thus D + E can only be a correct block when $D = B'$, thus D + E does not confer greater fitness than $D + B'$ and there can be no context where $f(A + c) > f(A + B + c)$.)

Note that when using random contexts, p is inversely related to the exponent of the size of the module B. But in SEAM contexts are built from other coevolving individuals. If all individuals in the population, including B, are correct modules of size k, and if the 0s kind of module and the 1s kind of module is equally represented in each partition, then the probability that a context built from this population will reveal an incorrect join to be incorrect is just the probability that the context will contain a correct module of size $2k$ in the $B' + E$ partition that is incompatible with B′. This probability is independent of blocks in other partitions since the partitions of correct modules are nonoverlapping. Thus $p = 1/4$ in this case: that is, there are four possible block combinations of size k that make candidate blocks of size $2k$, only one of which is a correct size-$2k$ block and incompatible with B′.

Since the test is symmetric, that is, we are looking for a context where $f(A + c) > f(A + B + c)$, or $f(B + c) > f(A + B + c)$, the number of contexts that need to be tested is limited by the size of whichever module is the smaller out of A or B. In general, the probability of a context assembled from other individuals revealing an incorrect join to be incorrect is $p = 1/2^{(2K/k)}$, where K is the size of the smaller of the two blocks in the proposed join, and k is the average size of blocks in the population in the partition of that block (assuming 0s and 1s are equally represented).

In practice, we cannot ensure that all members of the population are of about the same size because it may be the case that different partitions and different types of block within a partition are progressing at different rates. Let us assume that in general, different modules/blocks in the problem may be m hierarchical levels apart in size, that is, when the smallest block of A and B is of size K, the average size of other entities specifying blocks in the partition of that block and its neighboring partition is no less than $k = K/2^m$. This assumption asserts that different solutions to a module never get more than m hierarchical levels ahead of one another.

If some members of the population are of size $k = K/2^m$, then $2K/k = 2K/(K/2^m) = 2^{(m+1)}$, and the probability of a context revealing an incorrect join to be incorrect is $p = 2^{-2^{(m+1)}}$ for a join between modules of any size in the operation of SEAM. Note that this contextual testing scales up appropriately as the size of the modules being tested scales up—but testing joins in random contexts cannot do this, as seen in our control experiments (figure 7.7).

Thus, p is constant if the ratio of sizes of different solutions to a module in the population is constant. This is not an unreasonable assumption in HIFF and shuffled HIFF since the discovery of different solutions to a module are equally likely. Thus, given a constant upper bound for p, we arrive at a constant upper bound for C, the expected number of contexts required to determine the stability of a proposed join. Finally, a bound for C allows us to give an upper bound on the expected time to find a global optimum in HIFF using SEAM.

THEOREM 7: $T \leq O(N^2 lnN)$, where T is an upper bound on the expected time to find a global optimum in shuffled HIFF using the SEAM algorithm in figure 8.5 given a constant bound on the ratio of different-sized entities in the population as described above, and N is the problem size in bits.

Proof: Using $O(N^2 lnN)$ from theorem 6, which was based on $T \leq 3Cr$, we see from the above argument that in SEAM (as well as idealized SEAM) $C \approx O(1)$, and r is the same for SEAM as idealized SEAM, thus $T \approx O(N^2 lnN)$. ■

Summary of Analytic Results

The gist of the above analysis is that by testing an appropriate number of contextual groups we can ensure that only correct joins are made. This number of contexts is limited, regardless of the size of the modules being processed, simply because contexts are built from individuals of about the same size as the individuals being joined. Thus the operation of SEAM continues unhindered through successive hierarchical levels. Given this invariant property of the SEAM population, the expected time to solution in HIFF or shuffled HIFF is therefore polynomial in N, the size of the problem, despite there being difficult interdependencies between modules of all sizes right up to size $N/2$.

Note that in general, analytical results for complex population-based algorithms such as those analyzed here are very difficult because the way in which new individuals are created is dependent on the current state of the population. This dependency on the state of the population cannot be ignored since it is exactly this that allows compositional algorithms to change the way in which they move in the search space as evolution progresses. However, both here and in the proof for the GA on HIFF, an analytic time is provided by making assumptions about certain properties of the population rather than the exact composition of the population. For the GA I need to assume that appropriate diversity is maintained and given this invariant property of the population I can prove a polynomial solution time. In SEAM, the necessary invariant property of the population is less vague—I need only assume that the discovery of different solutions to a module do not get too far ahead of one another. If this holds, then a polynomial bound holds.

Of course this result is dependent on the problem class, HIFF. The property of HIFF that is critical here is that the dependencies of a module with its context are limited, and thereby it is not necessary to test a proposed module in all possible contexts but merely a sample of contexts. Nonetheless, the interdependencies that do exist between a module and its context are high order and must be resolved to find optimal solutions.

The important point to note is that the result given in the earlier section for composition based on sexual recombination showed the potential for compositional mechanisms to provide a divide-and-conquer style problem decomposition in this class of modular interdependency system, but that that result was conditioned on having *a priori* knowledge of which genes are dependent on which other genes so as to order them appropriately on the chromosome. The above result for SEAM is true for shuffled HIFF as well as HIFF and thus shows that the algorithmic advantage available from compositional mechanisms is *not*, in general, dependent on knowing this information in advance. Thus the algorithmic advantage available from compositional mechanisms in this class of modular interdependency system is *not* dependent on knowing in advance which genes are dependent on which other genes so as to order them appropriately on the chromosome.

8.3 Summary

This chapter supports the findings of the simulation results, showing that the distinction between the algorithmic classes of gradual and compositional evolutionary processes is fundamental in terms of the expected time to find fit genotypes. Specifically, the expected time for a genetic algorithm to optimize problems of this class is $O(N^2 \lg^2 N)$ in the size of the problem (given the assumption of appropriate population diversity), and the expected time for SEAM to solve this problem class is even closer to quadratic $O(N^2 lnN)$, even though it does not have any *a priori* information about the location of modules and is insensitive to the ordering of genes on the chromosome (given some related assumptions about population diversity) (see De Jong,

Watson, and Thierens 2005b for extended analysis). In contrast, the expected time for a mutation-based hill climber is exponential in N, at best $O(N^2 2^{N/2})$. In short, this means that systems of this type do not have to be very large before they are essentially impossible to evolve by random incremental improvements but may nonetheless remain easily evolvable by compositional mechanisms.

These analytic results agree with our normal intuitions. If a problem can be decomposed into smaller subproblems it is much easier to solve than one that cannot be decomposed. But in these models we have brought this simple idea of problem decomposition into the space of evolutionary mechanisms. The models of sexual recombination and symbiotic encapsulation show that an evolutionary process, based purely on natural selection, can provide the algorithmic advantages of problem decomposition. Whereas previously only the naive extremes were considered—either biological systems are arbitrarily complex and cannot be evolved, or they have few or weak interdependencies and can be evolved—now we have a third possibility. If dependencies are strong and significant but have a modular structure then they are evolvable if compositional mechanisms are available. The analyses in this chapter have used the language of computational complexity theory to give these concepts formal definition: to show that it is not merely the case that a sexual population sometimes evolves faster than an asexual one, for example, but to show that in some circumstances the adaptation of sexual and asexual populations belong to different algorithmic classes.

9 Scaling Up Evolution

A fitness saddle—the separation of a local optimum from a superior configuration of features—is a useful way to conceptualize the difficulty of a landscape for a gradual evolutionary mechanism. But, what scale of fitness saddle should we expect in a natural adaptive landscape? Intuitively, we might suspect that whatever scale of ruggedness is overcome, we could "zoom out," and see that a larger scale of ruggedness becomes the limiting characteristic of the adaptive landscape. If this is so, then there is no fixed scale of saddle-crossing ability that is sufficient for open-ended evolvability. In contrast, an adaptive mechanism that scales up as evolution continues, enabling larger and larger jumps in feature space, is not necessarily limited in the same way.

In this chapter I present the case that compositional evolution provides a means to scale up evolutionary processes. That is, whereas gradual evolutionary processes "tinker" with an evolving system using variation at the microscopic scale, compositional evolution can start by tinkering at the lowest level and, when useful subsystems start to become stable, it naturally scales up to tinker with assemblies of those, and so on through assemblies of increasing scale. After a while, the units that are being manipulated by a compositional mechanism are far removed from the original substrate. This is explicit in symbiotic encapsulation but is also present implicitly in compositional evolution based on sexual recombination.

For example, an evolutionary process might start by tinkering with the molecular sequence of self-replicating molecules, and then proceed by tinkering with the composition of groups of molecules in a hypercycle. Then, as their replication becomes synchronized to form chromosomes and is enclosed in a membrane to form a protocell, it becomes more useful to think of them as an individual unit, a single-celled organism. Following the sequence of major evolutionary transitions (Maynard Smith and Szathmary 1995), it is subsequent tinkering with assemblies of these simple cells that created the eukaryote cell with its organelles. So although evolution is a process of tinkering, by scaling up the units that are being tinkered with, compositional evolution escapes from the microscopic tinkering to which gradual evolution is wedded.

In this chapter I want to use the concrete models presented in previous chapters to discuss the underlying algorithmic principle that makes compositional evolution inherently scalable and leaves gradual evolution stuck at the starting blocks—both metaphorically and literally.

I start by pointing out that thinking about selection at different scales is in fact common in population genetics. Then I discuss the algorithmic advantage of selection at different scales, and an important bit of background work on this topic, Wright's shifting balance theory. Then I discuss how physical linkage in sexual populations implicitly permits selection on sets of coadapted alleles and how this relates to the ability of the sexual population to solve a problem with hierarchical modularity, like HIFF. In the second half of this chapter, I survey the concepts of scale invariance that are used in the SEAM model.

Nucleotides and Genes, Bits and Alleles

Thinking about evolutionary processes at different scales is natural and common, even though it is generally not explicit. In particular, population genetics models normally model changes in the variation and frequencies of alleles. These alleles are variants of genes. On the relatively short evolutionary timescales that population genetics models usually address, it is reasonable to suppose that there are only two variants of a gene in the population—hence most models are *biallelic* models. Now, these two alleles are different because they have different nucleotide sequences. And the differences between nucleotide sequences were created by spontaneous point mutation on individual nucleotides. But genes contain thousands of nucleotides and alleles of genes may differ at a great many nucleotide sites. Nonetheless, when we want to model the changes in frequency of variants in a population it is natural to abstract all these nucleotide differences into binary alleles for the gene. For example, two alleles might contain nucleotides like this: *ctgggcagagctcgactgagcctat...cgatcgatcgatttatactt* and *ctgggcccagcatgactttgcctat...cgttcgatcgatttataccc*; but we might simply refer to these as just *A* and *a*, for example. Using this kind of abstraction will be fine when we do not need to refer to any of the internal details. For example, on short timescales where new mutations are not a factor, if these two combinations of nucleotides are "particulate" under recombination then we may as well represent them quite simply as *A* and *a*—and this is what is done in most population genetics. Further, if, for example, *A* is a variant of *a* created by spontaneous mutation at a single nucleotide site, and all the other nucleotides of the allele are identical in *A* and *a*, then it does not really matter if we think of *A* and *a* as alleles of genes under selection, or as two single-nucleotide variants under selection.

But this is not sufficient justification for believing that there is really only one scale here. The units that are manipulated by recombination are sets of tightly linked nucleotides, and the units that are manipulated by spontaneous point mutation are individual nucleotides. It is so natural to switch back and forth between these two scales when talking about mutation and recombination that it is easy to miss that it is in fact quite natural to think about variational units of more than one scale. Notice that it will not be necessary to make a distinction between these scales unless we want to model two alleles that are not mutational neighbors—as might be the case, for example, when alleles from two semi-isolated subpopulations come together.

These two scales of unit are so conflated that it is really difficult to tell what unit it is that is supposed to be modeled by the genetic algorithm. Following the lead of population genetics models, it is normal to use biallelic loci in genetic algorithms and accordingly, individuals are represented by binary strings. But is each position in the string supposed to be the locus of a gene, or a nucleotide site? On the one hand, if it is supposed to be the locus of a gene then this is not consistent with the mutation model. That is, how is it that mutation spontaneously creates new alleles of only two types?—there should be many possible alleles for the gene (exponential in the number of nucleotide sites). We might be interested in alleles that are mutational neighbors in some circumstances, but subsequent mutational events cannot just go back and forth between two alleles. On the other hand, if each bit is supposed to be a nucleotide site, then this is incompatible with a recombination model like uniform recombination (allowing each bit to segregate independently), which would be nonsense biologically.

I suspect that some researchers would argue that it is merely a terminological discrepancy and that algorithmically it does not matter what names things have. But I suggest that this misses an important point: that it is natural to think about units of variation in biological evolution at more than one scale. By relabeling the units from one scale of metaphor to another we miss the fact that there really is more than one scale of variation taking place in natural evolution: variation at the scale of individual nucleotide sites produced by spontaneous point mutation, and variation at the scale of alleles of genes produced by exchanging alleles between different members of a sexual population. In recent work I have been developing a model for the benefit of sexual recombination that exploits the interaction between mutation on nucleotide sites and recombination of genes (Watson 2004, 2005). But the models in this book show composition acting over multiple hierarchical levels. In this chapter I look at how the compositional models provide evolution that operates on more than one scale of unit.

9.1 Units in Sexual Populations

In a genetic algorithm with uniform crossover, or a sexual population with free recombination of genes, different loci reproduce independently. In fact, from an algorithmic point of view, it makes little difference whether the evolution of two genes is implemented in the same population of individuals or two separate populations. We might just as well have explicitly separate populations for each locus and bring alleles together temporarily (with alleles drawn randomly from other populations for the other loci) for the purposes of evaluation (see Potter and De Jong 1994). In other words, a genetic algorithm with crossover is really a coevolutionary system even though there may be only one population in the implementation. When this is understood, it is easier to understand why the successful operation of the GA with crossover has quite a different set of conditions from the successful operation of the GA without crossover. For example, it makes it easier to understand that we will not achieve effective compositional evolution in a genetic algorithm just by throwing in a compositional operator like sexual recombination; sexual recombination completely changes the dynamics of change in an evolving population, and we need mechanisms to promote and maintain diversity among coevolving partitions of variables, for example, to get the most from it.

Selection on Bits or Wholes

So, which is best? Is it best to have selection act on individual alleles, or is it best to have selection act on whole genotypes? Here I want to address this question purely from an optimization point of view.

Consider two extreme cases: an asexual population and a sexual population with free recombination (uniform crossover). These two cases enable selection on whole genomes or individual alleles, respectively. In the asexual case, the individual variables within an individual coadapt to one another because they reproduce as a unit. In the sexual case, the reproductive units are single variables that coevolve with one another by virtue of being evaluated in the environment of one another. They are really quite different evolutionary scenarios, and the purpose of this subsection is to show that from an optimization point of view, neither scenario is necessarily an effective means of optimization.

Consider the fitness landscape defined by figure 9.1. In this system an individual with one hundred 1s is the most fit, an individual with no 1s is less fit, and an individual with fifty 1s is the least fit. This is a simple function rewarding a similarity of alleles, but for the sake of illustration, all 1s is higher fitness than all 0s (similar to a deceptive trap function, Deb and Goldberg 1993). Note also that a function just like this (but symmetric, see equation 4.1) is described by Dawkins to explain how genomes can appear to have coadapted genes even though selection acts on individual alleles (the "rowers" analogy, pp. 38–39 in Dawkins 1989).

With selection on individual alleles, a 1 allele will rise in frequency if the average number of 1 alleles in individuals it is evaluated in is greater than fifty. Otherwise it will decrease in frequency and 0 alleles will be selected for. Clearly, the average fitness of individuals in the population can be increased by this form of selection, but obviously, if the population should happen to start off with less than fifty 1s per indi-

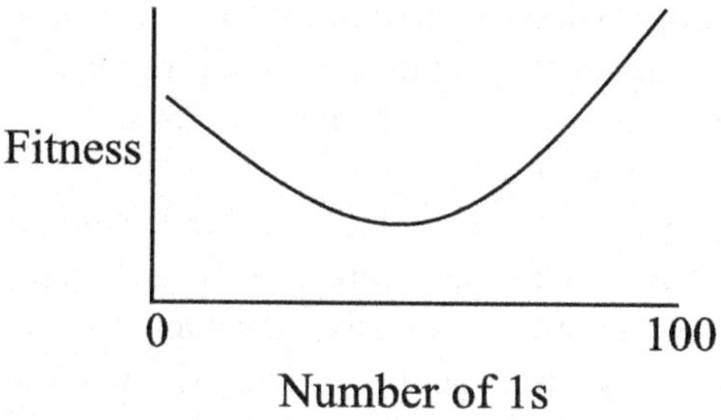

Figure 9.1
A simple challenge to extreme units of selection.

vidual on average then it will ultimately arrive at all 0s rather than the fitter all-1s configuration. If this was the case, then even if we were to (magically) introduce an individual that had a 1 allele at every locus, being significantly fitter than all other individuals in the population, it could not result in moving the population to the higher fitness configuration. In fact, since these alleles are selected for individually, and the average number of 1s in the individuals in which these alleles are evaluated is close to zero, these 1 alleles will appear less fit than 0 alleles and be very quickly removed from the population.

In contrast, in a population using selection on entire genomes, if an all-1s individual were (magically) introduced into a population then it would obviously rise in frequency and take over the population, even if all other individuals were all 0s. However, as I said, the introduction of such an individual would be quite magical. This individual is one of 2^{100} possible individuals; it could not arise by spontaneous mutation.

Disregarding new mutations for the moment, assuming that the initial population started out with individuals that were approximately half 0s and half 1s then a population with selection on individual alleles would arrive at either all 1s or all 0s just by selecting on the initial variation that was given in the population (assuming all alleles were present in at least one individual in the initial population and no alleles were lost by drift). In contrast, a population with selection on whole genomes would only be able to select for the fittest individual in the initial population, which will not be very fit if it has approximately half 0s and half 1s.

The point I want to make is that both selection schemes have their advantages but neither one is ideal. A population with selection on whole genomes could select for the fittest genotype if it was present in the population. But the space of possible genotypes is huge so this is unlikely and a random sample of individuals will not include very fit genotypes. On the other hand, a population with selection on individual alleles can use individual alleles that are present in the population much more efficiently to improve fitness, but it might not be the fittest genotype that rises to the top, even if the fittest genotype occurs in the population.

Algorithmically, a mix of the two would be sensible. If we did a few independent runs of populations using selection on individual alleles then some runs would arrive at all 0s and some would arrive at all 1s. If we then turned off sex, effectively "freezing" all the individuals so that they get selected as whole genotypes, and threw them all into one big population and applied selection again, then the individuals that were all 1s would win out. This way we could get the advantages of being able to select for individual alleles to find fit configurations of alleles quickly, and the advantages of being able to select for whole genomes so we could find the fittest genotypes. In short, a combination of selection on individual alleles and selection on whole genotypes makes sense algorithmically because the former is not guaranteed to find the fittest configurations, but the combinatorics of the latter is prohibitive in large problem spaces.

This is a simple scenario to illustrate the advantages and disadvantages of evolution in an asexual population and evolution in a population with free recombination. In this scenario, the reason that selection on individual alleles is useful is that the fitness contributions of individual alleles have lots of useful information in them—they create a smooth fitness gradient toward high-fitness configurations. But they do not have all the fitness information in them. Additional fitness contributions make the all-1s configuration higher fitness than the all-0s configuration but this difference is not noticeable unless comparing an individual that has a large number of 1s with an individual that has a large number of 0s. Conversely, selection on whole genomes can exploit these extra fitness contributions but cannot exploit the information in the fitness contributions of individual alleles.

So, how could we get selection on both parts and wholes in natural populations? In sexual populations, selection acts on individual alleles—under what circumstances would a population be able to select on combinations of alleles? This is not a new question in population genetics.

Shifting Balance Theory

For Sewell Wright, the motivation for shifting balance theory was to enable selection on coadapted sets of alleles, which he called "interaction systems." Wright agreed with Fisher that in large panmictic populations, "combinations [of alleles] are broken-up too rapidly to permit effective selection among interaction systems (unless the loci are so closely linked that alleles at different loci behave almost as if alleles of each other)." And thus selection is "restricted to the net effects of alleles" (Wright 1977, p. 470). It was the use of selection among different "demes" of a subdivided population that was supposed to rescue the possibility of selection on sets of co-adapted alleles in shifting balance theory (SBT).

SBT describes the adaptation of a population when subdivided into a number of semi-isolated demes. Wright suggests that the cumulative effect of a subdivided population is quite different from the effect of adaptation in a single panmictic (unstructured) population. Specifically, subdivision permits different subpopulations to differentiate by genetic drift (nonadaptive genetic change arising from stochastic selection processes in small populations) and arrive at different genetic combinations (see also Barton 1993; Slatkin 1981; Wakeley 2000). This parallel exploration of many demes increases the possibility that at least one subpopulation may discover a higher adaptive peak, and subsequent migration of the superior variants to other demes permits the whole population to shift to the superior peak (just like the scenario described above). Alternatively, a few demes may each discover different high-fitness adaptive peaks, and the mating of migrants from these subtypes may result in a superior integration of their characteristics.

Wright thus compares two possibilities for the "progress" of evolution: (1) selection among mutations, and (2) selection among "interaction systems." In the panmictic case, "progress of mass selection under a constant set of conditions is limited by the extremely rare occurrence of novel favourable mutations." But, although a mutation that is individually favorable might be rare, "[t]he fixation of a gene by mass selection tends, however, to be followed by a succession of favourable modifiers that build up a favourable interaction system." So, Wright suggests that finding fit combinations of alleles, interaction systems (together with the occasional new mutation), is more likely than the occurrence of mutations whose net effect is positive. Then, since a panmictic population provides no means to select among interaction systems, Wright employs the notions of subdivision and drift to enable localized adaptation where each deme can discover and focus on a different interaction system. Thus Wright states that "inferior interaction systems are replaced by superior ones" if a population is "divided into small populations, sufficiently isolated to permit wide stochastic deviations in numerous loci but not so isolated as to prevent excess diffusion from those centers that happen to have acquired the most adaptive interaction systems ..." (1977, p. 471).

Note that there are some important features of SBT that are in common with the models described in earlier chapters:

• Selection on interaction systems (i.e., modules).

• Semi-independent, parallel adaptation of many subsets of genetic material (i.e., an emphasis on diversity).

• Significantly localized selection (i.e., competition is predominantly between members within a subset).

• Significant among-subset variance in the effect of an allele/feature. Different demes contain different genetic backgrounds and therefore, through epistatic effects, produce different effects on a given allele.

• Possible assembly of "complex adaptations whose constituent parts arise via peak shifts in different demes" (Coyne, Barton, and Turelli 2000).

Wright's work on SBT provides an example of a population genetics model that explicitly addresses the evolution of interaction systems or modules, emphasizes the importance of mechanisms that can enable selection on interaction systems, and suggests that the rest of the genotype cannot be treated as a static backdrop to the adaptation of an individual locus. There is also some significant overlap between the motives of Wright's SBT and the motives of the work presented in this book. Specifically, in both cases mechanisms are investigated that enable an escape from local optima on the fitness surface. Additionally, there is some similarity in the mechanism modeled. Specifically, both SBT and my models of compositional evolution suggest that an escape from local optima can be facilitated by selection on sets of coadapted alleles.

However, there are also many significant differences in the mechanisms modeled—the compositional mechanisms modeled in this book are not models of SBT and are not subject to the same limitations as SBT. For example, a significant feature of Wright's SBT is the use of genetic drift, which is not featured in my models; Wright places relatively little emphasis on the bringing together of different interaction systems from different subpopulations whereas this is central to the compositional models; and whereas Wright uses population subdivision to facilitate selection on different interaction systems, my models of composition via sexual recombination use physical genetic linkage to enable selection on coadapted sets of alleles discussed below (and subdivision is primarily used just to maintain diversity).

Physical Linkage and Selection on Coadapted Alleles

The possibility that inversions (and possibly other mechanisms that rearrange gene order) could play a useful evolutionary role by bringing together coadapted gene complexes, preventing them from being broken up by crossover, is well-known

(Dobzhansky 1955; Kelly 2000). In the quote above, page 251, Wright acknowledges the notion that physical linkage could allow selection on sets of coadapted alleles, but in the same sentence he also dismisses it. Why is this?

Without chromosome-rearranging mechanisms there seems to be a good reason to dismiss the role that physical linkage plays in enabling selection on coadapted alleles. Specifically, alleles were defined as the "particulate units of inheritance." Usually this corresponded to the alleles of individual genes—what we now know as individual protein-coding regions. But if two genes should happen to be collocated and thus strongly physically linked then they are effectively one particulate unit of inheritance; it seems we may as well treat them as one locus, as Wright suggests. I suspect the reasoning goes like this: if two alleles are physically linked (enough to become coadapted) then we may as well abstract them into a single locus, and if they are not physically linked then they cannot become coadapted (because they cannot be reliably reproduced as a set). Either way, when a locus is defined with this sort of reasoning, there can never be coadapted alleles from physical linkage—either there are independent alleles or there is one allele.

Dawkins (1976), following Williams (1966), employs this reasoning in the definition of a gene. A gene is whatever unit reproduces faithfully and this is controlled by the rate of recombination. Under a high rate of recombination selection acts on relatively short sections of chromosome, under low rates of recombination selection acts on relatively long sections of chromosome. But whatever the unit is, there is no selection on groups of them—hence each gene optimizes its individual interests by definition of the selective unit (Dawkins 1976).

Is this way of looking at it sufficient? I think it is *if* you want to model the changes in frequency of variants only over short timescales. Ronald Fisher's background was in plant breeding, and Wright had a background in animal breeding—and the concerns of breeding experiments have relatively short timescales. Perhaps it is not surprising then that the research questions which were paramount at the formulation of the modern synthesis (of Mendelian genetics and the theory of natural selection) in the 1930s were short timescale questions such as the maintenance of variation under blending inheritance, and "the correlation between relatives on the supposition of Mendelian inheritance" (Fisher 1918). On these timescales there is very little new variation introduced by mutation—the sort of models that were most interesting for population genetics were those dealing only with selection on the standing variation within the population. In this case, whatever the combinations of genetic material may be within the selective unit, these combinations are essentially "atomic," "particulate," and "immutable" under recombination—in short, their internal details are irrelevant.

However, this is too simplistic. In reality, in sexual populations the linkage of different sites is not all or nothing. Under intermediate rates of recombination—that is, neither asexual populations, nor free recombination, but something in between—the genetic map causes selection to be applied more or less strongly to different sized units of genetic material simultaneously. There is significant structure in the linkage-disequilibrium patterns along the length of the chromosome at many scales, from single nucleotide differences within genes to haplotype blocks (McVean et al. 2004). Here selection can act on combinations of alleles that are tightly linked because they are unlikely to be separated during reproduction. However, selection can also act on sets of alleles that are less strongly linked, alleles at loci that are a bit further apart, though this selective unit will be less coherent because it is more likely to be disrupted during reproduction. In general, the strength of selection on a set of alleles will be inversely related to how distributed they are on the genome. All of these units of selection apply at all times, but on longer timescales smaller units will be processed more effectively. It is therefore not appropriate to take any particular length of genetic material and define this as the one true unit of selection.

So, in figure 9.1, as discussed, there was some useful information in the fitness contributions of individual alleles, but also some fitness contributions that only became apparent when comparing individuals that differed by very many alleles. But what happens in the more interesting case where fitness contributions are derived from allele combinations of various sizes? The experiments using HIFF showed that selection on whole genomes (RMHC or asexual GA) failed to find high-fitness configurations of the system. The experiments using a GA with uniform crossover showed that selection on individual alleles also failed to find high-fitness configurations of the system. Selection at either of these extremes of possible units failed. However, a GA with one- or two-point crossover succeeds easily in finding high-fitness configurations. This success can be understood by acknowledging that a population with a low rate of recombination (not asexual, and not free recombination) permits selection at many scales simultaneously—on sets of physically linked alleles, from individual alleles to whole genomes, in correspondence with the rate of recombination among alleles at different genetic distances in the genetic map.

This is what produces the successful result when the genetic algorithm (with diversity maintenance) is applied to HIFF. In HIFF, there is no single unit of selection that can efficiently find fit configurations. If selection is applied only on small units then these can be optimized well, but the interdependencies between these units cannot be resolved to find solutions to higher-level modules. If selection were applied only on large units then interdependent sets of smaller units within them could be selected for, but the bigger the unit the greater the combinatorial search space within each unit. It is a lock-step no-win trade-off in a hierarchically consistent problem like HIFF. However, if an evolutionary process can utilize selection on small blocks of alleles to resolve interdependencies between them and find good small blocks, and subsequently use selection on large blocks of alleles to resolve interdependencies between small blocks to find larger good blocks, and so on at all scales, then HIFF is easy. This is how a sexual population with a low recombination rate succeeds in finding fit configurations in HIFF. We can see that it is the physical linkage of appropriate groups of alleles that provides this advantage because the GA completely fails when this arrangement is randomized, and because it also fails when there is no recombination or too much recombination.

In short, the success of the sexual population in finding fit configurations in a hierarchically modular system such as HIFF derives from its ability to use multiple scales of selection (see also Watson 2005). However, as I have taken pains to point out, the ability of the genetic algorithm to do this depends entirely on the assumption of a fortuitous arrangement of the loci on the chromosome. In natural genomes this is not entirely hypothetical as I discuss in section 10.7.

In the GA with crossover the coevolution of schemata of different sizes is implicit—applied through the use of physical linkage in an appropriately ordered genetic map. SEAM makes the manipulation of schemata of increasing sizes quite explicit, and thereby alleviates the limitations exhibited by sexual recombination.

9.2 Scaling Up Evolution with Symbiotic Encapsulation

The way in which evolution is scaled up in the model of sexual recombination depends on the assumption of a favorable genetic map. Moreover, there is no sense in which the sexual population progresses incrementally from selection on individual alleles to selection on larger and larger groups of alleles—it is, more exactly, that selection acts on chunks of genetic material at all scales from the outset, and as evolution progresses this results first in good small blocks and then in good larger blocks and so on. Likewise, the unit of variation also does not change, variations occur by exchanging sections of genetic material of all sizes from the outset—however, fitness improvements are likely to result from large variations only toward the end of the process when large chunks of genetic material have been internally optimized.

In the model of symbiotic encapsulation things work differently. When a join is made between a symbiotic pair it does effectively become a new unit of selection. And since new entities are made by assembling extant entities, the unit of variation scales up too. Moreover, in SEAM this process is entirely independent of the genetic map. This makes SEAM a more interesting form of compositional evolution, and a more general and scalable approach to optimization. In the following subsections I discuss a number of component parts of SEAM to explain how symbiotic encapsulation enables scalable evolution.

Scale-Invariant Evolutionary Processes

The main features of an evolutionary algorithm are: variation, evaluation, and selection. In the RMHC, variation acts at the scale of the primitive problem variables, and evaluation and selection act on complete strings. In the GA with crossover, evaluation is applied to complete strings but variation (by crossover) and selection act on schemata of all sizes at all stages of search. In neither method does the scale of these processes (either variation, evaluation, or selection) increase progressively as search continues. Thus, even in an adaptive landscape that is scale invariant, like HIFF, it cannot be the case that these mechanisms properly escape the primitive variables of the problem domain. The RMHC continues to explore variations in the primitive variables throughout the process. And for example, in the genetic algorithm, even when all individuals contain only large fully optimized correct modules, crossover is still just as likely to exchange an order-1 schema as it was in the first generation of the run.

In contrast, in SEAM all three of these features scale up as search progresses (if the problem domain allows):

- Variation: Variation is performed by the assembly of extant entities. As extant entities increase in complexity, the variations that are explored are of the same scale. The size of the jumps that can be made (with respect to the original mutation-based landscape) scales with the complexity of extant entities. This frees the variation operator from the original primitive space of variations and allows search to move explicitly from the combinations of primitive variables to the combination of schemata of successively higher orders. (Notice that the addition of any explicit mutation breaks the scale-invariant quality of the variation in the algorithm. That is, spontaneous mutation is inherently tied to the original primitive variables.)
- Selection: In SEAM, when new entities are defined they encapsulate the pair of entities involved so that they always travel together as a whole in the future. Accordingly, the unit of selection is explicitly scaled up. And since new units are created from the assembly of extant units, the unit of selection continues to scale up appropriately.
- Evaluation: SEAM progresses by the identification of good modules rather than the direct identification of good complete solutions. The identification of good mod-

ules requires that we have good assemblies in which to test the value of a module. In SEAM the assemblies that are used to test a module are built from extant modules. Therefore, the quality of contexts used to evaluate modules improves in step with the quality of extant modules.

These observations show that all these major features of SEAM are scale free. When applied to a scale-free modular problem (Lipson 2004), such as HIFF, the modularity at all scales is equally utilizable by the evolutionary process.

Note that SEAM explicitly scales up the unit of selection because once a join is deemed stable it is permanent and not retested for stability in the future. This might seem to contravene the assumption that entities should act in their selfish interest—but I will discuss this later (p. 264). First I will address the mechanism of evaluation. It is all very well to say that we make contexts from assemblies of other entities but why is this the right thing to do? What stops suboptimal modules, such as ----1100--------, that are certainly above average fitness, from taking over in the population? How can it be that this complicated form of group evaluation selects for subsets of coadapted alleles that are not just above average fitness but in fact the right modules for making bigger modules? To understand the answers to these questions I want to first talk about some related phenomena.

From the Baldwin Effect to Symbiotic Scaffolding

The Baldwin effect (1896) describes how lifetime learning can guide the accumulation of heritable genetic variation. This does not involve the inheritance of acquired characteristics. Rather it describes how the presence of lifetime learning changes the shape of the fitness landscape in which subsequent genetic variation takes place. Moreover, it changes it in such a manner that it favors selection for heritable variations that increase innate ability at the learned task. This works on the assumption that learning enables rapid exploration in the space of phenotypic behaviors and is therefore much more likely to discover a complex behavior than the relatively slow genetic variations. However, assuming that the learning mechanism has some cost, for example it takes time to learn the task, then in the presence of such a learning mechanism, any genetic mutation that should reduce the learning overhead would be selected for. It is possible that through the accumulation of numerous such mutations the learning mechanism would eventually become redundant and the formerly learned behavior would become an innate behavior. It is said that the learned behavior has become *canalized* by the genetic variation (Waddington 1942), or *genetically assimilated* (Mills and Watson 2005). The important point is that without the learning mechanism, variations that reduce the learning overhead (and increase the innate ability) would not necessarily be valuable and would not rise in frequency. Accordingly, in such a scenario the complex behavior is unevolvable without the learning mechanism to guide evolution toward it—hence, "how learning can guide evolution" (Hinton and Nowlan 1987).

In previous work, I investigated the possibility of "symbiotic scaffolding" (Watson and Pollack 1999d), a symbiotic analogue of the Baldwin effect. The idea is that, instead of augmenting innate abilities with lifetime learning, the innate abilities of one organism may be augmented by lifetime interaction with other organisms in its vicinity, perhaps allowing it to live in an otherwise hostile habitat (Grieshaber and Völkel 1998). Under symbiotic scaffolding an organism may come to exhibit the characteristics of a symbiont without direct genetic transfer (in a manner analogous to the Baldwin effect where an organism may come to exhibit acquired characteristics without Lamarckian inheritance). The basic model demonstrated a symbiotic scaffolding effect, and subsequent investigations illustrated some interesting phenomena (Watson, Reil, and Pollack 2000b; see also Wiles, Tonkes, and Watson 2001, which uses HIFF and symbiotic scaffolding). This model illustrates that it is in principle possible for a complex adaptation to be discovered first by a symbiotic group, and subsequently be canalized by the heritable features of a member of that group. The bivalve *Solemya reidi* may be a natural example (Watson, Reil, and Pollack 2000b; Powell and Somero 1986).

In general, we can see that both the Baldwin effect and symbiotic scaffolding work by a mechanism of rapid variation guiding a mechanism of relatively slow variation. Crudely these correspond to nonheritable variation and heritable variation respectively (see Mills and Watson 2005). In both models the slow variation is genetic mutation, but the fast variation comes from different sources in the two models. In the Baldwin effect it comes from lifetime learning, in symbiotic scaffolding it comes from the transient formation of symbiotic groups. We know that one of the conditions for the Baldwin effect is that the space of variations available to these two mechanisms be in some sense correlated (Mayley 1996). If they are not, then the fact that the mechanism of rapid variation might discover a fit configuration does not provide a gradient that the mechanism of slow variation can follow. It needs to be the case that the slow variation mechanism can incrementally reduce the amount of rapid variation that is required in the lifetime of an organism (and thereby reduce the cost of lifetime learning/plasticity)—and if the space of variations in the two mechanisms is not correlated, then it is not possible for the heritable variation to canalize the nonheritable variation.

In Hinton and Nowlan's (1987) model of the Baldwin effect, lifetime variation is modeled by random completion of the partially specified string, and genetic variation is modeled by random variation in the specified features. Both mechanisms produce variants that are neighbors in the mutation-neighborhood metric. Accordingly, genetic variation is able to canalize acquired characteristics effectively. However, the symbiotic scaffolding model did not address the need for the rapid and slow variation mechanisms to move in correlated spaces. Fortunately, in the "needle on a plateau" adaptive landscape that we used, following Hinton and Nowlan, there are no local optima, and the effect was robust. But, in general, it should not be expected that the variations in feature combinations that can be produced by composing together symbiotic groups can be canalized by gradual mutational change within the entity of interest—they are very different variation mechanisms. In fact, in symbiotic scaffolding the assembly of transient symbiotic groups is a compositional mechanism, whereas genetic variation from mutation is, of course, a gradual mechanism.

From Symbiotic Scaffolding to Symbiotic Encapsulation

Algorithmically, this kind of process where a rapid variation mechanism guides a slow variation mechanism makes the best sense when both variation mechanisms are really the same—except that one is slow (heritable variation) and the other is fast (nonheritable variation). In Hinton and Nowlan's model of the Baldwin effect, lifetime learning and genetic variation are both gradual variation. In the earlier model of symbiotic scaffolding, symbiotic group formation is a compositional mechanism and genetic variation is a gradual mechanism—so it is fortunate that it worked. What if the rapid variation mechanism and the slow variation mechanism were both compositional?

This is what is implemented in SEAM. The formation of transient (nonheritable) groups for the purposes of evaluation uses exactly the same composition operator (on the same entities) that the formation of permanent joins uses. This means that the rapid compositional variation of transient groups necessarily operates in the right space to enable the relatively slow permanent joins to canalize successful groups. In the Baldwin effect, lifetime plasticity guides genetic variation, and genetic variation canalizes acquired traits. In SEAM, the evaluation of transient groups guides the genetic encapsulation of new entities, and the genetic encapsulation of new entities canalizes features of the more successful groups. In both cases, there is a mechanism of rapid nonheritable variation guiding a relatively slow, heritable variation mechanism. But in Hinton and Nowlan's model of the Baldwin effect the variation of both mechanisms is gradual, and in SEAM the variation of both mechanisms is compositional.

The benefit of this is that the evaluation of entities in contextual groups primes them for subsequent joins, or equivalently, solutions found first by groups are later

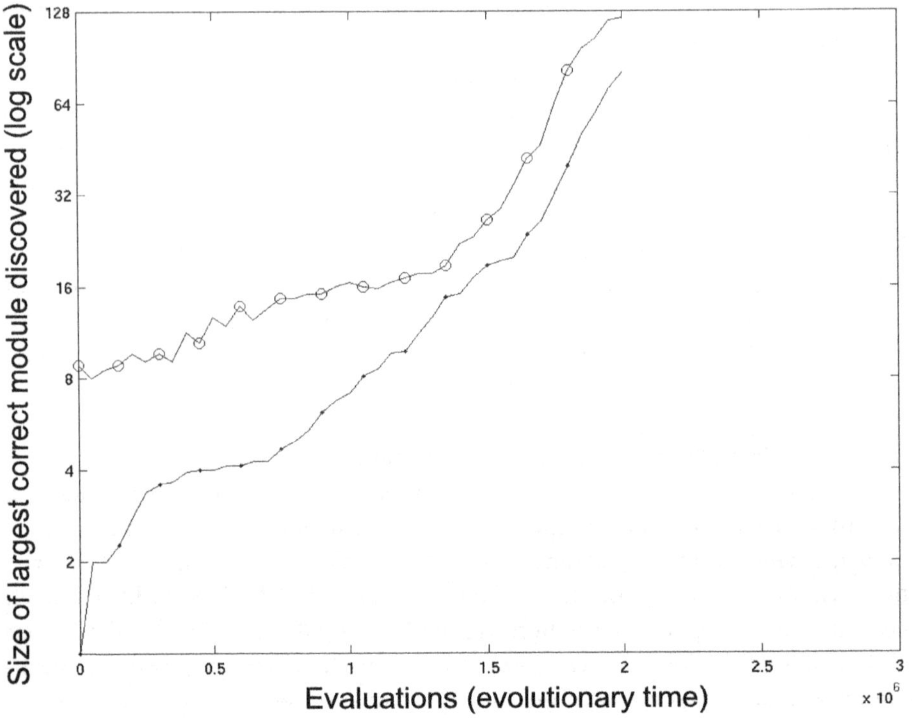

Figure 9.2
Size of modules in individuals and in groups in SEAM (log scale). The size axis shown in this figure uses a log scale—thus, if the increase in size is proportional to extant size the curve would appear as a straight line. We can see clearly in this figure that innovation by composition continues steadily in this problem, approaching a scale-invariant increase in the size of correct modules in individual entities.

canalized (Waddington 1942) by composite entities (see also Bull 1999). In figure 9.2, the "group curve" (shown with circle point markers) is the size of the largest correct module in any group of entities when they are evaluated together as a contextual environment (this corresponds to the curve shown for SEAM in figure 7.7). The "individual curve" (shown with dot point markers) seen running below the group curve is the size of the largest correct module in any stable individual entity. The individual curve shows how the discovery of correct building blocks by individuals follows behind the discovery of correct building blocks by groups. This shows how good modules found by groups are subsequently canalized by individual entities.

This discussion is intended to help explain why evaluating individuals in groups made from assemblies of other individuals from the population is the right way to evaluate entities for successful joins. But algorithmically this seems like a roundabout way to get what we are looking for. It does not explain why the discovery of modules first by groups and then by individuals is better than, say, just keeping the good groups. Algorithmically we are not prevented from doing this if it works, just like we are not prevented from using Lamarkian inheritance if it works. In fact, this roundabout way of doing things does make sense algorithmically. To see why this is the case, it is useful to view symbiotic encapsulation in SEAM (and the Baldwin effect) as an instance of the general mechanism of *stochastic lookahead.*

Symbiotic Scaffolding and Stochastic Lookahead

I call the general idea of allowing a fast nonheritable variation mechanism to guide a slow heritable variation mechanism "stochastic lookahead." This might sound unevolutionary for the same reason as the Baldwin effect sounds unevolutionary at first. However, the Baldwin effect is not unevolutionary; it does not use Lamarckian inheritance, but lifetime variation does guide subsequent genetic variation (see Watson, Reil, and Pollack 2000b for further discussion).

SEAM uses the idea of stochastic lookahead to enable the identification of good modules, as follows. We want to select for good modules, but what makes a "good module"? A good module is precisely the thing that, when used in assemblies in the future, will produce good assemblies. So, how do we find such an entity? By trying it in a number of assemblies and seeing how it does.

If we try a proposed module in a number of assemblies and it does well then it is precisely what we want from a module. But this raises two questions: (1) how can we expect to make a good assembly, with which to find good modules, before we have good modules? If we make poor assemblies then they will not reveal the potential utility of the proposed module; (2) if we already made a good assembly, then we are done—why should we be interested in the module? Why do we not just keep the good assembly?

These two questions and their answers are interrelated. The simple answer to the first question is that we do not know how to make good assemblies, but we can make many assemblies from the modules we have so far, and hopefully some will be sufficient to reveal the utility of a proposed new module. Note that the better our modules are so far, the better assemblies we can make, and the better assemblies we can make the better we can evaluate the utility of a module. The answer to the second question is that initially the best assembly we find will not be a very good one. Keeping the best assembly we have found so far is the "greedy" method that finds suboptimal configurations. We should not suppose that the assemblies we make are perfect, just that they are good enough to reveal good modules. Then when we have better modules, we can use these to build still better assemblies, which in turn are used to find larger modules, and so on.

These ideas are very similar to the ideas of the self-adaptive greedy estimate algorithm, SAGE (Juillé 1999, pp. 50–51). SAGE uses a partial solution as the beginning of a complete solution that is filled in at random or by using an incremental construction heuristic. The complete solutions built in the early stages are not very good, but they are good enough to determine the next incremental step for the partial solution.

Stochastic Lookahead Avoids the Need for Backtracking in Greedy Optimization

We can contrast the operation of stochastic lookahead with greedy approaches to finding good associations. Two possible greedy approaches might be: (1) to create new associations by selecting for any association that was better than not having an association at all (simple hill climbing in incremental construction); (2) selecting for associations that were the best on average of all possible associations (steepest ascent). Both these approaches would lead to suboptimal associations. For example, in HIFF the module ----1111 might provide a large fitness increase when added to the module --00----, perhaps the largest we can find at a given point in the search process, but it is not a correct join and making this join will prevent future joins that would have been higher fitness.

The classic artificial-intelligence search approach to overcome this problem is to "backtrack" and try a different path in the search space—in this case a different association. Evolution, of course, cannot backtrack—if it finds itself at a suboptimal configuration with no further improvements possible, then that is the end of the story. However, we can see the operation of group evaluation as providing a means to "lookahead" to avoid the need to backtrack. That is, by evaluating the fitness of a proposed join in many groups of individuals we are implicitly providing fitness feedback about the future consequences of the proposed join. We are not really making joins and backtracking, we are just evaluating a proposed join in many transient contexts. Because these contexts are built using the same join operator over the same individuals, they provide an accurate reflection of the future consequences for a join. This has the effect of discounting the immediate/short-term benefit of a proposed join with the future/long-term consequences of a join. And this in turn means that a greedy optimization *in this modified fitness landscape* provides an improved optimization. That is, the future-discounted fitness, the fitness coming from many group evaluations, modifies the fitness function for the individuals concerned so that, rather than forming the association that maximizes their immediate selfish interest, they are implicitly maximizing their long-term interests.

This use of future-discounted fitness is analogous to the use of "lookahead" in traditional game playing. In a board game, for example, heuristic search for a best move involves the use of a static evaluation function that assesses the value of static properties of the players' pieces and their positions. A common technique in game strategies is to look ahead in the space of possible moves following a proposed move to arrive at many possible future board states and apply the evaluation function to these board states instead of the immediate board state. Such lookahead is then used to assess the value of each proposed move. In SEAM, we do not explicitly assess the value of each possible association to find the best one—which would be unevolutionary—instead, for each proposed join, we stochastically assess whether there is any other join in a random sample of possibilities that would be better than this one and reject the proposed join if there is. This models the competition between a proposed composite and its free-living variants. Algorithmically, this is probably wasteful of evaluations and suggests a deterministic algorithm that may perform better (De Jong, Thierens, and Watson 2004).

Whenever it is the case that "a little lookahead plus the fitness function" is better than "the fitness function applied right now," SEAM will be better than greedy optimization under the same representation and variation operators. The HIFF function shows exactly when this will be the case. Of course, this will not always be the case. Like any heuristic, filling in the unspecified bits of a partial solution with other individuals and evaluating the full string is an imperfect heuristic for determining the value of a module, with or without lookahead. However, lemma 1 (in section 8.2), shows that, in principle, lookahead that covers all possible future joins is guaranteed to prevent suboptimal joins in this class of problem. The question then becomes—how much lookahead does a given problem require to prevent suboptimal joins? In separable problems, any join between good modules is a good join because there are no intermodule dependencies to be resolved. Thus no lookahead is required and a simple greedy method provides optimal solutions. In a problem containing arbitrarily high-order deceptive schemata, an arbitrarily large amount of lookahead is required to prevent suboptimal joins. But in problems with modular interdependency, where the context sensitivity of a module is significant but limited, a small amount of lookahead is sufficient (see section 8.2).

We can see that the stochastic lookahead enabled by group evaluation is necessary for SEAM because the control experiment using evaluation in random groups fails (see section 7.5). But this discussion has been intended to explain *why* this works by relating it to the underlying algorithmic principles of lookahead in search. The underlying algorithmic principles illustrated by SEAM show that the formation of symbiotic groups and their subsequent canalization by mechanisms of symbiotic encapsulation in nature is a fundamentally different form of evolutionary process and provides the ability for evolution to scale up in a much more principled manner than that enabled by sexual recombination.

Selfish Genes and the Evolution of Cooperation

Given the mention of symbiotic groups, group evaluation, scaling up the unit of selection, and maximising long-term (rather than immediate) payoffs in the previous subsections, I had better briefly mention how this relates to the evolution of cooperation. As section 7.3 described, an entity enters into an association because it is in its own best interest to do so. When entities discover a successful mutually beneficial group, they remain in it because there is no other individual they could be paired with (out of those sampled) that confers a better fitness improvement. Thus, to be sure, entities do not cooperate in this model out of the kindness of their hearts and any notion of altruism can therefore be dispensed with. To this extent, the model is in alignment with the selfish-gene model (Dawkins 1976).

However, I have also suggested that we can see the formation of high-fitness configurations through composition as the formation of hierarchical cooperative groups (see section 4.5), and it should be noted that a naive model of individual selection would not discover high-fitness configurations. Specifically, a model based on the (appropriately named) "greedy" selection strategy, selecting for an association whenever it is better on average than not having the association, fails to find high-fitness configurations in HIFF (see section 7.5). The point then is not whether entities remain in an association for altruistic or selfish motives—the point is how the immediate fitness landscape of the individual is modified such that the selfish fitness choices it makes now lead it to discover the mutually beneficial configurations rather than the mutual "defect" configurations. In SEAM this is achieved by the mechanism of group evaluation which guides the formation of associations toward those that are optimal, rather than just immediately satisfying, as discussed above.

However, although at a given point in time the union of any two entities in SEAM is in their selfish interest (under the fitness landscape modified by group evaluation), the identity of those entities varies over time. I noted earlier that SEAM explicitly scales up the unit of selection, because once a join is deemed stable it is permanent and not retested for stability in the future, and that this might seem to contravene the assumption that entities should act in their selfish interest. But in fact, if we continued to apply selection for components at lower levels, individuals would rechoose the same associations because the join that was in their selfish interest in the first instance remains in their selfish interest. This is evident because neither they nor their partner changes internally and the environment becomes only more stable over time.

Thus we could implement the algorithm using only primitive-unit selection. The point here is that although we *could* implement selection at only the primitive level this is unnecessary and, worse, misses the point that the selection of the primitives can be accurately abstracted into the selection of the composites in this class of problem. An analogy might be useful here: if we were modeling the movement of billiard balls on a billiard table we *could* model the individual atoms within each ball. This would be accurate but unnecessary. Moreover, this would miss the point that the balls are useful abstractions of the atoms in the system because in that scenario there are no pressures sufficient to make the bonds among atoms within a ball unstable. I suspect that this form of thinking might contribute to resolving some of the controversy that surrounds concepts of hierarchical selection (Keller 1999; Gould 1982a, 2002)—that is, the lower-level view is always accurate but also misses the point—but untangling the numerous issues in that topic will have to be for another book.

9.3 The Inherent Tension of Innovation and Reproductive Fidelity

Finally in this chapter, I would like to address how compositional evolution affects key components of evolution by natural selection. Heritability, variation, and differential reproduction are fundamental principles in evolution by natural selection. However, it is a familiar irony that random variation is the source of new innovation but also inherently opposed to the maintenance of extant complexity (heritability). We might refer to this as the inherent tension of innovation and reproductive fidelity—or the tension of change and nonchange. Evolution has created mechanisms, such as enzymatic repair, that reduce the *error rate* (Nowak and Schuster 1989) and increase reproductive fidelity. But this raises the question: how can it be the case that heritability may be increased (by whatever mechanism) without also suppressing the opportunity for innovation? Differential reproduction is also not such a simple concept as it might first appear. Specifically, it requires us to delineate the entities involved—to identify the entities whose reproduction could be differentiated. There are many biological cases where the relevant reproductive units are not so obvious.

Symbiotic encapsulation offers an intriguing perspective on these issues. It is perfectly reasonable that a number of entities may each be individually stable and yet, via the discovery of successful compositions of these entities, there is still opportunity for innovation at a higher level of organization (see Meyers and Fontana 2005, p. 137). Thus, composition presents no opposition between the stability or reproductive fidelity of the component entities and the opportunity for innovation in entities at the next level of organization. And interestingly, this view is enabled by a willingness to repeatedly redefine the boundary of the entities involved in processes of differential reproduction.

The tension between reproductive fidelity and the opportunity for innovation perhaps suggests an inherent limit to the complexity that can be evolved by gradual mechanisms—these notions being allied to the complexity ceiling imposed by the limits of reproductive fidelity (Eigen and Schuster 1979). In contrast, it seems from the above observations, and the discussions of this chapter, that compositional mechanisms are not necessarily subject to the same limitations and may be better able to provide continued increases in complexity. Indeed, the solution provided by Eigen and Schuster for the reproductive-fidelity problem is a compositional event; specifically, the formation of hypercycles from the assembly of formerly independent self-replicating molecules.

This chapter has discussed how sexual recombination enables evolution to scale up in some respects, and how the features of the symbiotic encapsulation model illustrate that a more principled scaling up is possible. These discussions touched on a large number of technical and conceptually tricky issues that require significant further investigation to attain formal clarity. But in the meantime, they serve to give some indication of how the compositional models relate to a number of important concepts, why the models have the exact features that they do, and in particular, how they address the existing intuition that compositional evolution is not merely different from gradual evolution but has the potential to overcome some of its formal limitations.

10 The Impact of Compositional Evolution

This concluding chapter discusses the impact of the findings of the previous models on our understanding of evolution. This includes discussion of several conceptual issues that affect the way we see evolution and what evolution is capable of: the possibility of large directed genetic changes, whether sex/symbiogenesis provides a fundamentally different source of adaptation, the consequences that this has on our concepts of evolutionary difficulty, and how these issues are all better understood by recognizing the possibility of a different underlying algorithmic paradigm for evolution by natural selection. The purpose of this book has been to illustrate these conceptual issues *in principle*, and to expand the possibilities for how evolution may operate—but, before summing up, I briefly discuss the availability of the main prerequisites for compositional evolution: the availability of compositional mechanisms, and the likelihood of modularity in natural adaptive domains.

Before getting started on this main concluding discussion, the next subsection discusses some specific areas for future research that are suggested by the previous models. These are discussed separately for evolutionary computation and evolutionary biology before discussing how they can be brought together, and I also comment on a possible cause for why it is that these two disciplines have more difficulty communicating than one might expect given their apparently similar subject matter.

10.1 Future and Ongoing Research

In Evolutionary Biology

The work of previous chapters has provided an operationalized model of compositional mechanisms. However, there is much to be done to properly integrate the findings of these models with existing frameworks. As it is, SEAM illustrates the maintenance of complementary coevolving lineages and their genetic integration into composites. However, a full model of evolutionary processes should include mechanisms of speciation that allow the usual "differentiation from a common ancestor" in addition to compositional "integration into a new whole." A general model of evolutionary change might provide a framework that incorporates both gradual and compositional mechanisms, perhaps acting on different timescales or across different ecosystem scales. The role of compositional mechanisms in the major evolutionary transitions suggests that gradual and compositional mechanisms might correspond to intra- and intertransitional mechanisms of change respectively. In such a framework, gradual mechanisms and competitive selection between noncomplementary entities might provide the common picture of microevolutionary change; whereas compositional mechanisms and the coexistence of complementary entities might provide a more macroscale framework into which the former can be fitted.

But there are also more fine-scale roles for compositional evolution, discussed below (section 10.6).

On the subject of integrating evolutionary change at different scales, it is notable that ecosystem dynamics models are currently not integrated well with population genetics models. Often "community models" incorporate the interactions of numerous species but do not model evolutionary changes in the interaction coefficients of the underlying "community matrix" (e.g., Arthur 1987)—that is, the competitive (or otherwise) relationship of species to one another is generally fixed, while the stability (or otherwise) of population dynamics are examined. In contrast, population genetics models do include changes in the genetic composition of a species but generally do not model the interaction of multiple species. In order to properly understand the balance of diversity and competitive exclusion necessary to properly model the diversification and integration of species under compositional mechanisms, it is necessary to integrate models of interspecies interaction and intraspecies genetic change. In the models this book has presented, some of the necessary machinery has been embedded in mechanisms such as deterministic crowding and selection based on Pareto dominance. A proper integration of the compositional mechanisms presented in this work with more conventional population genetics subdivision models on the one hand, and community stability models on the other, is required. I suggest that the multidimensional treatment of fitness used in SEAM could assist in modeling the balance of competitive exclusion and stable coexistence that is required in a general model of evolutionary change incorporating both compositional and gradual mechanisms. The relationship between the Pareto-dominance-based selection in SEAM, Nash equilibria and mixed strategies (e.g., see Ficici 2004), and evolutionary stable strategies (Maynard Smith 1982) requires further attention.

The models I have presented suggest that shifting balance theory and serial endosymbiosis theory are related in the sense that both are concerned with the evolution of interaction systems in different lineages and their subsequent integration. The difference between them at this level of abstraction is that the former addresses subdivision (usually spatial subdivision) within a population of a single species and their integration via sexual recombination, whereas the latter addresses the adaptation of multiple species and their integration via symbiotic encapsulation. Margulis (1993a) suggests we may view sexual recombination and symbiotic encapsulation as analogous mechanisms—the main difference being that the donor entities that create an offspring under sexual recombination share a closer common ancestor than the donor entities that create a new individual under symbiotic encapsulation. In my introduction of SEAM I suggested that another important factor is seen (therefore) in the expected overlap of characters. More work is necessary to properly integrate our understanding of the two mechanisms and provide a general model of compositional change.

Intrinsic to the scale-invariant properties of SEAM discussed in the previous chapter are the ideas of scaling up the unit of variation and scaling up the unit of selection. I have attempted to describe how the scaling up of selection implicit in SEAM is both consistent with individual selection/selection at the lowest level unit, and an appropriate abstraction for understanding selection in a compositional setting. It would be useful to draw out this point in simpler models in order to address the issues more clearly.

Ongoing research on the benefit of recombination shows that a polynomial-versus-exponential distinction in the time for a sexual and asexual population to evolve fit genotypes can be demonstrated for a single compositional event rather than a hierarchical process (Watson 2004, 2005). This focuses on the assembly of just two genes each containing numerous nucleotide sites. These sites have numerous epistatic interdependencies among them but also strong synergistic epistasis among the sites within each gene. This system exhibits the property that a good combination of sites for the first gene is easy to find by accumulating point mutations, but a good combination of sites for the second gene is then hard to find without causing fitness decreases through dependencies with the first gene. Thus the two genes are each easy to find individually in parallel, and from there they can be combined together compositionally, but they cannot be found in a single linear process. This work focuses on the interaction of variation on nucleotide sites by mutation, with variation on combinations of genes by recombination (Watson 2005). This forms a complementary part of the picture of compositional evolution writ large, progressing through many hierarchical levels, as shown in this book.

Other ongoing work on the benefit of recombination (Watson 2005b) discusses a model of hybridization and questions the supposed importance of "multidimensional epistasis" (Kondrashov and Kondrashov 2001) in determining the advantage of sex. These new models, and the models of sexual recombination in chapter 6, like many models in evolutionary computation, all adopt an "evolution as search process" approach (see p. 72, this vol.), employing the assumption that a population is far from equilibrium. Although it is useful to tackle the modeling of a complex process like sex from complementary directions, these models ultimately need to be reconciled with the majority of "frequency thinking" population genetics models addressing populations at equilibrium (e.g. Bergman, Otto, and Feldman 1995a, 1995b; Barton 1995; Bürger 2000).

Finally, the work in this book has addressed the capability of different evolutionary processes to evolve complex systems given that there is an inherent modularity in the epistatic dependencies among parts of the system. Processes where the modularity of epistatic dependencies is a result of adaptation, rather than a given (Wagner 1995, 1996; Wagner and Altenberg 1996; Orr 2000b; Lipson, Pollack, and Suh 2002), make things even more complicated but need to be addressed.

In Evolutionary Computation

There are a number of other theoretical works comparing mutation and crossover landscapes and examining the action of recombination, for example, Culberson 1995; Spears 1992, 2004; Aizawa 1997; Gitchoff and Wagner 1996; Stephens and Waelbroeck 1999; Wagner and Stadler 1997; Stadler and Wagner 1997. Armed with the concept of modular interdependency and the proofs developed for compositional mechanisms on HIFF, it would be beneficial to return to these works and make a thorough examination of the relationships and implications. Future work should also continue to formalize a description of the class of problem for which compositional mechanisms are well suited. In this book I have focused on a particular instance of this class, and described a way to generate similar hierarchically decomposable problems in the same class. But it is necessary to continue to elucidate the defining features of this class that are essential for the success of compositional mechanisms (De Jong, Watson, and Thierens 2005a).

An important means to validate theoretical understanding is to apply it to engineering-problem domains. Preliminary investigations suggest that an algorithm like SEAM may work well on a particular subclass of traditional hard combinatorial problems; for example, a subclass of traveling-salesperson problems where the distribution of delivery points is clustered at several scales into regions, districts, and cities, for example.

In principle, SEAM can be applied to any substrate that is amenable to a compositional construction of solutions. There is nothing in the algorithm that is dependent on, or makes use of the fact that, individuals are represented in bit strings (see De Jong, Thierens, and Watson 2004 for a discussion on generalized hierarchical GAs). Neither is SEAM restricted to fixed-length representations—components can be tested in many groups without the idea that the group provides a fully specified set of problem variables. Accordingly, future work may exploit aspects of modularity and interdependency in any number of different substrates. For example: graph partitioning (see Karypis and Kumar 1995; Karypis 1999; Toulouse, Thulasiraman, and Glover 1999), neural networks (see Potter and De Jong 1995), genetic programming (see Rosca 1997; Juillé and Pollack 1996; O'Reilly 1997), sorting networks (Juillé 1999), electronic circuit design (see Thompson 1998), robot controllers and morphologies (see Sims 1994; Lipson and Pollack 2000), and 3-D sketch interpretation.[1]

Applying SEAM to these domains potentially provides the opportunity to identify functional modules in the domain as well as optimize the given objective function.

I suspect that there are a number of algorithmic aspects to SEAM that may need attention in order for it to be applied as a robust engineering-optimization method. First, it may be the case in some domains that there is no join between a pair of components that is always in the interest of the two parties involved. In which case it may be necessary to relax the Pareto-dominance criterion and allow joins that are "nearly always good" or "preferred in nearly all contexts" to become stable. Second, in the current version of SEAM, initialization covers all the primitive components of the problem domain. In some domains, especially continuous substrates, it is not likely to be feasible to cover all required primitive components by initialization. Accordingly, it may be necessary to allow the creation of new primitive elements, perhaps gradually derived from existing elements. A different approach would be to define "subprimitives" that can be used to compose "primitives"—for example, using arithmetic operators with only the values 1 and 0 to make real-valued constants (as in some genetic-programming work).

Third, in the current version of SEAM, a primitive component is used only once. It seems likely that in general we will want to keep a component for reuse several times. If parent components are retained in the population after a join in SEAM then it is still able to solve HIFF effectively, but not so rapidly. It will be seen from section 8.2 that retaining small individuals in the population spoils the scale-invariant property of the algorithm. However, it may be pragmatically useful to do this in some domains. An alternative might be to use a number of copies of each primitive in the initial population. Fourth, in the current version of SEAM, structural information about component modules used in a composite individual are not maintained in the individuals after a join is made. However, this information could easily be stored and outputted so that SEAM could be used as a method to provide information about the modular structure of a problem domain, rather than just optimize it.

Fifth and finally, SEAM evaluates many groups of individuals in assessing the stability of a proposed join. If the join is eventually deemed unstable, then all the information from these evaluations is discarded. We know that it is not appropriate to keep a group just because it appears to give high fitness (this defeats the possibility of future compositions that may have found a higher fitness) but perhaps it may be possible to compromise in some circumstances—to use some of this information to bias future joins without excluding future exploration of alternatives. Specifically, it seems likely that a probabilistic form of association—or a strength of association—might be better able to utilize the feedback from evaluations than the discrete all-or-nothing kind of joins used in the current version of SEAM. Interestingly, this begins to converge with algorithms such as BOA (Pelikan, Goldberg, and Cantú-Paz 1999).

The Union of the Two

Before beginning to summarize the findings of this book in the remainder of this chapter, I would like to take a moment to share some thoughts on why interdisciplinary communication between evolutionary computation and evolutionary biology has not been as obvious and easy as one might think it ought to be.

The cross-fertilization of results between these disciplines is, for a start, made difficult by a history of differing assumptions. These come in part from the differing needs of two disciplines that, in one case, seeks to understand natural mechanisms as they are, and in the other, seeks to extract inspiration for computational problem solving and engineering purposes. But I suggest that there is a deeper more specific reason for the disconnection between these research fields that relates directly to the research topic of this book.

Specifically, the assumption of linear gradual change in evolutionary biology is directly at odds with what is interesting from a computational point of view. In computer science we recognize the algorithmic principle described by Darwin—the linear accumulation of small changes through random variation and selection—as *hill climbing*, more specifically *random mutation hill climbing*. However, we also recognize that hill climbing is the simplest possible form of optimization and is known to work well only on a limited class of problems. Accordingly, the problems that are interesting to a computer scientist tend to be problems that cannot be solved by hill climbing. This includes large problem spaces with complex interactions between the problem variables.

In contrast, if you think that evolution *must* behave like a hill climber, then problem spaces with complex interdependencies between them are simply not part of the space of systems to which natural evolution can adapt. In evolutionary biology, natural selection is not expected to find "best" solutions—only to show *some* propensity for adaptation. Accepting the limitations of a gradualist/hill-climbing process—accepting that that is just the way natural evolution is—promotes a focus on small systems and simple interactions that hill-climbing processes can optimize. This emphasis is seen very clearly in the way that Fisher formalized the operation of sex. Specifically, the assertion that selection must act on individual alleles because sexual recombination breaks up combinations of alleles is consistent with the assumption that evolution operates exclusively by the linear accumulation of small changes. Then, if selection acts on individual alleles, this legitimizes simplified models that focus on the additive effects of alleles. It is not that epistasis is assumed to be absent, but if selection cannot act on combinations of alleles then there is little need to model epistasis.

Accordingly, population genetics models tend to focus on individual alleles, often using single loci—or if epistasis among multiple loci is included, then it is often just between two loci, or else it has highly simplifying assumptions such as that it is epistasis that does not create any local optima. By assuming that evolution is a hill-climbing process, and consistent with this, that sex forces selection to act on individual alleles, it seems that population genetics has painted itself into a corner where it now becomes difficult to understand what sex is good for. That is, assumptions derived from the action of sex promote further assumptions about the type of epistasis that needs to be modeled for most purposes, and these assumptions about epistasis then preclude many interesting effects of sex. More generally, these assumptions and models make communication between the disciplines ever more difficult as they exclude many of the features that are interesting to computational optimization. And conversely, large multilocus systems with complex epistasis commonly used in evolutionary computation seem to bear little relevance to biological processes under normal population genetics assumptions.

But, there are other algorithmic possibilities, as discussed in section 10.5. If nothing else, computer science can at least contribute to evolutionary biology the knowledge that hill climbing is but one of a large space of possible optimization principles. The breakthrough that Darwin provided was to show that at least one form of optimization, or adaptation, could be provided by natural biological processes. Hill climbing is the simplest and most intuitive form of optimization process. But this does not mean that hill climbing is the *only* possible form of optimization that could be provided by natural biological processes. By going outside this algorithmic framework, we offer the possibility that the biological principles of natural evolution could be more interesting computationally, and that the large complex kinds of models that evolutionary computation finds interesting could become more relevant to evolutionary biology. This kind of interdisciplinary unification is a good deal more than that which can be handled in the scope of one book. But the good news is, instead of just shrugging our shoulders and resigning ourselves to the fact that different disciplines have different needs, there is a chance that a wealth of results in both disciplines could become more useful to the other. Hopefully, the union of ideas between the disciplines used in this book is itself an example of the principle of compositional innovation: in that case, the interdisciplinary exchange between computer science and biology promises innovation that neither discipline could achieve via small modifications within its own local population of theories and methods. Even in the happy case that this is so—there is still a lot of selection required to identify the most productive union.

10.2 Large Directed Adaptive Genetic Changes

I start the discussion of conceptual impact of compositional evolution by addressing whether large genetic changes can be directed and adaptive. I should be clear that under the neo-Darwinian theory of evolution by natural selection it is perfectly reasonable for natural selection to act on large genetic changes (Maynard Smith 1991) should they be available and beneficial. Indeed, this is how evolution by natural selection can exploit compositional mechanisms. The point is that the normal perception of evolutionary processes is that all genetic changes are random, or more exactly, undirected (see section 3.4). The real distinction between compositional evolution and gradual evolution is not that one is nongradual and one is gradual, but that one is compositional and the other is *linear*—that is, what I refer to as the "gradualist framework of evolution" assumes the linear sequential accumulation of undirected genetic changes (whatever size they may be). This is the proper comparison that the simulation models have addressed; the "gradual" evolutionary mechanisms explore the entire range of mutation rates and thereby do not assume that "gradual evolution" uses only *small* changes. The finding is that there is no scale of undirected genetic change that can evolve this class of complex system. If we are hoping to have large directed adaptive genetic changes that are not miraculous then they can only be directed by virtue of prior selection. But if we have only a single lineage or population, then all the genetic material available has been subject to the same selection as every other member of that population. So any genetic material introduced to a new individual is either the same as that it already has or is random/undirected. However, genetic material evolved in different lineages is not necessarily subject to the same selection (even if it is evaluated under the same fitness function) because epistatic dependencies with different genetic backgrounds produce different selective pressures. Genetic material that is subsequently transferred from one lineage is directed by prior adaptation but is not the same as the genetic material in another lineage. By this means, large adaptive genetic changes are possible through compositional mechanisms but are not available through the linear accumulation of changes in a single population. This is the distinction that is illustrated in the compositional and gradual mechanisms shown in the simulations.[2]

Thus when I argue that compositional mechanisms permit large adaptive genetic changes, I am not merely talking about the possibility that evolution by natural selection can act on large *undirected* changes if they should be beneficial. Compositional evolution allows large *directed* adaptive genetic changes. That is, these changes are a very specific subset of those possible under mutation; it is not the case that mutant genotypes produced by composition equally represent all genotypes that have a given genetic distance from the parent, and moreover, they are not just an arbitrary subset of possible genetic variations, but a subset that is more likely to include fitter variants than undirected variation (see p. 92). Nonetheless, I should be clear that the generation of compositional events is not biased in such a way that beneficial compositional events will be in any way overrepresented among the set of possible compositional events.[3] Rather the point is that, as the simulations show, there are conditions where the entire set of compositional events (though some are better than others) is more likely on average to be beneficial than is undirected variation as produced by mutation.

Thus compositional mechanisms afford adaptive capability that is not available under gradual mechanisms because they employ multiple inheritance. That is, under the gradualist framework, characters are inherited from one parent only (or very similar parents), and under compositional evolution, characters are inherited from more than one parent (exactly two, in all the models we have looked at). There are several possible genetic mechanisms that may produce highly nonrandom genetic variations from a *single* parent, such as inversion, translocation, or gene duplication. However, when nonrandom genetic material is introduced *across lineages* it may be wholly unrelated to the genetic material in the recipient lineage, not a rearrangement of existing genetic material—which as Ridley suggests, does not provide a real increase in complexity (2001, p. 43). This may be good or bad. It may be bad because new genetic material, selected for in a different genetic context, may be wholly useless or detrimental in the genetic context of the recipient individual. On the other hand, it provides an opportunity for innovation that is not available through mutational change or the rearrangement of genetic material within a lineage.

The important point is that the opportunity for innovation through the introduction of genetic material that has been preadapted in a parallel lineage is likely to be higher than it is through any system of stochastic variation within a single lineage. This depends on the assumption that there is limited context dependency for the genetic material involved. That is, in cases where epistatic dependencies do not restrict the fitness contribution of a subsequence to a unique context, that subsequence will confer a positive fitness contribution in some other contexts. And more important, that subsequence may be more likely to confer a positive fitness contribution than an undirected change in genetic material.

10.3 Symbiosis as a Source of Evolutionary Innovation

The intuition that symbiotic composition might afford large, relatively sudden, changes in the characters of an entity is not new (e.g., Margulis 1993a; Margulis and Fester 1991; Mehrezkovsky 1909; Wallin 1927). And many authors accept that symbiosis is a mechanism available for increasing complexity (e.g., Maynard Smith and Szathmary 1995; Ridley 1985, 2001). However, as I have discussed (section 1.5), there has been an underlying assumption for some that gradual mechanisms are, in some sense, primary—in that they provide the components that are later assembled.

However, the models in this book illustrate that this adherence to the primacy of gradual change is not required. First, the fact should not be overlooked that although the components may have been evolved gradually, the entity that they were assembled into was not evolved gradually, and the compositional models show that in principle there are conditions where complex adaptations could not have been evolved gradually. Moreover, it is not necessary that the components that are assembled were provided by gradual change; they may themselves have been assembled from subcomponents. This kind of "symbiosis all the way down" (or perhaps, "up") is reminiscent of serial endosymbiosis theory (Margulis 1993a). Using the notion of hierarchical encapsulation, I have provided a clear model of a class of systems that typifies those that cannot be evolved gradually but can be evolved compositionally, and the formal models illustrate the intuitions of compositional change evident in previous thinking.

In accord with the intuitions of Margulis, Wallin, and the earlier Russian biologists, my models support the possibility that symbiosis potentially provides a fundamentally different source of evolutionary innovation from the accepted norms of evolutionary change. Even if one is already happy with the idea that large adaptive genetic changes are provided by symbiogenesis, and that these are not miraculous, as Maynard Smith suggests (section 1.5), it is nonetheless a different thing to show that there are systems that symbiogenesis can evolve that gradual mechanisms cannot—moreover, to show that these systems can have all of the properties associated with evolutionary difficulty and still be easy for compositional mechanisms. This is not merely a trick, a sleight of hand, or an aberration, but rather reveals that such mechanisms belong fundamentally to a different class of optimization process than the hill-climbing model described by Darwin. The point is not merely to challenge an assumption of strict gradualism, but the broader underlying principle of linear improvement. The appropriate algorithmic principle underlying compositional mechanisms is divide-and-conquer problem decomposition, and this form of optimization has fundamentally different optimization capabilities.

10.4 Evolutionary Difficulty and Gradualism

I have argued that common concepts associated with evolutionary difficulty such as the ruggedness of a landscape, the existence of broad fitness saddles, the number of local optima, and notions of irreducible complexity are all based on an underlying assumption of gradual evolution (the linear accumulation of undirected genetic changes). The model landscape and compositional mechanisms that I have illustrated and analyzed show that gradual change is not the only nonteleological possibility for evolutionary mechanisms. Compositional mechanisms can, under certain conditions, enable efficient evolution in landscapes that exhibit all these characteristics.

Accordingly, I have illustrated a class of complex systems, normally considered unevolvable, that are easily evolvable under compositional mechanisms. This class of mechanisms would be *considered* unevolvable because it really *is* unevolvable *under gradual mechanisms*. But this kind of system is not in fact unevolvable because it is easily evolved by compositional mechanisms.

One conclusion from this, showing general contradiction with the above notions of evolutionary difficulty, is that certain kinds of complex adaptations may be easily evolvable despite the fact that there is no guaranteed path of small changes conferring monotonically increasing fitness approaching these systems. The simulation experiments included scenarios where gradualism is neither sufficient nor required to explain the evolution of a complex adaptation. The insistence on a path of small changes approaching a complex adaptation is therefore not essential in evolutionary explanation.

I emphasize the conclusion that compositional evolution does not present a challenge to the theory of evolution by natural selection in general, but does present a challenge to the assumption of linear improvement. It is not true that the Darwinian must reject a system of large changes (e.g., Ridley 1985) and it is not the case that all systems must have evolved only through the gradual accumulation of small changes. Accordingly, it is not essential that there be paths of small changes approaching a complex adaptation (e.g., Behe 1996), nor that we find or posit the existence of such paths in all cases (e.g., Dawkins 1996).

10.5 Algorithmic Principles of Adaptation

The issues discussed above—the possibility of large directed genetic changes, whether sex/symbiogenesis provides a fundamentally different source of adaptation, and the impact that this has on our concepts of evolutionary difficulty—are all better understood by recognizing the possibility of a different underlying algorithmic paradigm for evolution.

Darwin's masterful contribution was to show that there was *some* principle of optimization that could be implemented in biological systems. This provided an algorithmic model of how adaptation may take place. But the *hill-climbing* algorithmic principle that he described—the linear accumulation of random changes—is only one algorithmic possibility. Compositional evolution does not fit within the hill-climbing framework and provides a fundamentally distinct form of adaptational process because it is allied to a different underlying algorithm—namely, divide-and-conquer problem decomposition. It is because compositional evolution operates outside the hill-climbing framework that gradualist notions of evolutionary difficulty do not apply. And hence, I have been able to show that certain kinds of complex systems are in principle easily evolvable under compositional evolution despite the absence of a linear succession of protosystems.

Divide-and-conquer problem decomposition is not such a difficult concept. Top-down functional decomposition of a problem into semi-independent subproblems is a familiar and intuitive approach in design and engineering. When we approach almost any complex problem we naturally look for ways to break it up to make it easier. However, ordinarily, we think of problem decomposition only in the context of human design, where top-down domain knowledge of how to decompose a problem can be applied. But then, prior to 150 years ago, all design/optimization was believed to belong exclusively to the realm of personal (or at least personified) top-down intervention. The question is whether more than one algorithmic principle can be implemented in biological systems. The models described in this book show that, given a mechanism of compositional variation, evolution can provide divide-and-conquer optimization in principle. The analytic chapter supports these findings, providing proofs that the distinction between the algorithmic classes is fundamental in terms of the expected time to find fit genotypes.

Having identified the possibility that a particular form of optimization process could in principle operate in biological systems, the next logical question to ask is whether this form of optimization would do any good—that is, whether this form of optimization process is effective given the nature of the adaptive domain in which evolutionary systems reside. A hill-climbing process, for example, will be effective when the adaptive domain provides paths of gradually changing protosystems monotonically increasing in fitness. Under the gradualist framework of evolution this is the only possibility. The conditions under which a divide-and-conquer process will be effective will be different. Specifically, such a process will be useful when the adaptive domain is modular.

The next two subsections discuss the availability of compositional variation mechanisms in nature and the likelihood of modularity in natural adaptive domains. Although the goal of this book has been satisfied in showing that compositional evolution is a logical possibility for evolution in principle, it would be remiss not to discuss these topics.

10.6 The Availability and Impact of Compositional Mechanisms in Nature

The symbiogenic origin of eukaryote organelles, including those found in all plants and animals, is now accepted. However, the impact of symbiogenic events on evolutionary processes as a whole might seem minimal since such events appear to be rare. More generally, the "mergers and acquisitions" mode of complexity increase may still seem unlikely to be beneficial in most circumstances (Ridley 2001). I do not dispute that this mode is unlikely to be beneficial; it is, of course, very unlikely that a compositional event will produce a beneficial result. But, evolution by natural selection is used to dealing with unlikely events. The more important point is not whether the likelihood of a beneficial event is low in an absolute sense, but rather whether the likelihood of a beneficial change from a compositional event is greater or smaller than the likelihood of a beneficial change from an undirected mutational process such as spontaneous genetic mutation.

When a population is stuck on a local optimum and the closest point in sequence space with equal or higher fitness is far away, the chance of getting off this peak by a random change is very small. However, in some circumstances, depending on the structural properties of the landscape and the diversity of other lineages, a compositional event can provide much "smarter" genetic changes with a much higher likelihood of providing a fitness benefit. The purpose of the models in this book is to bring this intuitive argument into a concrete model where we can see the probabilities involved clearly and analytically. The models show an example set of sufficient conditions for this kind of reasoning to hold. This means that in principle, in the right circumstances, even though the likelihood of a beneficial compositional event might be small, it may be orders of magnitude more likely that a subsequent fitness improvement will be provided by a compositional event and not a gradual event.

I have also argued that symbiogenesis may be viewed as an instance of a general set of compositional mechanisms common to several of the major evolutionary transitions. Evidence for the involvement of compositional mechanisms is available for many of the transitions summarized by Michod (1999). So, composition is implicated in some of the most fundamental events in evolutionary history, but still, what about the complex adaptations that occur within a transitional level—the adaptation of metazoan features, for example, such as the eye or the wing? Maynard Smith and Szathmary (1995) explicitly exclude this type of adaptation from the list of fundamental evolutionary events precisely because they do not involve compartmentation or a change in the mechanism of information exchange (the units of inheritance). However, when we include items such as sexual recombination, hybridization, and allopolyploidy in our list of compositional mechanisms, we see that compositional mechanisms may act, albeit in a more subtle manner, on adaptations between the major transitions as well as causing the transitions themselves. I think it best to be clear, just in case, that I am not suggesting that organs like eyes and wings are appropriate components to be put together by compositional events. But the compositional capabilities of reasonably ordinary (perhaps slightly subdivided) sexual populations should not be dismissed. At the very least, the ability of sexual populations to manipulate genes as functional modules (being large sets of nucleotide sites grouped both functionally and physically, as discussed below) provides something that cannot be achieved by spontaneous point mutation (or sexual recombination in a panmictic population).

Potentially, the notion of acquiring symbiont characters *without* direct genetic transfer, as in the model of symbiotic scaffolding (Watson and Pollack 1999d; and section 9.2), further broadens the influence of compositional processes to situations where there are no mechanisms of direct genetic transfer available.

Finally on this topic, it is worth mentioning that the influence of compositional mechanisms should not necessarily be restricted to scenarios that ultimately result in full genetic integration (directly or via scaffolding). We have grown very accustomed to defining organisms by the common center of genetic material, but more general notions perhaps based on reproductive interdependence might be sufficient—consider the complex siphonophores (e.g., Gould 1985, p. 82), not to mention mitochondria.

10.7 Modularity in Natural Systems

Although the effectiveness of compositional mechanisms does not depend on the existence of a smooth path of gradually changing protosystems, it does depend on the existence of modularity in the adaptive domain. The modular interdependency structure defined in chapter 4 is a particular example of modularity *sufficient* for effective compositional evolution, but it is not yet clear exactly what the *necessary* conditions of modularity are for effective compositional evolution. The existence of appropriate modularity in nature is an empirical matter that is only now becoming testable (Segre et al. 2005), but there are a number of ideas about modularity discussed below that suggest that appropriate modularity in natural systems is not an entirely unreasonable possibility (Callebaut and Rasskin-Gutman 2005).

Note that although, in general, it is clear that each kind of adaptive mechanism is well suited to different classes of adaptive landscapes (Wolpert and Macready 1997), I have done more than simply show that gradual and compositional mechanisms are different. For example, we have learned a lot about the class of landscapes that discriminate the adaptive capacities of these mechanisms, why the different mechanisms behave differently in this class, about the properties of complex systems that create such landscapes, and about the conditions required for compositional mechanisms to operate effectively.

In chapter 4 I defined a system exhibiting modular interdependency precisely because that was the class of system that would distinguish the adaptive capacity of gradual and compositional mechanisms. It is not part of the claim of this book that natural adaptive landscapes may exhibit these precise characteristics. However, there are some observations that may be of interest on this topic.

On the most general level, one might argue that modular interdependency structure in adaptive domains might result from modular structure in the physical world (see "dynamical hierarchics," Lenaerts, Chu, and Watson 2005). That is, to the extent that the natural environment of an organism is neither an undifferentiated soup nor a collection of wholly unrelated independent objects, but rather is a system of more-or-less differentiated but interacting objects, the problem of adapting to, interacting with, controlling, or modifying natural environments is also implicitly modular in structure. (See also Bak 1996; Gordon 1993.)

Slightly more specific observations concerning modularity in natural systems include the fact that scale invariance and fractal structures are often associated with biological systems (e.g., Mandelbrot 1982) and the self-organization of dynamical systems (Kauffmann 1993). "Small world networks" (Watts 1999) exhibiting scale-invariant properties (Ravasz et al. 2002) occur in many different types of systems, biological and man-made, and seem to result from simple properties of incremental network construction (Slanina and Kotrola 2000).

For many (e.g., Holland 2000; Hartwell et al. 1999; Ravasz et al. 2002; Hartwell et al. 1999; Callebaut 2005), the modular nature of biological systems, and other systems (Simon 1969), is ubiquitous and obvious. For others, different assumptions are normal—for example, Kaufmann (1989, 1993) starts with the assumption that gene networks are largely random. Figure 10.1 sketches some different possibilities.

If the dependencies in biological systems are like figure 10.1a then this presents a problem for the science of biology. Arbitrarily complex interdependencies would mean that there is no higher-level abstraction of the system that can reduce the

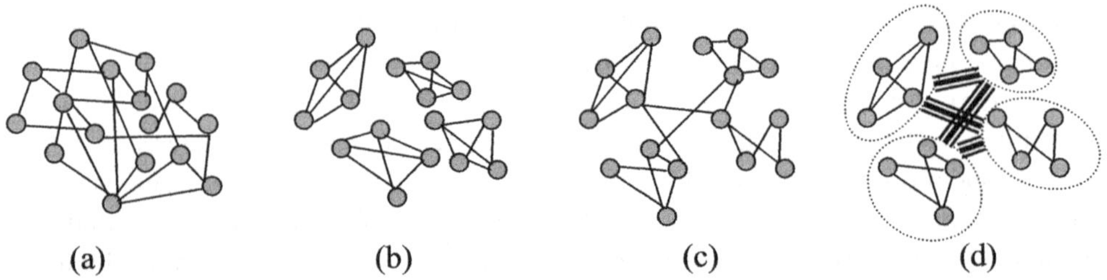

Figure 10.1
Possible interdependency structures. Nodes represent genes, edges represent dependencies between genes. (a) Random structure (as in *NK* landscapes). (b) Separable subgroups with only internal interdependencies (as in Royal Road, concatenated-trap functions). (c) Clustered dependency structure (as in *HDFs*, Holland 2000; and *NKC* landscapes). (d) Modular interdependency structure as in HIFF.

dimensionality of the model. Abstraction is really intrinsic to what it means to understand a system, I think. If this is the case, then we may as well give up now on trying to make sense of biological systems. If a biological system needs a specific, arbitrarily complex system of dependencies like this then neither gradual nor compositional mechanisms could optimize it well (not that evolution by natural selections demands optimal solutions). But I do not think biological systems are like that, and I think that anyone who has not given up on trying to understand biological systems also does not think they are too much like that.

At the other extreme, I do not think anyone believes that biological systems are anything like figure 10.1b either. A strict, simple kind of modularity, exhibiting fully independent modules, is also not biologically realistic. If this were the case then the subject of biology would be easy. And, if biology were like this then gradual mechanisms could accumulate additional modules linearly and compositional mechanisms would not be necessary to explain their evolution. The reality of biological systems is likely to be somewhere in between these two extremes.

One possibility is that biological networks can be represented with something like figure 10.1c. This depicts a clustered network of interdependencies with more links within clusters than between clusters. Here the dependencies between clusters are simple pairwise dependencies of the same type as dependencies within clusters. If biological systems are like this then gradual mechanisms would be able to do well enough, although they would not necessarily be able to optimize the remaining intermodule dependencies, and compositional mechanisms might do better at resolving intermodule dependencies but doing so would not necessarily be very important (if it were very important then the apparent modularity of the clusters would be misleading). This is a real possibility for biological systems (Segre et al. 2005).

Figure 10.1d shows something subtly different. Here the dependencies between modules are something new; some kind of higher-level interaction implemented via the emergent properties of the respective modules. If this were the case for biological systems then, as before, gradual mechanisms would not be very good at resolving intermodule dependencies, and compositional mechanisms could do better, but additionally, the fitness benefits of resolving the module interdependencies (available only to compositional mechanisms) could be arbitrarily important. Figure 10.1d corresponds to the system of modular interdependency used in my simulation experiments showing a strong advantage for compositional evolution.

The distinction between figure 10.1c and figure 10.1d is seen in the following example. Protein-interaction networks, in some respects, depend on quite specific binding affinities of proteins working in semi-independent pathways, but additionally, a protein may bind with a protein in another, functionally different, protein pathway, modifying the operation of that conceptually distinct function. In this system, the interactions between pathways are the same type as the interactions within pathways, figure 10.1c. But now consider the functional dependencies between the nucleotides that code for the proteins in this network. The nucleotides of a given gene are functionally interdependent by virtue of shared transcription and translation machinery. But the nucleotides of different genes are functionally interdependent by virtue of the interactions between the proteins that they code for. So there are sequence-specific dependencies between the nucleotides within a gene that certainly produce highly epistatic effects on the shape and form of the protein and thus its function and fitness effects. Also there are sequence-specific dependencies between the nucleotides of one gene and another, producing highly epistatic effects through the positioning of active domains and the binding affinities with other proteins and thus with fitness.

However, the fitness interactions between nucleotides of the same gene are different from the fitness interactions between nucleotides of different genes. The former involve, for example, the energy-minimization constraints of the rapid folding of the amino-acid chain, and the latter are mediated, for example, through the three-dimensional structure of the resultant protein. In short, the interprotein interactions are not simply sparse interactions of the same type as the intraprotein interactions, but depend (at least in part) on the emergent properties of the protein structure such as shape and the synergistic effects that the intraprotein interactions create such as binding affinities.

Such a hierarchical understanding of interdependencies is natural in our everyday understanding of biological systems (see, e.g., Holland 2000; Hartwell et al. 1999; Lenaerts, Chu, and Watson 2005). If this is an appropriate way to understand modularity in biological systems then compositional mechanisms can provide a profound impact for the evolvability of such systems. The difficult part is understanding what the implications of a structure like this are for the fitness interactions among the components (rather than the functional interactions). This is an empirical question that is not easy to answer with today's technology, but it is coming closer.

This understanding of the different forms that modularity can take is provided by the models of chapter 4. And the impact of this kind of modularity for the benefit of compositional mechanisms was explored in the simulation experiments of chapters 5 through 7. However, chapters 6 and 7 also illustrated the distinction between the adaptive capabilities of sex and the adaptive capabilities of symbiotic encapsulation. These distinctions depended not on the properties of modularity in fitness dependencies (which were required for both types of compositional mechanisms) but on the correspondence of these fitness dependencies with the ordering of genes in the genetic map. Specifically, the ability of sex to provide compositional evolution required not only modular fitness dependencies but also that this modular structure correspond well with the physical linkage of the genetic material that produced these dependencies (see figures 1.9 and 6.10). This is required, at one level or another, for sex to provide effective compositional evolution.

In prokaryotes, groups of genes known as operons are functionally and physically linked. Although prokaryotes do not undergo meiotic sex, this functional grouping of genes (Overbeek et al. 1999) could assist in supporting the efficacy of lateral gene transfer. In eukaryotes functionally related genes are often not collocated, which presents a problem for compositional evolution via sexual recombination. As I mentioned earlier, the relationship between functional interdependency and fitness interdependency is not a simple one, but I cannot have it both ways. In the absence of evidence to the contrary, I am inclined to believe that fitness interdependencies are correlated with functional interdependencies. I think a more important level of modularity for compositional evolution under sexual recombination is the gene itself (rather than groups of genes).

In all organisms, the nucleotide sites within a gene are grouped both functionally (as discussed above) and also physically by virtue of shared transcription and translation machinery. This is a basic level of modularity that is so obvious in genomes it is often taken for granted and abstracted away (as when the gene is modeled as a single binary variable—see earlier discussion on nucleotides and genes, p. 246). This level of modularity alone is sufficient to provide an advantage to a mechanism that can select on combinations of tightly linked nucleotide sites, as per a sexual population, as opposed to mutational change that operates on the scale of individual nucleotide sites.

This basic modularity of genomes is quite profound but generally abstracted away before its significance is appreciated. It is common to think about evolution as a hill-climbing process acting on individual sites (varied by mutation), and it is common to think about evolution acting on individual alleles (varied by recombination). The combinations of alleles produced by recombination are random combinations of alleles, but they are not random combinations of nucleotides because sex manipulates blocks of sites adapted by prior selection on individual mutations. It is not necessarily the case therefore that a hill-climbing model at either one of these scales is sufficient to explain the evolution of fit genotypes when these two processes are considered together (Watson 2005).

10.8 Conclusions

The evolutionary biology motivations for this work come from intuitions that are quite straightforward. It has been observed by many that symbiosis is involved in some of the most important transitions in evolutionary history (Maynard Smith and Szathmary 1995; Buss 1987; Michod 1999; Sapp 1994). However, symbiosis is not generally incorporated into models of adaptation, and it is not properly understood how changes like the evolutionary transitions should be integrated with our common understanding of evolutionary change. The basic intuition is that if two coadapted symbionts are joined together into a new entity then this may be a means toward increases in complexity (e.g., Margulis 1993a). But it has not been at all clear whether there are any circumstances where entities evolved in this manner could not have been evolved otherwise, and what difference this might make to our understanding of evolutionary difficulty.

The experiments presented in this book have operationalized the intuitive notions coming from evolutionary biology into a working model using components from evolutionary computation. The simulation models show that there is a fundamental distinction to be made between compositional evolution and gradual evolution.

Compositional evolution refers to evolution enabled by variation mechanisms that combine together systems or subsystems of genetic material that have been semi-independently preadapted in parallel. Examples of compositional mechanisms in nature include normal mechanisms of sexual recombination (under particular conditions of population diversity and genetic linkage), mechanisms of interspecific combination such as horizontal gene transfer, and also mechanisms of symbiotic encapsulation (such as endosymbiosis or other mechanisms that encapsulate a group of simple entities into a complex entity at a higher level of organization), as exhibited in some of the major transitions in evolution.

In contrast, the familiar gradualist framework of evolution refers to the linear sequential accumulation of random variations in genetic material, that is, linear incremental improvement. The primary form of gradual variation mechanism in nature is spontaneous genetic mutation. Clearly, unlike compositional mechanisms, the new genetic material introduced by each such change has not been preadapted elsewhere as a set. The fact that each such change is undirected leads to the normal understanding that evolution is driven predominantly by small modifications, that is, "successive slight modifications" (Darwin 1859). But the gradualist framework of evolution does not depend on this "strict gradualism" and may in principle include undirected genetic changes of any size.

The models in this book serve to illustrate the fundamental distinction between gradual and compositional evolution by drawing analogies with different algorithmic paradigms—namely simple optimization methods such as hill climbing and divide-and-conquer problem decomposition, respectively.

This is the basis of the computational motives for this research. These are also based on intuitions that are quite straightforward: specifically, that by evolving things in parts and putting them together we can exploit the well-known principle of breaking a problem into parts and solving the parts semi-independently so as to make the problem more manageable and the computational expense more tractable. Like the intuitions about symbiogenesis in evolutionary biology, this intuitive idea is also well-known in evolutionary computation, only here it is more commonly associated with the operation of sexual recombination. However, despite some well-known previous attempts to show what it is that a genetic algorithm with sexual crossover is good for, the problem decomposition capabilities of sex have not clearly been shown in previous evolutionary computation models. Two important issues contributed to this failure: (1) without a sufficiently developed concept of modularity, compositional mechanisms are unecessary. In particular, if modules are assumed to be separable, omitting significant intermodule dependencies, then gradual evolution may be sufficient to accumulate the solutions to modules linearly; (2) merely adding a compositional variation mechanism to a linear model of evolution does not necessarily provide compositional evolution. Unless we understand the need to maintain diversity and promote individuals with complementary modules, then a compositional variation mechanism cannot provide compositional evolution. Accordingly, a genetic algorithm with sexual crossover and fitness-proportionate selection applied to a separable building-block problem was not sufficient to illustrate the intuitive ideas of problem decomposition in a GA. Accordingly, one of the two main contributions to the evolutionary computation literature provided by this book is to show how some form of GA with crossover, on some form of modularity, can show the intuition of problem decomposition that was sought after in previous work.

The second main contribution to evolutionary computation is to show that this problem decomposition advantage, that has always been assumed to depend on the correspondence of epistatic dependencies with tight physical linkage, is in fact available in more general circumstances. I provide a new model, the symbiogenic evolutionary adaptation model, of an evolutionary process that solves this class of problem without the need for favorable gene ordering. This model takes biological inspiration from symbiogenesis and the major evolutionary transitions and also benefits significantly from ideas provided by models such as cooperative coevolution, the messy GA, multiobjective optimization algorithms, and other computational methods for explicit module acquisition and reuse.

However, none of these previous models have shown the explicit encapsulation of modules over successive hierarchical levels, or identified the properties of a problem domain that clearly exemplify the benefit of such an approach. Together these results help us to better understand what the genetic algorithm is good for, and what crossover in the genetic algorithm is good for, and they also go beyond the genetic algorithm to provide a new algorithmic method of problem decomposition and module acquisition.

So, compositional and gradual mechanisms enable effective adaptation in different classes of adaptive domains, and in fact, in general, it is clear that different kinds of adaptive mechanisms will be well suited to different classes of adaptive landscapes. But this book has done more than simply show that gradual and compositional mechanisms are different. Chapter 4 described a class of complex systems based on modular interdependency that exemplifies the difference in the adaptive capacities of these mechanisms by utilizing intuitive concepts of interdependency, modularity, and hierarchical modularity. The ideas of hierarchy and modularity are highly pervasive in our thoughts about biological and artificial systems, and Simon (1969) provides some concepts that have been very important in this work. Chapter 4 developed his intuitions about "nearly decomposable systems" into the more formal notion of "modular interdependency," by clearly distinguishing the idea of separability from decomposability. This has been critical in identifying the class of systems that are amenable to compositional evolution.

The fact that gradual and compositional evolution offer fundamentally different algorithmic processes causes us to modify our intuitions about what is evolvable or unevolvable, and the class of landscapes in which continued adaptation is possible or not possible. The simulations showed how a system possessing modular interdependency may exhibit all the usual characteristics of evolutionary difficulty: creating a fitness landscape which is highly rugged, possessing an exponential number of local optima; where the width of fitness saddles is large with respect to the number of variables in the system; where high-fitness configurations of the system appear to be irreducibly complex—that is, any small change is catastrophically deleterious; and finally, where there is no path of gradual changes conferring monotonically increasing fitness that approaches the optima in the landscape. And yet, I have also illustrated a sufficient set of conditions under which such systems are easily evolvable via compositional evolution. First, I illustrated this using sexual recombination—investigating necessary conditions of population diversity and properties of the genetic map. Second, I illustrated a compositional mechanism based on symbiotic encapsulation—which requires appropriate diversity conditions provided by a particular selection model. However, the latter model, SEAM, shows that the adaptive advantage of compositional mechanisms does not, in principle, depend on *a priori* knowledge of genetic dependencies as is required to provide favorable gene ordering under sexual recombination.

Thus, the prevailing notions of evolutionary difficulty are dependent on the assumption of gradual change. In the presence of compositional mechanisms, the existence of a path of small genetic changes conferring monotonically increasing fitness is not necessarily required to explain a complex adaptation. In fact, the existence of a path of genetic changes conferring monotonically increasing fitness, each one a plausible modification of the last under any source of undirected genetic variation, is not essential to explain a complex adaptation. Instead of thinking about evolution exclusively as incremental improvement we need to be more accommodating. Specifically, we need to be open to the fact that hill climbing is not the only algorithmic principle that could be implemented in biological processes. The models in this book show that mechanisms of sexual recombination and symbiotic encapsulation can (under some circumstances) provide adaptation better understood as divide-and-conquer problem decomposition. These mechanisms still act within the framework of evolution by natural selection—this is not in question here—but outside the gradualist framework. It is perhaps the assumption that evolution by natural selection is synonymous with linear incremental improvement that has motivated proponents of natural selection to unnaturally force sexual recombination, symbiogenesis, and the major evolutionary transitions into a gradualist model. But perhaps once it is seen that rejecting gradualism does not require rejecting evolution by natural selection, it will be possible to welcome more natural interpretations of these phenomena.

Thus, instead of treating such events as curios—as some kind of hiccup in the long chain of successive slight modifications—we can accommodate such events and processes in a different algorithmic paradigm. Instead of trying to write exceptions into the gradualist framework, we can undo the assumption that evolution by natural selection must be exclusively gradual. It does not have to be gradual; large, nonrandom genetic changes that are beneficial (i.e., more likely to be beneficial than undirected random genetic changes of the same magnitude) are not magical but a natural product of evolution by natural selection when compositional mechanisms are included.

Perhaps the clearest consequence of this shift in perspective is the following. When someone attacks the plausibility of evolution by attacking the plausibility of a gradual succession of protosystems (e.g., Paley 1802; Behe 1996) the normal response is to assert that there *is* a succession of protosystems but that that person just missed it, or was not imaginative enough to see it (Dawkins 1996). This may be the case. But now there is another logical alternative: we may, if it be the case, accept that there is *no* succession of gradually improving protosystems and yet maintain that this does *not* impinge on the plausibility of this systems evolution. A succession of gradually improving protosystems is not a logical requirement for a system produced under evolution by natural selection.

In summary, no algorithmic concept has had greater impact on the way we view ourselves and the world around us than the theory of evolution by natural selection. Darwin's masterful contribution was to provide an algorithmic model of how adaptation may take place in biological systems. However, the hill-climbing algorithm that he described—linear incremental improvement—is only one algorithmic possibility. The proposal made in this book, that other algorithmic processes could be implemented in biological systems, does not challenge the theory of evolution by natural selection. But it does challenge the assumption that evolution must proceed by a linear hill-climbing process as described by the gradualist framework of evolution. Mechanisms of compositional evolution in nature do not fit within the gradualist framework and provide a fundamentally distinct form of adaptational process.

Accordingly, Darwin's famous assertion needs revision: even if it could be demonstrated that a complex adaptation existed which could not possibly have been formed by numerous, successive, slight modifications, (or even random modifications of any size), Darwin's theory of evolution by natural selection would *not* break down.

Evolution by natural selection is bigger than that. Accordingly, when faced with the existence of a particular complex system in nature, perhaps possessing many complex interdependent parts, even those where any small change in the system causes the system to cease functioning, it is not strictly necessary to show that there exists a linear succession of protosystems that are gradually increasing in function. If such a succession can be found, or reasonable hypotheses about the plausible existence of such a path can be upheld, then all well and good. But other explanations are possible.

Notes

Chapter 1

1. See Callebaut and Rasskin-Gutman 2005 for a wide-ranging collection of works on modularity that are very valuable in understanding the broader meanings and details of modularity in biological systems.

2. I should qualify that "can evolve" and "cannot evolve" are more exactly understood as "is very easy to evolve" and "is very difficult to evolve"—but, in the framework of combinatorial optimization, these terms are not as subjective as they might appear. See chapter 8.

Chapter 2

1. "Saltation": evolutionary change within a species originated by sudden, drastic mutations that reorganize the whole genome. Although most such reorganizations are deleterious, a few of those "hopeful monsters" would be progenitors of new groups, Goldschmidt argued. (The viability of "hopeful monsters" was later resurrected by Gould [1982b, 1977], drawing on the observation that changes in phenotype are strongly nonrandom, as we shall briefly discuss.)

2. More specifically, *random mutation hill climbing* (figure 5.2).

3. Because certain effects of natural selection (such as the change in frequency of a beneficial allele) are controlled by the ratio of fitnesses of two competing alleles not the absolute difference in the fitnesses of the two alleles, fitness epistasis is sometimes defined as any deviation from multiplicative fitness effects rather than as a deviation from additive fitness effects (see Phillips, Otto, and Whitlock 2000). Such a deviation from multiplicative fitnesses is equivalent to a deviation from additivity in the log of fitness effects (as in figure 3.11).

4. In fact, as the "long path" problems attest (Horn, Goldberg, and Deb 1994), we also need this path to be short, as it is possible to construct problem spaces that have exponentially long paths of monotonically increasing fitness to the global optima.

Chapter 3

1. Other possibilities for large changes include mechanisms that enable large changes in phenotype from small changes in genotype, and mechanisms for large genetic changes that involve the duplication of genetic material within one individual. I will briefly discuss these later.

2. The chromosomes are replicated before meiotic divisions begin, then there are two meiotic divisions (halving the number of chromosomes in each division), so there are in fact four haploids produced from each diploid cell. But here and in the following figures I have drawn only two of them.

3. The appropriateness of this model depends in part on whether the bits in a bit-string individual are supposed to represent genes or nucleotides, a topic I discuss later.

4. A notable exception in Michod's list above is the transition to multicellularity. However, the existence of slime molds that spend part of their life cycle as colonies of single-celled organisms, and part as multicellular fruiting bodies, is of interest here.

5. Note that Dawkins, like I have done in this book, assumes that the mechanism of reproduction is a given—as though it were not subject to evolutionary change. The evolution of sex is a more complicated subject altogether, and in a framework that acknowledges the possibility of alternate reproductive mechanisms, the units of reproduction are as much a *product* of the evolutionary process as they are the *objects* of the evolutionary process.

6. "Panmictic": unstructured or freely mixed. Wright is introducing the assumptions behind "shifting balance theory" (which we will discuss later), where in contrast, he addresses the action of small subpopulations within a spatially subdivided population.

7. "Polymorphic": containing different alleles (in different individuals).

8. Wright uses "interaction system" to refer to sets of coadapted alleles.

9. The BBH per se concerns the operation of the simple GA (with crossover). The ability of the hypothesis to explain the operation of the simple GA is a quite different issue from whether or not there is some useful intuition about how a GA-like algorithm *could* work. More specifically, I am going to argue that the idea described here, if it can be made to work (for some type of EA on some class of problem), would be a valuable process—even if it does not explain the operation of the simple GA on problems in general.

10. Other definitions of random strings, and random changes, may be derived from different neighborhood metrics and different notions of uniformity in the space of possible strings. For our purposes, we may as well define random change to be whatever kind of changes spontaneous mutation produces. But the definitions given here reflect quite natural meanings for "random string" and "random change."

11. Although, in some of our analysis of recombination (see section 6.5) we will consider properties (such as the absence of local optima) of the fitness landscape defined by the recombinative neighborhood metric by using "invariants" of the population.

Chapter 4

1. For example, this is the case in the second version of the Royal Road problems, RR2 (Mitchell, Forrest, and Holland 1992),—i.e., even though there are epistatic interactions between blocks in this problem, the blocks are nonetheless separable by this definition. The inadequacy of the linear-sum definition of separability is apparent in the observation that the interblock epistasis in RR2 creates no local optima in the fitness landscape.

2. I will also consider a random-linkage or "shuffled" version of HIFF in later experiments.

3. Where $[s1, s2 \rightarrow s3, s4]$ means that values $s1$ and $s2$ will have a tendency to change to the values $s3$ and $s4$ in the next time step. The actual new state of a variable in the system can be taken to follow the majority of these tendencies coming from all connections. $[s1, s2 \rightarrow s3, s4 \text{ or } s5, s6]$ means that two variables will change to either the values $s3$ and $s4$ or the values $s5$ and $s6$ with equal probability.

4. Ising models are usually defined with a regular one-, two-, or three-dimensional lattice connectivity structure. But Ising models on scale-invariant lattices, such as on a graph described by the edges in a Sierpinski triangle, are an item of study in and of themselves.

Chapter 5

1. This is on the order of $1/H$, where H is the number of hierarchical levels in the system.

2. This function is written using "big-O" notation to describe the asymptotic behavior of the function. It gives an asymptotic upper bound for the magnitude of a function, and basically means that for large N this term dominates other terms in the exact result.

Chapter 6

1. I am particularly grateful to Martin Oates for investigating many different "restricted mating" types of diversity maintenance for GAs on HIFF, and to Christopher Ronnewinkel who brought deterministic crowding to my attention in this effort.

2. Figure 5.4 in Altenberg 2005 provides an interesting comparison with this representation. Altenberg stresses dimensional reduction in his figure but does not assume a strict tree of dependencies.

Chapter 7

1. Parts of this chapter are reprinted with minor revisions from *Biosystems*, vol. 69, Richard Watson and Jordan B. Pollack, "A Computational Model of Symbiotic Composition in Evolutionary Transitions," pp. 187–209, copyright 2003, with permission from Elsevier.

2. The "null" value used in the implementation of SEAM cannot reasonably be characterized as a third allele since it is not heritable in the same way as nonnull values.

3. A couple of implementational details: the implementation used in these experiments checks for $A + B \gg A$ using a separate set of contexts from the check for $A + B \gg B$. This is wasteful of evaluations since it evaluates $A + B$ in twice as many contexts as necessary. Also, this implementation does not test whether $A + B \equiv A$ or $A + B \equiv B$—if such a test is possible, which it is using a binary representation as here, then this could be used to avoid 200 wasted evaluations every time this occurs. The following results therefore provide an upper limit on the number of evaluations necessary.

4. "From square one, we would like to be able to evaluate the fitness of a part without possessing a whole" (Goldberg, Korb, and Deb 1989).

5. See the Pareto hill climber (Knowles and Corne 1999, 2000; Knowles, Watson, and Corne 2001), and the multiobjective messy GA (Van Veldhuizen and Lamont 2000).

Chapter 8

1. Parts of section 8.1 are reprinted with minor revisions from *Foundations of Genetic Algorithms VI*, Richard Watson, "Analysis of Recombinative Algorithms on a Non-Separable Building-Block Problem," pp. 69–89, copyright 2001, with permission from Elsevier.

2. In Wright and Zhao 1999, time, T, is measured in steps of the algorithm shown in figure 8.1, but note that each step requires two evaluations.

3. This proof is a direct adaptation of that provided by Wright and Zhao (1999).

4. Though in this section we are assuming tight linkage.

5. We can view this as the decomposition of the single-objective HIFF problem into a two-objective problem—specifically, the "find modules of 0s" dimension, and the "find modules of 1s" dimension (see Knowles, Watson, and Corne 2001 for an explicit multiobjective treatment of HIFF). These two dimensions can be seen as the "ideal trainers" (Juillé and Pollack 1998) for the two underlying dimensions inherent in the HIFF problem (thanks to Edwin de Jong for this observation).

6. Note that when A and B form a correct join there cannot be any context in which the superposition B causes a decrease in fitness that has not already been caused by the presence of A.

Chapter 10

1. SEAM has already been implemented with some modifications and applied to this domain (personal communication Hod Lipson, 2002).

2. In some cases, the distinction between one lineage and another does not necessarily require distinct populations. The use of the diversity maintenance method in the experiments with the GA, for example, is sufficient.

3. However, if endosymbiotic events are more likely to occur among mutualist symbionts than among arbitrary pairs of organisms then this possibility cannot be ruled out.

Glossary

Adaptation An evolved feature made *adaptive* by action of natural selection.

Adaptive Providing a benefit or an increase in *fitness.*

Adaptive peak *Local optimum.*

Adaptive surface *Fitness landscape.*

Additive effect An effect (or component of an effect) that does not exhibit *epistasis.*

Algorithm A formal step-by-step procedure or methodological process (as in a computer program, but not specific to any particular programming language).

Algorithmics The study and design of *algorithms.*

Allele A variant of a *gene.*

Allele frequency The frequency of an *allele* in a *population.*

Allopolyploidy *Polyploidy* resulting from *hybridization* of two *species.*

Assortment Mixing of *alleles* (at different *loci*) from different parental *haplotypes* during *sexual reproduction* (producing new combinations of *alleles*; see *genetic recombination*).

Average excess Of an *allele*, the ratio of the average *fitness* of individuals who have the *allele* to the *population* mean *fitness.*

Bottom-up An approach to *optimization* or design characterized by starting with raw materials or primitive components and putting them together in different ways to see if they provide a solution (antonym of *top-down*).

Building block A chunk of useful genetic material—formally, a *schema* of above average *fitness* and short defining length.

Building block hypothesis The hypothesis that *genetic algorithms* work by processing *building blocks.*

Chloroplast An intracellular *organelle* in plants, containing chlorophyll.

Chromosome A portion of the *genome* comprising a single DNA molecule. Most *genomes* contain two copies (see *diploid*) of several chromosomes.

Coadapted Adapted to one another, as in finger and thumb, or butterfly and flower.

Codon A triplet of *nucleotides* coding for one amino acid (of a protein).

Coevolution Evolution of two entities (usually *populations* of separate *species*) where each evolves to the environment provided by the other, as in butterfly and flower. In *evolutionary computation*, may include cases having a single *population* of individuals engaged with one another via a two-player game, e.g., coevolved chess players. If the improvement of one implies the failure of the other this is adversarial coevolution. If the two work together to solve a problem this is *cooperative coevolution.*

Combinatorial explosion The rapid increase in the number of possible combinations that can be drawn from a set with (even modest) increases in set size.

Competing conventions problem The notion that if two individuals solve a problem by different methods (different conventions) then crossing them is unlikely to produce a useful result.

Competitive exclusion The process whereby an increase in one type forces another to extinction.

Complexity theory The theoretical science assessing the computational expense of *algorithms.*

Compositional evolution Evolutionary processes involving the combination of systems or subsystems of semi-independently preadapted genetic material.

Concatenated trap function A test problem composed of several deceptive (but independent) subfunctions joined together.

Cooperative coevolution *Coevolution* of two or more entities that each provide a part of a collective solution.

Credit assignment problem The problem of determining which members of a group or which parts of a system are responsible for the overall performance of the group or system.

Crossover In genetics, *sexual recombination* via the *assortment* of subsections of *chromosome*; in *evolutionary computation*, any form of *sexual recombination.*

Crossover point In *sexual recombination*, the interlocal (between two *loci*) position where a subsection of *chromosome* from one parent ends, and a subsection of *chromosome* from the other parent begins.

Crowding A computational method of *fitness sharing* where only similar individuals compete.

Deme One subpopulation in a subdivided *population.*

Deterministic crowding A particular method of *crowding* where offspring replace existing individuals if and only if they are fitter. See *niche.*

Diploid Organisms that possess two copies of every *chromosome*, one paternally inherited and one maternally inherited. Describes nearly all plants, animals, and fungi.

Disjoint Of two sets, having no members on common.

Diversity Amount of *variation* in a *population.*

Divide-and-conquer problem decomposition The method of solving a problem by breaking it into smaller subproblems; algorithmic analogue of *compositional evolution.*

Dominance The extent in *diploids* to which one *allele* masks its *homologous allele* (distinct from *Pareto dominance*).

Drift See *genetic drift.*

Dynamical system Informally, a system composed of interacting parts that change state in response to one another over time; a system where future state is a function of current state.

EA *Evolutionary algorithm.*

Ecosystem A community of organisms (including many *species*), their interaction, and their environment.

Endosymbiosis A symbiosis where one organism lives inside the other.

Epistasis Functional interactions between *alleles* at different *loci*, meaning that the effect of a *mutation* at one *locus* depends on the *allelic* state at one or more other *loci*. See also *frustration of variables.*

Eukaryote A class of organisms having cells with, among other distinguishing features, a membrane-bound nucleus and *organelles* (includes all plants, animals, and fungi).

Evolutionary algorithm A computational problem-solving and design method based on a population of candidate solutions undergoing repeated *variation* and selection. Includes: *genetic algorithms*, genetic programming, evolutionary strategies, and evolutionary programming.

Evolutionary computation The broad class of computational techniques inspired by evolution. See *evolutionary algorithm.*

Evolvability Of a system, how easy or difficult it is for that system to evolve or become well adapted.

Evolvable/unevolvable Informally, can/cannot be evolved; formally, evolution of such a system requires a process that has subexponential/*exponential complexity* in the size of the system, and therefore the evolution of large systems is feasible/infeasible.

Exaptation The co-option of an *adaptation* evolved for one purpose into service for some other purpose.

Exhaustive search An *algorithm* that searches for a (good) solution by examining every possible candidate solution systematically.

Exon A subsection of genetic material within a *gene* that is translated into protein.

Exponential complexity The property of an *algorithm* that the number of computational steps required to carry it out is an exponential function of the problem size to which it is applied.

Feature A phenotypic characteristic.

Fitness Informally, the quality of an organism; formally, the probability of survival and reproduction of an organism; in *evolutionary computation*, the value returned by the *objective fitness function.*

Fitness function *Objective fitness function.*

Fitness landscape The surface defined over genotypes space where the height of each point indicates the *fitness* of each genotype.

Fitness saddle The region of a *fitness landscape* between the current point and the nearest point of equal or higher *fitness.*

Fitness sharing A method for maintaining *population diversity* in *evolutionary algorithms* by dividing a finite share of *fitness* among similar members of the *population*, thus helping to prevent too many copies of each type.

Fitness surface *Fitness landscape.*

Fixation (loss) of an allele Change in *allele frequency* in a *population* to 100% (0%).

Free recombination In genetics, *sexual recombination* where each *locus* undergoes *independent assortment*; known in *evolutionary computation* as *uniform crossover.*

Frequency dependent fitness In *population genetics*, the condition that *fitness* is sensitive to the abundance of a type; known in *evolutionary computation* as *fitness sharing.*

Frustration of variables The condition that the problem variables cannot be optimized independently (see *optimization*); in *population genetics*, analogous to *epistasis.*

GA *Genetic algorithm.*

Gametes Sex cells (e.g., sperm or egg) produced by *meiosis.*

Gene A portion of DNA encoding a single protein or RNA molecule.

Gene duplication A genetic *mutation* (general sense) resulting in a *gene* being copied to another (usually neighboring) part of the *chromosome.*

Genetic algorithm A type of *evolutionary algorithm* usually using binary *genotypes* and *variation* from *mutation* and *crossover.*

Genetic drift Effects on *allele frequencies* due to stochastic sampling in selection/reproduction (e.g., beneficial *alleles* may be *lost*, or deleterious *alleles* may *fix*).

Genetic linkage In genetics, *physical linkage*.

Genetic map The physical position/ordering of *loci* on the *chromosome*. Can be inferred from observations about the frequency of *genetic recombination* between *loci*.

Genetic recombination In genetics: during *meiosis*, the process whereby *alleles* at two or more *loci* are brought together from different *haplotypes* into the same *haplotype*, or are disassociated from a *haplotype* into separate *haplotypes*. In *evolutionary computation*: the creation of a new (*haploid*) *genotype* by taking parts from each of two parental (*haploid*) *genotypes*.

Genome The total genetic material of an organism.

Genotype An exact specification of *allelic* state at all *loci* in the *genome*.

Gradual evolution Informally, evolution via incremental improvement or successive slight *variations*; formally, evolution via the linear successive accumulation of random genetic changes.

Gradualism/gradualist framework Doctrine of *gradual evolution*.

Greedy algorithm An *algorithm* that incrementally builds or improves a solution by repeatedly taking the best immediate or local improvement (without considering all the combinations of alternatives).

Hamming distance A measure of the difference between two bit strings, equal to the count of bits that differ.

Haploid Organism or cell (e.g., *gametes*) having one set of *chromosomes* (compare *diploid*). Individuals in *genetic algorithms* have *haploid genomes* (of one *chromosome*).

Haplotype Exact specification of *allelic* state at all *loci* in a *haploid genotype*.

Heritability Informally, how well a feature is passed from parent to offspring; formally, the observation of a correlation between relatives for some trait value. The strength of correlation gives insight into the genetic contribution to the trait.

Hierarchical if and only if A hierarchical version of *if and only if* defining a complex system with *hierarchical modularity*.

Hierarchical modularity The property of a system that it is composed of *modules* each (or some) of which is composed of submodules, and so on.

HIFF *Hierarchical if and only if.*

Hill climbing A *greedy algorithm* that accumulates improvements in a candidate solution by accepting small modifications only if they are beneficial; equivalently, a search process that traverses a *fitness landscape* by following local upward gradients.

Homologous Of *chromosomes*, the two members of a *diploid* pair of *chromosomes*; of *genes*, two corresponding *alleles* in homologous *chromosomes*.

Hopeful monster The result of a radical random genetic change that is evolutionarily successful, presumed to be exclusively the realm of wishful thinking.

Horizontal gene transfer Transport of genetic material from one cell to another that is not the result of direct (vertical) descent. May occur across *species* boundaries. Most common in single-celled organisms.

Hybridization *Sexual recombination* between different *species*.

If and only if The logical (Boolean) function of equality. That is, if A is true *if and only if* B is true, then A and B are either both true or both false. (i.e., 00—true, 01—false, 10—false, 11—true.) In *HIFF*, *if and only if* is used to create pairwise *interdependency*.

Independent assortment Mendel's second rule, which is that the *alleles* in a *haploid* produced by *meiosis* are taken from either the paternal or maternal *haplotype* independently and with equal probability.

Interdependency Of two variables, the condition that the optimal setting for each variable is dependent on the setting of the other. A particular form of *epistasis*, or *frustration of variables*.

Interspecific Between two (or more) *species*.

Irreducible complexity The property that no small part of a system can be removed without causing it to cease functioning.

Lateral gene transfer *Horizontal gene transfer.*

Lineage Informally, a line of descendents.

Linear complexity The property of an *algorithm* that the number of computational steps required to carry it out is a linear function of the problem size to which it is applied.

Linkage In genetics, usually refers to *physical linkage*, but see also *linkage disequilibrium*; in *evolutionary computation, physical linkage* (see also *linkage learning*).

Linkage disequilibrium A statistical property of *populations* referring to the nonrandom association of *alleles* at two or more *loci*.

Linkage learning *Evolutionary computation* method that attempts to rearrange *genetic map* such that *physical linkage* provide *tight linkage*; more generally, a method that attempts to deduce which *genes* are epistatically dependent on which other *genes* (see *epistasis*).

Local optimum Informally, a substandard solution; formally (in *evolutionary computation*), a position in a *fitness landscape* where all neighboring *genotypes* are lower in *fitness*; formally (in *optimization*), a candidate solution which has the property that all small modifications produce inferior solutions.

Locus Position in the *genome* of a unit of Mendelian inheritance. Often equivalent to an entire *gene* in the pregenomic era; now may be as small as a *nucleotide site*. Plur. *loci*.

Meiosis Division of *diploid* cells producing *haploid* cells (*gametes*).

Meiotic sex *Sexual reproduction* involving *meiosis*.

Messy GA A type of *genetic algorithm* using (among other features) a partially specified moving *locus* representation of individuals—that is, individuals do not keep *genes* in prespecified locations (enabling *variation* in their *physical linkage*), and they are not required to specify *alleles* for all *genes*.

Migration The movement of an individual or individuals from one *deme* to another.

Mitochondrion Intracellular *organelle* producing energy in *eukaryote* cells. Mitochondria contain DNA, are self-replicating, and have an *endosymbiotic* origin.

Modular interdependency Informally, a system that is modular but has *interdependencies* between the *modules*; formally, the property of a system that it is decomposable into *modules* that are not *separable*.

Module A subpart of a system (see *hierarchical modularity*; *modular interdependency*; *building block*).

Monomorphic State of being genetically converged: at a *locus*, all individuals in the *population* exhibit the same *allele* at this *locus*; of a *population*, all individuals are genetically identical at all *loci*.

Monotonically increasing Increasing or staying the same, but not decreasing.

Mutation Generally, any spontaneous genetic change (including translocation, *gene duplication*, inversion, recombination, etc.); specifically (in this book) synonymous with *point mutation*.

Nearly decomposable Simon's notion of a system that has almost *separable* subparts.

Neutral evolution Evolution (i.e., changes in the *allele frequencies* of a *population*) that confers no change in *fitness* (or more generally, no change in *phenotype*). For example, involving *mutations* at *nucleotide sites* that are not transcribed and translated into proteins, but also translated *mutations* that have negligible *fitness* effect.

Neutral theory The doctrine that most *variation* in a *population* is neutral with respect to *fitness*, and that (therefore) most evolution is *neutral evolution*.

Niche The specific habitat of an organism; *niched*: having numerous niches imposed or provided (implies competition restricted to cohabitants; see *crowding*).

NK landscape A random *fitness landscape* defined over N variables composed by the sum of N *fitness* contributions each an *epistatic* function of K variables.

Nucleotide site A single residue of DNA in the *genome*.

Objective fitness function A computable function returning the quality of a candidate solution.

One-point crossover *Sexual recombination* involving a single *crossover point*.

Optimization A process that seeks values of problem variables that optimize some function over those variables (e.g., to seek maximum *fitness*).

Organelle Small intracellular body (situated outside the nucleus) such as a *mitochondrion* or *chloroplast*.

Panmictic Freely mixing *population* (not subdivided).

Pareto coevolution A method of *coevolution* using *Pareto dominance* to select individuals where criteria are provided by other *coevolved* individuals.

Pareto dominance Pareto's notion of superiority under multiple criteria. Formally: A Pareto dominates B if and only if A is at least as good as B in all criteria and better in at least one.

Partial specification In *evolutionary computation*, the use of individuals that specify a subset of the problem variables or a subset of the *alleles* for the entire *genome*.

Partition A subset of *loci* (unlike a *schema*, a partition does not specify *alleles* for those *loci*; it is just a subset of positions in the *genome*).

Phenotype Informally, the physical form of an organism; formally, a detectable physical characteristic of an organism's *genotype*.

Phylogeny The ancestral lineage or evolutionary history of an organism or organisms.

Physical linkage The propensity for *genes* to remain together during *sexual recombination* due to their physical proximity in the *chromosome* (see also *linkage*).

Point mutation A spontaneous genetic change affecting a single *locus*; point mutations (plural) may affect several *loci* but in an independent manner.

Polymorphic Presence of multiple *alleles* at a *locus* in a *population*; antonym of *monomorphic*.

Polynomial complexity The property of an *algorithm* that the number of computational steps required to carry it out is a polynomial function of the problem size to which it is applied.

Polyploidy Having an extra set of *chromosomes* (over and above *diploidy*). May result from incorrect *meiosis* that fails to halve *chromosome* number in production of *gametes.*

Poor linkage Informally, the property that *physical linkage* is not favorable, such as when the *loci* of a would-be *building block* are scattered along the *chromosome*; formally, the property that *physical linkage* of *loci* does not correspond well to the epistatic dependencies of those *loci* (see *epistasis*).

Population In evolutionary biology, an independent collection of organisms (of the same *species*); in *evolutionary computation*, a set of candidate solutions in an *evolutionary algorithm.*

Population genetics The mathematical study of evolution/genetic *variation* in a *population.*

Premature convergence In *evolutionary computation*, the loss of genetic *diversity* from a *population* prior to finding the desired solution.

Prokaryote A simple organism lacking a differentiated nucleus (and *organelles*), e.g., a bacterium.

Proto-system First-formed, early, ancestral, or intermediate system.

Punctuated equilibria, theory of The theory that evolution proceeds at a nonuniform rate having periods of rapid change and also long periods of stasis.

Random mutation hill climber A *hill climbing algorithm* where new candidate solutions are produced by random *mutation* of the best solution found so far.

Random search A primitive *optimization algorithm* that generates candidate solutions entirely at random (not by *variation* of best so far) and records best found.

Recombination *Sexual recombination.*

RMHC *Random mutation hill climber.*

Royal road function An idealized test problem composed of several *irreducible* (but not deceptive) subfunctions joined together.

Saltation An evolutionary jump; an instantaneous evolutionary change originated by sudden, drastic genetic changes, especially changes that reorganize the whole *genome* structure.

SBT *Shifting balance theory.*

Schema The exact specification of *allelic* state at a subset of *loci* in the *genome*; more formally, the set of all possible *genotypes* that exhibit this partial specification. Plur. *schemata.*

SEAM *Symbiogenic evolutionary adaptation model.*

Segregating allele An *allele* that is expressed by a fraction of the individuals in a *population*, i.e., not fixed (see *fixation [loss] of an allele*).

Segregation The separation of an *allele* from its *homologous allele* in *meiosis*. See also *independent assortment* and *segregating allele.*

Separable Of two variables or *modules*: informally, one is independent of the other; formally, the effect of the two variables/*modules* together can be expressed as a linear sum of functions on each variable/*module* separately (see *epistasis*). Specifically (in this book), the condition that the optimal (or maximum *fitness*) setting for one variable/*module* is independent of the setting of the other variable/*module.*

Serial endosymbiosis theory The theory that organisms have arisen via the repeated encapsulation of *endosymbionts* (see *symbiotic encapsulation*).

Sexual recombination *Sexual reproduction* involving *genetic recombination.*

Sexual reproduction Reproduction involving the coming together of genetic material from more than one parent.

Shifting balance theory The theory that in a *subdivided population* one *deme* may (via *genetic drift*) leave a *fitness* peak, discover a peak of higher *fitness*, and subsequently (via outward *migration* of successful members) recruit other *demes* to shift over to the higher *fitness* peak.

Shuffled HIFF A variant of *HIFF* where the *genetic map* is randomly reorganized so as to destroy the *tight linkage* of *building blocks* (does not affect the modular structure of epistatic interdependencies in *HIFF*; see *epistasis* and *interdependency*).

Site See *locus*; *nucleotide site.*

Species A group of organisms capable of freely interbreeding.

Stochastic Of a process, containing randomized steps, or dependent on a random variable.

Strict gradualism Evolution via the linear accumulation of random genetic changes that are exclusively small.

Subdivided population A *population* divided into multiple subpopulations (or *demes*) with low rate of *migration* between them.

Symbiogenesis The creation of a new *species* via the genetic integration of *symbionts.*

Symbiogenic evolutionary adaptation model A model of evolution based on *symbiotic encapsulation.*

Symbiosis The living together of organisms; hence, *symbiont*, an organism in a symbiotic relationship.

Symbiotic encapsulation The joining together of two symbiotic partners into a new whole, as in: *endosymbiosis* followed by genetic integration; *symbiogenic* origin of *eukaryote organelles*; and some (other) major evolutionary transitions.

Syngamy Joining of *haploid* cells (*gametes*) to produce a *dilpoid* cell (zygote).

Tight linkage Informally, the property that *physical linkage* is favorable, such as when the *loci* of a *building block* are close together on the *chromosome*; formally, the property that *physical linkage* of *loci* corresponds well to the epistatic dependencies of those *loci* (see *epistasis*).

Top-down An approach to *optimization* or design characterized by starting with the desired solution and decomposing the design into simpler and smaller parts until each can be provided by a raw material or primitive component (antonym of *bottom-up*).

Trait A character of the *phenotype*, e.g., blue eyes, smooth seeds (may or may not be a response to a single *allele*).

Uniform crossover *Evolutionary computation* synonym for *free recombination*, i.e., *genetic recombination* where *alleles* are taken from either parent with equal probability independently at each *locus.*

Variation Of an individual, a change in *genotype*; in a *population*, the genetic differences the *population* contains.

XOR The logical function of "exclusive OR" or inequality (i.e., 00—false, 01—true, 10—true, 11—false).

References

Aizawa, A. 1997. "Fitness Landscape Characterization by Variance of Decompositions." In *Foundations of Genetic Algorithms 4*, ed. R. K. Belew and M. D. Vose, 225–245. San Francisco: Morgan Kaufmann.

Altenberg, L. 1995. "The Schema Theorem and Price's Theorem." In *Foundations of Genetic Algorithms 3*, ed. D. Whitley and M. D. Vose, 23–49. San Francisco: Morgan Kaufmann.

Altenberg, L. 2005. "Modularity in Evolution: Some Low-Level Questions." In *Modularity: Understanding the Development and Evolution of Natural Complex Systems*, ed. W. Callebaut and D. Rasskin-Gutman, 99–128. Cambridge, Mass.: MIT Press.

Angeline, P. J., and J. B. Pollack. 1993. "Evolutionary Module Acquisition." In *Proceedings of the Second Annual Conference on Evolutionary Programming*, ed. D. B. Fogel and W. Atmar, 154–163. San Diego: Evolutionary Programming Society.

Arnold, M. L. 1997. *Natural Hybridization and Evolution*. Oxford: Oxford University Press.

Arthur, W. 1987. *The Niche in Competition and Evolution*. New York: Wiley and Sons.

Arthur, W. 1997. *The Origin of Animal Body Plans: A Study in Evolutionary Developmental Biology*. Cambridge: Cambridge University Press.

Bäck, T., F. Hoffmeister, and H. P. Schwefel. 1991. "A Survey of Evolutionary Strategies." In *Proceedings of the Fourth International Conference on Genetic Algorithms*, ed. R. Belew and L. Booker, 2–9. San Francisco: Morgan Kaufmann.

Bak, P. 1996. *How Nature Works: The Science of Self-Organized Criticality*. New York: Copernicus.

Baldwin, J. M. 1896. "A New Factor in Evolution." *American Naturalist* 30: 441–451.

Barricelli, N. A. 1957. "Symbiogenetic Evolution Processes Realised by Artificial Methods." *Methodos* 9: 143–182.

Barricelli, N. A. 1963a. "Numerical Testing of Evolution Theories. Part 1, Theoretical Introduction and Basis Tests." *Acta Biotheoretica* 16(1–2): 70–98.

Barricelli, N. A. 1963b. "Numerical Testing of Evolution Theories. Part 2, Symbiogenesis and Terrestrial Life." *Acta Biotheoretica* 16(3–4): 99–126.

Barry, A. 1996. "Hierarchy Formation within Classifier Systems—A Review." In *Proceedings of the First International Conference on Evolutionary Algorithms and Their Application*, ed. E. G. Goodman, V. L. Uskov, and W. F. Punch, 195–211. Moscow: The Presidium of the Russian Academy of Sciences.

Barton, N. H. 1993. "The Probability of Fixation of a Favoured Allele in a Subdivided Population." *Genetic Research* 62: 149–157.

Barton, N. H. 1995. "A General Model for the Evolution of Recombination." *Genetic Research* 65: 123–144.

Barton, N. H. 2001. "The Role of Hybridization in Evolution." *Molecular Ecology* 10: 551–568.

Behe, M. J. 1996. *Darwin's Black Box: The Biochemical Challenge to Evolution*. New York: The Free Press.

Bergman, A., S. P. Otto, and M. W. Feldman. 1995a. "On the Evolution of Recombination in Haploids and Diploids. I. Deterministic Models." *Complexity* 1: 49–56.

Bergman, A., S. P. Otto, and M. W. Feldman. 1995b. "On the Evolution of Recombination in Haploids and Diploids. II. Stochastic Models." *Complexity* 1: 57–67.

Bermudes, D., and L. Margulis. 1985. "Symbiosis as a Mechanism of Evolution: Status of the Symbiosis Theory." *Symbiosis* 1: 101–124.

Birdsell, J. A., and C. Wills. 2003. "The Evolutionary Origin and Maintenance of Sexual Recombination: A Review of Contemporary Models." In *Evolutionary Biology*, vol. 33, ed. R. J. MacIntyre, and M. T. Clegg, 27–138. New York: Kluwer Academic.

Bucci, A., and J. B. Pollack. 2002. "Order-Theoretic Analysis of Coevolution Problems: Coevolutionary Statics." In *Proceedings of Understanding Coevolution: Theory and Analysis of Coevolutionary Algorithms Workshop, (GECCO) 2002*, ed. A. M. Barry, 229–235. New York: AAAI Press.

Bucci, A., and J. B. Pollack. 2003. "Focusing versus Intransitivity: Geometrical Aspects of Co-evolution." In *Proceedings of the Genetic and Evolutionary Computation Conference (GECCO) 2003*, ed. E. Cantú-Paz et al., 250–261. Berlin: Springer-Verlag.

Bucci, A., J. B. Pollack, and E. D. De Jong. 2004. "Automated Extraction of Problem Structure." In *Proceedings of the Genetic and Evolutionary Computation Conference (GECCO) 2004*, ed. K. Deb et al., pp. 501–512. Berlin: Springer-Verlag.

Bull, L. W. 1997. "On the Evolution of Eukaryotes: Computational Models of Symbiogenesis and Multicellularity." In *Mathematical and Computational Biology: Hierarchical Complexity and Digital Evolution*, ed. C. H. Nehaniv, 31–46. Providence, R.I.: American Mathematical Society.

Bull, L. W. 1999. "On the Evolution of Multicellularity and Eusociality." *Artificial Life* 5(1): 1–15.

Bull, L. W., and T. C. Fogarty. 1995. "Artificial Symbiogenesis." *Artificial Life* 2(3): 269–292.

Bull, L. W., and T. C. Fogarty. 1996. "Horizontal Gene Transfer in Endosymbiosis." In *Artificial Life V: Proceedings of the Fifth International Workshop on the Synthesis and Simulation of Living Systems*, ed. C. G. Langton and T. Shimohara, 77–84. Cambridge, Mass.: MIT Press.

Bull, L. W., T. C. Fogarty, and A. G. Pipe. 1995. "Artificial Endosymbiosis." In *Advances in Artificial Life—Proceedings of the Third European Conference on Artificial Life*, ed. F. Moran, A. Moreno, J. J. Merelo, and P. Chaon, 273–289. Berlin: Springer-Verlag.

Bürger, R. 2000. *The Mathematical Theory of Selection, Recombination, and Mutation.* Chichester: Wiley.

Buss, L. W. 1987. *The Evolution of Individuality*. Princeton: Princeton University Press.

Callebaut, W. 2005. "The Ubiquity of Modularity." In *Modularity: Understanding the Development and Evolution of Natural Complex Systems*, ed. W. Callebaut and D. Rasskin-Gutman, 3–28. Cambridge, Mass.: MIT Press.

Callebaut, W., and D. Rasskin-Gutman (eds.). 2005. *Modularity: Understanding the Development and Evolution of Natural Complex Systems.* Cambridge, Mass.: MIT Press.

Campbell, N. 2004. "Genome Evolution: Give and Take." *Nature Reviews Genetics* 5: 638–639.

Cavicchio, D. J. 1970. "Adaptive Search Using Simulated Evolution." Ph.D. dissertation, University of Michigan, Ann Arbor, Michigan.

Chen, S. 1999. "Is the Common Good? A New Perspective Developed in Genetic Algorithms." Ph.D. dissertation, Robotics Institute, Carnegie Mellon University, Pittsburgh, Pennsylvania.

Christiansen, F. B., S. P. Otto, M. W. Feldman, and A. Bergman. 1998. "Waiting with and without Recombination: The Time to Production of a Double Mutant." *Theoretical Population Biology* 53: 199–215.

Cipra, B. A. 1987. "An Introduction to the Ising Model." *American Mathematical Monthly* 94: 937–959.

Coello Coello, C. A. 1999. "An Updated Survey of Evolutionary Multiobjective Optimization Techniques: State of the Art and Future Trends." In *Congress on Evolutionary Computation*, ed. P. J. Angeline, Z. Michalewicz, M. Schoenauer, X. Yao, and A. Zalzala, 3–13. Piscataway, N.J.: IEEE Press.

Cormen, T. H., C. E. Leiserson, and R. L. Rivest. 1991. *Introduction to Algorithms.* Cambridge, Mass., and New York: MIT Press and McGraw-Hill.

Coyne, J. A., N. H. Barton, and M. Turelli. 2000. "Is Wright's Shifting Balance Process Important in Evolution?" *Evolution* 54(1): 306–317.

Culberson, J. C. 1992. "Genetic Invariance: A New Paradigm for Genetic Algorithm Design." Technical report TR92-02, University of Alberta.

Culberson, J. C. 1995. "Mutation-Crossover Isomorphisms and the Construction of Discriminating Functions." *Evolutionary Computation* 2: 279–311.

Darwin, C. 1859. *On the Origin of Species by Means of Natural Selection.* London: John Murray.

Davies, J. 1996. "Origins and Evolution of Antibiotic Resistance." *Microbiologia* 12: 9–16.

Dawkins, R. 1976. *The Selfish Gene.* New York: Oxford University Press.

Dawkins, R. 1989. *The Selfish Gene*, second edition. New York: Oxford University Press.

Dawkins, R. 1996. *Climbing Mount Improbable*. New York: W. W. Norton.

Deb, K., and D. E. Goldberg. 1989. "An Investigation of Niche and Species Formation in Genetic Function Optimization." In *Proceedings of the Third International Conference on Genetic Algorithms*, ed. J. D. Schaffer, 42–50. San Francisco: Morgan Kaufmann.

Deb, K., and D. E. Goldberg. 1992. "Sufficient Conditions for Deceptive and Easy Binary Functions." *Annals of Mathematics and Artificial Intelligence* 10: 385–408. (Also IlliGAL Report No. 91009, University of Illinois.)

Deb, K., and D. E. Goldberg. 1993. "Analyzing Deception in Trap Functions." In *Foundations of Genetic Algorithms 2*, ed. D. Whitley, 93–108. San Francisco: Morgan Kaufmann.

De Bary, A. 1887. *Comparative Morphology and Biology of the Fungi, Mycetozoa, and Bacteria*. Oxford: Clarendon Press.

De Jong, E. D. 2004a. "Intransitivity in Coevolution." In *Proceedings of the 8th International Conference on Parallel Problem Solving from Nature PPSN-04*, ed. Xin Yao et al., 843–851. Berlin: Springer-Verlag.

De Jong, E. D. 2004b. "The Incremental Pareto-Coevolution Archive." In *Proceedings of the Genetic and Evolutionary Computation Conference (GECCO) 2004*, ed. K. Deb et al., 525–536. Berlin: Springer-Verlag.

De Jong, E. D., and J. B. Pollack. 2004. "Ideal Evaluation from Coevolution: Evolutionary Computation." *Evolutionary Computation* 12(2): 159–192.

De Jong, E. D., D. Thierens, and R. A. Watson. 2004. "Hierarchical Genetic Algorithms." In *Proceedings of the 8th International Conference on Parallel Problem Solving from Nature PPSN-04*, ed. Xin Yao et al., 232–241. Birmingham, U.K.: Springer-Verlag.

De Jong, E. D., R. A. Watson, and J. B. Pollack. 2001. "Reducing Bloat and Promoting Diversity Using Multi-Objective Methods." In *Proceedings of the Genetic and Evolutionary Computation Conference (GECCO) 2001*, ed. L. Spector, E. Goodman, A. Wu, W. B. Langdon, H.-M. Voigt, M. Gen, S. Sen, M. Dorigo, S. Pezeshk, M. Garzon, and E. Burke, 11–18. San Francisco: Morgan Kaufmann.

De Jong, E. D., R. A. Watson, and D. Thierens. 2005a. "A Generator for Hierarchical Problems." In *Proceedings of the GECCO 2005 Workshop on Theory of Representations*, ed. M. Toussaint, A. H. Wright, and E. D. De Jong, 321–326.

De Jong, E. D., R. A. Watson, and D. Thierens. 2005b. "On the Complexity of Hierarchical Problem Solving." In *Proceedings of the Genetic and Evolutionary Computation Conference (GECCO) 2005*, ed. H.-G. Beyer and U.-M. O'Reilly, 1201–1208. New York: ACM.

De Jong, K. A. 1975. "An Analysis of the Behavior of a Class of Genetic Adaptive Systems." Ph.D. dissertation, University of Michigan, Ann Arbor, Michigan.

De Jong, K. A. 1988. "Using Genetic Algorithms to Learn Task Programs: The Pitt Approach." *Machine Learning* 3: 2–3.

De Jong, K. A. 2002. *Evolutionary Computation: A Unified Approach*. Cambridge, Mass.: MIT Press.

De Jong, K. A., and M. A. Potter. 1995. "Evolving Complex Structures via Cooperative Coevolution." In *Proceedings of the Fourth Annual Conference on Evolutionary Programming*, ed. J. R. McDonnell, R. G. Reynolds, and D. B. Fogel, 307–317. Cambridge, Mass.: MIT Press.

De Jong, K. A., and W. Spears. 1990. "An Analysis of the Interacting Roles of Population Size and Crossover in Genetic Algorithms." In *Proceedings of the First International Conference on Parallel Problem Solving from Nature*, ed. H.-P. Schwefel and R. Maenner, 38–47. Berlin: Springer-Verlag.

DeVries, H. 1909. *The Mutation Theory: Experiments and Observations on the Origin of Species in the Vegetable Kingdom*. Chicago: Open Court.

Dobzhansky, T. 1955. "A Review of Some Fundamental Concepts and Problems of Population Genetics." *Cold Spring Harbour Symposium on Quantitative Biology* 20: 1–15.

Doncaster, C. P., G. E. Pound, and S. C. Cox. 2000. "The Ecological Cost of Sex." *Nature* 404: 281–285.

Doolittle, W. F. 1980. "Revolutionary Concepts in Evolutionary Cell Biology." *Trends in Biochemical Sciences* 5(6): 146–149.

Doolittle, W. F. 2000. "Uprooting the Tree of Life." *Scientific American* 282: 90–95.

Dorigo, M., G. Di Caro, and L. M. Gambardella. 1999. "Ant Algorithms for Discrete Optimization." *Artificial Life* 5(2): 137–172.

Dumeur, R. 1996. "Evolution through Cooperation: The Symbiotic Algorithm." In *Proceedings of Artificial Evolution European Conference 1995 (AE95)*, ed. J.-M. Alliot, E. Lutton, E. M. A. Ronald, M. Schoenauer, and D. Snyers, 145–158. Berlin: Springer-Verlag.

Ebner, M., M. Shackleton, and R. Shipman. 2001. "How Neutral Networks Influence Evolvability." *Complexity* 7(2): 19–33.

Ebner, M., R. A. Watson, and J. Alexander. 2000. "Co-evolutionary Dynamics on a Deformable Landscape." In *Proceedings of the 2000 Congress on Evolutionary Computation*, vol. 2, ed. B. Bosacchi, D. B. Fogel, and J. C. Bezdek, 1284–1291. La Jolla, Calif.: IEEE Press.

Eigen, M., and P. Schuster. 1979. "The Hypercycle: A Principle of Natural Self-Organisation." Berlin: Springer-Verlag.

Elena, S. F. 1999. "Little Evidence for Synergism among Deleterious Mutations in a Nonsegmented RNA Virus." *Journal of Molecular Evolution* 49: 703–707.

Elena, S. F., and R. E. Lenski. 1997. "Test of Synergistic Interactions among Deleterious Mutations in Bacteria." *Nature* 390: 395–398.

Eshelman, L. J., K. E. Mathias, and J. D. Schaffer. 1996. "Convergence Controlled Variation." In *Foundations of Genetic Algorithms 4*, ed. R. K. Belew and M. D. Vose, 203–224. San Francisco: Morgan Kaufmann.

Famintsyn, A. 1907. "The Role of Symbiosis in the Evolution of Organisms." *Transactions of the Academy of Sciences*, series 8, Physical-Mathematical Division 20(3): 1–14.

Felsenstein, J. 1974. "The Evolutionary Advantage of Recombination." *Genetics* 78: 737–756.

Ficici, S. G. 2004. "Solution Concepts in Coevolutionary Algorithms." Ph.D. dissertation, Brandeis University, Waltham, Massachusetts.

Ficici, S. G., and J. B. Pollack. 2000. "A Game-Theoretic Approach to the Simple Coevolutionary Algorithm." In *Parallel Problem Solving from Nature VI*, ed. M. Schoenauer et al. Berlin: Springer-Verlag.

Ficici, S. G., and J. B. Pollack. 2001. "Pareto Optimality in Coevolutionary Learning." In *Sixth European Conference on Artificial Life*, ed. J. Kelemen. Berlin: Springer-Verlag.

Ficici, S. G., and J. B. Pollack. 2003. "A Game-Theoretic Memory Mechanism for Coevolution." In *Proceedings 2003 Genetic and Evolutionary Computation Conference*, ed. E. Cantú-Paz et al., 286–297. Berlin: Springer-Verlag.

Fisher, R. A. 1918. "The Correlation between Relatives on the Supposition of Mendelian Inheritance." *Transactions of the Royal Society of Edinburgh* 52: 399–433.

Fisher, R. A. 1930. *The Genetical Theory of Natural Selection*. New York: Dover.

Fisher, R. A. 1958. *The Genetical Theory of Natural Selection*, second ed. New York: Dover.

Fogel, L. J., A. J. Owens, and M. J. Walsh. 1966. *Artificial Intelligence through Simulated Evolution*. New York: Wiley.

Fonseca, C. M., and P. J. Fleming. 1995. "An Overview of Evolutionary Algorithms in Multiobjective Optimization." *Evolutionary Computation* 3(1): 1–16.

Forrest, S., and M. Mitchell. 1993a. "Relative Building Block Fitness and the Building Block Hypothesis." In *Foundations of Genetic Algorithms 2*, ed. D. Whitley. San Francisco: Morgan Kaufmann.

Forrest, S., and M. Mitchell. 1993b. "What Makes a Problem Hard for a Genetic Algorithm? Some Anomalous Results and Their Explanation." *Machine Learning* 13: 285–319.

Frank, S. A. 1997. "Models of Symbiosis." *American Naturalist* 150: 80–99.

Gitchoff, P., and G. P. Wagner. 1996. "Recombination Induced Hypergraphs: A New Approach to Mutation-Recombination Isomorphism." *Complexity* 2: 37–43.

Goldberg, D. E. 1989. *Genetic Algorithms in Search, Optimization, and Machine Learning*. Reading, Mass.: Addison-Wesley.

Goldberg, D. E., K. Deb, H. Kargupta, and G. Harik. 1993. "Rapid, Accurate Optimization of Difficult Problems Using Fast Messy Genetic Algorithms." IlliGAL Report No. 93004, Illinois Genetic Algorithms Laboratory, University of Illinois at Urbana-Champaign, Urbana, Illinois.

Goldberg, D. E., K. Deb, and B. Korb. 1990. "Messy Genetic Algorithms Revisited: Studies in Mixed Size and Scale." *Complex Systems* 4: 415–444.

Goldberg, D. E., and J. Horn. 1994. "Genetic Algorithm Difficulty and the Modality of Fitness Landscapes." In *Foundations of Genetic Algorithms 3*, ed. D. Whitley. San Francisco: Morgan Kaufmann.

Goldberg, D. E., and J. Richardson. 1987. "Genetic Algorithms with Sharing for Multimodal Function Optimization." In *Genetic Algorithms and Their Applications: Proceedings of the Second International Conference on GAs*, ed. J. J. Grefenstette, 41–49. Hillsdale, N.J.: Lawrence Erlbaum.

Goldberg, D. E., B. Korb, and K. Deb. 1989. "Messy Genetic Algorithms: Motivation, Analysis, and First Results." *Complex Systems* 3: 493–530.

Goldschmidt, R. 1940. *The Material Basis of Evolution*. New Haven: Yale University Press.

Gordo, I., and B. Charlesworth. 2000. "On the Speed of Muller's Ratchet." *Genetics* 156: 2137–2140.

Gordon, R. 1993. "The Fractal Physics of Biological Evolution." In *Dynamical Phenomena at Interfaces, Surfaces, and Membranes*, ed. D. Beysens, N. Boccara, and G. Forgacs, 99–111. Commack, N.Y.: NOVA Science Publishers.

Gould, S. J. 1982a. "The Meaning of Punctuated Equilibrium and Its Role in Validating a Hierarchical Approach to Macro Evolution." In *Perspectives on Evolution*, ed. R. Milkman, 83–104. Sunderland, Mass.: Sinauer.

Gould, S. J. 1982b. "The Uses of Heresy." Introduction to R. Goldschmidt, *The Material Basis of Evolution*, xiii–xlii. New Haven: Yale University Press.

Gould, S. J. 1985. *The Flamingo's Smile*. New York: W. W. Norton.

Gould, S. J. 2002. *The Structure of Evolutionary Theory*. Cambridge, Mass.: Harvard University Press.

Gould, S. J., and N. Eldredge. 1977. "Punctuated Equilibria: The Tempo and Mode of Evolution Reconsidered." *Paleobiology* 3: 115–151.

Gould, S. J., and R. C. Lewontin. 1979. "The Spandrels of San Marco and the Panglossian Paradigm: A Critique of the Adaptationist Programme." *Proceedings of the Royal Society of London B* 205: 581–598.

Gould, S. J., and E. Vrba. 1982. "Exaptation—A Missing Term in the Science of Form." *Paleobiology* 8: 4–15.

Gregor, M. 1866. "Versuche über Pflanzenhybriden [Experiments in plant hybridization]." *Verhandlungen des naturforschenden Vereines in Brünn*, Bd. IV, 1865, Abhandlungen, 3–47.

Grieshaber, M. K., and S. Völkel. 1998. "Animal Adaptations for Tolerance and Exploitation of Poisonous Sulfide." *Annual Review of Physiology* 60: 33–53.

Gruau, F. 1994. "Neural Network Synthesis Using Cellular Encoding and the Genetic Algorithm." Ph.D. dissertation, Ecole Normale Superieure de Lyon.

Haeckel, E. 1876 (1868). *The History of Creation*, 2 vols. Trans. E. R. Lankester. London: King. (First German publication 1868.)

Hallinan, J. 2004. "Gene Duplication and Hierarchical Modularity in Intracelluar Interaction Networks." *Biosystems* 74(1–3): 51–62.

Hamilton, W. D., R. Axelrod, and R. Tanese. 1990. "Sexual Reproduction as an Adaptation to Resist Parasites." *Proceedings of the National Academy of Science USA* 87: 3566–3573.

Harik, G. R., and D. E. Goldberg. 1996. "Learning Linkage." In *Foundations of Genetic Algorithms 4*, ed. R. K. Belew and M. D. Vose, 247–262. San Francisco: Morgan Kaufmann.

Harik, G. R. 1997. "Learning Gene Linkage to Efficiently Solve Problems of Bounded Difficulty Using Genetic Algorithms." Ph.D. dissertation, Department of Computer Science and Engineering, University of Michigan, Ann Arbor, Michigan.

Harrison, R. G. 1990. "Hybrid Zones: Windows on Evolutionary Processes." In *Oxford Surveys in Evolutionary Biology*, vol. 7, ed. D. J. Futuyma and J. Antonovics, 69–128. Oxford: Oxford University Press.

Hartwell, L., J. Hopfield, S. Leibler, and A. Murray. 1999. "From Molecular to Modular Cell Biology." *Nature* 402 (suppl.): C47–C52.

Harvey, I. 1993. "The Puzzle of the Persistent Question Marks: A Case Study of Genetic Drift." In *Genetic Algorithms: Proceedings of the Fifth International Conference on Genetic Algorithms*, ed. S. Forrest, 15–22. San Francisco: Morgan Kaufmann.

Harvey, I. 1996. "The Microbial Genetic Algorithm." Unpublished paper.

Harvey, I. 2001. "Artificial Evolution: A Continuing SAGA." In *Evolutionary Robotics: From Intelligent Robots to Artificial Life, Proceedings of Eighth International Symposium on Evolutionary Robotics (ER2001)*, ed. T. Gomi. Springer-Verlag Lecture Notes in Computer Science LNCS 2217. Berlin: Springer-Verlag.

Hill, W. G., and A. Robertson. 1966. "The Effects of Linkage on Limits to Artificial Selection." *Genetic Research* 8: 269–294.

Hillis, W. D. 1992. "Coevolving Parasites Improve Simulated Evolution as an Optimization Procedure." In *Artificial Life II*, ed. C. G. Langton, C. Taylor, J. D. Farmer, and S. Rasmussen, 313–324. Reading, Mass.: Addison-Wesley.

Hinton, G. E., and S. J. Nowlan. 1987. "How Learning Can Guide Evolution." *Complex Systems* 1: 495–502.

Hirasawa, K., J. Hu, J. Murata, and J. Mao. 2001. "Genetic Symbiosis Algorithm." *Machine Intelligence and Robotic Control* 3(1): 27–34.

Hoffmeister, M., and W. Martin. 2003. "Interspecific Evolution: Microbial Symbiosis, Endosymbiosis, and Gene Transfer." *Environmental Microbiology* 5: 641–649.

Hofmeyr, S., and S. Forrest. 1999. "Immunity by Design: An Artificial Immune System." In *Proceedings of the Genetic and Evolutionary Computation Conference (GECCO) 1999*, ed. W. Banzhaf, J. Daida, A. E. Eiben, M. H. Garzon, V. Honavar, M. Jakiela, and R. E. Smith, 1289–1296. San Francisco: Morgan Kaufmann.

Höhn, C., and C. Reeves. 1996. "Are Long Path Problems Hard for Genetic Algorithms?" In *Proceedings of the Fourth Conference on Parallel Problems Solving from Nature (PPSN IV)*, vol. 1141 of LNCS, ed. H. M. Voigt, W. Ebeling, I. Rechenberg, and H. P. Schwefel, 134–143. Berlin: Springer-Verlag.

Holland, J. H., and J. S. Reitman. 1978. "Cognitive Systems Based on Adaptive Algorithms." In *Pattern Directed Inference Systems*, ed. D. A. Waterman and F. Hayes-Roth, 313–329. New York: Academic Press.

Holland, J. H. 1975. *Adaptation in Natural and Artificial Systems*. Ann Arbor: The University of Michigan Press.

Holland, J. H. 1993. "Royal Road Functions." *Internet Genetic Algorithms Digest* 7(22). Available via ftp (Aug. 1993) from ftp.santafe.edu in pub/terry/jhrr.tar.gz.

Holland, J. H. 2000. "Building Blocks, Cohort Genetic Algorithms, and Hyperplane-Defined Functions." *Evolutionary Computation* 8(4): 373–391.

Horn, J., D. E. Goldberg, and K. Deb. 1994. "Long Path Problems." In *Parallel Problem Solving from Nature—PPSN III*, ed. Y. Davidor, H. P. Schwefel, and R. Manner, 149–158. Berlin: Springer-Verlag.

Horn, J., N. Nafpliotis, and D. E. Goldberg. 1994. "A Niched Pareto Genetic Algorithm for Multiobjective Optimization." In *Proceedings of the First IEEE Conference on Evolutionary Computation*, vol. 1, ed.

Z. Michalewicz, J. D. Schaffer, H.-P. Schwefel, D. B. Fogel, and H. Kitano, 67–72. New York: IEEE Press.

Hornby, G. S. 2003. "Generative Representations for Evolutionary Design Automation." Ph.D. dissertation, Department of Computer Science, Brandeis University, Waltham, Massachusetts.

Husbands, P. 1993. "An Ecosystems Model for Integrated Production Planning." *International Journal of Computer Integrated Manufacturing* 6(1–2): 74–86.

Hutchinson, G. E. 1965. *The Ecological Theatre and the Evolutionary Play*. New Haven: Yale University Press.

Huynen, M. A., P. F. Stadler, and W. Fontana. 1996. "Smoothness within Ruggedness: The Role of Neutrality in Adaptation." *Proceedings National Academy of Sciences USA* 93: 397–401.

Ilachinski, A. 2001. *Cellular Automata: A Discrete Universe*. Singapore: World Scientific.

Jansen, T., and I. Wegener. 1999. "On the Analysis of Evolutionary Algorithms—A Proof That Crossover Really Can Help." In *Proceedings of the Seventh Annual European Symposium on Algorithms (ESA'99)*, LNCS 1643, ed. J. Nesetril, 184–193. Berlin: Springer-Verlag.

Jansen, T., and I. Wegener. 2001. "Real Royal Road Functions—Where Crossover Provably Is Essential." In *Proceedings of the Genetic and Evolutionary Computation Conference (GECCO) 2001*, ed. L. Spector, E. Goodman, A. Wu, W. B. Langdon, H.-M. Voigt, M. Gen, S. Sen, M. Dorigo, S. Pezeshk, M. Garzon, and E. Burke, 1034–1041. San Francisco: Morgan Kaufmann.

Jones, T. 1995. "Evolutionary Algorithms, Fitness Landscapes, and Search." Ph.D. dissertation, University of New Mexico, Albuquerque.

Juillé, H. 1999. "Methods for Statistical Inference: Extending the Evolutionary Computation Paradigm." Ph.D. dissertation, Department of Computer Science, Brandeis University, Waltham, Massachusetts.

Juillé, H., and J. B. Pollack. 1996. "Coevolving Intertwined Spirals." In *Proceedings of the Fifth Annual Conference on Evolutionary Programming*, 461–468. Cambridge, Mass.: MIT Press.

Juillé, H., and J. B. Pollack. 1998. "Coevolving the 'Ideal' Trainer: Application to the Discovery of Cellular Automata Rules." In *Proceedings of the Third Annual Genetic Programming Conference*, ed. J. R. Koza, W. Banzhaf, K. Chellapilla, K. Deb, M. Dorigo, D. B. Fogel, M. H. Garzon, D. E. Goldberg, H. Iba, and R. L. Riolo. San Francisco: Morgan Kaufmann.

Kargupta, H. 1995. "Signal-to-Noise, Crosstalk, and Long-Range Problem Difficulty in Genetic Algorithms." In *Proceedings of the Fifth International Conference on Genetic Algorithms*, ed. S. Forrest, 193–200. San Mateo, Calif.: Morgan Kaufmann.

Kargupta, H. 1997. "Gene Expression: The Missing Link in Evolutionary Computation." In *Genetic Algorithms in Engineering and Computer Science*, ed. Q. Quagliarella, J. Periaux, and G. Winter. New York: John Wiley.

Karypis, G. 1999. "Multilevel Algorithms for Multi-Constraint Hypergraph Partitioning." University of Minnesota, Department of Computer Science, Technical Report no. 99-034.

Karypis, G., and V. Kumar. 1995. "A Fast and High Quality Multilevel Scheme for Partitioning Irregular Graphs." University of Minnesota, Department of Computer Science, Technical Report no. 95-035.

Kauffman, S. A. 1986. "Autocatalytic Sets of Proteins." *Journal of Theoretical Biology* 119: 1–24.

Kauffman, S. A. 1989. "Adaptation on Rugged Fitness Landscapes." In *Lectures in the Sciences of Complexity*, vol. 11, ed. D. L. Stein, 527–618. Reading, Mass.: Addison-Wesley.

Kauffman, S. A. 1993. *The Origins of Order*. Oxford: Oxford University Press.

Kauffman, S. A., and S. Johnsen. 1989. "Coevolution to the Edge of Chaos: Coupled Fitness Landscapes, Poised States, and Coevolutionary Avalanches." In *Artificial Life II*, ed. C. Langton, C. Taylor, D. Farmer, and S. Rasmussen, 325–370. Reading, Mass.: Addison-Wesley.

Keller, L. 1999. *Levels of Selection in Evolution*. Princeton: Princeton University Press.

Kelly, J. K. 2000. "Epistasis, Linkage, and Balancing Selection." In *Epistasis and Evolutionary Process*, ed. J. Wolf, E. D. Brodie III, and M. J. Wade. Oxford: Oxford University Press.

Khakhina, L. N. 1992. *Concepts of Symbiogenesis: Historical and Critical Study of the Research of Russian Botanists*, ed. L. Margulis and M. McMenamin, trans. S. Merkel and R. Coalston. New Haven: Yale University Press.

Kim, J., and B. A. Salisbury. 2001. "A Tree Obscured by Vines: Horizontal Gene Transfer and the Median Tree Method of Estimating Species Phylogeny." *Pacific Symposium on Biocomputing* 571–582.

Kimura, M. 1983. *The Neutral Theory of Molecular Evolution*. Cambridge: Cambridge University Press.

Knowles, J. D., and D. W. Corne. 1999. "The Pareto Archived Evolution Strategy: A New Baseline Algorithm for Pareto Multiobjective Optimisation." In *Proceedings of the 1999 Congress on Evolutionary Computation (CEC'99)*, vol. 1, ed. P. J. Angeline, Z. Michalewicz, M. Schoenauer, X. Yao, and A. Zalzala, 98–105. Piscataway, N.J.: IEEE Press.

Knowles, J. D., and D. W. Corne. 2000. "Approximating the Nondominated Front Using the Pareto Archived Evolution Strategy." *Evolutionary Computation* 8(2): 149–172.

Knowles, J. D., and R. A. Watson. 2002. "On the Utility of Redundant Encodings in Mutation-based Evolutionary Search." In *Parallel Problem Solving from Nature PPSN VII*, ed. Juan J. Merelo-Guervós, Panagiotis Adamidis, Hans-Georg Beyer, and José-Luis Fernández-Villiacañas, and Hans-Paul Schwefel, 99–98. Berlin: Springer-Verlag.

Knowles, J. D., R. A. Watson, and D. W. Corne. 2001. "Reducing Local Optima in Single-Objective Problems by Multi-objectivization." In *Proceedings of the First International Conference on Evolutionary Multi-criterion Optimization (EMO'01)*, ed. Eckart Zitzler, Kalyanmoy Deb, Lothar Thiele, Carlos A. Coello Coello, and David Corne, 269–283. Berlin: Springer-Verlag.

Kondrashov, A. S. 1982. "Selection against Harmful Mutations in Large Sexual and Asexual Populations." *Genetic Research* 40: 325–332.

Kondrashov, A. S. 1988. "Deleterious Mutations and the Evolution of Sexual Reproduction." *Nature* 336: 435–440.

Kondrashov, A. S. 1993. "Classification of Hypotheses on the Advantage of Amphimixis." *Journal of Heredity* 84: 372–387.

Kondrashov, F. A., and A. S. Kondrashov. 2001. "Multidimensional Epistasis and the Disadvantage of Sex." *Proceedings National Academy of Sciences USA* 98: 12089–12092.

Koza, J. R. 1992. *Genetic Programming: On the Programming of Computers by Means of Natural Selection*. Cambridge, Mass.: MIT Press.

Koza, J. R. 1994. *Genetic Programming II: Automatic Discovery of Reusable Programs*. Cambridge, Mass.: MIT Press.

Kozo-Polyansky, B. M. 1921. "The Theory of Symbiogenesis and Pangenesis, Provisional Hypothesis." In *Journal of the first All-Russian Congress of Russian Botanists in Petrograd in 1921*. Peterograd. (In Russian; see Khakhina 1992 for translation.)

Kvasnicka, V. 2000. "An Evolutionary Model of Symbiosis." In *Quo Vadis Computational Intelligence?*, ed. P. Sincak and J. Vascak, 293–304. Heidelberg: Physica-Verlag.

Lawrence, J. G., and H. Ochman. 1998. "Molecular Archaeology of the Escherichia coli genome." *Proceedings National Academy of Sciences USA* 95: 9413–9417.

Lenaerts, T., D. Chu, and R. A. Watson. 2005. "Dynamical Hierarchies." *Artificial Life* 11(4). To appear.

Levins, R., and R. C. Lewontin. 1985. *The Dialectical Biologist*. Cambridge, Mass.: Harvard University Press.

Lewis, E. 1978. "A Gene Complex Controlling Segmentation in Drosophila." *Nature* 276: 565–570.

Lewontin, R. C. 1982. "Organism and Environment." In *Learning, Development, Culture*, ed. H. Plotkin, 151–170. New York: John Wiley.

Lewontin, R. C. 1983. "The Organism as the Subject and Object of Evolution." *Scientia* 118: 65–82.

Lewontin, R. C. 2000. *The Triple Helix: Gene, Organism, and Environment*. Cambridge, Mass.: Harvard University Press.

Li, W.-H., and D. Graur. 1991. *Fundamentals of Molecular Evolution.* Sunderland, Mass.: Sinauer.

Liepins, G. E., and M. D. Vose. 1991. "Deceptiveness and Genetic Algorithm Dynamics." In *Foundations of Genetic Algorithms*, ed. G. Rawlins, 36–52. San Francisco: Morgan Kaufmann.

Lindell, D., M. B. Sullivan, Z. I. Johnson, A. C. Tolonen, F. Rohwer, and S. W. Chisholm. 2004. "Transfer of Photosynthesis Genes to and from Prochlorococcus Viruses." *Proceedings National Academy of Sciences USA* 101: 11013–11018.

Lipson, H. 2004. "Principles of Modularity, Regularity, and Hierarchy for Scalable Systems." In *Genetic and Evolutionary Computation Conference (GECCO'04): Workshop on Modularity, Regularity, and Hierarchy*, ed. H. Lipson, E. D. De Jong, and J. Koza. Seattle, Washington, June 26–30.

Lipson, H., and J. B. Pollack. 2000. "Automatic Design and Manufacture of Artificial Lifeforms." *Nature* 406: 974–978.

Lipson, H., J. B. Pollack, and N. P. Suh. 2002. "On the Origin of Modular Variation." *Evolution* 56(8): 1549–1556.

López-García, P., and D. Moreira. 1999. "Metabolic Symbiosis at the Origin of Eukaryotes." *Trends in Biochemical Sciences* 24: 88–93.

Louis, S. J., and G. J. E. Rawlins. 1991. "Designer Genetic Algorithms: Genetic Algorithms in Structure Design." In *Proceedings of Fourth International Conference on Genetic Algorithms*, ed. L. Booker and R. Belew, 53–60. San Francisco: Morgan Kaufmann.

MacArthur, R. H. 1968. "The Theory of the Niche." In *Population Biology and Evolution*, ed. R. C. Lewontin. Syracuse: Syracuse University Press.

Mahfoud, S. 1995. "Niching Methods for Genetic Algorithms." Ph.D. dissertation, University of Illinois. (Also IlliGAl Report No. 95001.)

Mandelbrot, B. B. 1982. *The Fractal Geometry of Nature.* San Francisco: Freeman.

Mao, J., K. Hirasawa, J. Hu, and J. Murata. 2001. "Genetic Symbiosis Algorithm for Multiobjective Optimization Problems." *Transactions of the Society of Instrument and Control Engineering* 37(9): 894–901.

Margulis, L. 1970. *Origin of Eukaryotic Cell.* New Haven: Yale University Press.

Margulis, L. 1993a. *Symbiosis in Cell Evolution: Microbial Communities in the Archean and Ptroterozoic Eons*, second ed. New York: W. H. Freeman.

Margulis, L. 1993b. "Origins of Species: Acquired Genomes and Individuality." *BioSystems* 31(2–3): 121–125.

Margulis, L. 1995. "Gaia Is a Tough Bitch." In *The Third Culture*, ed. J. Brockman. New York: Simon and Schuster.

Margulis, L., and R. Fester, eds. 1991. *Symbiosis as a Source of Evolutionary Innovation.* Cambridge, Mass.: MIT Press.

Mayley, G. 1996. "Landscapes, Learning Costs, and Genetic Assimilation." In *Evolution, Learning, and Instinct: 100 Years of the Baldwin Effect*, special issue of *Evolutionary Computation* 4(3), ed. P. Turney, D. Whitley, and R. Anderson, 213–214.

Maynard Smith, J. 1978. *The Evolution of Sex.* Cambridge: Cambridge University Press.

Maynard Smith, J. 1982. *Evolution and the Theory of Games.* Cambridge: Cambridge University Press.

Maynard Smith, J. 1991. "A Darwinian View of Symbiosis." In *Symbiosis as a Source of Evolutionary Innovation*, ed. L. Margulis and R. Fester, 26–39. Cambridge, Mass.: MIT Press.

Maynard Smith, J., and E. Szathmary. 1993. "The Origin of Chromosomes. I. Selection of Linkage." *Journal of Theoretical Biology* 164: 437–466.

Maynard Smith, J., and E. Szathmary. 1995. *The Major Transitions in Evolution.* New York: W. H. Freeman.

Mazodier, P., and J. Davies. 1991. "Gene Transfer between Distantly Related Bacteria." *Annual Review of Genetics* 25: 147–171.

McVean, G. A., T. McVean, S. R. Myers, S. Hunt, P. Deloukas, D. R. Bentley, and P. Donnelly. 2004. "The Fine-Scale Structure of Recombination Rate Variation in the Human Genome." *Science* 304: 581–584.

Merezhkovsky, K. S. 1909. "The Theory of Two Plasms as the Basis of Symbiogenesis: A New Study or the Origins of Organisms." In *Proceedings of the Studies of the Imperial Kazan University*. Publishing Office of the Imperial University. (In Russian; see Khakhina 1992 for translation.)

Meyers, L. A., and W. Fontana. 2005. "Evolutionary Lock-In and the Origin of Modularity in RNA Structure." In *Modularity: Understanding the Development and Evolution of Natural Complex Systems*, ed. W. Callebaut and D. Rasskin-Gutman, 129–141. Cambridge, Mass.: MIT Press.

Michod, R. E. 1999. *Darwinian Dynamics: Evolutionary Transitions in Fitness and Individuality*. Princeton: Princeton University Press.

Michod, R. E., and B. R. Levin. 1988. *The Evolution of Sex*. Sunderland, Mass.: Sinauer.

Mills, R. M., and R. A. Watson. 2005. "Genetic Assimilation and Canalisation in the Baldwin Effect." In *Advances in Artificial Life, Eighth European Conference (ECAL 2005)*, Lecture Notes in Artificial Intelligence (LNAI 3630), ed. M. S. Capcarrere, A. A. Freitas, P. J. Bentley, C. G. Johnson, and J. Timmis, 353–362. Berlin: Springer-Verlag.

Mitchell, M. 1996. *An Introduction to Genetic Algorithms*. Cambridge, Mass.: MIT Press.

Mitchell, M., S. Forrest, and J. H. Holland. 1992. "The Royal Road for Genetic Algorithms: Fitness Landscapes and GA Performance." In *Toward a Practice of Autonomous Systems: Proceedings of the First European Conference on Artificial Life*, ed. F. J. Varela and P. Bourgine, 245–254. Cambridge, Mass.: MIT Press.

Mitchell, M., J. H. Holland, and S. Forrest. 1995. "When Will a Genetic Algorithm Outperform Hill-Climbing?" *Advances in Neural Information Processing Systems* 6: 51–58. San Francisco: Morgan Kaufmann.

Moriarty, D. E. 1997. "Symbiotic Evolution of Neural Networks in Sequential Decision Tasks." Ph.D. dissertation, University of Texas at Austin.

Muhlenbein, H. 1992. "How Genetic Algorithms Really Work: I. Mutation and Hill-Climbing." In *Parallel Problem Solving from Nature 2*, ed. R. Manner and B. Manderick, 15–25. Amsterdam: Elsevier.

Muller, H. J. 1964. "The Relation of Recombination to Mutational Advance." *Mutation Research* 1: 2–9.

Nix, A. E., and M. D. Vose. 1992. "Modeling Genetic Algorithms with Markov Chains." *Annals of Mathematics and AI* 5: 79–88.

Noble, J., and R. A. Watson. 2001. "Pareto Coevolution: Using Performance against Coevolved Opponents in a Game as Dimensions for Pareto Selection." In *Proceedings of the Genetic and Evolutionary Computation Conference (GECCO) 2001*, ed. L. Spector, E. Goodman, A. Wu, W. B. Langdon, H.-M. Voigt, M. Gen, S. Sen, M. Dorigo, S. Pezeshk, M. Garzon, and E. Burke, 493–500. San Francisco: Morgan Kaufmann.

Nowak, M., and P. Schuster. 1989. "Error Thresholds of Replication in Finite Populations: Mutation Frequencies and the Onset of Muller's Ratchet." *Journal of Theoretical Biology* 137: 375–395.

Numaoka, C. 1995. "Symbiosis and Coevolution in Animats." In *Proceedings of the Third European Conference on Artificial Life (ECAL'95)*, ed. F. Moran, A. Moreno, J. J. Merelo, and P. Chacon. Berlin: Springer-Verlag.

Oates, M., and D. Corne. 2001. "Overcoming Fitness Barriers in Multi-modal Search Spaces." In *Foundations of Genetic Algorithms VI*, ed. W. N. Martin and W. M. Spears, 37–50. San Francisco: Morgan Kaufmann.

Ochman, H., J. G. Lawrence, and E. A. Groisman. 2000. "Lateral Gene Transfer and the Nature of Bacterial Innovation." *Nature* 405: 299–304.

Ohno, S. 1970. *Evolution by Gene Duplication*. New York: Springer-Verlag.

Ohta, T. 1968. "Effect of Initial Linkage Disequilibrium and Epistasis on Fixation Probability in a Small Population, with Two Segregating Loci." *Theoretical and Applied Genetics* 38: 234–248.

O'Reilly, U. 1997. "The Impact of External Dependency in Genetic Programming Primitives." In *Emerging Technologies*, ed. C. Clack, K. Vekaria, and N. Zin, 45–58. London: University College London.

Orr, H. A. 2000a. "The Rate of Adaptation in Asexuals." *Genetics* 155: 961–968.

Orr, H. A. 2000b. "Adaptation and the Cost of Complexity." *Evolution* 54(1): 13–20.

Otto, S. P., and N. H. Barton. 1997. "The Evolution of Recombination: Removing the Limits to Natural Selection." *Genetics* 147(2): 879–906.

Otto, S. P., M. W. Feldman, and F. B. Christiansen. 1994. "Some Advantages and Disadvantages of Recombination. In *Lecture Notes in Biomathematics*, ed. S. A. Levin, 198–211. New York: Springer-Verlag.

Overbeek, R., M. Fonstein, M. D'Souza, G. D. Pusch, and N. Maltsev. 1999. "The Use of Gene Clusters to Infer Functional Coupling." *Proceedings of the National Academy of Sciences USA* 96(6): 2896–2901.

Paley, W. 1802. *Natural Theology, or Evidences of the Existence and Attributes of the Deity Collected from the Appearances of Nature*. London: Faulder.

Pelikan, M., and D. E. Goldberg. 2000. "Hierarchical Problem Solving by the Bayesian Optimization Algorithm." In *Proceedings of the Genetic and Evolutionary Computation Conference (GECCO) 2000*, ed. D. Whitley et al., 267–274. San Francisco: Morgan Kaufmann. (Also IlliGAL Report No. 2000002.)

Pelikan, M., and D. E. Goldberg. 2001. "Escaping Hierarchical Traps with Competent Genetic Algorithms." In *Proceedings of the Genetic and Evolutionary Computation Conference (GECCO) 2001*, ed. L. Spector, E. Goodman, A. Wu, W. B. Langdon, H.-M. Voigt, M. Gen, S. Sen, M. Dorigo, S. Pezeshk, M. Garzon, and E. Burke, 511–518. San Francisco: Morgan Kaufmann.

Pelikan, M., and D. E. Goldberg. 2003. "A Hierarchy Machine: Learning to Optimize from Nature and Humans." *Complexity* 8(5): 36–45.

Pelikan, M., D. E. Goldberg, and E. Cantú-Paz. 1999. "BOA: The Bayesian Optimization Algorithm." In *Proceedings of the Genetic and Evolutionary Computation Conference (GECCO) 1999*, vol. 1, ed. W. Banzhaf, J. Daida, A. E. Eiben, M. H. Garzon, V. Honavar, M. Jakiela, and R. E. Smith, 525–532. San Francisco: Morgan Kaufmann.

Phillips, P. C. 1998. "The Language of Gene Interactions." *Genetics* 149: 1167–1171.

Phillips, P. C., S. P. Otto, and M. C. Whitlock. 2000. "Beyond the Average: The Evolutionary Importance of Epistasis and the Variability of Epistatic Effects." In *Epistasis and the Evolutionary Process*, ed. J. Wolf, E. D. Brodie III, and M. J. Wade. Oxford: Oxford University Press.

Pollack, J. B., and A. D. Blair. 1998. "Co-Evolution in the Successful Learning of Backgammon Strategy." *Machine Learning* 32(3): 225–240.

Poon, A., and S. P. Otto. 2000. "Compensating for Our Load of Mutations: Freezing the Meltdown of Small Populations." *Evolution* 54(5): 1467–1479.

Potter, M. A., J. K. Bassett, and K. A. De Jong. 2003. "Visualizing Evolvability with Price's Equation." In *Proceedings of the 2003 Congress on Evolutionary Computation*, ed. R. Sarkar, R. Reynolds, H. Abbass, T. Kay-Chen, R. McKay, D. Essam, and T. Gedeon, 2785–2790. Canberra: IEEE Press.

Potter, M. A., and K. A. De Jong. 1994. "A Cooperative Coevolutionary Approach to Function Optimization." In *Proceedings of the Third Conference on Parallel Problem Solving from Nature*, ed. Y. Davidor, H. P. Schwefel, and R. Manner, 149–158. Berlin: Springer-Verlag.

Potter, M. A., and K. A. De Jong. 1995. "Evolving Neural Networks with Collaborative Species." In *Proceedings of the 1995 Summer Computer Simulation Conference*, 340–345. San Diego: The Society for Computer Simulation.

Potter, M. A., and K. A. De Jong. 2000. "Cooperative Coevolution: An Architecture for Evolving Coadapted Subcomponents." *Evolutionary Computation* 8(1): 1–29.

Potter, M. A. 1997. "The Design and Analysis of a Computational Model of Cooperative Coevolution." Ph.D. dissertation, George Mason University, Fairfax, Virginia.

Powell, M. A., and G. N. Somero. 1986. "Hydrogen-Sulfide Oxidation Is Coupled to Oxidative-Phosphorilation in Mitochondria of Solemya reidi." *Science* 233: 563–566.

Radcliffe, N. J. 1991. "Formal Analysis and Random Respectful Recombination." In *Proceedings Fourth International Conference on Genetic Algorithms*, ed. R. Belew and L. Booker. San Francisco: Morgan Kaufmann.

Raff, R. A. 1996. *The Shape of Life: Genes, Development, and the Evolution of Animal Form*. Chicago: University of Chicago Press.

Ravasz, E., A. L. Somera, Z. N. Oltvai, and A.-L. Barabasi. 2002. "Hierarchical Organization of Modularity in Metabolic Networks." *Science* 297: 1551–1555.

Reidys, C., P. Stadler, and P. Schuster. "Generic Properties of Combinatory Map—Neutral Networks of RNA Secondary Structures." *Bulletin of Mathematical Biology* 59: 339–397.

Reynolds, C. W. 1994. "Competition, Coevolution, and the Game of Tag." In *Proceedings of Artificial Life IV*, ed. R. Brooks and P. Maes, 59–69. Cambridge, Mass.: MIT Press.

Ridley, M. 1985. *The Problems of Evolution*. Oxford: Oxford University Press.

Ridley, M. 2001. *The Cooperative Gene*. New York: The Free Press.

Rieseberg, L. H., O. Raymond, D. M. Rosenthal, Z. Lai, K. Livingstone, T. Nakazato, J. L. Durphy, A. E. Schwarzbach, L. A. Donovan, and C. Lexer. 2003. "Major Ecological Transitions in Wild Sunflowers Facilitated by Hybridization." *Science* 301(5637): 1211–1216.

Rivera, M. C., and J. A. Lake. 2004. "The Ring of Life Provides Evidence for a Genome Fusion Origin of Eukaryotes." *Nature* 431: 152–155.

Rogers, A., and A. Prügel-Bennett. 2001. "A Solvable Model of a Hard Optimisation Problem." In *Proceedings of Theoretical Aspects of Evolutionary Computing*, ed. L. Kallel et al., 207–221.

Rosca, J. P. 1997. "Hierarchical Learning with Procedural Abstraction Mechanisms." Ph.D. dissertation, University of Rochester, Rochester, New York.

Rosenberg, R. S. 1967. "Simulation of Genetic Populations with Biochemical Properties." Ph.D. dissertation, University of Michigan, Ann Arbor, Michigan.

Rouzine, I., J. Wakeley, and J. M. Coffin. 2003. "The Solitary Wave of Asexual Evolution." *Proceedings of the National Academy of Sciences USA* 100: 587–592.

Saffo, M. B. 1990. "Symbiosis within a Symbiosis: Intracellular Bacteria within the Endosymbiotic Protist Nephromyces." *Marine Biology* 107: 291–296.

Sapp, J. 1994. *Evolution by Association: A History of Symbiosis*. New York: Oxford University Press.

Segre, D., A. Deluna, G. M. Church, and R. Kishony. 2005. "Modular Epistasis in Yeast Metabolism." *Nature Genetics* 37(1): 77–83.

Shackleton, M. A., R. Shipman, and M. Ebner. 2000. "An Investigation of Redundant Genotype–Phenotype Mappings and Their Role in Evolutionary Search." In *Proceedings of the International Congress on Evolutionary Computation, CEC-2000*, ed. A. Zalzala, C. Fonseca, J.-H. Kim, A. Smith, and X. Yao. Piscataway, N.J.: IEEE Press.

Shapiro, J., and A. Prügel-Bennet. 1997. "Genetic Algorithm Dynamics in a Two Well Potential." In *Foundations of Genetic Algorithms 4*, ed. R. K. Belew and M. D. Vose, 101–116. San Francisco: Morgan Kaufmann.

Shipman, R., M. Shackleton, M. Ebner, and R. A. Watson. 2000. "Neutral Search Spaces for Artificial Evolution: A Lesson from Life." In *Proceedings of the Seventh International Conference on Artificial Life*, ed. M. A. Bedau, S. Rasmussen, J. S. McCaskill, and N. H. Packard, 162–169. Cambridge, Mass.: MIT Press.

Shnol, E. E., and A. S. Kondrashov. 1993. "The Effect of Selection on the Phenotypic Variance." *Genetics* 134(3): 995–996.

Sigmund, K. 1998. "The Population Dynamics of Conflict and Cooperation." Proceedings of the International Congress of Mathematicans 1998. *Documenta Mathematica* 1: 487–506.

Simon, H. A. 1969 (1996). *The Sciences of the Artificial.* Cambridge, Mass.: MIT Press.

Simon, H. A., and A. Ando. 1961. "Aggregation of Variables in Dynamic Systems." *Econometrica* 29: 111–138.

Sims, K. 1994. "Evolving 3D Morphology and Behaviour by Competition." In *Artificial Life* 1: 353–372.

Slanina, F., and M. Kotrola. 2000. "Random Networks Created by Biological Evolution." *Physical Review E* 62(5): 6170–6177.

Slatkin, M. 1981. "Fixation Probabilities and Fixation Times in a Subdivided Population." *Evolution* 35(3): 477–488.

Smith, M. W., D. F. Feng, and R. F. Doolittle. 1992. "Evolution by Acquisition: the Case for Horizontal Gene Transfers." *Trends in Biochemical Sciences* 17(12): 489–493.

Smith, R. E., S. Forrest, and A. S. Perelson. 1993. "Searching for Diverse, Co-operative Populations with Genetic Algorithms." *Evolutionary Computation* 1(2): 127–149.

Spears, W. M. 1992. "Crossover or Mutation?" In *Foundations of Genetic Algorithms 2*, ed. D. Whitley, 221–237. San Mateo, Calif.: Morgan Kaufmann.

Spears, W. M. 2004. *Evolutionary Algorithms: The Role of Mutation and Recombination.* Berlin: Springer-Verlag.

Spears, W. M., and K. A. De Jong. 1991. "On the Virtues of Parameterized Uniform Crossover." In *Proceedings of the Fourth International Conference on Genetic Algorithms*, ed. R. K. Belew and L. B. Booker, 230–236. San Mateo, Calif.: Morgan Kaufmann.

Stadler, P. F., and G. P. Wagner. 1997. "Algebraic Theory of Recombination Spaces." *Evolutionary Computation* 5: 241–275.

Starkweather, T., D. Whitley, and K. Mathias. 1991. "Optimization Using Distributed Genetic Algorithms." In *Parallel Problem Solving from Nature*, ed. H. Schwefel and R. Maenner, 176–186. Berlin: Springer-Verlag.

Stephens, C. R., and H. Waelbroeck. 1998. "Analysis of the Effective Degrees of Freedom in Genetic Algorithms." *Physical Review* D57: 3251.

Stephens, C. R., and H. Waelbroeck. 1999. "Schemata, Evolution, and Building Blocks." *Evolutionary Computation* 7(2): 109–124.

Syswerda, G. 1989. "Uniform Crossover in Genetic Algorithms." In *Proceedings Third International Conference on Genetic Algorithms*, ed. J. Schaffer, 2–9. Los Altos, Calif.: Morgan Kaufmann.

Syswerda, G. 1990. "A Study of Reproduction in Generational and Steady-State Genetic Algorithms." In *Foundations of Genetic Algorithms*, ed. G. Rawlins. San Francisco: Morgan Kaufmann.

Syvanen, M., and C. I. Kado. 1998. *Horizontal Gene Transfer.* Boston: Kluwer Academic.

Thierens, D., and D. Goldberg. 1993. "Mixing in Genetic Algorithms." In *Proceedings of the Fifth International Conference on Genetic Algorithms*, ed. S. Forrest, 38–45. San Mateo, Calif.: Morgan Kaufmann.

Thompson, A. 1998. *Hardware Evolution: Automatic Design of Electronic Circuits in Reconfigurable Hardware by Artificial Evolution.* Berlin: Springer-Verlag.

Tomlinson, A., and L. Bull. 2001. "Symbiogenesis in Learning Classifier Systems." *Artificial Life* 7(1): 33–62.

Toulouse, M., K. Thulasiraman, and F. Glover. 1999. "Multi-Level Cooperative Search: A New Paradigm for Combinatorial Optimization and an Application to Graph Partitioning." In *Proceedings of the Fifth International European Parallel Computing Conference (EUROPAR'99)*, LNCS no. 1685, ed. P. Amestoy et al., 533–542. Berlin: Springer-Verlag.

Tsujimura, Y., Y. Mafune, and M. Gen. 2001. "Effects of Symbiotic Evolution in Genetic Algorithms for Job-Shop Scheduling." In *34th Annual Hawaii International Conference on System Sciences (HICSS-34)*, ed. Ralph H. Sprague, Jr. and J. F. Nunamaker. Piscataway, N.J.: IEEE Press.

Valenzuela, C. L., and A. J. Jones. 1994. "Evolutionary Divide-and-Conquer (I): A Novel Genetic Approach to the TSP." *Evolutionary Computation* 1(4): 313–334.

Van Hoyweghen, C., D. E. Goldberg, and B. Naudts. 2001. "Building Block Superiority, Multimodality, and Synchronization Problems." In *Proceedings of the Genetic and Evolutionary Computation Conference (GECCO) 2001*, ed. L. Spector, E. Goodman, A. Wu, W. B. Langdon, H.-M. Voigt, M. Gen, S. Sen, M. Dorigo, S. Pezeshk, M. Garzon, and E. Burke, 694–701. San Francisco: Morgan Kaufmann. (Also IlliGAL Report No. 2001020.)

Van Hoyweghen, C., D. E. Goldberg, and B. Naudts. 2002. "From TwoMax to the Ising Model: Easy and Hard Symmetrical Problems." In *Proceedings of the Genetic and Evolutionary Computation Conference (GECCO) 2002*, ed. W. B. Langdon, E. Cantú-Paz, K. E. Mathias, R. Roy, D. Davis, R. Poli, K. Balakrishnan, V. Honavar, G. Rudolph, J. Wegener, L. Bull, M. A. Potter, A. C. Schultz, J. F. Miller, E. Burke, and N. Jonoska. San Francisco: Morgan Kaufmann. (Also IlliGAL Report No. 2001030.)

Van Hoyweghen, C., and B. Naudts. 2001. "H-iff versus Ising: Analysis of a Recombinative Algorithm." Technical Report, University of Antwerp.

Van Nimwegen, E., and J. P. Crutchfield. 2000. "Metastable Evolutionary Dynamics: Crossing Fitness Barriers or Escaping via Neutral Paths?" *Bulletin of Mathematical Biology* 62: 799–848.

Van Veldhuizen, D. A., and G. B. Lamont. "Multiobjective Optimization with Messy Genetic Algorithms." In *Proceedings of the 2000 ACM Symposium on Applied Computing*, ed. J. Carroll, E. Damiani, H. Haddad, and D. Oppenheim, 470–476. New York: ACM Press.

Variano, E. A., J. H. McCoy, and H. Lipson. 2004. "Networks, Dynamics, and Modularity." *Physical Review Letters* 92(18).

Vekaria, K., and C. Clack. 1998. "Selective Crossover in Genetic Algorithms." In *Proceedings of Parallel Problem Solving from Nature V*, ed. A. E. Eiben, T. Back, M. Schoenauer, and H.-B. Schweffel, 438–447. Berlin: Springer-Verlag.

Vose, M. D. 1999. *The Simple Genetic Algorithm: Foundations and Theory*. Cambridge, Mass.: MIT Press.

Waddington, C. H. 1942. "Canalization of Development and the Inheritance of Acquired Characters." *Nature* 150: 563–565.

Wagner, G. P. 1995. "Adaptation and the Modular Design of Organisms." In *Advances in Artificial Life*, ed. F. Morán, A. Morán, J. J. Merelo, and P. Chacón, 317–328. Berlin: Springer-Verlag.

Wagner, G. P. 1996. "Homologues, Natural Kinds, and the Evolution of Modularity." *American Zoologist* 36: 36–43.

Wagner, G. P. 2002. "To Epistasis—and Beyond!" *Evolution* 56(4): 852–855.

Wagner, G. P., and L. Altenberg. 1996. "Complex Adaptations and the Evolution of Evolvability." *Evolution* 50(3): 967–976.

Wagner, G. P., M. D. Laubichler, and H. Bagheri-Chaichian. 1998. "Genetic Measurement Theory of Epistatic Effects." *Genetica* 102: 569–580.

Wagner, G. P., J. Mezey, and R. Calabretta. 2005. "Natural Selection and the Origin of Modules." In *Modularity: Understanding the Development and Evolution of Natural Complex Systems*, ed. W. Callebaut and D. Rasskin-Gutman, 33–49. Cambridge, Mass.: MIT Press.

Wagner, G. P., and P. F. Stadler. 1997. "Complex Adaptations and the Structure of Recombination Spaces. In *Algebraic Engineering*, ed. C. Nehaniv and M. Ito, 96–115. London: World Scientific.

Wakeley, J. 2000. "The Effects of Subdivision on the Genetic Divergence of Populations and Species." *Evolution* 54: 1092–1101.

Wallin, I. E. 1927. *Symbionticism and the Origin of Species*. Baltimore: Williams and Wilkins.

Watson, J. D., and F. H. C. Crick. 1953. "A Structure for Deoxyribose Nucleic Acid." *Nature* 171: 737–738.

Watson, R. A. 1996. "A Study of the Effect of Group Formation on Evolutionary Search." M.Sc. dissertation, Sussex University.

Watson, R. A. 2001. "Analysis of Recombinative Algorithms on a Non-Separable Building Block Problem." *Foundations of Genetic Algorithms VI*, ed. W. N. Martin and W. M. Spears, 69–89. San Francisco: Morgan Kaufmann.

Watson, R. A. 2004. "A Simple Two-Module Problem to Exemplify Building-Block Assembly Under Crossover." In *Proceedings of Parallel Problem Solving from Nature—(PPSN VIII)*, ed. Xin Yao et al., 160–169. Berlin: Springer-Verlag.

Watson, R. A. 2005a. "On the Unit of Selection in Sexual Populations." In *Advances in Artificial Life, Eighth European Conference (ECAL 2005)*, Lecture Notes in Artifical Intelligence (LNAI 3630), ed. M. S. Capcarrere, A. A. Freitas, P. J. Bentley, C. G. Johnson, and J. Timmis, 895–905. Berlin: Springer-Verlag.

Watson, R. A. 2005b. "Multidimensional Epistasis and the Advantage of Sex." In *Proceedings of the 2005 Congress on Evolutionary Computation (CEC 2005)*, 2792–2799. Portland, Oregon: IEEE Press.

Watson, R. A., S. G. Ficici, and J. B. Pollack. 2002. "Embodied Evolution: Distributing an Evolutionary Algorithm in a Population of Robots." *Journal of Robotics and Autonomous Systems* 39(1): 1–18.

Watson, R. A., G. S. Hornby, and J. B. Pollack. 1998. "Modeling Building Block Interdependency." In *Proceedings of Parallel Problem Solving from Nature V*, ed. A. E. Eiben, T. Back, M. Schoenauer, and H.-B. Schweffel, 97–106. Berlin: Springer-Verlag.

Watson, R. A., and J. B. Pollack. 1999a. "Hierarchically Consistent Test Problems for Genetic Algorithms." In *Proceedings of 1999 Congress on Evolutionary Computation, CEC-99*, ed. P. J. Angeline, Z. Michalewicz, M. Schoenauer, X. Yao, and A. Zalzala, 1406–1413. Piscataway, N.J.: IEEE Press.

Watson, R. A., and J. B. Pollack. 1999b. "Hierarchically-Consistent GA Test Problems: Summary and Additional Results." In *GECCO-99 Late Breaking Papers*, ed. S. Brave and A. S. Wu, 292–297. San Mateo, Calif.: Morgan Kaufmann.

Watson, R. A., and J. B. Pollack. 1999c. "Incremental Commitment in Genetic Algorithms." In *Proceedings of 1999 Genetic and Evolutionary Computation Conference (GECCO) 1999*, ed. W. Banzhaf, J. Daida, A. E. Eiben, M. H. Garzon, V. Honavar, M. Jakiela, and R. E. Smith, 710–717. San Francisco: Morgan Kaufmann.

Watson, R. A., and J. B. Pollack. 1999d. "How Symbiosis Can Guide Evolution." In *Proceedings of European Conference on Artificial Life (ECAL) V*, ed. D. Floreano, J.-D. Nicoud, and F. Mondada, 29–38. Berlin: Springer-Verlag.

Watson, R. A., and J. B. Pollack. 2000a. "Symbiotic Combination as an Alternative to Sexual Recombination in Genetic Algorithms." In *Proceedings of Parallel Problem Solving from Nature (PPSN) VI*, ed. M. Schoenauer et al., 425–434. Berlin: Springer-Verlag.

Watson, R. A., and J. B. Pollack. 2000b. "Recombination without Respect: Schema Combination and Disruption in Genetic Algorithm Crossover." In *Proceedings of the 2000 Genetic and Evolutionary Computation Conference*, ed. D. Whitley et al., 112–119. San Francisco: Morgan Kaufmann.

Watson, R. A., and J. B. Pollack. 2001a. "Symbiotic Composition and Evolvability." In *Proceedings of European Conference on Artificial Life (ECAL) VI*, ed. J. Kelemen and P. Sosík, 480–490. Berlin: Springer-Verlag.

Watson, R. A., and J. B. Pollack. 2001b. "Coevolutionary Dynamics in a Minimal Substrate." In *Proceedings of Genetic and Evolutionary Computation Conference (GECCO) 2001*, ed. L. Spector, E. Goodman, A. Wu, W. B. Langdon, H.-M. Voigt, M. Gen, S. Sen, M. Dorigo, S. Pezeshk, M. Garzon, and E. Burke, 702–709. San Francisco: Morgan Kaufmann.

Watson, R. A., and J. B. Pollack. 2003. "A Computational Model of Symbiotic Composition in Evolutionary Transitions." *BioSystems* 69(2–3): 187–209.

Watson, R. A., and J. B. Pollack. 2005. "Modular Interdependency in Complex Dynamical Systems." *Artificial Life* 11(4). To appear.

Watson, R. A., T. Reil, and J. B. Pollack. 2000b. "Mutualism, Parasitism, and Evolutionary Adaptation." In *Proceedings of Artificial Life VII*, ed. M. Bedau, J. McCaskill, N. Packard, and S. Rasmussen, 170–178. Cambridge, Mass.: MIT Press.

Watts, D. J. 1999. *Small Worlds: The Dynamics of Networks between Order and Randomness*. Princeton: Princeton University Press.

Weinreich, D. M., R. A. Watson, and L. Chao. 2005. "Perspectives: Fitness Landscapes, Sign Epistasis, and Evolution by Natural Selection." *Evolution* 59(6): 1165–1174.

Wiegand, R. P., W. C. Liles, and K. A. De Jong. 2001. "An Empirical Analysis of Collaboration Methods in Cooperative Coevolutionary Algorithms." In *Proceedings of the Genetic and Evolutionary Computation Conference (GECCO) 2001*, ed. L. Spector, E. D. Goodman, A. Wu, W. B. Langdon, H.-M. Voigt, M. Gen, S. Sen, M. Dorigo, S. Pezeshk, M. H. Garzon, and E. Burke, 1235–1242. San Mateo, Calif.: Morgan Kaufmann.

Werth, C. R., S. I. Guttman, and W. H. Eshbaugh. 1985. "Recurring Origins of Allopolyploid Species in Asplenium." *Science* 228: 731–733.

West, S. A., A. D. Peters, and N. H. Barton. 1998. "Testing for Epistasis between Deleterious Mutations." *Genetics* 149(1): 435–444.

Whitley, D., R. Beveridge, C. Graves, and K. Mathias. 1995a. "Test Driving Three 1995 Genetic Algorithms: New Test Functions and Geometric Matching." *Heuristics* 1: 77–104.

Whitley, D., K. Mathias, S. Rana, and J. Dzubera. 1995b. "Building Better Test Functions." In *ICGA-6*, ed. L. Eshelman, 239–246. San Francisco: Morgan Kaufmann.

Wiles, J., B. Tonkes, and J. R. Watson. 2001. "How Learning Can Guide Evolution in Hierarchical Modular Tasks." In *Proceedings of the 23rd Annual Conference of the Cognitive Science Society (CogSci 2001)*, ed. J. D. Moore and K. Stenning, 1130–1135. Mahwah, N.J.: Lawrence Erlbaum.

Williams, G. C. 1966. *Adaptation and Natural Selection: A Critique of Some Current Evolutionary Thought*. Princeton: Princeton University Press.

Wilson, K. G. 1979. "Problems in Physics with Many Scales of Length." *Scientific American* 241(2): 158–179.

Wilson, S. W., and D. E. Goldberg. 1989. "A Critical Review of Classifier Systems." In *Proceedings of the Third International Conference on Genetic Algorithms and Their Applications*, ed. J. D. Schaffer, 244–255. San Francisco: Morgan Kaufmann.

Wolf, J. B., E. D. Brodie III, and M. J. Wade, eds. 2005. *Epistasis and the Evolutionary Process*. Oxford: Oxford University Press.

Wolpert, D., and W. Macready. 1997. "No Free Lunch Theorems for Optimization." *IEEE Transactions on Evolutionary Computation* 1(1): 67–82.

Wright, A. H., and J. E. Rowe. 2001. "Continuous Dynamical System Models of Steady-State Genetic Algorithms." In *Foundations of Genetic Algorithms*, vol. 6, ed. W. Spears, T. Fogarty, and W. Martin. San Francisco: Morgan Kaufmann.

Wright, A. H., and Y. Zhao. 1999. "Markov Chain Models of Genetic Algorithms." In *Proceedings of the Genetic and Evolutionary Computation Conference (GECCO) 1999*, ed. W. Banzhaf, J. Daida, A. E. Eiben, M. H. Garzon, V. Honavar, M. Jakiela, and R. E. Smith, 734–741. San Francisco: Morgan Kaufmann.

Wright, S. 1931. "Evolution in Mendelian Populations." *Genetics* 16: 97–159.

Wright, S. 1935. "Evolution in Populations in Approximate Equilibrium." *Journal of Genetics* 30: 257–266.

Wright, S. 1967. "Surfaces of Selective Value." *Proceedings National Academy of Sciences* 58: 165–179.

Wright, S. 1977. *Evolution and the Genetics of Populations*, vol. 3. Chicago: University of Chicago Press.

Index